Stravinsky and the Russian Period

Van den Toorn and McGinness take a fresh look at the dynamics of Stravinsky's musical style, from a variety of analytical, critical, and aesthetic angles. Starting with processes of juxtaposition and stratification, the book offers an in-depth analysis of works such as *The Rite of Spring*, *Les Noces*, and *Renard*. Characteristic features of style, melody, and harmony are traced to rhythmic forces, including those of metrical displacement. Along with Stravinsky's formalist aesthetics, the strict performing style he favored is also traced to rhythmic factors, thus reversing the direction of the traditional causal relationship. Here, aesthetic belief and performance practice are seen as flowing directly from the musical invention. The book provides a counter-argument to the criticism and aesthetics of T. W. Adorno and Richard Taruskin, and will appeal to composers, critics, and performers as well as scholars of Stravinsky's music.

PIETER C. VAN DEN TOORN is Professor of Music at the University of California at Santa Barbara. He is the author of *The Music of Igor Stravinsky* (1983), *Stravinsky and "The Rite of Spring"* (1987), and *Music, Politics, and the Academy* (1995). *Stravinsky and "The Rite of Spring"* won the Deems Taylor Award (1989) and the Outstanding Publication Award of the Society for Music Theory (1990).

JOHN MCGINNESS is an Associate Professor of Music Theory at the Crane School of Music, State University of New York at Potsdam. His essays and articles on topics including the music of Debussy, Stravinsky, and Ives have appeared in *The Musical Quarterly*, *Music Theory Spectrum*, and *Cahiers Debussy*, among other publications. As a pianist specializing in contemporary music, he has premiered more than twenty-five new works and has recorded for CRS and Radio Nederland.

Music Since 1900

GENERAL EDITOR Arnold Whittall

This series – formerly *Music in the Twentieth Century* – offers a wide perspective on music and musical life since the end of the nineteenth century. Books included range from historical and biographical studies concentrating particularly on the context and circumstances in which composers were writing, to analytical and critical studies concerned with the nature of musical language and questions of compositional process. The importance given to context will also be reflected in studies dealing with, for example, the patronage, publishing, and promotion of new music, and in accounts of the musical life of particular countries.

Titles in the series

Jonathan Cross
The Stravinsky Legacy

Michael Nyman
Experimental Music: Cage and Beyond

Jennifer Doctor
The BBC and Ultra-Modern Music, 1922–1936

Robert Adlington
The Music of Harrison Birtwistle

Keith Potter
Four Musical Minimalists: La Monte Young, Terry Riley, Steve Reich, Philip Glass

Carlo Caballero
Fauré and French Musical Aesthetics

Peter Burt
The Music of Toru Takemitsu

David Clarke
The Music and Thought of Michael Tippett: Modern Times and Metaphysics

M. J. Grant
Serial Music, Serial Aesthetics: Compositional Theory in Post-War Europe

Philip Rupprecht
Britten's Musical Language

Mark Carroll
Music and Ideology in Cold War Europe

Adrian Thomas
Polish Music since Szymanowski

J. P. E. Harper-Scott
Edward Elgar, Modernist

Yayoi Uno Everett
The Music of Louis Andriessen

Ethan Haimo
Schoenberg's Transformation of Musical Language

Rachel Beckles Willson
Ligeti, Kurtág, and Hungarian Music during the Cold War

Michael Cherlin
Schoenberg's Musical Imagination

Joseph N. Straus
Twelve-Tone Music in America

David Metzer
Musical Modernism at the Turn of the Twenty-First Century

Edward Campbell
Boulez, Music and Philosophy

Jonathan Goldman
The Musical Language of Pierre Boulez: Writings and Compositions

Pieter C. van den Toorn and John McGinness
Stravinsky and the Russian Period: Sound and Legacy of a Musical Idiom

Stravinsky and the Russian Period: Sound and Legacy of a Musical Idiom

Pieter C. van den Toorn
John McGinness

CAMBRIDGE
UNIVERSITY PRESS

CAMBRIDGE UNIVERSITY PRESS
Cambridge, New York, Melbourne, Madrid, Cape Town,
Singapore, São Paulo, Delhi, Mexico City

Cambridge University Press
The Edinburgh Building, Cambridge CB2 8RU, UK

Published in the United States of America by Cambridge University Press, New York

www.cambridge.org
Information on this title: www.cambridge.org/9781107021006

First published 2012
3rd printing 2013

Printed and bound in the United Kingdom by the MPG Books Group

A catalogue record for this publication is available from the British Library

Library of Congress Cataloguing in Publication data
Van den Toorn, Pieter C., 1938-
Stravinsky and the Russian period : sound and legacy of a musical idiom / Pieter C. van
den Toorn, John McGinness.
   p.   cm. – (Music since 1900)
Includes bibliographical references.
ISBN 978-1-107-02100-6
1. Stravinsky, Igor, 1882-1971 – Criticism and interpretation.   I. McGinness, John.
II. Title.
ML410.S932V39   2012
780.92–dc23

                                                                                            2011049747

ISBN 978-1-107-02100-6 Hardback

To Henry Mishkin, Nadia Boulanger, Joseph Kerman, John Baron, Allen Forte, and Lilian Kallir

And to Richard Taruskin, PA, PP

Contents

Acknowledgments page xi

Introduction 1

1 Meter and metrical displacement in Stravinsky 13
Meter and its definitions 13
Metrical displacement in Stravinsky 18
Displacement, location, and intensity 28
Earlier examples of displacement 30
The concept of metrical dissonance 38

2 The octatonic scale 42
Octatonic–diatonic interaction 48

3 A brief survey 53
The Russian folk wedding 56
The scenario 60
Musical sources in *Les Noces* 66
Renard (1915–16) 73
The Soldier's Tale (1918) 78

4 Meter, motive, and alignment in *Les Noces*: Stravinsky's block and layered structures 82
Metrical displacement in the first tableau 89
Block structures in the second tableau 96
Layered structures in the second tableau 103
Additional layered structures 107
Conclusions 111

5 Melody and harmony in *Les Noces* 114
Melody and the folk element 117
Preliminary remarks; a *Tonnetz* for *Les Noces* 131
Octatonic–diatonic interaction in the first and third tableaux 147
Interactions in the fourth tableau 159
Octatonic fever 167

6 Meter, text, and alignment in *Renard* (1916): Stravinsky's "rejoicing discovery" 173
Origins of displacement 174
Pribaoutka 177
The role of articulation in processes of metrical displacement: Stravinsky's slurs, beams, and accent markings 183
Stravinsky contra Schoenberg 194

7   **Allegro!** *Renard* **reconsidered 196**
     Extra eighth-note beats 201
     Substructure 206
     Structure in the large 208
     Pitch relations 214
     Coda: the Royal March in *The Soldier's Tale* (1918) 220

8   **Melodic repeat structures in the music of Stravinsky, Debussy, and Rimsky-Korsakov: another look at the** *Symphonies of Wind Instruments* **(1920) 225**
     The conservative alternative 232
     Antecedents in the music of Debussy and Rimsky-Korsakov 235
     Continuity and discontinuity 245

9   **Issues of performance practice and aesthetic belief 252**
     Expressive timing 254

10   **Stravinsky and his critics 267**
     T. W. Adorno 269
     Critical indictments 271
     Rebuttals 275
     Stravinsky the person 284
     Full cycle: *Les Noces* and *The Rite of Spring* revisited 291
     Conclusions 299

     Selected bibliography 304
     Index 313

Acknowledgments

We wish to thank the Paul Sacher Foundation in Basel, Switzerland, for their permission to examine the sketches of numerous Stravinsky works, including those of *Les Noces* and *Renard*. We are indebted as well to the Interdisciplinary Humanities Center at the University of California, Santa Barbara, for the award of a research grant some years ago, and to the Society for Music Theory and the Dragan Plamenac Endowment of the American Musicological Society for their generous subventions to cover the cost of realizing the musical examples. The staff of the Music Library at the University of California, Santa Barbara, proved immensely resourceful during the period of research, and we are grateful for their expertise.

At Cambridge University Press, Arnold Whittall, General Editor of the current series, "Music Since 1900," examined the manuscript on several occasions, while Victoria Cooper, Rebecca Taylor and Christina Sarigiannidou offered invaluable assistance during the production process. Cattarina van den Toorn devoted countless hours to some of the technical challenges of the project, and the musical illustrations were set with great skill by Andre Mount. Helpful less directly but no less crucially were Virginia, Anna-Marie, Linnea, and Christine van den Toorn, together with Cate and Hendrik Dibble.

We would also like to thank the following publishers for permission to reproduce excerpts taken from copyrighted works: Boosey & Hawkes, Inc., for Béla Bartók's String Quartet No. 3 (SZ85, U.S. only); Hawkes & Son (London), Ltd., for Bartók's *Mikrokosmos* No. 101, Bartók's Violin Concerto No. 2, and for Igor Stravinsky's *Symphonies of Wind Instruments* and *The Rite of Spring*; Universal Edition A.G. for Bartók's String Quartet No. 3 (outside U.S., copyright 1929, Wien/UE34310; copyright renewed 1956 by Boosey & Hawkes, Inc.); and Chester Music, Ltd., for Stravinsky's *L'Histoire du soldat, Les Noces*, and *Renard*.

Introduction

For the greater part of the twentieth century Igor Stravinsky and Arnold Schoenberg stood at opposite ends of a musical divide. Although it was not entirely of their own making, two camps of followers emerged during the 1920s and 30s who were oriented toward one or the other of these two composers: their styles, pitch languages, and methods of composition. On an even broader scale, the two sides came to represent, on the one hand, alternatives to atonality and the Second Viennese School (consisting, as with neoclassicism, of extensions of the diatonic and tonal foundations of the past), and, on the other, the atonal and serial initiatives themselves. Tradition and the past played a role on both sides of this fence, even if they were angled quite differently.[1]

The two sides were not equal. In the 1940s, 50s, and 60s, especially, the atonalists, serialists, and total serialists tended to hold sway. The accepted wisdom at the time seems to have been that theirs was indeed the music of the future. Pierre Boulez, Darmstadt, *Die Reihe*, and T. W. Adorno's *Philosophy of Modern Music* (1949) come to mind in this regard, as do Milton Babbitt and the Princeton School. Following Schoenberg's death in 1951, Stravinsky's gradual adoption of serial methods had the effect of confirming the direction that had long been suspected. In the United States, the serial conversion of Aaron Copland and of several other composers took place at about the same time.[2]

---

[1] Among other qualifications to our bird's eye view of twentieth-century music (or a sizeable chunk thereof), the neoclassical dimension to Schoenberg's twelve-tone works has long been a focus of critical and historical attention; see, for example, J. Peter Burkholder, "Schoenberg the Reactionary," in Walter Frisch, ed., *Schoenberg and His World* (Princeton University Press, 1999), 162–94. For Stravinsky's own later reflections on the celebrated Stravinsky–Schoenberg split, see Igor Stravinsky and Robert Craft, *Dialogues and a Diary* (Garden City, NY: Doubleday, 1963), 56–59. To judge from the recollections of Pierre Suvchinsky, a close friend of the composer's, the mood toward Schoenberg and his school was one of outright hostility during the 1920s and 30s. Alban Berg's *Wozzeck* was regularly dismissed by Stravinsky as "une musique boche," while Mahler was mispronounced as "Malheur"; anyone favorably disposed toward the Mahler–Schoenberg–Berg line was disowned as a "traitor." See Igor Stravinsky and Robert Craft, *Retrospectives and Conclusions* (New York: Knopf, 1969), 193. For a concise chronicle of the Stravinsky–Schoenberg divide, see Scott Messing, *Neoclassicism in Music: From the Genesis of the Concept through the Schoenberg/Stravinsky Polemic* (University of Rochester Press, 1996), 87–149. A brief personal history of the relationship appears in Robert Craft, *Down a Path of Wonder: Memoirs of Stravinsky, Schoenberg and other Cultural Figures* (London: Naxos, 2006), 3–12.
[2] Copland's Piano Quartet, a twelve-tone work, was begun in 1950. For an insightful account of the underlying musical dynamics of this era, see Richard Taruskin, *The Oxford History of Western Music* (Oxford University Press, 2005), vol. V: 103–73.

All this changed in the late 1960s and 70s, however. With the birth of a number of counter-currents, including American minimalism, the pendulum began to swing wildly in the opposite direction. Almost overnight, the musical processes that had been scorned at such length by the progressives acquired a new lease. In open revolt against the academies, serialism, and "difficult" music, composers such as Steve Reich and Philip Glass turned to the repetitive patterns, layered structures, and modal harmonies of Stravinsky's Russian-period works as one of several options. The static, non-developmental, repetitive, ritualistic, and impersonal qualities of these processes proved antidotal; the key to a liberation of sorts.

Putting aside Reich's early phase-shifting music, his *City Life* (1995) can come to mind in this connection, with its octatonic scale passages and syncopated, percussive use of the piano. So, too, his more recent *You are (Variations)* (2005) can remind the listener of the four pianos in the final version of *Les Noces* (1917–23), and of the vocal style, staccato and heavily syncopated, in Stravinsky's *Symphony of Psalms* (1930), third movement. John Adams and Louis Andriessen have been drawn more persistently to the block and stratified textures in Stravinsky's Russian-period works.[3] Unmistakable in the opening pages of Adams's *El Dorado* symphony (1991) are the superimposed strands of the first of Stravinsky's *Three Pieces for String Quartet* (1914), a veritable primer in the use of superimposed rhythmic pedals. Block structures are more conspicuous in Andriessen's *De Staat* (1976), even if the pitch language, heavily chromatic and atonal at times, differs markedly from that of Reich or Adams.[4]

The politics of Stravinsky's music can seem to have changed as well. The cosmopolitan of the previous half-century – austere formalist with a snooty

---

[3] By block structure is meant a vertical *juxtaposition* of distinct units or *blocks* of material, one that is abrupt and lacking in transitions. When repeated, the individual blocks may be lengthened, shortened, or reshuffled, but their content is apt to remain fixed. Block structures have been compared to techniques of "cutting and pasting," montage, collage, and Cubism in painting early in the twentieth century. In contrast, a layered structure is a horizontal *stratification* of two or more fragments. Fixed in register and often instrumentally as well, these superimposed fragments repeat according to varying cycles or spans. Illustrations of both approaches are examined in the ensuing chapters. For additional descriptions, see Pieter C. van den Toorn, *Stravinsky and "The Rite of Spring": The Beginnings of a Musical Language* (Berkeley: University of California Press, 1987), 97–101. In this earlier study, block and layered structures were labeled "Type 1" and "Type 2," respectively.

[4] Connections between Stravinsky's block structures and minimalist or post-minimalist repertories are discussed in Jonathan Cross, *The Stravinsky Legacy* (Cambridge University Press, 1998), 170–89. Not all critics have viewed early minimalism as a complete negation of the serial methods that preceded it. Stressed in Keith Potter, *Four Musical Minimalists* (Cambridge University Press, 1995), 10–11, is the commitment, on the part of both integral serialism and minimalism, "to the consequences of rigorous application of processes independent, to a significant degree, of the composer's note-to-note control." See, too, Arnold Whittall, *Serialism* (Oxford University Press, 2008), 142–44.

sense of entitlement, as one critic would have it[5] – has been replaced by something more down-to-earth and even democratic. To follow Andriessen on this, Russian-period works such as *Les Noces* and *Renard* (1916), founded in popular verse, custom, and even vocal and instrumental sonority, are to some degree populist.[6] The marches, waltzes, and ragtimes of *The Soldier's Tale* (1918) are common, garden-variety adaptations, full of clichés and stretched out instrumentally to the bone. They resemble street music in this, the antithesis of elite concert music, in any case as measured against nineteenth- and twentieth-century standards. Even today, as a form of caricature, they can seem fresh and provocative.

The composer's image has also undergone something of an adjustment, mostly from the grim to the fundamentally happy. The private world of composition he inhabited may have shielded him somewhat from the political and personal upheaval that accompanied his relocations from St. Petersburg to Switzerland (1914–19), and from there to France (1919–39) and the United States (1939–71). The description of him in Robert Craft's most recent book of recollection is that of a happy man, a "divertimento composer."[7] What kept him going, evidently, were strict rules capable of inspiring as well as circumscribing (something concrete to compose against),[8] an abstract sense of order or construction, and aesthetic bliss.

These and other developments in recent years have led us to want to revisit the music of Stravinsky's Russian period, and by way of a number of underlying processes. Chief among these are the following:

---

[5] See Richard Taruskin, "Stravinsky and Us," in Jonathan Cross, ed., *The Cambridge Companion to Stravinsky* (Cambridge University Press, 2003), 282–83.

[6] See Louis Andriessen and Jonathan Cross, "Composing with Stravinsky," in Cross, ed., *The Cambridge Companion to Stravinsky*, 254–59. On Andriessen's own methods of fusing art music with contemporary popular idioms, see Yayoi Uno Everett, *The Music of Louis Andriessen* (Cambridge University Press, 2006), 61–76.

[7] See Craft, *Down A Path of Wonder*.

[8] Stravinsky acknowledged his need for strict compositional guidelines on several occasions; see, in particular, Igor Stravinsky, *Poetics of Music in the Form of Six Lessons*, trans. Arthur Knodel and Ingolf Dahl (New York: Vintage Books, 1956), 68: "My freedom ... consists in my moving about within the narrow frame that I have assigned to myself for each one of my undertakings. I shall go even further: my freedom will be so much the greater and more meaningful the more narrowly I limit my field of action and the more I surround myself with obstacles. Whatever diminishes constraint, diminishes strength." Some of the wording here may have been borrowed from a 1904 lecture-essay of André Gide's, "The Evolution of the Theater"; see André Gide, *My Theater: Five Plays and an Essay*, trans. Jackson Matthews (New York: Knopf, 1952). "Art is born of constraint," Gide writes, "lives by struggle, and dies of freedom" (263). The convergence of a number of artistic and aesthetic ideals shared in one way or another by Gide, Paul Valéry, and Stravinsky is pursued in Maureen A. Carr, *Multiple Masks: Neoclassicism in Stravinsky's Works on Greek Subjects* (Lincoln: University of Nebraska Press, 2002), 5–8. Underscored by Carr are the "amazing coincidences of chronology." Although it is not known if Stravinsky heard or read Gide's early lecture-essay, a version thereof reappeared in a critical edition in 1939, the year in which Stravinsky's own lectures, subsequently published in the form of his *Poetics of Music*, were formulated.

1. Metrical displacement (*rhythm*).
2. Block and layered (or stratified) textures ("*form*").
3. A modal diatonicism that is subject to specific forms of octatonic intervention (*pitch*).

Readers familiar with the critical and analytical-theoretical literature surrounding Stravinsky's music will doubtless already have encountered some of these terms, although with meanings not always equivalent to the ones we will be adopting here. Introduced in Edward T. Cone's essay, "Stravinsky: the Progress of a Method,"[9] the term *stratification* (along with *stratified* and *strata*) was applied broadly at first to both the *vertical* juxtaposition of distinct blocks of material and the *horizontal* layering of distinct patterns of repetition. In keeping with more recent studies, however, we will be applying *stratification* and *layering* only to the second of these two modes of construction, the horizontal mode.[10] Narrowing the scope of these terms will allow us to deal a bit more effectively with the individual detail in moving from one context to the next.

Yet the bulk of our analytical-theoretical energies will be directed toward the first of the processes listed above, the metrical displacement of repeated motives, themes, and chords. This, too, is a subject that has been dealt with previously, although differently from the way we intend to be approaching it here. Seeking a fuller account of this process of displacement, we will be focusing on meter, alignment, and psychological effect, the nature of the conflict that is triggered by this phenomenon.[11] Our interests rest as well with the extent and variety of the uses of displacement in music of the Russian era.

The interaction between these various factors will also concern us. With pitch relations generally, the nature of the interplay is loose and informal. The modal and octatonic structures mentioned above can exist independently of

---

[9] In Benjamin Boretz and Edward T. Cone, eds., *Perspectives on Schoenberg and Stravinsky* (New York: W. W. Norton, 1972), 155–64.

[10] See, for example, Cross, *The Stravinsky Legacy*. Similar distinctions in terminology, drawn between Stravinsky's vertical juxtapositions and horizontal layerings, are applied in van den Toorn, *Stravinsky and "The Rite of Spring."*

[11] Our point of departure on issues of metrical displacement in Stravinsky's music generally is Pieter C. van den Toorn, "Stravinsky, Adorno, and the Art of Displacement," *The Musical Quarterly* 87, no. 3 (2004): 468–509. Excerpts from this essay, revised, are reproduced here in Chapters 1 and 10. Included in Chapter 9 are passages from Pieter C. van den Toorn, "Stravinsky, *Les Noces (Svadebka)*, and The Prohibition Against Expressive Timing," *Journal of Musicology* 20, no. 2 (2003): 285–304. The present volume is in many ways an attempt to extend and amplify ideas introduced in these earlier studies. Essential, too, as a departure point in matters of periodic repetition and alignment in Stravinsky's stratifications, is Gretchen Horlacher, "The Rhythms of Reiteration: Formal Development in Stravinsky's Ostinati," *Music Theory Spectrum* 14, no. 2 (1992): 171–87. See, too, Gretchen Horlacher, *Building Blocks: Repetition and Continuity in the Music of Stravinsky* (New York: Oxford University Press, 2011).

the processes of displacement, juxtaposition, and stratification as well as vice versa. On the other hand, relations between these three processes are intimate. Stratification actually implies a form of displacement. If the super-imposed fragments of a layered structure repeat according to varying spans, then their alignment will shift (be displaced). And it will shift not only between the fragments themselves but also in relation to the meter. And to the extent that, in passages exhibiting a form of juxtaposition, individual blocks are lengthened, shortened, and/or reordered, they, too, will shift (be displaced) in relation to an established meter.

In this way, metrical displacement surfaces as the most basic of the various processes cited above, operating in works of the Russian period as a kind of stylistic common denominator. Nearly always present (and abundantly so) in these works, displacement can account for many of the more informal features we tend readily to identify with Stravinsky's music. As we shall see in Chapters 1–5, it can account for the literal nature of the repetition, the lack of variation or development along traditional lines. And it can account for much of the articulation as well, the beams, staccato, and non-espressivo markings in his scores.

Even the strict performance style on which the composer placed such emphasis can be traced to the displacement process. The tendency among Stravinsky's critics has been to look to the outside, of course, to attribute this and other features of Stravinsky's idiom to extraneous forces. Modernist fashion in the world of conducting has been cited in connection with the strict performance style,[12] as has the notorious bluntness of the composer's formalist convictions. The specter of an anti-humanistic, autocratic person-ality has been raised. Yet there is a better way of explaining the strict style and its rationale, and it consists of starting with the music and fanning out from there, as it were, allowing the materials themselves to stand as the catalyst that set (and that continues to set) this and many other ideas, traits, and practices in motion. From such a perspective, neither the composer's insistence on a strict approach to the performance of his music nor the bare-knuckled character of his formalism can reliably be regarded as a starting point. Far more readily, both the strict style and the formalist aesthetics fall into place as effects and consequences of the musical processes alluded to above.

To condense but one small segment of this line of reasoning: if the metrical displacement of a fragment, configuration or block of material is to have its effect, then (1) the repetition must be kept fairly literal, and (2) the beat must

---

[12] See, for example, Robert Fink, "'Rigoroso ($\flat$ =126)': The Rite of Spring and the Forging of a Modernist Performing Style," Journal of the American Musicological Society 52, no. 2 (1999): 299–350.

be maintained fairly strictly. This sounds innocent enough (the specifics of Stravinsky's performance practice are worked out in Chapter 9), yet the implications are far reaching. While a steady beat will lack much in the way of expressive timing and nuance, it will make up for this by its ability to project a clear sense of metrical placement and displacement. And the latter is essential in a performance of Stravinsky's music. Without it, much of the point of the invention is lost. And so there is little reason why listeners and performers should feel themselves put out by a beat of this kind, unable to come to grips with an underlying rationale, and at the mercy therefore of a conductor's or composer's "ethic of scrupulous submission," as one critic has charged.[13] On the contrary, a relatively strict beat is likely to leave that much more of the rhythmic play exposed to the ear. Timing and the element of surprise are apt to be felt that much more keenly.

Whether any of these Stravinskian features – metrical displacement, literal repetition, or the need for a strictly maintained beat – is not ultimately reflective of something base and sinister (as Adorno and several others have argued), is a matter to which we will be turning in Chapter 10. The point here is that an explanation can be sought in musical terms. A logic may be inferred: one which, sensed by the listener, is capable of endowing these features with a certain integrity. The anti-expressive in Stravinsky's music can be expressive, in other words, as can the ritualistic and the near-absence of expressive nuance. The meaning and significance of these features are not etched in stone, but can vary subtly from one setting to the next. (The role played by unity and even "organic unity" in an approach of this kind has come under attack, and primarily because of the restrictions that would seem to be placed on the analytical process. Analysis would seem to be confined to a determination of the unity of this or that part in relation to an assumed whole.[14] By *organic*, however, we mean to underscore the natural rather than artificial character of these phenomena, the sense of their being integral rather than forced or arbitrary. And while an overreaching purpose or train of thought is undoubtedly implied by this reasoning [a unity of sorts], it is so dynamically rather than passively. As this larger whole has

---

[13] Taruskin, "Stravinsky and Us," 283.

[14] See Joseph Kerman "How We Got into Analysis, and How to Get Out," in Joseph Kerman, *Write All These Down* (Berkeley: University of California Press, 1998), 12–32. To follow Kerman, the emphasis on unity or "organic unity" in contemporary analysis (and especially in Schenkerian analysis), has had the effect of slighting "salient" and expressive features, along with issues of contrast and critical value. More recently, arguments directed at the teleological bias of much analysis have sought to promote aspects of non-linearity and intertextuality. See, in this connection, Kevin Korsyn, *Decentering Music: A Critique of Contemporary Musical Research* (Oxford University Press, 2003).

generally been understood, it works both ways. In the process of defining the various features alluded to above, the whole is defined by them as well.)

But the content of this new expression of Stravinsky's – what his "musical manners" can be said to be expressive of – must remain somewhat in the shadows.[15] In the case of *Les Noces*, no doubt, we can point to a great many descriptive factors, grace notes that can imitate a gasp or a sob, octatonic scale patterns that, coloring the diatonic, can mimic the sound of a peasant band. Often enough, too, the repetition in Stravinsky's music can seem unrelenting, to project an air of rigidity, stasis, and intractability. Beyond these metaphorical descriptions and analogies, however, the expressive qualities of his music and the ability of these qualities to stir emotionally (passionately) are matters not readily open to verbal translation. We are moved synthetically and essentially by what a piece of music is, evidently, not by what it could or might possibly represent. And the aesthetic rapture that can take hold can do so regardless of a piece's character, be it one of sadness, joy, exhilaration, longing, or intractability. Whatever the character, the source of our delight would seem to lie elsewhere.

The expressive qualities associated with Stravinsky's music are not something external to the music, in other words, impulses which, lying to the outside, have obtained a form of portrayal within. They are inherent. They defy scrutiny not because they are too definite or too indefinite for words, but because their definiteness is entirely musical. They are feelings at all only by virtue of their expression in music.[16]

This is part and parcel of a formalist approach, no doubt, an aesthetics of the "specifically musical," as Eduard Hanslick characterized it in 1854, [17]

---

[15] See Stravinsky and Craft, *Dialogues and a Diary*, 10.

[16] For an excellent, brief explanation of the formalist approach to music and music appreciation, see Carl Dahlhaus, "Fragments of a Musical Hermeneutics," trans. Karen Painter, *Current Musicology* 50: 8–10. No less relevant here is the historical perspective outlined in Carl Dahlhaus, *The Idea of Absolute Music*, trans. Roger Lustig (Chicago University Press, 1989), and in Lydia Goehr, *The Imaginary Museum of Musical Works* (Oxford University Press, 1992), 148–75. In Nicholas Cook, "Theorizing Musical Meaning," *Music Theory Spectrum* 23 (2001): 170–95, formalists are dubbed "neo-Hanslickians" who stand in opposition to "neo-Adornians." Ideas about an "enhanced formalism" are pursued in Peter Kivy, *Music, Language, and Cognition* (Oxford: Clarendon Press, 2007), 199–201, and at greater length in Peter Kivy, *Music Alone: Philosophical Reflections on the Purely Musical Experience* (Ithaca: Cornell University Press, 1990), 124–223. To follow Kivy, even were expressive properties such as "sadness" and "mournfulness" to be judged a part of the fabric of absolute music ("music alone," as he calls it), such music would still ultimately be devoid of semantic or representational content. In his view, listeners moved by this literature are moved by something other than these expressive properties. Our opinion here is that much music other than absolute is quite capable of drawing attention to itself as music (of being listened to for its own sake, as it were), music that would include (at times) works with extra-musical content (opera, lieder, ballet, and so forth), and music irrespective of its genre, style, idiom, age, or national (or ethnic) origin.

[17] Eduard Hanslick, *The Beautiful in Music*, trans. Gustav Cohen (New York: Liberal Arts Press, 1957), 47. The "beautiful in music" depends not on "the accurate expression of feelings,"

and the sort of understanding to which Stravinsky himself subscribed with stubborn insistence for nearly half a century. We should note in caution, however, that the listening experience (or, more generally, our ability to summon the presence of a musical context) is not hereby abandoned for the sake of analysis and theory. Even between immediate experience and reflection, there is no wall of separation, in actuality, only a form of interplay that, as it happens, is there from the start. Limited time-wise in our ability to focus or attend, we are forced to give way at some point. Seeking to capture something of what is felt in immediacy, we construct an image thereof, doing so by moving back and forth, alternating between states of attunement (rapturous, self-forgetting immersion) and analytical reflection. The interaction can prompt a "second immediacy." (Immediacy in the raw "knows nothing of itself," as Carl Dahlhaus remarked some time ago.)[18] And it is in this way that analysis and theory are able to emerge as formal extensions of what may transpire informally at the earliest point of contact.

Overview

Stravinsky and the Russian Period begins with *Les Noces* and the complicated history of its conception. Extending through much of the Russian era, the story of this ballet seemed appropriate as a point of departure. We then move on to parts of *Renard, The Soldier's Tale* (very briefly), and the *Symphonies of Wind Instruments* (1920). Other Stravinsky works are cited in the course of our inquiry, yet, for the purposes at hand, these four works seemed ideal as a means of illustration.[19]

Turning first to rhythm and then to pitch, Chapters 1 and 2 set the analytic-theoretical stage for the inquiry as a whole. Metrical displacement hinges on meter, obviously, meter as a "mental construct" (understood psychologically or cognitively, in other words, as a form of motor

---

Hanslick argued, but rather on "sounds artistically combined," on processes specific to music. See the account of Hanslick's formalism (as his ideas came to be known) in Carl Dahlhaus, *Esthetics of Music*, trans. William W. Austin (Cambridge University Press, 1982), 52–57.

[18] Dahlhaus, *Esthetics of Music*, 72–73, 85. Suspicious of aesthetic immediacy, Dahlhaus stresses the analytical and historical assumptions that underlie a subsequent, "second immediacy," one informed by reflection.

[19] Alternatively, *The Rite of Spring* could have served as our starting point, as could, quite possibly, an even earlier work. The subject of three monographs in recent years, however, *The Rite* has been covered exhaustively: see Allen Forte, *The Harmonic Organization of "The Rite of Spring"* (New Haven: Yale University Press, 1978), van den Toorn, *Stravinsky and "The Rite of Spring,"* and Peter Hill, *Stravinsky: "The Rite of Spring"* (Cambridge University Press, 2000). It seemed advantageous not only to begin with a work other than *The Rite*, but to do so with *Les Noces*, in fact, something that was a bit more centrally located from the standpoint of the Russian era as a whole. *The Rite* is discussed at length in Chapter 5, however, and primarily as a means of comparison in matters of pitch relations.

behavior),[20] as well as a form of notation. A working definition seemed in order, therefore, one that could lay the groundwork for much of our discussion in the coming chapters. Chapter 1 starts with a short section on meter and then proceeds to a theory of metrical displacement in Stravinsky's music. Several types of listener responses to displacement are discussed, along with a method of classification according to metrical location. A few earlier examples of displacement are introduced for the purpose of further highlighting the particulars of Stravinsky's approach.

The octatonic scale seemed likewise in need of a few preliminary remarks. In Chapter 2 we structure the scale in such a way as to reflect not only its particular emphasis in Stravinsky's Russian-period works, but also, in the same works, the specific ways in which the octatonic aligns itself with the diatonic.

Chapter 3 offers a brief account of the historical background of the Russian period. We turn first to the Russian wedding play that underlies *Les Noces*, and then to the libretto and a number of musical sources. *Renard* and *The Soldier's Tale* are treated in much the same fashion, although on a smaller scale.

Whether the music of Stravinsky's Swiss years (1914–19) is "Turanian" in conception (a product of Eurasianist ideas and ideals, as Richard Taruskin has claimed)[21] is a matter about which we remain uncertain. Difficult to prove or disprove, the question of the composer's ties to the Eurasianists is no less difficult to weigh in its musical consequences. (The Eurasianist movement of the 1920s and 30s, consisting in large part of Russian émigrés, espoused the eventual establishment of a Slavic homeland called "Turania.") An entry in the diary of Romain Rolland, dated March 1914, would seem to identify the composer with ideas central to the Eurasianist cause,[22] and some of Stravinsky's closest friends at the time were Eurasianists. Yet the evidence of a compositional or artistic commitment in this direction is slim. There are no references to the Eurasianists in Stravinsky's writings or in the correspondence surrounding the composition and early performances of works such as *Les Noces*, *Renard*, and *The Soldier's Tale*. And the Eurasianist vision of an idyllic "symphonic society" can seem at odds not only with the abstract qualities of the fourth and final version of *Les Noces* (at which point Stravinsky had long adopted constructivist and formalist methods), but

---

[20] Fred Lerdahl and Ray Jackendoff, *A Generative Theory of Tonal Music* (Cambridge: MIT Press, 1983), 18. See, too, Justin London, *Hearing in Time: Psychological Aspects of Meter* (Oxford University Press, 2004), 3–14.

[21] See Richard Taruskin, *Defining Russia Musically: Historical and Hermeneutical Essays* (Princeton University Press, 1997), 393–460.

[22] Romain Rolland, *Journal des années de guerre 1914–1919* (Paris: Editions Albin Michel, 1952), 59. Cited in Taruskin, *Defining Russia Musically*, 411–12.

with the more ethnically driven features of the earlier versions as well.[23] We shall be returning to this issue a bit more closely in Chapter 10.

Discussed at the outset in Chapter 4 are features of ritual in the text and music of *Les Noces*. Several patterns of displacement in the first tableau are given a preliminary review. Of primary concern, however, are the block and layered structures of *Les Noces*, the means by which a larger sense of form is established.

The role of the "folk element" in Stravinsky's melodic style is discussed in Chapter 5, "Melody and Harmony in *Les Noces*." Issues of direct borrowing and the composer's technique of simulation are also addressed. The whole of *Les Noces* is viewed from the perspective of a comprehensive model of octatonic–diatonic relations, sketched along the lines of a *Tonnetz* and featuring intersecting cycles of perfect fifths, minor thirds, and major seconds. Unlike the neo-Riemannian tables that have been designed to accommodate some of the triadic yet non-tonal passages in the music of composers such as Wagner and Liszt, however, the unit of vocabulary traversing these interval cycles is the (0 2 3 5) Dorian tetrachord and its (0 2 5) trichordal subset. The (0 2 3 5) tetrachord and its embedded subset are of particular relevance to *Les Noces* and other works of the Russian period.

Our more detailed analysis of pitch relations in the opening tableaux of *Les Noces* elaborates on a number of passages of transition and stratification. This includes the lengthy stratified texture at Rehearsal Nos. 68–72 in the third tableau, a remarkable network of reiterating fragments and chords, all superimposed over a basso ostinato that is no less remarkable for its intricacy. Interactions between the diatonic and octatonic sets, relatively straightforward at the beginning of *Les Noces*, grow more novel as the piece unfolds. At the outset of the fourth tableau, the results on the octatonic side of this referential interaction are a tour de force,[24] as we suggest, the climactic point of a kind of "octatonic fever." With an explicit octatonic hand exposed early on in *Les Noces*, the temptation on Stravinsky's part seems to have been to push the envelope in later sections. The octatonicism is as lively and inventive here as it is anywhere in twentieth-century music.[25]

---

[23] Taruskin, *Defining Russia Musically*, 404.

[24] The term *reference* or *referential* is applied to pitch-class sets or collections which, like the octatonic and the diatonic and their orderings as scales in Stravinsky's music, play a dominant role in sections, pieces, and even stylistic periods; the subsets of these sets acquire the status of a *vocabulary*. In contrast, superset and subset are the more general, all-encompassing terms. See the earlier discussion of this terminology in Pieter C. van den Toorn, *The Music of Igor Stravinsky* (New Haven: Yale University Press, 1983), 49. Or see Benjamin Boretz, *Meta-Variations: Studies in the Foundations of Musical Thought* (Red Hook, NY: Open Space, 1995), 174–89.

[25] The octatonic or octatonic-diatonic approach to pitch relations in Stravinsky's music, introduced earlier in van den Toorn, *The Music of Igor Stravinsky*, is thus extended in this present volume.

Featured in Chapter 6 is the first *Renard* music to be composed, the *pribaoutka* at Rehearsal Nos. 64–67. Our discussion centers on the relationship between the flexible stresses in Stravinsky's text-setting and those resulting from the metrical displacement of repeated themes and fragments in his scores. The composer's habit of fixing the articulation of a given motive and its displaced repeats, a crucial element in the displacement process, is discussed at length. A concluding section, "Stravinsky contra Schoenberg," contrasts the composer's art of displacement with a number of assumptions underlying the Classical style.

Chapter 7 focuses on two stretches of music in *Renard*, the opening allegro at Rehearsal Nos. 0–9 and the con brio section accompanying the entrance of the Cat and Goat at No. 24. Another form of stratification, the allegro proved ideal as a way of bringing together the issues of rhythm, meter, pitch, and form introduced in previous chapters. Displacements at intermediate ranges are distinguished from those located to the background of the metrical grid. The intervention of octatonic relations is traced from the tritone transposition at Rehearsal No. 13 to the full implementation at Rehearsal No. 24. Chapter 7 ends with a discussion of the "Royal March" from *The Soldier's Tale*, where the particulars of displacement mirror those at the opening of *Renard*.

Melodic repeat structures are addressed in Chapter 8, as they appear not only at the opening of the *Symphonies of Wind Instruments*, but also, as a form of precedent, in the music of Debussy and Rimsky-Korsakov. Distinctions are drawn along the following lines: the metrical displacement that invariably inflects the repeated motive in Stravinsky's structures rarely does so in Debussy's or Rimsky-Korsakov's. Block structures in the *Symphonies* and the technique of juxtaposition more generally are examined from the standpoint of the implied discontinuity. Radical interpretations of these structures, reflecting a form of metrical parallelism, imply either an absence of meter or a constant interruption thereof.

Chapter 9 turns to a number of issues involving aesthetics and the strict performance style as it applies to Stravinsky's music. As key to the strict style, we stress the curtailment in the use of expressive timing or rubato, along with the musical processes that may be credited with having triggered

---

The approach is derived in part from Arthur Berger, "Problems of Pitch Organization in Stravinsky," in Benjamin Boretz and Edward T. Cone, eds., *Perspectives on Schoenberg and Stravinsky* (New York: W. W. Norton, 1972), 123–54. For an alternative perspective, see Dmitri Tymoczko, "Stravinsky and the Octatonic: A Reconsideration," *Music Theory Spectrum* 24 (2002): 68–102. Largely in place of the octatonic, Tymoczko infers a great many orderings and hybrid orderings of the diatonic set, including the harmonic and melodic minor scales. His views are debated in Pieter C. van den Toorn, "The Sounds of Stravinsky," *Music Theory Spectrum* 25, no.1 (2003): 167–87. See, too, in the same issue of *Music Theory Spectrum*, Tymoczko's reply, "Stravinsky Reconsidered Again," 187–202.

these innovations. Our concluding chapter, "Stravinsky and His Critics," focuses on several critical approaches, including those of T. W. Adorno, Richard Taruskin, Jonathan Kramer, and Hans Keller. (Kramer and Keller are also featured briefly in Chapter 8.) The socio-political understanding shared by Adorno and Taruskin encompasses a form of embodiment; the repetitive, static, and ritualistic features of Stravinsky's music are alleged to harbor autocratic, anti-humanistic, and even fascist impulses. In Taruskin's account, these impulses are traced to the composer himself and, more specifically, to Stravinsky's "objectivist aesthetics."[26] With particular reference to the music and scenario of *Les Noces*, we challenge these interpretations, offering an alternative view of the repetition, ritual, and immobility that so strongly inflect the music of Stravinsky's Russian era.

Two concluding sections in Chapter 10 return the discussion full cycle to *Les Noces* and *The Rite of Spring* and to the matter of their expressive content. Here, too, we offer an alternative to the prevailing accounts, to the harsh light in which the various stylistic features mentioned above have been cast, the indifference and "anti-humanism" for which they have been made to stand.

[26] Taruskin, "Stravinsky and Us," 282.

1 Meter and metrical displacement in Stravinsky

> Nothing is fecund save the strife versus the obstacle; there is no creation save the action of overcoming resistance ... Stravinsky has never destroyed the measured bar; he struggles against it, he disarticulates it, he multiplies and hooks up the different meters, but he never permits himself once, and for good and all, to get rid of this bothersome fiction, for he needs the annoyance, the resistance, against which to leap and surge, for there is no rhythmic diversity without stability.
>
> (Boris de Schloezer, "An Abridged Analysis," in Edwin Corle, ed., *Igor Stravinsky*)

Meter and its definitions

Even with the uniformly spaced beats of a given level of metrical pulsation idealized as "points in time" and distinguished as such from the grouping of motives, themes, and phrases,[1] the implications for meter need not be mechanical. Meter is a form of habit, no doubt, measurement internalized by the listener. As introduced by Fred Lerdahl and Ray Jackendoff in their *A Generative Theory of Tonal Music*, meter consists of a hierarchy or grid of five or so interacting, nested levels of pulsation.[2] If the number of such levels is reduced to two, the nature of the interaction is made apparent: the slower level marks off the faster one in equally spaced time-spans of two or three units. Yet the engagement presupposed by such a conception need not be the passive or perfunctory one questioned at length in critiques of the Lerdahl-Jackendoff approach.[3] Not only is the regularity of meter invariably tempered by the traditional liberties of performance (indeed, even with relatively strict

---

[1] Fred Lerdahl and Ray Jackendoff, *A Generative Theory of Tonal Music* (Cambridge: MIT Press, 1983), 18.

[2] *Ibid.*, 17–25. The Lerdahl–Jackendoff approach to meter has been sustained in a host of subsequent publications, including Joel Lester, *The Rhythms of Tonal Music* (Carbondale: Southern Illinois University Press, 1986), and William N. Rothstein, *Phrase Rhythm in Tonal Music* (New York: Schirmer Books, 1989). In Justin London's *Hearing in Time: Psychological Aspects of Meter* (Oxford University Press, 2004), the thesis is also largely consistent with Lerdahl's and Jackendoff's, even if London's point of departure is psychological or cognitive rather than linguistic.

[3] See Christopher F. Hasty, *Meter as Rhythm* (Oxford University Press, 1997), 148–49, 168–74. In search of a new theory of meter as process, one that would allow for greater degrees of "spontaneity," "freedom," and "metrical particularity" (instead of "metrical type"), Hasty argues against "formality" and the conception of beats as durationless points in time. He deplores "the

applications of the beat), but its assimilation by the listener is deeply physical in nature.[4]

Internalized, meter is synchronized with our "internal clock mechanisms," biological and cognitive in function.[5] These mechanisms are oscillations in the main, back-and-forth motions described metaphorically as "wave-like" by Victor Zuckerkandl.[6] Complementary parts move in a periodic fashion ("rhythmically," to use the psychologist's term). And they are varied as well as manifold. At an early age (six months), infants rock back and forth "rhythmically." And they suck "rhythmically," too.[7] And this, also, is reflexive. Infants inhale and exhale, and are also likely to walk rhythmically and at a moderate pace; rocking, breathing, and walking are motor behaviors. Indeed, the analogy of these behaviors is not only to the regular strong-weak alternation of metrical beats, but also to the middle range of a metrical hierarchy, the moderate tempos that are typically the most salient for the listener.

At an even more elementary level, neurons are transmitted by impulse. Pointing to "the human mind" rather than to biological rhythms, Robert Gjerdingen has examined "the regular up-and-down oscillation" of neural populations; the "rhythmic" ebb and flow of such populations.[8] This is what internalization is, evidently: the synchrony of meter with alternating states of excitation and inhibition. Musical meter engages "our psychobiologic beings" in this way.[9] As a particular kind of motor behavior, it becomes *entrained*, synchronized with aspects of our internal selves. Made physically a part of us,

---

reduction of meter to the mechanical repetition of equal durations conceived as habit," or the idea that our "actions" are coordinated "by an independent mechanism conceived as an internal clock or set of clocks" (168–69).

[4] *Ibid.*, 168–74. Some of Hasty's concerns about the "mechanical" conception of meter in the Lerdahl–Jackendoff approach are anticipated in Victor Zuckerkandl, *Sound and Symbol: Music and the External World*, trans. Willard R. Trask (Princeton University Press, 1956), 170–71. More specifically, Zuckerkandl contemplates the "merging" of meter and rhythm, the "transformation" of meter "into rhythm." The idea is rejected, however, and because of the "clearly distinguishable" principles of meter and rhythm. And the rejection comes even as Zuckerkandl freely admits that the regularity or periodic nature of meter is not one of "mechanical strictness" or accuracy, but is subject "to constant slight alterations" in performance. "[Meter] seems to be made of rubber not of steel." On the question of expressive timing in performance, see the remarks on "meter and expressive variation" in London, *Hearing in Time*, 164–73. London notes as well that, in the mind of the listener, a meter will often fluctuate "from relatively rich patterns of expectation with several additional levels of structure above and below the beat and/or measure to patterns that are relatively sparse, a bare bones series of beats." The periodicities of some levels may remain invariant, while others on the musical surface "may come and go." These shifts, "from thick to thin, may be as dramatic [as] changes in the basic pattern of beats" (104–05).

[5] David Epstein, *Shaping Time: Music, the Brain, and Performance* (New York: Schirmer Books, 1995), 138.

[6] See Zuckerkandl, *Sound and Symbol*, 169–80.

[7] On the early "rhythmic" behavior of infants, see Paul Fraisse, "Rhythm and Tempo," in Diana Deutsch, ed., *The Psychology of Music* (New York: Academic Press, 1982), 151–53.

[8] Robert Gjerdingen, "Meter as a Mode of Attending: A Network Simulation of Attentional Rhythmicity in Music," *Intégral* 3 (1989): 67–92. See, too, the discussion of this in London, *Hearing in Time*, 12–28.

[9] Neil Todd, "A Model of Expressive Timing in Tonal Music," *Music Perception* 3, no. 1 (1985): 35.

it becomes a "mode of attending,"[10] one of focusing and of "continually casting ourselves forward by rhythmically anticipating future events that may occur within smaller and larger time intervals."[11] The dynamic mode of engagement made possible by such means of attunement is not deterred all that easily. Once established in the mind of the listener, a meter is abandoned or "renounced" only "in the face of strong contradictory evidence."[12]

At the same time, the levels of a metrical hierarchy are not equally salient. At a moderate range of about 80–100 beats per minute (BPM),[13] one level is likely to stand out against the others. This is the *tactus*, the level at which feet are tapped, batons waved, and so forth.[14] Following this, the minimal requirement for meter is that "the tactus be coordinated with one other level of pulsation."[15] In Justin London's *Hearing in Time*, the ideal meter consists of a tactus flanked on either side by one or more additional levels. The rapid, moderate, and relatively slow rates of pulsation resulting from this balanced framework correspond to a "subdivision of the tactus, the tactus level itself, and a higher level ordering of beats in measures."[16] Alternatively, in Harold Krebs's study of metrical conflict in the music of Schumann and others, the levels of the metrical hierarchy are broken down into a "pulse level" and one or more "interpretative levels." The pulse level is "the fastest level," Krebs explains, while "the slower levels are interpretive in the sense that they impose a metrical interpretation on the pulse level."[17]

---

[10] Gjerdingen, "Meter as a Mode of Attending," 67–92.

[11] Mari Riess-Jones, "Only Time Can Tell: On the Topology of Mental Space and Time," *Critical Inquiry* 7, no. 3 (1981): 571. Reiss-Jones's argument extends to our ability to attend or focus more generally. In attending to an event or object, "we can cast ourselves cognitively toward a good vantage point," and do so "rhythmically" (*metrically*, in other words), in a fashion "that is regularly spaced in time." We program events "rhythmically," which in turn allows us to anticipate accurately.

[12] Lerdahl and Jackendoff, *A Generative Theory*, 17. See, also, London, *Hearing in Time*, 25: "We actively seek and generate temporal structure through our attending behaviors. The way we attend to the present is strongly affected by our immediate past; once we have established a pattern of temporal attending we tend to maintain it in the face of surprises, noncongruent events, or even contradictory invariants. Music often depends on our making an effort to project and maintain an established meter in passages that involve things like syncopation and hemiola."

[13] The rate of the tactus can vary significantly from one context to the next, to be sure, yet the range of about 80–100 BPM would seem to be "maximally salient" for the listener; see London, *Hearing in Time*, 31. London cites several empirical studies in this regard, including Richard Parncutt, "A Perpetual Model of Pulse Salience and Metrical Accent in Musical Rhythms," *Music Perception* 11, no. 4: 409–64. More particularly, in empirical study, a distinct preference manifests itself for pulsation at about 100 BPM, "a pronounced peak of maximum pulse salience" (31). The range within which beat perception and entrainment can occur is about 30 to 240 BPM. Beats can be assimilated in an integrated fashion within those limits, "holistically" rather than analytically. At the same time, beat perception would seem to require "at least the potential of hearing a subdivision" (35), a stipulation that would mean an extension on both sides of this range.

[14] See Lerdahl and Jackendoff, *A Generative Theory*. "Perceptually the most salient metrical level" (284), the tactus is the level at which "the regularities of metrical structure are most stringent" (27).

[15] London, *Hearing in Time*, 17.   [16] *Ibid.*, 18.

[17] Harold Krebs, "Some Extensions of the Concepts of Metrical Consonance and Dissonance," *Journal of Music Theory* 31, no. 1 (1987): 101.

Both London's and Krebs's approaches will concern us in subsequent chapters.

Given its built-in constraints, which include the ability of the listener to entrain and the salience of the middle range of the metrical hierarchy, meter is inevitably "a relatively local phenomenon."[18] In moving above the bar line (hypermeter) or below the tactus (subtactus levels of pulsation), meter begins to recede. The sense of an upbeat-downbeat, weak-strong alternation (and hence ultimately of a higher- or lower-level division) dims and then disappears altogether. And the implications here are crucial where metrical displacement is concerned. As we shall see in forthcoming chapters, as meter dims, so, too, does displacement and the disruptive effect it can have on the meter. The effect of disruption is a *potential*, we should stress, subject to a great many variables in any given instance. And it is not, strictly speaking, the displacement of a repeated fragment or chord that triggers the disruption, but rather the expectations of *metrical parallelism* that are thwarted in the process.

Metrical parallelism is another important concept where meter is concerned.[19] When a melody is repeated, the normal expectation is that the repeat will occur at a metrically parallel location. When this expectation is met, both the original alignment *and* the meter are confirmed.[20] When it is not (when the repeated melody is metrically displaced), a form of syncopation is apt to result. Most often in the common-practice music of the eighteenth and nineteenth centuries, the forces of meter override those of metrical parallelism, and the repeated melody is read as metrically displaced or non-parallel.

Conflicts of this kind between meter and the forces of metrical parallelism underlie Stravinsky's settings of displacement. Yet the threat of an actual interruption of the meter is far more pervasive in Stravinsky's settings than it is in more traditional contexts. A number of factors may be cited in this connection, most notably tempo and the increasingly shallow locations of the meter at which a displacement may occur (*metrical location*).

---

[18] Lerdahl and Jackendoff, *A Generative Theory*, 21.

[19] See Lerdahl and Jackendoff, *A Generative Theory*, 74–75. The authors treat metrical parallelism as a "metrical preference rule." In passages of displacement or non-parallelism, this rule comes into conflict with "well-formedness rules" stipulating that the beats of a metrical level of pulsation must be equally spaced. Most often in the traditional contexts examined by Lerdahl and Jackendoff, the latter trumps the former; the more "global" demand for meter and equally spaced beats overrides the "local" one for metrical parallelism. The perceptual-cognitive implications of metrical parallelism and non-parallelism in traditional tonal contexts are discussed in David Temperley, "Motivic Perception and Modularity," *Music Perception* 13, no. 2 (1995): 141–69.

[20] Parallelism can play a vital role in both the establishment and confirmation of a meter. See the detailed study of this in David Temperley and Christopher Bartlette, "Parallelism as a Factor in Metrical Analysis," *Music Perception* 20, no. 2 (2002): 117–49.

Example 1.1. *Renard*, opening allegro, mm. 7–13

By way of illustration, see Example 1.1. Taken from the opening section of *Renard*, the passage is one to which we shall be returning in Chapter 7. The metrical analysis applied directly below the musical quotation follows the familiar Lerdahl-Jackendoff path; beats, analogous to points in time, are represented by dots. Reading from top to bottom, the inferred hierarchy starts with the level of the sixteenth-note beat and is followed by that of the eighth-note beat, the quarter-note beat (the likely tactus at 126 BPM), the half note beat or bar line and, hypermetrically, the whole-note or two-measure beat. The latter is in large part a reflection of the two-measure span of the ostinato pattern. In addition, the excerpt exhibits a form of *stratification*.[21] The irregularly spaced entrances of the clarinet fragment, displaced relative to the 2/4 bar line already at m. 9, are superimposed over the conflicting two-measure span of the basso ostinato.[22]

Of more immediate concern here, however, is the application to Stravinsky's music of a theory of meter drawn in large part from the tonal repertories of the eighteenth and nineteenth centuries. Critical above all is the sharp distinction Lerdahl and Jackendoff draw between *meter* and *grouping*.[23]

---

[21] See note 3 in the Introduction for a brief description of stratification or layering. Registrally and often instrumentally fixed, fragments and chords repeat according to varying spans or cycles. Alignment will shift between the fragments and chords themselves and as they relate to the meter (displacement).

[22] We use the term *fragment* to underscore the short, open-ended character of melody in *Les Noces*, *Renard*, and other Russian-period works. When repeated, as fragments invariably are in these contexts, they become *motivic*; *fragment* and *motive* are used very nearly interchangeably in this study. *Segment*, the more general term, underscores a bit more forcefully the idea of a division of the melodic surface. Its use here covers fragment, motive, as well as lengthier spans of melodic material.

[23] Lerhdahl and Jackendoff, *A Generative Theory*, 25–30. The distinction between meter and grouping, more specifically between beats conceptualized as durationless "points in time" and groupings (motives, themes, and the like) defined in terms of duration, is critical to a hearing and understanding of the processes and stylistic features we will be examining in this volume.

Grouping, the more universal of the two concepts, entails the "chunking" or segmenting of musical materials into motives, themes, phrases, periods, and so forth. While the resultant groups possess duration, metrical beats do not. Beats are separated from each other by distances, intervals which are termed *time-spans*. While meter and grouping interact, they are intrinsically separate and independent phenomena.

By the same token, metrical accents are not *phenomenal* accents.[24] While relatively strong beats are metrical accents, local stresses such as attack points and long-held notes are phenomenal. Along with slurs, dots, and dynamic shadings, phenomenal accents are often a part of what we will be referring to as *articulation*. The latter, too, can play a crucial role in processes of displacement and stratification.

Metrical displacement in Stravinsky

A central concern of Stravinsky's settings of displacement is not the motive and the elaboration of its features (as it often is with the music of the Classical and Romantic eras, to follow Schoenberg's account of "the style of developing variation"),[25] but just the opposite, namely the literal repetition of a motive's features. Repetition itself follows a different logic. In works of Stravinsky's Russian period above all, motives, themes, and chords are repeated not to be elaborated upon along traditional lines, but to be

Hence, as a framework for this discussion, our preference for the accounts of meter in Lerdahl and Jackendoff's *A Generative Theory* and London's *Hearing in Time*, where the meter–grouping distinction is underscored markedly.

[24] *Ibid.*, 17–18.

[25] Arnold Schoenberg, *Fundamentals of Musical Composition*, ed. Gerald Strang and Leonard Stein (London: Faber and Faber, 1967), 8. In spelling out the implications of the concept of "developing variation," Schoenberg divided the "features of the motive" into four large categories, namely, *rhythm, intervals, harmony*, and *melody*. The means by which these features were varied were spelled out in considerable detail; a melody could be altered "by transposition," "by semi-contrapuntal treatment of the accompaniment," and so forth (10). "Homophonic music can be called the style of developing variation. This means that in the succession of motive-forms produced through variation of the basic motive, there is something that can be compared to development, to growth" (8). Or see the description of "developing variation" in Arnold Schoenberg, *Style and Idea: Selected Writings of Arnold Schoenberg*, ed. Leonard Stein, trans. Leo Black (Berkeley: University of California Press, 1985): "Criteria for the Evaluation of Music," 129–31. Ideas encompassed by Schoenberg's use of the term "developing variation" underlie much current understanding not only of Schoenberg's music but also of the Classical or "homophonic" style generally: see, for example, Carl Dahlhaus, "What is 'developing variation'?", in Carl Dahlhaus, *Schoenberg and the New Music*, trans. Derrick Puffett and Alfred Clayton (Cambridge University Press, 1987), 128–34; and Carl Dahlhaus, *Between Romanticism and Modernism* , trans. Mary Whittall (Berkeley: University of California Press, 1980), 40–52. The concept is further explored in Walter Frisch, *Brahms and the Principle of Developing Variation* (Berkeley: University of California Press, 1983). The continuing role of "developing variation" in Schoenberg's atonal and twelve-tone repertories is examined in Jack Boss, "Schoenberg's Op. 22 Radio Talk, and Developing Variation in Atonal Music," *Music Theory Spectrum* 14, no. 2 (1992): 125–49; and Ethan Haimo, "Developing Variation and Schoenberg's Twelve-Tone Music," *Music Analysis* 16, no. 3 (1997): 349–65.

displaced metrically. And in the displacement of such entities, features other than alignment are retained in order that alignment itself (and its shifts) might be set in relief. The literalness of the repetition acts as a foil in this respect. As features of pitch, interval, duration, and articulation are retained, alignment shifts.

This is not the whole of it, however. Literalness in the repetition of a fragment acts as a counterforce, too, a way of referring the listener back to the fragment's original placement. With all other features of the motive retained, the expectation is that its original alignment will be repeated as well. And the more that is repeated literally, the more fully aroused are these conflicting expectations of metrical parallelism likely to be.

The implications here are fiendish. To repeat a theme, motive, or chord literally and without variation so as to highlight and expose its displacement is to undermine that displacement at the same time. It is to raise a conflicting signal of metrical parallelism. Typically, and with varying degrees of intensity, listeners are caught off guard by this. Unable to commit themselves initially to a reading of displacement or to one of metrical parallelism, they are apt to lose their metrical bearings. And the disruption has to do not with one or the other of these two signals, but with their conflict, with the fact that there is insufficient evidence for an easy, automatic ruling in favor of one or the other.

And the experience may be repeated. The conflict may be relived from one hearing to the next. Listeners can "go through pretty much the same motions," suffer something of the same consequences.[26] In this respect, conscious memory can indeed be independent of on-the-spot processing. Overexposure can breed fatigue and inattention, to be sure, while subsequent hearings can benefit in some measure from seepage. To a remarkable degree, however, listeners are

[26] Ray Jackendoff, "Musical Parsing and Musical Affect," *Music Perception* 9, no. 2 (1991): 227. According to Jackendoff, along the lines indicated in J. A. Fodor, *Modularity of Mind* (Cambridge: MIT Press, 1983), "the parser is modular and 'informationally encapsulated' from musical memory. It does not care whether the piece is familiar or not, and goes through pretty much the same motions regardless." Hence, "whatever structure is retrieved from memory in the course of producing a musical image, the processor goes dumbly to work on it, recreating the structure already being stored in and retrieved from long-term memory ... In essence, the parser is always hearing the piece for the first time" (227–28). For a discussion of this and other theories of the relevant cognitive processes, as well as of the implications of these theories for music listening and music theory, see Mark DeBellis, *Music and Conceptualization* (Cambridge University Press, 1995), 80–116. Needless to say, there are competing theories about the listener's ability to relive repeatedly the experiences associated with phenomena such as metrical displacement. In Bob Snyder, *Music and Memory: An Introduction* (Cambridge: MIT Press, 2000), 88, this ability to relive is attributed to the uniqueness of expressive nuance in performance, the fact that such nuance is not "easily rehearsed" and "by-passes the function of long-term memory." Circumventing "explicit long-term memory," expressive timing is "ineffable," and "this is probably the major reason why recordings, which freeze the details of particular performances, can be listened to many times and continue to seem vital and interesting." For an earlier discussion of these issues, see Leonard Meyer, *Music, the Arts, and Ideas* (University of Chicago Press, 1967), 46–53.

able "to be taken in" by a given displacement upon repeated hearings, to experience something of the same jolt.[27]

In Example 1.1 from the opening of *Renard*, the principal fragment in the clarinet is introduced on the first quarter-note beat of a 2/4 measure, only to be displaced to the second quarter-note beat two measures later. In half-note beats, it falls first on and then off the beat. How is this shift likely to be interpreted? Will listeners read through the displacement with the steady 2/4 meter sustained as a frame of reference? Or, alternatively, will they be taken in by the literalness of the repetition, by the fixed character of the articulation (the phrase markings)? Will they attempt to match that literalness with the fragment's original placement on the half-note beat? And will they do so by interrupting the meter at the half-note beat, adding an irregular (or "extra") quarter-note beat to the count at m. 8?[28]

The first of these two interpretations is *conservative*. An established meter is sustained (*conserved*) in order that the "same" fragment might be read through placed and displaced. The second is *radical*. The meter is interrupted in order that the repeat of the fragment might be aligned as before.[29] The reciprocity of the relationship between these two metrical interpretations is summarized graphically in Figure 1.1. Reading from left to right, conservative listeners adjust the alignment of a repeated theme, motive, or chord ("change") by holding on to an established meter ("no change"), while radical listeners do the

---

[27] Jackendoff, "Musical Parsing," 227. The ability "to be taken in" repeatedly by a musical phenom- enon such as displacement is examined from the standpoint of the deceptive cadence. "Because the parser is independent of conscious memory," Jackendoff concludes, "it will be taken in every time by a deceptive cadence, which will produce its characteristic affect." See note 26 above.

[28] The notion of the "extra" beat is borrowed from Andrew Imbrie, "'Extra' Measures and Metrical Ambiguity in Beethoven," in Alan Tyson, ed., *Beethoven Studies* (New York: Norton, 1973): 45–66. In Imbrie's studies of metrical irregularity in Beethoven's music, however, "extra" beats are beats at the level of the bar line and above (hypermeter), not, as here in *Renard*, at the level of the tactus.

[29] The distinction between "conservative" and "radical" responses, between allowing the meter to be sustained and allowing it to be interrupted, was first made in Imbrie, "'Extra' Measures and Metrical Ambiguity in Beethoven," 45–66. Imbrie stressed the "conservative force" of meter: "[Meter] is the principle that attempts to reduce to 'law and order' the rhythmic complexities of the musical surface ... the frame of reference by which we try to measure and judge relative values ... Our desire for security prompts us to accept the simplest, most nearly regular interpretation ..." The distinction was then introduced in Lerdahl and Jackendoff, *A Generative Theory*, 23–25, as a way of classifying alternative readings of hypermeter at the opening of Mozart's G minor symphony, K. 550. It has also been applied to various types of responses to displacement in *The Rite of Spring*; see Pieter C. van den Toorn, *Stravinsky and "The Rite of Spring": The Beginnings of a Musical Language* (Berkeley: University of California Press, 1987), 67. And see Gretchen Horlacher, "Metric Irregularity in *Les Noces*: The Problem of Periodicity," *Journal of Music Theory* 39, no. 2 (1995): 285–310. There are obvious correspond- ences here as well to the distinctions drawn between "accentual meter" and "metric grouping" in Candace Brower, "Memory and the Perception of Rhythm," *Music Theory Spectrum* 15, no. 1 (1993): 27–33. Conservative interpretations correspond to Brower's "accentual meter," radical interpretations to her "metric grouping." The first of these categories involves the sustaining of a regular meter, while the second involves adjusting "to changes in the spacing of events by simply adding or subtracting measures" (28–29). Brower sees the two as representing "fundamentally different ways of organizing and perceiving rhythm."

	change	no change
conservative →	placement (displacement)	meter
radical ⟶	meter	placement

Figure 1.1. Alternative responses to displacement

Figure 1.2. Figure and ground

reverse, adjust their metrical bearings ("change") in order to persevere with an established alignment ("no change"). A measure of *conservation* thus underlies both interpretations, whether it be meter in the case of the conservative response, alignment in that of the radical one.

There are obvious correspondences here to the figure-and-ground experiments of Gestalt psychology. The well-known Rubin vase shown in Figure 1.2 may be viewed either as a white vase with two opposing profiles as a background (unfocused) or as two profiles with the vase as background (unfocused).[30] And although readers may switch from one of these orientations to the other, they cannot attend to both simultaneously. Even as they attend, they are unlikely to do so all that firmly. For the evidence in support of a flip-flop, of allowing what is figure (focused) to become ground (unfocused) and vice versa, is in no way eliminated by their attention. A certain precariousness is likely to qualify the experience.

More specifically with the clarinet fragment in the opening allegro of *Renard*, the alternative barrings in Examples 1.2a and b are taken from the finished score and an early sketch of Stravinsky's, respectively. Typical of Stravinsky's methods of cutting and pasting, the fragment is sliced up into smaller segments or "cells," units which are then repeated independently of one another. As the brackets indicate in Example 1.2a, the series of irregularly spaced entrances that results from this segmentation spans 5+2+5 quarter-note beats. (The quarter-note beat is the likely tactus here with a marking of 126 BPM.) In the finished score, Example 1.2a, the resultant displacements lie exposed to the eye. The assumption here is that the passage will be heard and understood conservatively, that is, with the clarinet fragment newly placed at m. 9 and m. 10. The steady 2/4 meter on which these displacements hinge is introduced and then maintained in large part by the basso ostinato, which acts as a metrical backdrop. Further support for the notated meter is lent by the clarinet fragment's stressed Gs on the downbeats of m. 7 and m. 8, and by the metrical squareness of the accompanying fragment in the cimbalom (not shown in Example 1.2a).

The radical alternative outlined in Example 1.2b stems from an early sketch of Stravinsky's.[31] One of the many in the *Renard* sketchbook that would seem to indicate the composer's awareness of these conservative and radical options, the sketch follows several drafts in which the conservative solution of the finished score is already in place. (The sketch may have arisen as an afterthought, in fact, with the composer having wanted to test the radical option on paper.) Here, the bar line shifts in order that the repeats of the clarinet fragment might be aligned in a parallel fashion. All repeats fall on the downbeat, with the assumption that the passage will be read radically, with the half-note beat or 2/4 bar line interrupted at m. 8 and m. 11. And much of the motivation for the notated metrical irregularity in Stravinsky's music may be traced accordingly; that is, to attempts to expose these opposing forces of metrical parallelism. Still more radical from this perspective is the parallel

---

[30] See the discussion of these balanced figure and ground images in Aron Gurwitsch, *The Field of Consciousness* (Pittsburgh: Duquesne University Press, 1964), 117–21.

[31] The available sketches of *Renard* are housed at the Paul Sacher Foundation in Basel, Switzerland. The passage in Example 1.2b is transcribed and transposed from p. 5 of the composer's sketchbook.

alignment in the analytical notation of Example 1.2c. In this final illustration, only the entrances of the clarinet fragment fall on the downbeats of the shifting bar lines.

No doubt, as outlined in Examples 1.2a and b, the distinction between these conservative and radical interpretations is clearcut. On the conservative side, the 2/4 meter is entrained and the repeats of the clarinet melody and its initial segment are heard as displacements. In contrast, radical listeners, unable to capture something of a higher-level beat (specifically here, the half-note beat or bar line), will hear the passage as essentially meterless. The irregularly spaced entrances of the clarinet fragment will be absorbed as a form of grouping or phrasing.

Yet many listeners may find themselves not at one or the other of these two poles, but rather betwixt and between. For them, the experience of reading through this passage in *Renard* is likely to be a good deal more conflicted than the alternative barrings in Examples 1.2a and b imply. In a more nuanced reading, conservative listeners might yet infer the half-note beat, to be sure, but not all that securely. Although not shown in Example 1.2a, the 2/4 meter of Stravinsky's conservative notation is preceded by an irregular 5/8 measure, one of the many complications we will be addressing in our more extended coverage of this opening section of *Renard* in Chapter 7. Further along at mm. 9–13, the disruptive potential of the displaced repeats of the clarinet fragment is apt to be heightened. Should the first of these displacements at m. 9 prove disruptive of the half-note beat, listeners would be forced to consider a number of alternatives. Shifting gears, they could acquiesce to the extra quarter-note beat imposed by the parallelism. Having done so, however, they might also seek to reinstate the half-note beat as a higher-level marker for the quarter-note beat as the tactus. (See, in this connection, the return of the stressed Gs and the 2/4 measure in Stravinsky's radical barring of Example 1.2b; the attempt at restoration might last a second or so.) In this way, a radical reading of this passage would emerge *by default*, as it were, the result of the listener's inability to follow through continuously (and hence conservatively) with the 2/4 bar line.

In a more conflicted setting of this kind, the disturbance of the half-note beat might inflect the quarter-note pulse as well, although theoretically this would not be the case. The quarter-note beat would continue unaffected by the disruption of the half-note beat. We would estimate the greater sense of conflict described directly above to be fairly common as a response to displacement more generally in Stravinsky's music.

In fact, as a way of accounting for this greater complexity of the listening experience, compromises have often been worked out in the notation. Many

Example 1.2. *Renard*, opening allegro, clarinet fragment, mm. 7–13

(a) score (conservative)
(b) early sketch (radical)
(c) rebarred (still more radical)

of these notational strategies involve crossings of the bar line with beams, attempts, at least on paper, to preserve both an established alignment (parallelism) and an established meter. Such solutions cannot alter perception, of course, or the role played by a frame of reference. Given sufficient cause, listeners will orient themselves as a matter of course, seeking a reliable groove, a *context* or backdrop against which to organize "events." Nor can these compromises alter the fact that, while listeners may orient themselves conservatively or radically in response to a displacement, they cannot do so both ways simultaneously. However much, by means of a crossing of the bar line, the notation may imply the possibility of such an option, opposing forces are set in motion, forces which are not ultimately reconcilable.[32] Attending to one of these forces, listeners can keep the other at bay, allowing it to be experienced dimly as a threat to the prevailing order.[33] But they cannot orient themselves both ways at the same time.

Yet the equivocation implied by the crossing of a bar line is not without perceptual implications. In the first split seconds of a response, the experience of a displacement may be confused, as we have observed. A displacement is felt not in isolation, obviously, but as it relates to a previously established placement. Intimations of that earlier alignment surface not as part of an evolving sense of structure (an overriding pattern inferred by the listener, in other words), but as something which conflicts with such a sense. And this is crucial. The feeling is that of a prevailing assumption gone amiss, and of being taken unawares by this. Assumptions about meter and the metrical alignment of a repeated fragment or chord, inferred reflexively and internalized at some earlier point, cannot be sustained. The process may be likened to that of a rug being pulled suddenly and unexpectedly from under the listener's feet. Although a part of the listener's unfocused environment at first, the rug, upsetting expectations by being pulled, is suddenly thrust to the surface of consciousness. (A few split seconds of disorientation may ensue before an awareness of these circumstances sets in.) And this is likely to be the case even with highly conservative readings, in which established levels of metrical pulsation may be clung to tenaciously. If only for a split second, a change in the metrical alignment of a repeated theme, motive, or chord is apt to bring about a slight disruption of that which underlies alignment, namely, meter.

---

[32] See London, *Hearing in Time*, 50. Empirical study would seem to indicate that "on any given presentation we tend to hear a passage under one and only one metric framework." When confronted with conflicting or "dissonant" levels of pulsation, "listeners will either (a) extract a composite pattern of all of the streams present, or (b) focus on one rhythmic stream and entrain to its meter while ignoring the metric implication of the other rhythmic streams" (84).

[33] The general premise here is that, while oriented or focused on a given interpretation or structure, whether conservative or radical in nature, listeners are still able to hold competing interpretations or structures at bay. Not only are they able to sense the challenge of an opposing interpretation or structure and be interrupted by it, but they can switch "in midstream" without having to backtrack to a beginning. See, in this connection, Jackendoff, "Musical Parsing": 214–17, 220–28. According to Jackendoff, listeners keep "multiple" or "parallel" interpretations at bay unconsciously while attending to one interpretation alone. "If subsequent events in the musical surface lead to a relative reweighing of the analyses," he writes, the selection process "can change horses in the midstream, jumping to a different analysis" (223). What Jackendoff overlooks, however, is the uncertainty and disruption the opposition of alternative metrical interpretations or structures can cause. Listeners may switch "in midstream" from one conservative or radical interpretation to another, but not without conflict or, often enough, real confusion and disorientation. It is not solely a matter of switching interpretations, in other words.

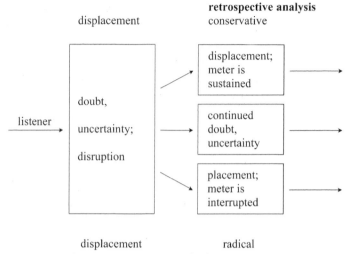

Figure 1.3. Alternative responses to displacement

At the first signs of change, then, confusion may reign. While the specific nature of the disturbance may not be known at first, it is likely to be sensed all the same. Figure 1.3 traces three possible response-patterns from an initial point of contact. Lasting anywhere from a split second to the lifetime of a listener's engagement with the context in question, an initial state of confusion is followed by a retrospective scramble to re-establish the lost frame of reference. Since the feeling is indeed likely to be that of an assumption gone amiss, assumptions in general may be put to the test: Was the fragment's earlier alignment correctly inferred? Was the meter correctly inferred? Should it be sustained, allowing for a perception of displacement? Alternatively, should it be interrupted, allowing for a parallel alignment? Much of this can pass in a few seconds.

What listeners seek is a *relationship*, a way of *relating* the old with the new. Sought is a means of connecting the various placements, acknowledging all as part of an overreaching train of thought.

In this way, too, metrical displacements and the conflict they initiate are largely unexpected. The listener is taken by surprise, as we have noted already, and the responses traced in Figure 1.3 correspond to those of the surprise more generally. To follow David Huron's account of the latter, surprises are the opposite of expectations, given that they occur after rather than before an event.[34] Consistent with the idea outlined in Figure 1.3 of an initial disorientation that is followed by a retrospective analysis, surprises

[34] David Huron, *Sweet Anticipation: Music and the Psychology of Expectation* (Cambridge: MIT Press, 2006), 19–40.

trigger two types of responses, an immediate "reaction response" and a slower "appraisal response." Unthinking, confused, and "deeply pessimistic," the reaction response puts the subject on high alert.[35] From the standpoint of the brain, information flows first to the thalamus, from which another pathway proceeds to the cerebral cortex, where the situation is appraised. The two pathways then converge in the lateral nucleus of the amygdala. Huron's conclusion is that, while musical surprises are capable of initiating the two responses, they are "short-lived because the ensuing appraisal ultimately judges the stimuli as non-threatening." The full expression of the "primordial behaviors of fight, flight, and freeze" is inhibited by the appraisal response.[36]

Observe, too, that the timings of the initial confused and subsequent analytical stages outlined in Figure 1.3 are left open. They can vary not only from one context to the next, but also from one listener to the next. Some displacements may be sensed fairly readily. Evidence in their support may be overwhelming, and the listener's initial doubt may be momentary and scarcely conscious. At other times, however, considerable thought and analysis may be required before the listener, retrospectively and with repeated hearings, is able to arrive at a conservative or radical reading, an integration of the disputed passage with an evolving sense of structure. (Worst-case scenarios involve outright dismissals, cases in which a disturbance of the meter is never made a part of such an emerging sense. Radical responses can arise *by default*, as we have observed; upset by the forces of parallelism, the listener is unable to persevere conservatively with an established meter.)

So, too, the details are likely to vary from one listener to the next. The same listener may react conservatively to one context, radically to another. And still another may switch in midstream, succumbing quite suddenly to the conflicting evidence which, up to that point, had served merely as a form of opposition.[37] And the possibility of a conservative or radical predisposition cannot be discounted either. The degree to which steady meters are internalized and made physically a part of the listener, synchronized with the listener's "internal clock mechanisms," may vary. Some listeners may be more susceptible than others in this regard. And their conservative responses may be a function of that susceptibility. Quite apart from the musical context in question, in other words, listeners may be predisposed to respond in the way they do. Figure 1.4 takes this possibility into account, rearranging Figure 1.3 accordingly. Listeners arrive on the scene inclined to react conservatively or radically, to sustain an established meter or to yield in this respect.

---

[35] *Ibid.*, 19–21.   [36] *Ibid.*, 39.   [37] See note 33 above.

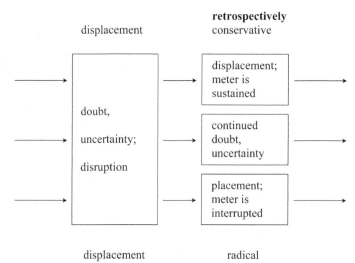

Figure 1.4. Alternative responses to displacement (with predisposition)

The variables are numerous and the complexity interwoven. While, as we have seen, specific ranges of tempo and metrical location can play a decisive role in determining the disruptive potential of a displacement, other factors can enter the equation, including the reiterated motive itself, and the length as well as regularity of the spans defined by its displacement. No single factor or combination of factors can work as a master key, determining the emergence of a conservative or radical reading from one setting to the next. Not all contexts invite the ultimate as far as a disruption is concerned, and it would be naive to insist that they should. As another part of the mix, too, there is the experience of the individual, a question of his/her disposition, as we observed.

Displacement, location, and intensity

Shown in Figure 1.5 is a way of classifying displacements on the basis of their location within a given metrical hierarchy or grid. (The given hierarchy here derives from the opening allegro of *Renard* at Rehearsal Nos. 0–9; see Example 1.2a.) Location is defined by two interacting levels of pulsation, a slower level which "interprets" or marks off the beats of a faster, "pulse" level.[38] The pulse level is the highest level at which the placed and

---

[38] Some of these terms are borrowed from Krebs, "Some Extensions," 101. Krebs concludes that the various "levels of motion . . . break down into a 'pulse level' and one or more 'interpretive levels.' The pulse level is the fastest level. The slower levels are interpretative in the sense that they impose a metrical interpretation on the pulse level."

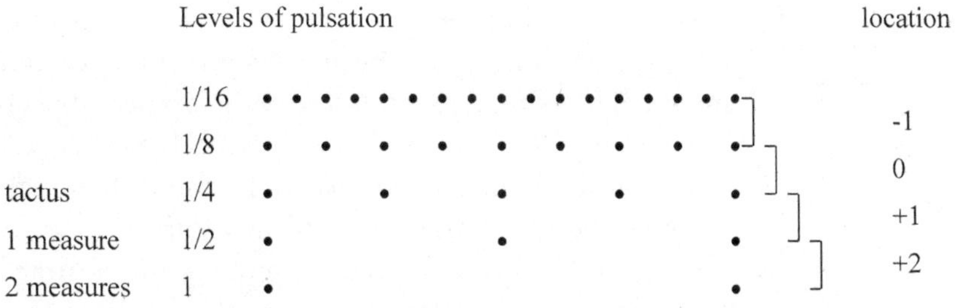

Levels of pulsation   location

Figure 1.5. *Renard*, Nos. 0–9; metrical displacement and metrical location

displaced entrances of a given fragment are beats, while the interpretative level is the next highest level at which those beats are marked off as onbeats or offbeats. In this way, displacement follows meter. At least two levels of pulsation must interact to meet its conditions, even if the effect of displacement may be felt at levels above and beyond any such initial interaction.

The levels of pulsation in Figure 1.5 are grouped in overlapping twos. At midpoint, at the degree marked "0," beats at the level of the tactus interpret those at the subtactus level just below. Here, the disruptive effect of a displacement is potentially at its highest: repeated fragments fall on and off the tactus, specifically in Figure 1.5, on and off the quarter-note beat. And, traditionally, this is where meter is centered, with the regularity of the tactus. This is where "the beat" is, so to speak, and where, as a result, the sense of a steady alternation between downbeats and upbeats, onbeats and offbeats, is most vivid. So, too, entrainment is likely to be at its deepest.

At the location marked +1, beats at the level just above the tactus interpret the tactus. Here, repeated fragments fall on and off the half-note beat (or bar line) rather than the quarter-note beat. Half-note rather than quarter-note beats are subject to interruption (quarter-note beats may continue uninterrupted), the disruptive effect of which is likely to be milder. This concerns time and timing as well as human psychology. The actual disturbance of the half-note beat at the degree of +1 may equal that of the quarter-note beat at the degree of 0. At a slower pace, however, displacement or the radical alternative of adding beats to the meter may be negotiated with greater ease.

Then, as this acute sense of meter fades when moving away from the tactus or the bar line, displacement fades, too. Extended beyond the immediate degrees of 0 and +1 and in the direction of either hypermeter or additional subtactus levels, displacement is felt less keenly. The listener's internalization of the meter is less marked, so that, when a fragment is displaced and the meter threatened or interrupted as a result, the sense of conflict is less severe; adjustments can be made more readily. (In Figure 1.5, locations above the degree of 0 are signified with a plus sign, degrees below, with a minus sign.)

Degrees higher than +2 at exclusively hypermetrical levels are possible, of course, but the impact of a displacement is likely to be increasingly faint. Similarly, degrees at exclusively subtactus levels are of little implication. There are practical considerations at work, in other words, limits to the extent to which the degrees of intensity, extended beyond those indicated in Figure 1.5, can take effect. These considerations involve structure not in the abstract, obviously, but structure as a reflection of the psychological processes of attention and engagement detailed above.

Shown in Examples 1.3a–d are the displaced repeats of another fragment from the opening allegro in *Renard*, arranged here according to the graduated scale of locations of Figure 1.5. The initial placement is followed by three displacements at increasingly shallow locations: introduced on the beat of a two-measure span in Example 1.3a, the fragment falls off the beat of that span in Example 1.3b. It then falls off the half-note beat or bar line in Example 1.3c, and finally off the quarter-note beat in Example 1.3d. While the last of these alignments is purely analytical in conception, the first three do indeed occur in Stravinsky's score, and in the order given here: following the initial placement, the degrees are progressively more shallow, the displacements themselves progressively more disruptive in their potential.

Earlier examples of displacement

Shifts in the metrical alignment of a motive or theme and the disturbance they can cause are not in themselves unique to Stravinsky's music. In the music of the Classical and Romantic eras, exact or near-exact restatements of thematic units may frequently be found falling on and off hypermetrical beats spanning two, three, and four measures. In the opening of Mozart's G minor Symphony, K. 550, for example, the repeat of the principal theme at m. 21 implies a reversal from even- to odd- numbered measures. At some point prior to the repeat, the steady hypermetrical level of two measures is shortened or lengthened by an extra measure, its alignment with the bar line displaced as a result.[39] And in the Menuetto of the same symphony (see Example 1.4), the three-measure module that may be inferred at the start of this movement fails to arrive "on target" with the start of the sequence at m. 15. A conflicting four-measure module intervenes at mm. 7–15, causing the

---

[39] See the metrical analysis of the opening of Mozart's G minor Symphony in Lerdahl and Jackendoff, *A Generative Theory*, 22–25.

Example 1.3. *Renard*, opening allegro, fragment of the combined soloists, displacements

falling-third sequence to begin not at m. 13 or m. 16 (as might have been expected had the three-measure module continued), but rather at m. 15.[40]

No doubt, as we have indicated, beats at hypermetrical levels of pulsation are spaced further apart, so that displacements are apt to be less intrusive. In

---

[40] Notice the hemiola rhythm in the first and second measures of the three-measure unit at mm. 1–9. Some long-term consequences of these and other metrical details are traced in Richard Cohn, "Metric and Hypermetric Dissonance in the Menuetto of Mozart's Symphony in G minor, K. 550," *Intégral* 6 (1992): 1–33. A number of general definitions and models of the hemiola are also introduced by Cohn, starting from other metrical and hypermetrical standpoints. The analogy between conflicting (and therefore "dissonant") levels of pulsation in hemiola passages and the concept of dissonance in pitch theory generally has been drawn repeatedly in analytic-theoretical venues. Cohn's point of departure is Krebs, "Some Extensions."

Example 1.4. Mozart, Symphony in G minor, K. 550, Menuetto, opening

radical interpretations, adding or subtracting beats to or from established levels of pulsation can be handled with less difficulty. Nor is the source of the disruption in older, hypermetrical examples always the start of the restatement or displaced repeat. In the passage cited in Example 1.4, the conflict begins at the second quarter-note beat of m. 9, the point at which the parallelism with the established three-measure module is broken. The motive reserved for the second beat of the second measure of the three-measure module reappears on the second beat of the third measure. And it does so as part of a chain, a process of sequential development, one that involves tonal transposition and hence a degree of modification (not the literalness that so often typifies the repetition of motivic features in Stravinsky's music).

And it is just here, in fact, with a view toward this element of motivic development, that the distinctions between displacement in the music of the Classical style and in that of Stravinsky come readily to the fore. In more traditional settings, where metrical alignment is but one of the many features of a motive that may be subject to development, changes in alignment can blend into the larger whole. They are often obscured by the variation that can affect virtually all aspects of the invention. In

Stravinsky's music, however, features other than alignment are often held constant, and for the reasons cited above. Melodic elaboration, transposition, and articulation are sacrificed in order that a fragment's displacement might be highlighted. As a result, displacement can play a larger and more prominent role. And Stravinsky's compositional feat – one of transferring to the salient middle range of the metrical hierarchy processes of alignment and realignment that had earlier been confined largely to the background (hypermeter) – can thus be seen as having ushered in a great many large-scale changes in melodic, harmonic, and instrumental language.

If only briefly, however, and as a means of further exposing Stravinsky's methods, the parallels with earlier contexts are worth exploring. At m. 9 in the Menuetto of Mozart's G minor Symphony (see Example 1.4), the hyper-metrical conflict or "dissonance" is "indirect" (as Harold Krebs has described "dissonances" of this kind in traditional contexts).[41] Although, on paper, the three- and four-measure modules succeed one another, traces of the former may persist in the mind of the listener well beyond the actual point of succession. Maintained conceptually in this way, these traces collide with the new four-measure module. The metrical conflict is felt "subliminally."[42] So, too, if the measures of the three-measure module are identified by the letters A, B, and C, then the first ten measures of the Menuetto would read as follows: ABC, ABC, and ABBB (where BBB is a tonal sequence built on the motives of the second measure).

At the same time, however, metrical displacement in more traditional contexts is not always confined to the background. A number of conditions seem to have invited shifts in alignment at shallower levels of structure; among these, the hemiola. Typically in passages featuring the latter, the bar line itself is challenged temporarily, while the level just below (possibly the tactus) is left undisturbed. In 3/4 contexts, half-note beats challenge the dotted half-note beat of the bar line. While, as the tactus, the quarter-note beat may continue uninterrupted, its interpretation by the bar line (the dotted half-note beat) is challenged by quarter-note beats grouped in twos (the half-note beat).

Curiously, however, discussions of the hemiola rhythm in Classical contexts have consistently ignored the key role played by displacement. For it is often the metrical realignment of a short motive, segment or chord that provides both the motivation and the necessary accentuation for the conflict.

Shown in Example 1.5a is the theme of the Minuet from Mozart's Serenade, *Eine Kleine Nachtmusik*, K. 525. Here, subsequent repeats of a rising two-note motive are transposed and displaced (see the brackets in

---

[41] See Krebs, "Some Extensions," 105.   [42] *Ibid.*, 106.

Example 1.5. Mozart, *Eine kleine Nachtmusik*, Minuet, opening theme

Example 1.5a). Introduced initially as a segment at the tail end of an ascending stepwise motion, the motive is first repeated on the third quarter-note beat of a 3/4 measure (over the bar line at mm. 2–3), only to be displaced to the second beat at m. 3. Spans between these repeats, while initially numbering three quarter-note beats, are narrowed to two beats, a process of compression which is carried a step further in the consequent phrase at mm. 6–7. In the latter, the motive is repeated four times as part of a descending sequence, falling on the third, second, and first beats, respectively, before it regains its initial alignment on the third beat. In the form of a hemiola cadence, a patterned cycle of displacement is thus forged, with repeats of the motive uniformly spaced and beginning and ending over the bar line. Incomplete and tentative at mm. 1–4, motivic repeats gain momentum at mm. 5–8, where they are further embellished and accentuated by turns.

What is thus missing routinely in Stravinsky's settings of displacement – a form of motivic elaboration – is here conspicuously evident. Displacements of the tiny two-note motive figure as part of a development. In a fashion consistent with Schoenberg's definition of "homophonic" or Classical music (the style of developing variation),[43] a segment, detached from a thematic configuration, is subjected to an elaboration. Repeats of the two-note motive, initially defined by a half step but transposed tonally to include whole steps, are not strictly literal but are developed in accord with an overriding descending motion, one which ends with a half cadence at m. 4 and a full cadence at m. 8. A useful comparison here might again be to the repetition of the clarinet fragment in the opening allegro of *Renard*, as marked off by the brackets above the treble stave in Example 1.2a. Repeats of this fragment are literal,

---

[43] See note 25 above.

untransposed, and instrumentally fixed. And in place of the uniform spacing between the repeats of the ascending two-note motive in the hemiola pattern of Example 1.5a, the spans between repeats of the clarinet fragment in the initial tutti section of *Renard* number 5+2+5+5+4 quarter-note beats.

Also useful as a comparison at this juncture is the repetition of the D-E motive over the bar line in the opening block of *Les Noces*, as bracketed below the soprano stave in Example 4.1. Here, too, repeats of the motive are literal and instrumentally unvarying. And although, in accord with our conservative rebarring of the block (see Example 4.3b), Stravinsky's pattern of displacement is also a cycle, the spans between repeats of the D-E motive are wildly irregular (see Example 4.2d).

In the Schenkerian graph of the Minuet theme in Example 1.5b, an "initial ascent" to the third scale degree (the B) is followed by a descending third progression. The latter is "interrupted" at the end of the antecedent phrase, only to be completed at the end of the consequent. The proverbial conflicts in segmentation between the Schoenbergian and Schenkerian approaches are here readily at hand, in the form of the motivic grouping of Example 1.5a and the harmonic-contrapuntal network of Example 1.5b. In the Schenkerian graph, the motive is defined by the descending third from the C as a neighbor to the B, and subsequently from the B and the A as well. The motivic grouping of the descending third is harmonic and contrapuntal rather than merely melodic in design, tied in this fashion to the graph as a whole.

Of concern here, however, is less the issue of motivic grouping than the larger sense of direction and purpose that is very much a part of both analytical approaches. The two-note motive bracketed in Example 1.5a may be compared to any number of similarly bracketed motives in the analytical portions of Schoenberg's *Style and Idea* and *Fundamentals of Musical Composition*. (Its analytical pursuit in Example 1.5a is owing to the crucial role that over-the-barline motives play in initiating cadential hemiolas.) In Schoenberg's *Fundamentals*, the idea of the motive is constrained only by size. Motives are the smallest "building blocks," the "lowest common denominators," and their ample multiplication, even when in conflict with structural boundaries of one kind or another, is viewed as evidence of depth and connectedness.[44]

No doubt, the metrical challenge posed by the half-note beats in the hemiola cadence of Example 1.5a is modest. The 2+2+2 pattern straddling the 3/4 bar line at mm. 6–7 is more like a grouping, a syncopation modestly tugging at the signature. The listener's sense of engagement may be

---

[44] Schoenberg, *Fundamentals*, 8.

heightened, but the prevailing dotted half-note beat is unlikely to be disrupted. The pattern intersects or arrives "on target" with the bar line after only two measures. And apart from the effect of displacement, the issue is one of persistence. Although regular, the pattern is insufficiently persistent to allow for an actual overturning of the bar line and a possible switch to the half-note beat. Perhaps the most that can be expected along these lines is an orientation toward the dotted whole-note beat, the beat spanning two 3/4 bars and the point of intersection between the two conflicting levels of interpretation.

The passages cited in Examples 1.6 and 1.7 are likely to be more strenuous in this regard. Both are drawn from minuet movements by Haydn. Each passage features a segment which, falling on the third beat of the measure and straddling the bar line as a result, is detached and is made the subject of an elaboration. Reappearing at the outset of the consequent phrase, the segment initiates a patterned cycle of displacement identical to the one examined in Example 1.5a. Indeed, features of this kind are typical of the hemiola in Classical contexts, even when, as in the case here, the hemiola is transferred from the cadence to a more formative stage of the phrase.[45] In Example 1.6 the cycle itself, uniformly spaced by the half-note beat, consists of four transposed repeats. Falling on the third, second, first, and third quarter-note beats, respectively, the motive begins and ends over the bar line. In Example 1.7, the sequence is a complete

Example 1.6. Haydn, String Quartet, Op. 17, No. 5/ii, mm. 21–29

[45] For an insightful account of the hemiola in the music of Haydn and the Classical era generally, see Floyd Grave, "Metrical Dissonance in Haydn," *Journal of Musicology* 12, no. 3 (1995): 168–202. The passages cited here in Examples 1.6 and 1.7 are both examined by Grave (180–84), although from a different perspective. The motivic segmentation is different in Grave's study from what it is here, while the element of displacement and its implications are largely ignored.

Example 1.7. Haydn, Symphony No. 104/iii, mm. 17–26

descending-fifth chain. Two fifth-related steps are paired (as is invariably the case with such chains), allowing for a canonic imitation of the cycle in the violas and cellos. The latter further underscores the half-note beat.

But it is the hemiola in the Minuet of Haydn's London Symphony (Example 1.7) that is apt to be the most demanding of these two examples. Initiating each phrase is the familiar over-the-bar line figure, here, a motive consisting of an arpeggiated triad. However, the initial cycle of four repeats is followed, with the overlapping of a single step, by another cycle. And there are no transpositions of the motive within these cycles, no changes in harmony. The repetition is literal from a melodic, harmonic, and articulative standpoint. Even more significantly, the harmonic change from the first to the second cycle accompanies the motivic repeat itself on the third beat of the measure. Indeed, the threes of the 3/4 signature are abandoned at mm. 21–25, triggering a form of indirect dissonance that is apt to be felt intensely by the listener.

All these features of the hemiola in Example 1.7 are indeed likely to lead to a disturbance of the bar line or dotted half-note beat. Several moments of disorientation and even a possible switch to the half-note beat are likely to follow for the listener, with the disruptive potential of the hemiola about as ferocious here as it is anywhere in the Classical tradition of Haydn, Mozart, and Beethoven.

The concept of metrical dissonance

In line with Harold Krebs's theory of "metrical dissonance," the hemiola patterns cited in Examples 1.5a, 1.6, and 1.7 are "grouping dissonances."[46] A pattern of repetition is "dissonant" with an interpretative level as defined by the meter. In the hemiola pattern of Mozart's Minuet theme (see Example 1.5a), a "2-layer" conflicts with the "3-layer" of the 3/4 signature (to continue here with Krebs's terminology);[47] above the quarter-note beat as the tactus (or, in this instance, the "pulse layer"), a pattern of half-note beats conflicts with the dotted half-note beat or bar line. Crucially, the two conflicting levels of interpretation intersect or arrive "on target" at regularly recurring points, here every two bars.

In Example 1.8 from the "Préambule" of Schumann's *Carnaval*, a two-note motive in the accompaniment by the left hand of the piano part ("oom-pah") outlines a complete cycle of displacement before reaching a cadence in the fifth measure, at which point the cycle is repeated. Beginning and ending on the beat, each of these cycles consists of four repeats of the two-note motive. In turn, the twos of these motivic repeats conflict with the threes of the steady 3/4 meter, the latter supported by, among other variables, the harmonic rhythm. The result is another grouping dissonance. The "cardinalities" of the two levels of metrical interpretation conflict, yielding regularly spaced points of intersection. In contrast, the right hand consists of another pattern of repetition, one which, although spanning three beats, begins on the second beat of the 3/4 measure. Here, the conflict with the 3/4 signature is a "displacement dissonance."[48] While the "cardinalities" of the meter and conflicting level of interpretation are the same (both

Example 1.8. Schumann, "Préambule," *Carnaval*, mm. 28–32

---

[46] See Krebs, "Some Extensions," 103–07. The application of the concepts of "grouping" and "displacement" to metrical "dissonance" in Schumann's music more generally is pursued at greater length in Harold Krebs, *Fantasy Pieces: Metrical Dissonance in the Music of Robert Schumann* (Oxford University Press, 1999). The terms "grouping" and "displacement" were borrowed from Peter Kaminsky, "Aspects of Harmony, Rhythm and Form in Schumann's *Papillons, Carnaval* and *Davidsbündlertänze*" (Ph.D. diss., Eastman School of Music, 1989). Earlier, in "Some Extensions," Krebs used the designations "Type A" and "Type B" for grouping and displacement, respectively.

[47] Krebs, *Fantasy Pieces*, 31–33.   [48] *Ibid.*, 33–36.

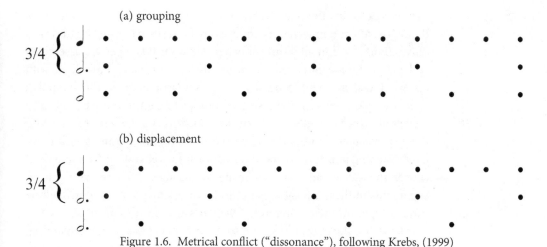

Figure 1.6. Metrical conflict ("dissonance"), following Krebs, (1999)

are 3-layers), there are no points of intersection between the two. Both types of metrical conflict, grouping and displacement, are outlined in Figure 1.6.[49]

Crucial from our perspective is the metrical displacement that, often enough, is as much a part of Krebs's grouping structures as it is of his displacement ones. The labels can be misleading from this standpoint, in fact, given that the conflicting level of interpretation in both grouping and displacement dissonances is often defined by a pattern of metrical realignment. In the "Préambule" from Schumann's *Carnaval* (Example 1.8), the conflicting 2-layer in the left-hand part involves the metrical displacement of a two-note motive. And in the consequent phrase of the Minuet theme from Mozart's *Eine Kleine Nachtmusik* (Example 1.5a), the 2-layer consists likewise of a cycle of displacement.

Krebs is careful to note that only rarely in Schumann's music do conflicts of the kind illustrated in Example 1.8 lead to a disruption of the meter. "The two conflicting levels are rarely heard as being equal in significance," he writes.[50] There is a "primary metrical consonance consisting of a pulse level" and its interpretation at slower levels of pulsation.[51] Established early on, such an interaction serves as a constant frame of reference. Internalized by the listener, the frame is an orientation, in relation to which the conflicting level of interpretation is sensed and felt as a form of syncopation – a pulling and tugging.

---

[49] For further discussion, see Krebs, *Fantasy Pieces*, 33.
[50] *Ibid.*, 31. Because of the inequality of the two conflicting levels of pulsation, the metrical framework is termed "metrical" while the opposing, secondary level is termed "anti-metrical."
[51] *Ibid.*, 30.

Needless to say, the many types of metrical displacement in contexts of the eighteenth and nineteenth centuries are far from exhausted by these few illustrations.[52] All in all, however, when these various types are assembled and placed beside Stravinsky's, three distinctions stand out. First, with cycles of displacement generally (including instances of the hemiola): while the spans between the displaced repeats of a given motive tend to be regular in earlier contexts, in Stravinsky's music they are often irregular, and often spectacularly so. As a rule, passages of irregular spanning lack regularly recurring points of intersection between the reiterating fragments and chords themselves and as they relate to the meter. There are no fixed alignments in these passages, periodically recurring points at which all the various superimposed, reiterating fragments and chords converge.

Indeed, it is the irregularity (and sometimes unevenness) of the spanning between successive repeats of motives, chords, and blocks of material in Stravinsky's music that accounts for the difficulty in applying the grouping and displacement dissonances outlined by Krebs. For the metrical dissonance in Krebs's schemes consists of a shadow meter, a conflicting level of interpretation above a shared pulse. And in much of the music to be examined here, the alternative to the prevailing meter (notated or not) is not another meter, strictly speaking, but only an interruption of a meter, a radically shifting bar line that mirrors the irregular spans of the repetition and, in so doing, is a form of metrical parallelism.

All of which is not to imply, on the other hand, that the spans defined by the reiterating fragments and chords in Stravinsky's stratifications are invariably irregular or uneven. Many of his layered structures are mixed in this regard, combining layers of irregular spanning with ostinatos (indeed, some of these structures are composed entirely of ostinatos).[53] This is true of the "Ritual of the Rival Tribes" at Nos. 64–71 in *The Rite of Spring* (see Example 6.9), where, early on, the patterns of repetition in the violins and bass drum span four and three quarter-note beats, respectively, outlining a grouping dissonance. The 4-layer in the violins, as reflected by the notated 4/4 meter, intersects regularly every three bars with the 3-layer in the bass drum. Beginning already at Rehearsal No. 65+3, however,

---

[52] In connection with Brahms's music, see the revealing analysis of a number of displacement dissonances in Peter H. Smith, "You Reap What You Sow: Some Instances of Rhythmic Ambiguity in Brahms," *Music Theory Spectrum* 28, no. 1 (2006): 57–98.

[53] See, in Chapter 4, our discussion of the hemiola in the lament of the second tableau of *Les Noces*, a form of grouping dissonance. Or see, in Gretchen Horlacher, "The Rhythms of Reiteration; Formal Development in Stravinsky's Ostinati," *Music Theory Spectrum* 14, no.2 (1992), the discussion of Rehearsal No.2 in the final movement of the *Symphony of Psalms*, where all the competing spans are ostinatos. Alongside the regularity of the individual spans and their intersections in this latter passage, Horlacher is able to trace recurring harmonic coincidences as well.

grouping and displacement dissonances of this kind are apt to be broken up in the mind of the listener, overwhelmed by the irregularly spaced entrances of the horn fragment. Only at the conclusion of this dance movement, in a passage to which we will be referring in Chapter 10, is the horn fragment made to repeat at regular intervals.

Second, earlier displacements are typically situated in the background of a metrical structure (see Example 1.4). And, third, earlier examples of displacement exhibit forms of motivic elaboration, processes that involve extensive changes in the melodic, harmonic, and rhythmic features of a motive. In Schoenberg's *Fundamentals of Musical Composition*, such changes are categorized under four headings, namely, rhythm, intervals, harmony, and melody.[54] Under each of these headings, features of the motive are varied in a number of ways; listed under melody, for example, are "transposition," the "addition of passing harmonies," and the "semi-contrapuntal statement of the accompaniment."[55]

Developing variations of this kind can soften the effect of a displacement, as we have noted already. Transposed tonally, a semitone can become a tone, a minor third, filled in and embellished, a major third. With fewer *specific* features of a motive retained, fewer are ultimately displaced. And such is the nature of these checks and balances, the trade-offs that occur when one dimension is weighed against another. Leaving many of a motive's more familiar features unchanged, Stravinsky set metrical alignment and realignment in relief. The sacrifices entailed by this exchange, pursued in the interests of a rhythmic-metric invention, are those against which Stravinsky's critics have directed much of their hostility. These issues will concern us briefly in Chapter 6 and more extensively in Chapter 10.

---

[54] Schoenberg, *Fundamentals*, 8–15.   [55] *Ibid.*, 10.

2 The octatonic scale

Earlier, in the Introduction, we noted that the processes of displacement, juxtaposition, and stratification in Stravinsky's music could exist without the octatonic set and its interaction with the diatonic. Each side of this equation could do without the other. But this was not to deny the existence of meaningful ties. If, in the main, Stravinsky's stratifications are static and self-enclosed conceptions, then, so, too, from a different perspective, is the octatonic scale and its symmetries. Especially in Russian-period works, octatonic fragments and chords are transposed literally along the minor-third cycle particular to a given collection or transposition. Motion of this kind, entirely circular, harbors a form of immobility of its own.

Confined to the octave and arranged in scale formation, the eight pitch classes of the octatonic set yield a scale of alternating 1s and 2s (half and whole steps). Such an arrangement yields two possible orderings, a 1–2 half-step–whole-step ordering, and a 2–1 whole-step–half-step ordering. These are shown in Example 2.1, with the 1–2 ordering and consequent (0 1 3 4 6 7 9 10 (0)) pitch numbering *ascending* on the left side, the reverse 2–1 ordering and (0 2 3 5 6 8 9 11 (0)) numbering *descending* on the right. And the issue as to which of these orderings might pertain to a given context hinges on questions of priority (centricity) and vocabulary.[1]

Thus, the Dorian (0 2 3 5) tetrachord and its 2–1–2 ordering, prevalent as a cohesive grouping in much music of Stravinsky's Russian era, implies the 2–1 ordering as cited on the right side in Example 2.1. And octatonic contexts which are (0 2 3 5) tetrachordally oriented will tend to suggest this 2–1 ordering as the most favorable approach in scale formation. (Notice the 0–11 interval span of this 2–1 ordering and consequent (0 2 3 5 6 8 9 11 (0)) numbering.) On the other hand, the root-positioned major and minor triads will tend more readily to suggest the 1–2 ordering on the left side of Example 2.1. This is true of the (0 1 3 4) tetrachord as well, although the latter is of only slight consequence in Russian-period works.

The set is limited to three transpositions of distinguishable content. These are also shown in Example 2.1, and labeled I, II, and III. Thus, respecting

---

[1] Examples 2.1 and 2.2 are derived in part from several illustrations in Pieter C. van den Toorn, *The Music of Igor Stravinsky* (New Haven: Yale University Press, 1983), 48–60. Here at the outset of this chapter, we have felt the need to reacquaint the reader with a number of essentials regarding the two versions of the octatonic scale and their relevance to Stravinsky's music.

Example 2.1. Octatonic orderings, numberings, transpositions

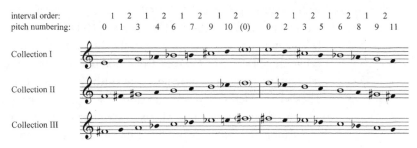

interval order: 1 2 1 2 1 2 1 2   2 1 2 1 2 1 2
pitch numbering: 0 1 3 4 6 7 9 10 (0) 0 2 3 5 6 8 9 11

Collection I

Collection II

Collection III

Collection I with the 1–2 ordering on the left side in Example 2.1; had we, following the initial E, transposed beyond F and F♯ to G, this final transposition would have duplicated the initial collection (Collection I), starting only with the G rather than the E. Moreover, since this transposition to G defines the interval of 3 (the minor third), transpositions at 6 and 9 will entail similar duplications. And it follows that this minor-third (0, 3, 6, 9) symmetrically defined partitioning is fundamental to the integrity of the single octatonic collection: given an octatonic fragment, transpositions at 3, 6, and 9 will remain confined to that collection.

Observe, too, that the 1–2 ordering on the left side in Example 2.1 ascends, while the reverse 2–1 ordering on the right descends. This is in principle to allow representation of longer spans of material, spans that, confined to a single collection, may nonetheless in vocabulary implicate both orderings. In other words, respecting Collection I again, with the ascending 1–2 ordering at E on the left side: were we to switch to the 2–1 ordering and yet remain committed to the customary ascending approach in scale presentation, the resultant scale would no longer represent Collection I but, rather, Collection III. However, by *descending* with the 2–1 ordering from E, not only do we remain confined to Collection I, but the (0, 3, 6, 9) symmetrically defined partitioning elements in terms of (E, G, B♭, D♭) remain the same as well.

Still, the descending formula, the reading-down situation on the right side of Example 2.1, is not wholly a question of analytical convenience. In Russian-period pieces such as *The Rite of Spring* and *Les Noces*, it is often an "upper" (0 2 3 5) tetrachord along with an "upper" pitch number 0 that assumes priority by means of doubling, metric accentuation, and persistence in moving from one block or section to the next. And if the scalar ordering and pitch numbering are to reflect these conditions, the descending formula is the logical course. Throughout the opening blocks of *Les Noces* and their subsequent restatements, for example, a punctuating E, along with an incomplete or gapped (E D (C♯) B) tetrachord with which this E is identified, assume priority. And it is by descending from E with the (0 2 3 5) tetrachordal numbering synchronized with the principal (E D C♯ B) unit, that the priority of these units is properly represented: (0 2 3 5) (6 8 9 11) in terms of (E D C♯ B)(B♭ A♭ G F), Collection I. (Again, to *ascend* from the E with the 2–1 ordering would yield a different octatonic collection, in this case, Collection III.) Moreover, the symmetry of the relevant groupings and orderings conveniently allows for options of this kind. The 2–1–2 ordering and consequent (0 2 3 5) pitch numbering of this present tetrachord remain the same whether ascending or descending.[2]

Turning in summary to the Russian period, all three collections are partitioned at three successive levels in Example 2.2, by their (0, 3, 6, 9) partitioning elements at the first level, their (0 2 3 5) tetrachords at the second, and their triads and dominant sevenths at the third.[3] At the first of these levels, (0, 3, 6, 9) is not a chordal sonority, but the transpositional path of the tetrachords, triads, and dominant sevenths at the second and third levels. In general, the (0 2 3 5) tetrachords of the second level are melodic or linear in conception, while the triads and dominant sevenths of the third are vertical.[4] At the final level, the 2–1 ordering of the scale, descending for the reasons cited, may be imagined as a form of encapsulation, an embodiment of Russian particularity where the octatonic set and its uses are concerned.

---

[2] For an earlier and more detailed discussion of the need, apropos of Stravinsky's Russian-period works, for a descending approach to the 2–1 ordering of the octatonic scale, see van den Toorn, *The Music of Igor Stravinsky*, 59–60.

Two recent publications on *The Rite of Spring* have made reference to a top-to-bottom reading of Stravinsky's materials. In Daniel K. L. Chua, "Rioting with Stravinsky: A Particular Analysis of *The Rite of Spring*," *Music Analysis* 26 (March 2007): 69, the author points to the upside-down character of the notorious "Augurs of Spring" chord at Rehearsal No. 13 of the score, and to the E-flat major key signature of the movement in question. And Matthew McDonald, in his attempt to link the intervals of various configurations in *The Rite* to rhythmic patterns, has also applied a descending form of representation; see Matthew McDonald, "*Jeux de Nombres*: Automated Rhythm in *The Rite of Spring*," *Journal of the American Musicological Society* 63, no. 3 (2010): 511.

[3] In addition to the units of vocabulary cited in Example 2.2, the (0, 3, 6, 9) partitioning elements of each octatonic collection are the roots of minor-seventh, half-diminished seventh, and dominant minor-ninth chords. Although all three of these sonorities may occasionally be found in Stravinsky's neoclassical contexts, they are evident scarcely at all in music of the Russian category. And such is very nearly the case with the minor triad as well. Although placed beside the major triad at the third level of each of the three partitionings in Example 2.2, it, too, is seldom present in octatonic or octatonic–diatonic passages in Russian-period works.

[4] We should mention the historical issue: the ease with which the octatonic vocabulary cited at the second and third levels of the models in Example 2.2 can be traced back to the music and notebooks of Stravinsky's predecessor, Nicholai Rimsky-Korsakov. As Richard Taruskin has shown in detail, even the association of the melodic (0 2 3 5) tetrachord and the harmonic triad with the 2–1 and 1–2 orderings of the octatonic scale, respectively, figured as part of the octatonic perspective shared by Rimsky-Korsakov and his circle of composers in the later part of the nineteenth century. See Richard Taruskin, *Stravinsky and the Russian Traditions: A Biography of the Works through "Mavra,"* 2 vols. (Berkeley: University of California Press, 1996); and Taruskin, "Catching Up with Rimsky-Korsakov," *Music Theory Spectrum* 33 (Fall 2011): 169–85. See, too, the earlier review of these historical matters in Pieter C. van den Toorn, *Stravinsky and "The Rite of Spring": The Beginnings of a Musical Language* (Berkeley: University of California Press, 1987), 115–31.

Example 2.2. Octatonic collections (transpositions); (0 2 3 5) tetrachords, triads, scales

Crucially, the descending 2–1 ordering of Example 2.2 incorporates the triads and dominant sevenths of the opposing conception. A subset of the (0 2 3 5) tetrachord, the (0 2 5) trichord is the connecting link in this exchange, with its pitch numbers 0, 2, and 5 becoming the root, seventh, and fifth, respectively, of the dominant seventh. Typical of Russian-period works as well is the $^6_5$ position or (0 2 5 8) ordering (reading down) of the dominant seventh (see, especially, Part I in *The Rite of Spring*), with the pitches of the (0 2 5) connecting link bunched together and exposed as such.[5]

The hyper-octatonic network pictured in Figure 2.1 sums up much of what we have been surveying in this section about the octatonic scale and its uses in works such as *The Rite of Spring* and *Les Noces*. While the network incorporates certain features of Richard Cohn's "hyper-hexatonic systems," it ignores Cohn's emphasis on neo-Riemannian operations and "maximally smooth cycles."[6] Instead, it is the octatonic *scale* that is represented by the circles in Figure 2.1, the three transpositions of the scale, which are again labeled I, II, and III. The upper case pitch letters surrounding each of the three circles are the (0, 3, 6, 9) partitioning elements outlined for each collection in Example 2.2, the first pitches of the (0 2 3 5) tetrachords and the roots of the triads and dominant sevenths. Both forms of the octatonic scale are represented by the circles, the descending 2–1 and the ascending 1–2 form, reading clockwise and counter-clockwise, respectively. Only the 2–1 form is represented by the pitch numbers inside each circle, however, that particular form to which much of the octatonic material in Stravinsky's Russian-period works makes reference.

---

[5] For further discussion of the dominant seventh and its characteristic disposition, see van den Toorn, *The Music of Igor Stravinsky*.

[6] Richard Cohn, "Maximally Smooth Cycles, Hexatonic Systems, and the Analysis of Late-Romantic Triadic Progressions," *Music Analysis* 15, no. 1 (1996): 9–40. With Cohn's hexatonic systems, the circles representing the four transpositions of set class 6–20 are *triadic* rather than *scalar*. They include a separate notch for the minor triad or parallel relationship (P), and as a means of securing a "maximally smooth cycle." (In the latter cycle, the two common tones between third-related and parallel triads are sustained while the third tone moves by tone or semitone.) The binary chain PR, with the P relationship alternating with the relative R, is octatonic, of course, but parsimonious voice-leading of this kind is seldom if ever an issue in Stravinsky's octatonic settings of the Russian period. Rather, the units of vocabulary shown at the second and third levels of each octatonic collection in Example 2.2 are transposed (often literally) along the minor-third or 3-cycle, the (0, 3, 6, 9) partitioning at the first level, and without reference to the P relationship (see note 3 above). Parsimonious graphs of the octatonic set and its transpositions, sketched along the lines of Cohn's hexatonic systems, are termed "octacycles" in Jack Douthett and Peter Steinbach, "Parsimonious Graphs: A Study in Parsimony, Contextual Transformations and Modes of Limited Transposition," *Journal of Music Theory* 42, no. 2 (1998): 247. See, too, the map of "triadic/octatonic chordal/regional space" in Fred Lerdahl, *Tonal Pitch Space* (Oxford University Press, 2001), 257.

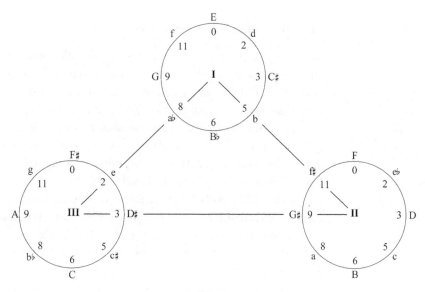

Figure 2.1. Hyper-octatonic network, with a view toward Stravinsky's Russian period

Circles can be effective in demonstrating the cyclical nature of the octatonic set's three chains of minor-third related (0 2 3 5) tetrachords and triads. Holding the pitch numbers within each circle constant, we can rotate the upper case pitch letters clockwise or counter-clockwise at 15, 30, and 45 degree angles, allowing the remaining three uppercase pitch letters to serve as pitch number 0, representing a form of localized pitch-class priority.

The term "hyper" in the title of Figure 2.1 refers to its regional or inter-regional character. Each circle or octatonic transposition corresponds to a single region (analogous to a key area in tonal music), while each region represents, roughly, a block or section of Stravinsky's music. In moving from the first to the second circle, the lower case pitch letters of the first become the upper case letters of the second (the (0, 3, 6, 9) partitioning elements of Collection II), a maneuver that is duplicated when moving from the second circle to the third, and from the third back to the first. Transformed at each turn is a 3-cycle or diminished-seventh chord; in pitch-specific terms, each of the octatonic collections in Figure 2.1 shares a diminished seventh with its two transpositions. The role assumed by this cycle or chord in linking trans-positions of the octatonic set 8–28 is analogous to that assumed by the 4-cycle or augmented triad in linking the four transpositions of the hexatonic set 6–20. The difference, however, is that, while each octatonic collection shares a 3-cycle with its two transpositions, a hexatonic collection shares a 4-cycle with only two of its three transpositions.

Octatonic–diatonic interaction

With the exception of a few passages in *The Rite of Spring* and *Les Noces*, superimpositions involving two or more octatonic collections are virtually non-existent in Stravinsky's oeuvre. The normal course is for one octatonic transposition to succeed another, and to do so at a distance.

On the other hand, interactions between the octatonic and diatonic sets are pervasive in Russian and neoclassical works, coming either in the form of a superimposition or succession. The interaction shown in Example 2.3 is typically Russian in conception. At Rehearsal No. 11 in *Les Noces*, the tritone-related (0 2 3 5)(6 8 (9) 11) tetrachords are superimposed, with G♯-A-F♯-B in Pianos I and III and E♭-C-E♭-F-E♭ in the bass solo. Implicating Collection II, the configuration is later joined by D-B-D-E-D in the soprano solo, another (0 2 (3) 5) tetrachord, but in terms of (E D (C♯) B). In the upper registers, a Dorian scale or D-scale is formed in terms of (B A G♯ F♯)(E D (C♯) B); (B A G♯ F♯) is the connecting link, that which is shared between the two octatonic and diatonic scales. Sketched in Figure 2.2, the specifics of this transaction are straightforward.

See, too, the four staves of analytical commentary below the musical quotation in Example 2.3. The dotted vertical line extending through the analysis implies octatonic-diatonic interaction, here between Collection II and the D-scale on B. The format itself mirrors that in Example 2.2; the (0, 3, 6, 9) partitioning elements of the octatonic set come first, followed by a vocabulary of (0 2 3 5) tetrachords and triads. At the final level, the vocabulary yields the given diatonic and octatonic scales, which, by means of beams, are made to incorporate something of the segmentation of the upper levels. The shared, octatonic-diatonic connecting links are either bracketed or may be inferred by their inclusion on both sides of the dotted vertical line.

In connection with Examples 2.1–2.3, however, the problematic nature of notions of scale step and pitch-class priority where the octatonic scale is concerned should be stressed. In keeping with the scale's symmetry, its 2–1 (or 1–2) scale pattern is repeated four times within the octave, leaving the (0, 3, 6, 9) partitioning elements "undifferentiated" from one another.[7] In an equal division of the octave of this kind, the elements themselves can embody little individuality or "uniqueness."[8] Priority thus becomes a matter of

[7] Lerdahl, *Tonal Pitch Space*, 269.

[8] *Ibid.*, 50. See, too, the discussion of pitch-class priority and the (0, 3, 6, 9) partitioning elements of the octatonic set in van den Toorn, *The Music of Stravinsky*, 49–54. In Arthur Berger, "Problems of Pitch Organization in Stravinsky," in Benjamin Boretz and Edward T. Cone, eds., *Perspectives on Schoenberg and Stravinsky* (New York: W. W. Norton, 1972), 133, the same elements are treated as "potential tone centers of equal weight and independence."

Example 2.3. *Les Noces*, first tableau, octatonic–diatonic interaction

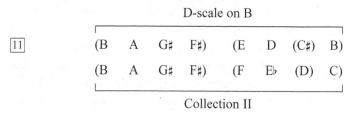

Figure 2.2. *Les Noces*, first tableau, octatonic–diatonic interaction

salience, of the prominence or persistence with which a given pitch class or unit of vocabulary asserts itself within a block or section of music. These conditions contrast sharply with the asymmetry of the diatonic collection, where, to follow Fred Lerdahl's wording, "the ordered set of step sizes that begins from each pitch [is] different in each case." The asymmetrical interval ordering ("step configurations") allows for an unambiguous "position-finding."[9]

[9] Lerdahl, *Tonal Pitch Space*, 50.

a) the basic space [following Lerdahl (2001), Figure 2.4]

level *a*:	0											(12 = 0)
level *b*:	0						7					(12 = 0)
level *c*:	0			4			7					(12 = 0)
level *d*:	0		2	4	5		7		9		11	(12 = 0)
level *e*:	0	1	2	3	4	5	6	7	8	9	10 11	(12 = 0)

b) triadic/octatonic basic space [following Lerdahl (2001), Figure 6.4]

level *a*:	0										
level *b*:	0						7				
level *c*:	0			4			7				
level *d*:	0	1		3	4		6	7		9	10
level *e*:	0	1	2	3	4	5	6	7	8	9	10 11

Figure 2.3. Models of pitch space

Indeed, as we have noted already, our discussion will at times be abandoning the scales introduced in Examples 2.1–2.3 and replacing them with the intersecting interval cycles of various *Tonnetze*. Floating free of the more traditional concepts associated with scales and scalar orderings will be the (0 2 3 5) tetrachords, triads, and dominant sevenths of Examples 2.2 and 2.3, along with the (0 2 7 9) tetrachords and (0 2 3 5 7 9) hexachords to which we will be referring in Chapters 5 and 7. Much of this vocabulary will be plotted octatonically along minor-third or 3-cycles, and diatonically along the 7-cycle or circle of fifths (with the fifth-related (0 2 (3) 5)s of the D-scale subsumed accordingly). The octatonic–diatonic interaction revealed by such means can be made to reflect global conditions of collectional transposition as well as local ones of vocabulary.

It might be useful to close our introductory remarks on pitch relations with Lerdahl's models of diatonic and octatonic "space" (see Figures 2.3a and b, respectively),[10] and with the idea of revising these models in accord with the vocabulary and scales particular to the music of Stravinsky's Russian period. Each level in Lerdahl's format represents a different kind of "space," starting with the octave and then moving down through the fifth, triad, scale, and chromatic scale. The levels are strictly hierarchical; elements at one level are subsumed by those at "lower" levels; in reverse, the stabler elements at one level are retained by succeeding levels. Crucially, the diatonic and octatonic

[10] *Ibid.*, 47, 253.

a) diatonic space, (0 2 3 5) tetrachordal

level												
level *a*:	0											
level *b*:	0				5							
level *c*:	0		2	3	5							
level *d*:	0		2	3	5		7		9	10		
level *e*:	0	1	2	3	4	5	6	7	8	9	10	11

b) octatonic space, (0 2 3 5) tetrachordal

level												
level *a*:	0											
level *b*:	0				5							
level *c*:	0		2	3	5							
level *d*:	0		2	3	5	6		8	9		11	
level *e*:	0	1	2	3	4	5	6	7	8	9	10	11

Figure 2.4. Models of diatonic and octatonic space

worlds intersect at all levels save level d, the level of the scale: featured in Figure 2.3a is the major-scale or C-scale ordering of the diatonic set; in figure 2.3b, the 1–2 half step-whole step ordering of the octatonic.

The octatonic–diatonic intersection represented by these models may be traced to the latter 1–2 ordering of the octatonic scale; in Figure 2.3b, reference is to the interval of a fifth and the triad, divisions obviously at odds with those introduced above in Examples 2.2 and 2.3. Emphasis here has been placed on the interval of a fourth and its enclosure of the (0 2 3 5) Dorian tetrachord, units implicating the 2–1 ordering of the scale. In Stravinsky's music, distinctions of this kind in scalar ordering (in the "rhythm" of the octatonic intervals, as one commentator has described it),[11] can reflect distinctions not only in vocabulary and priority but also in stylistic orientation. They can point to the larger ways in which, in pitch-relational terms, whole repertories may be distinguished from one another, in the present case, Stravinsky's Russian period from the neoclassical.[12]

Thus, while Stravinsky's neoclassical works can often seem to imply the more familiar major and minor orderings of the diatonic set, the emphasis in Russian-period works is decidedly modal. In Lerdahl's models of "the basic space" (see Figures 2.3a and b), the C-scale ordering of the diatonic set is

[11] Berger, "Pitch Organization in Stravinsky," 148.
[12] The two possible orderings of the octatonic scale and their relationship to the three familiar stylistic orientations of Stravinsky's music are discussed at length in van den Toorn, *The Music of Igor Stravinsky*, 48–72. See, also, Pieter C. van den Toorn, *Music, Politics, and the Academy* (Berkeley: University of California Press, 1995), 179–93.

made to relate to the triadic 1–2 ordering of the octatonic set. With a more specific view toward *Les Noces* and Stravinsky's Russian period, however, the same models can be made to feature the interval of a fourth and the (0 2 3 5) tetrachord as forms of intersection (connecting links between the diatonic and the octatonic), and along the lines already pursued in Example 2.3. Figures 2.4a and b incorporate designs of this kind, but with the distinction that, in both, the pitch-numbering is meant to descend.

As reproduced in Figures 2.3a and b, Lerdahl's models of diatonic and octatonic space are transformed at three successive levels, the level of the pitch class, chord, and region. Cited in support of this tripartite division of the diatonic universe are Carol Krumhansl's empirical studies documenting the "cognitive proximity" of pitch classes, chords, and regions relative to an induced tonic, tonic triad, and key, respectively.[13] In this present inquiry, the looser term *vocabulary* (or unit of vocabulary) will be used for chord, with *vocabulary* incorporating melodic trichords, tetrachords, and even hexachords as well as triads and dominant sevenths. Corresponding roughly to Lerdahl's idea of a region or key area is that of an octatonic collection or transposition (see Figure 2.1), along with the block or section to which the collection adheres. Especially in Chapters 5 and 7, the distinctions embodied by these terms will prove useful.

---

[13] Lerdahl, *Tonal Pitch Space*, 47. In addition, see C. L. Krumhansl, *Cognitive Foundations of Musical Pitch* (New York: Oxford University Press, 1990).

3 A brief survey

I became aware of an idea for a choral work on the subject of a Russian peasant wedding early in 1912; the title, *Svadebka, Les Noces*, occurred to me almost at the same time as the idea itself. As my conception developed, I began to see that it did not indicate the dramatization of a wedding or the accompaniment of a staged wedding spectacle with descriptive music. My wish was, instead, to present actual wedding material through direct quotations of popular – i.e., non-literary – verse. I waited two years before discovering my source in the anthologies of Afanasyev and Kireyevsky, but this wait was well rewarded, as the dance-cantata form of the music was also suggested to me by my reading of these two great argosies of the Russian language and spirit. *Renard* and *Histoire du soldat* were adapted from Afanasyev, *Les Noces* almost entirely from Kireyevsky.[1]

From the time of its early drafts and revisions to that of the postmodern era, enthusiasts of Stravinsky's music have harbored a special fondness for *Les Noces*. "*Svadebka (Les Noces)* ranks high in the by no means crowded company of indisputable contemporary masterpieces," wrote Robert Craft in 1972.[2] Even Constant Lambert, a critic of Stravinsky's music earlier in the past century, felt compelled to acknowledge the special status of this music: "*Les Noces* is one of the masterpieces of this [Russian] period and possibly the only really important work that Stravinsky has given us."[3]

Today, the success of *Les Noces* within Stravinsky's oeuvre can seem so incontrovertible as to render scarcely believable the modesty and even obscurity of its history (Craft mentions its "slender biography" at the time of the composer's death in 1971).[4] At the same time, however, issues of style, interpretation, and reception remain controversial. For no other work occupied Stravinsky for as long, beginning as a Russian spectacle

[1] Igor Stravinsky and Robert Craft, *Expositions and Developments* (Garden City, NY: Doubleday, 1962), 130.

[2] Robert Craft with William Harkins, "Stravinsky's *Svadebka*: An Introduction," *New York Review of Books*, December 14, 1972: 23.

[3] Constant Lambert, *Music Ho! A Study of Music in Decline*, 3rd edn. (London: Faber and Faber, 1966), 91. *Music Ho!* was first published in 1934.

[4] Craft and Harkins, "Stravinsky's *Svadebka*": 28. Recent contributions include Margarita Mazo, "Igor Stravinsky's *Les Noces*, the Rite of Passage," in *Les Noces (Svadebka): Scènes chorégraphiques russes avec chant et musique* (London: Chester Music, c. 2005), and "Stravinsky's *Les Noces* and Russian Folk Wedding Ritual," *Journal of the American Musicological Society* 43, no. 1 (Spring 1990): 99–142. See, too, Richard Taruskin, *Stravinsky and the Russian Traditions: A Biography of the Works through "Mavra,"* 2 vols. (Berkeley: University of California Press, 1996), Vol. II: 1319–86.

in the fashion of Sergei Diaghilev, and metamorphosing over a period of ten years into the pared-down, austere vision that premiered in 1923. Of all of Stravinsky's works, *Les Noces* took the longest time not only to complete, but, in aggregate, quite possibly to compose as well. The process of refinement, affecting matters of production, composition, staging, decor, and choreography, as well as instrumentation and text, stands as an emblem of the composer's deepening commitment to the abstract, the concise, and the impersonal.

The entirety of the conception may still offer today's listeners something new and different, whether viewed from a musical perspective – its battery of percussion with four "elephantine" pianos – or as a "cantata-ballet."[5] The prolonged process of instrumentation, given Stravinsky's general practice of orchestrating while he composed, may suggest novelty, in any case, a musical-dramatic inspiration for which there was no ready settlement along lines even remotely traditional. Indeed, the indecision can seem all the more extraordinary given the self-imposed interruptions for *Renard, The Soldier's Tale, Pulcinella* (1920), and the *Symphonies of Wind Instruments* (1920). For once Stravinsky was assured of a rhythmic or melodic "find," his instinct was to persevere from start to finish, without interruptions. As he later explained, the future seemed never to furnish the certainty of the present. Ideas were best encouraged when new and fresh.

To condense Craft's timeline, work on the libretto for *Les Noces* commenced in May or June of 1914. A trip to Russia (Ustilug and Kiev) in July 1914 provided an opportunity for additional texts, at which time Stravinsky acquired P. V. Kireyevsky's volume of Russian wedding songs, which would serve as the principal source.[6] Then, "back in Switzerland," Stravinsky's residence during the war years, "the song cycle *Pribaoutki* [1914] came

---

[5] Stravinsky and Craft, *Expositions and Developments*, 133. Stravinsky refers to the "elephantine" pianos in a discussion of the original staging: "At the first performance, the four pianos filled the corners of the scene, thus being separated from the percussion ensemble and the chorus and solo singers in the pit. Diaghilev argued for this arrangement on aesthetic grounds – the four black, elephantine shapes were an attractive addition to the *décors* – but my original idea was that the whole company of musicians and dancers should be together on the stage as equal participants."

[6] *Pesni sobrannïye P.V. Kireevskim. Novaya seriya. Izdanï Obshchestvom Lyubiteley Rossiyskoy Slovesnosti pri Imperatorskom Moskovskom Universitete* [Songs collected by P.V. Kireyevsky. New Series. Published by the Society of Lovers of Russian Philology at the Imperial Moscow University], vol. I *(Pesni obriadovïye)*, ed. V. F. Miller and M. N. Speransky (Moscow: Pechatnya A. I. Snegiryovoy, 1911). Also, Stravinsky collected several volumes from his father's library in Ustilug, including V. I. Dahl's *Tolkovïy slovar' zhivogo velikorusskogo yazïka* [Explanatory Dictionary of the Living Great-Russian Language], I. P. Sakharov's *Skazaniya russkogo naroda* [Legends of the Russian People], and A.V. Tereshchenko's *Bït russkogo naroda* [Manners and Customs of the Russian People].

first."[7] But by October 1914, a first version of the libretto had been "pieced together." And by the end of November, "Stravinsky had drafted some, possibly most, of the music of the first tableau."[8]

Much of 1915 passed with *Les Noces* and *Renard* "incubating" in what Craft describes as Stravinsky's "amazingly compartmental mind."[9] In January 1916 he accepted a commission for the "chamber opera" *Renard*, and *Les Noces* was put aside for seven months.[10] Not until 1917 was the whole of *Les Noces* "unveiled" for Diaghilev (to whom the work is dedicated), and not until October of that year was the sketch score completed.[11]

There then followed nearly five years of experiments with varied instrumental ensembles and an assortment of smaller works. The final score, with its four pianos providing the "perfectly homogeneous, perfectly impersonal, and perfectly mechanical" effect that Stravinsky desired, was not completed until April 1923, just weeks before the premiere.[12] Each diversion, each interruption, altered the composer's perspective, left him greatly changed. And this appears especially to have been the case with *The Soldier's Tale*, the preoccupation here with percussion and small ensemble dramatically reducing the sizable orchestral cloak in which *Les Noces* was first conceived.

Stretching through the heart of the Russian period, then, *Les Noces* offers the listener a decisive formulation of this period's uniquely conceived preoccupation with the substance and rhythm of Russian popular verse. The stem that emerged early on proved too rich and varied in its implications, necessitating, as a way of ensuring its future growth, a weeding-out process, one that was gradually to result in a prodigious, diversionary harvest, quite simply, the Russian period itself. For the springboard role *Les Noces* assumes for much Russian music is unmistakable. *Pribaoutki*, *Berceuses du chat*, and portions of *Renard* and *The Soldier's Tale* are clearly

---

[7] Craft and Harkins, "Stravinsky's *Svadebka*": 23. The timeline set forth by Craft and Harkins is, for the most part, identical to that of Mazo, "Igor Stravinsky's *Les Noces*," and Taruskin, *Stravinsky and the Russian Traditions*. On those occasions when inconsistencies arise, we will follow Taruskin.

[8] *Ibid.*, 23–24.   [9] *Ibid.*, 24.   [10] *Ibid.*, 24–25.

[11] The autograph date of the first complete draft of the work, finished in Morges, Switzerland, is October 11, 1917.

[12] Stravinsky and Craft, *Expositions and Developments*, 134. *Les Noces* was premiered in Paris, June 13, 1923, at the Théâtre de la Gaieté-Lyrique. It was produced by Sergei Diaghilev, choreographed by Bronislava Nijinska, and conducted by Ernest Ansermet. Stage design and costumes were by Natalya Goncharova. For Nijinska's account of her role, see "Creation of *Les Noces*," trans. Jean M. Serafetinides and Irina Nijinska, *Dance Magazine* (December 1974): 59. For Goncharova's account of her lengthy involvement, see "The Creation of *Les Noces*," *Ballet and Opera* 8 (Sept. 1949): 23, and "The Metamorphoses of the Ballet *Les Noces*," *Leonardo* 12 (1979): 137–43.

supplementary in this regard.[13] Indeed, the prolonged indecision in instrumentation is itself symptomatic of an important development in Stravinsky's Russian musical thought: from 1914 onward, a shift occurred from the immense orchestral resources that had been harnessed on behalf of *The Firebird*, *Petrushka*, and *The Rite of Spring* ("the Russian orchestral school in which I had been fostered," as Stravinsky later noted) to the "solo-instrumental style" of *Renard*, *The Soldier's Tale*, and *Les Noces*.[14] From a starting point in the ethnographic reality of the Russian village wedding ritual, *Les Noces* would transcend its early nationalistic source, communicating, almost paradoxically, a high degree of expressive intensity within a "perfectly impersonal" modernist frame.[15]

The Russian folk wedding

Diaghilev's initial enthusiasm for *Svadebka* – only later *Les Noces* – was doubly grounded. It lay not only in his nostalgic affection for the motherland, but also in the proven theatrical success of the subject matter.[16] For, notwithstanding the novelty of *Les Noces* and striking uniqueness of its final incarnation, portrayals of the Russian folk wedding had for some time been an established part of Russian musical culture. Beginning in the late eighteenth century, two popular singspiels, Alexander Ablesimov's *The Miller Who was a Wizard, a Cheat, and a Matchmaker* and Mikhail Matinsky's *St. Petersburg Bazaar*, had featured representations, with special emphasis on the *devichnik* or, loosely translated, the bride's wedding shower.[17] During the nineteenth century, a renewed interest in an "authentic," if romanticized, Russian identity was expressed in wedding depictions by Arensky, Mussorgsky, Rimsky-Korsakov, and Tchaikovsky,

---

[13] Stravinsky himself suggested as much: "My profound emotion on reading the news of war ... found some alleviation in the delight with which I steeped myself in Russian folk poems ... I culled a bouquet from among them all, which I distributed in three different compositions that I wrote one after the other, elaborating my material for *Les Noces*. They were *Pribaoutki*, for voice, with the accompaniment of a small orchestra; then *Les Berceuses du chat*, also for voice, accompanied by three clarinets; and, lastly, four little choruses for women's voices a cappella ['Saucers']"; see Igor Stravinsky, *An Autobiography* (New York: W. W. Norton, 1962), 53–55.

[14] Stravinsky and Craft, *Expositions and Developments*, 103–04.   [15] *Ibid.*, 134.

[16] In 1914, near the end of the summer season of the Ballets Russes, Diaghilev began a steady, prodding series of inquiries about Stravinsky's progress on *Les Noces*; see Robert Craft, ed., *Stravinsky: Selected Correspondence* (New York: Alfred A. Knopf, 1984), vol. II: 12, 14. The title "*Svadebka*" is the diminutive form of the standard noun, *svad'ba* (wedding). Stravinsky used the diminutive to indicate the wedding's peasant roots: "'Little Wedding' would be the best English equivalent, if 'little' could be made to mean not 'small' but 'peasant'"; see Stravinsky and Craft, *Expositions and Developments*, 130, n. 24. The work's subtitle, "Russian Choreographic Scenes with Singing and Music," also alludes to Russian peasant usage: by tradition, only music played on instruments was referred to as music.

[17] Alexander Ablesimov, *Mel'nik–koldun, obmanshchik i svat*, 1779; Mikhail Matinsky, *Sankt-peterburgskiy gostinnïy dvor*, 1782, later recomposed by Vasily Paskevich.

among others.[18] Glinka's *A Life for the Czar* (1836) and *Ruslan and Ludmila* (1843) both contain wedding scenes. The Wedding Chorus in Act I of *Ruslan and Ludmila*, "Lel' tainstvennyi," so closely resembles actual folk song that it is all the more remarkable for having been staged as opera.[19]

Yet the earliest performances of *Les Noces* are unlikely to have been affected by this early history. On the contrary, audiences are likely to have been startled by what they saw and heard. In place of a form of pageantry, a picturesque wedding festival *à la russe*, *Les Noces* opens with a type of singing that could equally well have served a funeral. In the true spirit of the Russian folk wedding play, the *svadebnaya igra*, Stravinsky begins with the bride's wailing (*plach*), an essential requirement of the ritual.

> Accompanying her laments with sobbing, at certain places [the bride] articulates a wail, loud and futile, "i-akh!" and simultaneously she collapses to the floor or to the table, beating herself with the whole weight of her body; not infrequently she repeats this procedure until the lower parts of her arms … become swollen and bruised.[20]

Wedding plays and funerals were rites of passage, in essence, celebrations marking the end of one stage of life (or being) and the beginning of another. As such, they featured forms of lament, elaborate vocalizations with many of the same melodic formulae.[21] In the opening tableaux of *Les Noces* the effect of this can be severe and even harsh, marking an intensity of expression quite unlike anything in the many adaptations of Stravinsky's predecessors.[22]

---

[18] See Mazo, "Stravinsky's *Les Noces*": 111.

[19] According to Mazo, Glinka's choruses represented a contribution to the development of compositional technique; see Mazo, "Stravinsky's *Les Noces*": 111. Taruskin provides more specific detail, however, showing that it was Glinka who managed to successfully render an authentic folk – quintuple – meter by setting the syllables to his texts isochronously (" … a powerful precedent"); see Taruskin, *Stravinsky and the Russian Traditions*, vol. II: 1355–57.

[20] F. M. Istomin and G. O. Dyutsh, *Pesni Russkogo naroda, sobranï v guberniyakh Arkhangelskoy i Olonetskoy v 1886 godu* (St. Petersburg: Imperial Russian Geographical Society, 1894), xviii; cited in Mazo, "Stravinsky's *Les Noces*": 108. Based on her own interviews in the Nikol'sk district (Vologda province), Mazo notes that this ritual behavior was performed until World War II.

[21] Mazo discusses the relationship between wedding and funeral laments in "Stravinsky's *Les Noces*": 121.

[22] Stravinsky's production, cast, and planned staging omitted priests and other figures and symbols of the Russian Orthodox Church. This was because the *igra* was grounded in pre-Christian ritual, with its most significant elements residing outside the realm of the Christian sacrament. At the same time, however, neither the text nor music of *Les Noces* was affected by these issues. Allusions to the Church and its symbols occur in both, frequently and often ingeniously. At Rehearsal No. 44 in the second tableau, for example, the divided basses command the Virgin Mary: "Pod'na svad'bu," or, loosely translated, "Off to the wedding with you!" Ordinarily, Christian saints are not commanded to perform, of course, only supplicated to intercede. A conflation of sorts is at work, in other words, a confusion of pagan and Christian ritual. What might have applied to, say, an "ancient fertility goddess" is being applied to "the mother of our

No single ethnographic source could have served as the foundation for the scenario. The variations, embellishments, local traditions, and forms of the *svadebnaya igra* were virtually endless. Always, however, a large cast was required, including the bride (*nevesta*), groom (*zhenikh*), parents (or their surrogates), friends, and, indispensable to the proceedings, two match-makers, the male *svat* and female *svakha*. In addition, a "best man" or *druzhko* served as a kind of master of ceremonies, a chief organizer of the ritual (which could extend over a period of several weeks).[23] Every player was obliged to fulfill his/her role as handed down by tradition, from the prescribed courtesy of the matchmakers to the solicitous attention of the bride's parents to their daughter. Above all, the bride was expected to weep bitterly, even if she were marrying for love.[24]

The wailing of the bride and her companions – a repetition of fixed behavior as a way of establishing a connection to the past – was not, despite its ubiquitous presence in folk weddings, a pretense. Professional weepers, women with a talent for improvisation within the particular rules of local convention, were often employed "to awaken specific emotions and thoughts," to compose psychologically moving laments of "striking power."[25] In her study of *Les Noces*, Margarita Mazo has discussed the three main properties of lament as they occur in Russian village ritual: *vopl'*, the natural voice gesture of wailing; *prichitaniye*, a form of uninterrupted rhythmic recitation; and *plach*, the actual weeping. Example 3.1 reproduces Mazo's transcriptions of these formulae as sung by the bride and her bridesmaids. The "correct proportions" between *vopl'*, *plach* and *prichitaniye* were prescribed by local tradition, and performers were expected to be able to distinguish between lamenting (*vopl'* and *plach*), as identified by vocalized breathing and loose pitch structure, and singing (*prichitaniye*), as identified by fixed pitches. The two approaches embodied distinct types of vocalization.[26]

Savior." Consistent with the collage-like construction of Stravinsky's text, in which lines of verse were often pieced together from a large assortment of wedding songs, one of these figures has replaced the other. For a discussion of the pre-Christian elements of the *igra*, see Simon Karlinsky, "Igor Stravinsky and Russian Preliterate Theater," in *Confronting Stravinsky: Man, Musician, and Modernist*, ed. Jann Pasler (Berkeley: University of California Press, 1986), 9.

[23] Information not otherwise credited here is derived from Taruskin's account of the *svadebnaya igra* in "Survey of Present-day Wedding Rites" in Tereshchenko's *Bït russkogo naroda*, 7 vols. (St. Petersburg, 1848), vol. II: 116–42. Tereshchenko notes that the *svat*, *svakha*, and the *druzhko* form the "essential trio" responsible for arranging and carrying out the ceremony; see Taruskin, *Stravinsky and the Russian Traditions*, vol. II: 1325.

[24] Y. M. Sokolov, "Wedding Ceremonials and Chants," in *Russian Folklore*, trans. Catherine Ruth Smith (Hatboro, Pa.: Folklore Associates, 1966), 212.

[25] *Ibid.*, 213–14.

[26] Example 3.1 is taken from Mazo, "Stravinsky's *Les Noces*": 122; originally published in "Nikol'skie prichitaniia v sootnosheniis drugimi zhanrami mestnoi pesennosti," *Musykal'naia folkloristika*, ed. Alexander Banin, vol. II (Moscow, 1978). The discussion of *vopl'*, *plach* and *prichitaniye* is based on Mazo, "Stravinsky's *Les Noces*": 122–126.

Example 3.1. Forms of lament

a) The Bride's *vopl'* superimposed over the bridesmaids' (chorus) *prichitaniye*

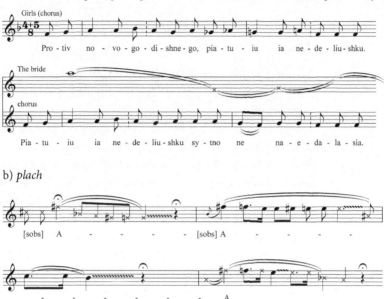

b) *plach*

Observe, too, in Example 3.1, the superimposition or *layering* of one distinct type of lament (specifically, *vopl'*, as sung by the bride) over the syllabic setting of another (*prichitaniye*) in the chorus. Such layering in the performance of these laments can bring to mind the many features of stratification in *Les Noces* and in Stravinsky's oeuvre as a whole. Stratification is emblematic, as we have indicated already, one of the principal means by which a larger sense of form is imposed in works of the Russian era above all.

During the *devichnik*, or bridal shower, which usually took place on the day prior to the wedding, the weeping of the bride and her entourage reached its peak. A married woman would lead the maidens in the singing of the *prichitaniye* while covering the bride's head with a veil. The center-piece of the ceremony was the undoing and combing out of the bride's braid (*kosa*), which was then redone in two plaits, wound around her head, and covered with the kerchief that would remain part of her dress for the remainder of her married life.[27] At the end of the evening or on the morning of the wedding, the girls would lead the bride to the bathhouse for her ritual bath (*bania*). The final required *plach* was that of the bride's mother, heard

---

[27] By the early nineteenth century (the time period in which *Les Noces* was set) much of this action – the binding of the bride's hair and the tying of the braids around her head to signify the married state – was already, as Stravinsky put it, "ritual for ritual's sake"; see Stravinsky and Craft, *Expositions and Developments*, 131.

as the bride and her attendants departed for the church ceremony (*vencha-niye*) in the morning.[28]

The scenario

The underlying source for all that *Les Noces* was to become can be summarized in a single phrase: "In the beginning was the word."[29] And the inexhaustible spring from which Stravinsky drew his inspiration was P. V. Kireyevsky's collection of folk verse, compiled during the first half of the nineteenth century.[30] Kireyevsky and his many contributors, among whom were poets and literary figures as distinguished as Alexander Pushkin and Nicholas Gogol, were motivated by the nationalist conviction that "the residual wisdom" of the Russian character could be found within the heritage of peasant life.[31] A new scholarly method emerged as one of the by-products of this reverence for folk authenticity. Kireyevsky transcribed the verses word for word, without regard for any perceived awkwardness or, in his own words, "apparent lack of sense."[32] In addition, he organized his collections geographically, going so far as to include, whenever possible, notes on the performance traditions of different regions. A virtually

---

[28] As many as seventeen ritual episodes, often varying widely in number, sequence, and duration from one Russian locality to the next, may be summarized in the following terms:

1. *svatan'ye* (the matchmaking)
2. the *smotrinï* (the bride-show)
3. the inspection of the groom's household
4. *rukobit'ye* and *sgovor* (confirmation of an unwritten contract, bargaining, and betrothal)
5. the *devichnik* (girls' gathering, a sort of bridal shower)
6. the *bania* (purifying bath)
7. the arrival of the groom and his *poyezd* (ritual personages from the groom's side)
8. the blessing by the bride's parents
9. the seeing off of the bride and the departure of the wedding train to church
10. the *venchaniye* (crowning, church ceremony)
11. the arrival of the wedding train at the groom's house, greeting the newly wedded couple
12. the blessing by the groom's parents
13. the *krasniy stol*
14. the newly-weds' departure from the feast
15. the *vykup posteli* (the ritualistic purchase of the wedding bed by the groom)
16. the verification of the young woman's chastity prior to the wedding and checking her household skills
17. the visiting of her parents

See Mazo, "Stravinsky's *Les Noces*": 117–18.

[29] Craft and Harkins, "Stravinsky's *Svadebka*": 26.

[30] Although the texts for *Les Noces* were drawn almost exclusively from Kireyevsky's anthology, Stravinsky also borrowed from Dahl's Dictionary, Sakharov's *Skazaniya russkogo naroda*, and Tereshchenko's *Bït russkogo naroda*. See Roberta Reeder, "Stravinsky's *Les Noces*," *Dance Research Journal* 18, no. 2 (Winter 1986–87): 38–49; and Taruskin, *Stravinsky and the Russian Traditions*, 1140–41.

[31] Reeder, "Stravinsky's *Les Noces*": 32.   [32] *Ibid.*

complete script of the *svadebnaya igra* thus lay at Stravinsky's disposal when, in late summer, 1914, he turned in earnest to a selection of the texts.

Only very few verses from Kireyevsky's vast collection appeared in print during his lifetime. The volume used by Stravinsky, published in 1911, consists primarily of wedding songs (1,043 of them), and was the result, in part, of "the great wave of new interest in native Russian art" that occurred from 1907 to 1917. [33] Many of the composer's earlier works – *The Firebird, Petrushka,* and *The Rite of Spring* – had incorporated Russian folk tales and legends, of course, yet none with a deeper sense of the reality of this Russian folk past than *Les Noces.* This is not to discount the many other staged re-creations of folk ritual at the time, including some that were a good deal more scrupulous, ethnographically speaking. Among these, *Scenes of Folk Festivals in Old Russia* (1913) by the folk music specialist Alexander Kastalsky had sought to recreate folk ritual based on ethnographic description and field-collected folk song. Many of the musical sources at Stravinsky's disposal had been available to Kastalsky as well, with the result that occasional musical correspondences can be identified between *Scenes of Folk Festivals* and *Les Noces.*[34]

The point here, however, is not that Stravinsky might initially have been attempting something similar to Kastalsky, but only that the interest in Russian folk art and ritual at the time was felt widely and in many diverse ways. The composer seems not to have heard Kastalsky's *Scenes of Folk Festivals.* But even if he had, it seems doubtful that it would have made much of a difference. For the reality that interested him was not solely that of the Russian folk past, but that of his own powers of appropriation as well, the reshaping of that heritage in a musical and psychological image of his own. Qualities and sensibilities were doubtless shared in one way or another: stiff, repetitive, and incantatory features, for the most part. But the audiences to which he sought to appeal were not ultimately those of the distant past (or the nostalgic present), but rather those of the contemporary world, the here-and-now, as it were.

---

[33] Karlinsky, "Igor Stravinsky and Russian Preliterate Theater," 5.

[34] Kastalsky's *Kartinï narodnïkh prazdnovaniy na Rusi* remained unpublished until 1960, *Stat'i. Vospominaniia. Materialy* (Moscow, 1960). An outline of his preface, containing ideas about the work as a whole, was, however, published in 1914 in *Muzïka*; see Mazo, "Stravinsky's *Les Noces*": 112. Among others, Mitrofan Pyatnitsky and Evgeniya Linyova also presented "unprocessed" folk song on stage. This attempt at "exact" recreation, especially through the use of recording technology, came, in part, as a reaction to the treatment of folk song in nineteenth century art music. Karlinsky observes, for example, that Glinka's setting of *Ruslan and Ludmila* "weds Russian and Tatar folk songs to musical textures borrowed from Rossini and Weber"; see Karlinsky, "Igor Stravinsky and Russian Preliterate Theater," 5.

As a collection of clichés and quotations of typical wedding sayings [*Les Noces*] might be compared to one of those scenes in *Ulysses* in which the reader seems to be overhearing scraps of conversation without the connecting thread of discourse. *Les Noces* might also be compared to *Ulysses* in the larger sense that both works are trying to *present* rather than to *describe*.[35]

Although *Les Noces*'s libretto would eventually evolve into a discourse of "Joycean" abstraction (as Stravinsky later described it), it did not begin that way. In the initial sketches for the scenario, the composer attempted to locate a point of aesthetic equilibrium between the ethnographically "true" and the dramatically effective.[36] An early plan for the scenario is given below:[37]

LES NOCES: Fantasy in Three Acts and Five Scenes
Act I
The Inspection [*Smotrini*]
Act II
  Scene 1
  The Bargain [*Sgovor*]
    a. At the Bride's
    b. At the Groom's (An Incantation against Sorcery – see page 49 in Kireyevsky)
  Scene 2
    a. *Devichnik* (The Bride's Party)
    b. The Girls Take Her to the Bath
  Scene 3
  In the Bride's House Before the Departure for the Church
Act III
  The Beautiful Table [*Krasnïy stol*]

---

[35] Stravinsky and Craft, *Expositions and Developments*, 130–31.
[36] Stravinsky's sketches include numerous reminders to himself to look up words in Dahl's Dictionary; see Vera Stravinsky and Robert Craft, *Stravinsky in Pictures and Documents* (New York: Simon and Schuster, 1978), 619, n. 235. As Taruskin points out, "he toyed briefly (Notebook, p. 5) with a six-part plan" taken directly from its pages:

1. *Bol'shoy propoy* (The Great Toast, i.e., the culmination of the *sgovor*)
2. *Plach i korovai* (lament and wedding loaf ceremonies)
3. *Devichnik* (bridal shower)
4. *Venchaniye* (church ceremony)
5. *Otvod* (exorcism)
6. *Krasnïy stol* (wedding feast)

See Taruskin, *Stravinsky and the Russian Traditions*, vol. II: 1342–43.
[37] Reproduced from Vera Stravinsky and Craft, *Pictures and Documents*, 145–46. See also, in slightly different form in Craft and Harkins, "Stravinsky's *Svadebka*": 29. The sketch is on page 2 of the twenty-four page notebook in which Stravinsky began making notes for *Svadebka* in 1914 (no. 84/2 in the Rothschild catalogue, in the Paul Sacher Stiftung). For details about this source, see Taruskin, *Stravinsky and the Russian Traditions*, vol. II: 1337–38.

With subject matter of such dramatic potential, Stravinsky may well have been contemplating a theatrical undertaking on a scale matching that of his opera *The Nightingale*.[38] Tellingly, the early sketches for *Les Noces* contain musical characterizations and dramatic action conceived along quasi-operatic lines. Especially in his copious notes for the second act, conceived realistically from an ethnographical standpoint, Stravinsky makes reference to specific pages and song verses in the Kireyevsky anthology.[39] As we have remarked already, his attachment to folk sources of this kind during the Swiss years was neither new nor exceptional. What changed during the course of *Les Noces*'s composition was his handling of these sources, the way he came to view them as a natural resource, a vein of inspiration that could be mined and processed at will. At the conclusion of his notes for this early three-act scenario, an "oily-voiced" tenor brings the narrative to a close by singing a conflation of Kireyevsky Nos. 514 and 465. As the libretto for *Les Noces* took shape, textual alterations of all kinds – a mixing of geographic areas and purpose, neologisms, conflations – became the rule.

The verse below, from the collection submitted to Kireyevsky by Pushkin (No. 142, lines 1–4), provides a typical example of Stravinsky's treatment of his textual sources (the rhyme scheme here, it should be noted, results from syntactic parallelism, and is unusual in this respect):

> Iagoda s iagodoi sokatilasia!
> Iagoda iagode poklonilasia!
> Iagoda s iagodoi slovo molvila!
> Iagoda ot iagody ne vdali rosla!
>
> A berry to a berry rolled near!
> A berry to the berry bowed!
> A berry with the berry a word spoke!
> A berry from the berry did not grow far![40]

---

[38] Premiered in May 1914 and staged by Alexandre Benois and Alexander Sanin, it should also be noted that the nature of *The Nightingale*'s triumph had been essentially *visual*. By general critical consensus, Stravinsky's music had not fared as well, having been overshadowed by the decor and the production itself. The composer's reaction to this seems not to have been entirely benign. During a September 1914 conversation with the French musicologist Romain Rolland, Stravinsky, in an oblique reference to Benois's work on *The Nightingale*, criticized the way in which the set design had tended "to limit [the] music by making its expression too specific." Romain Rolland, *Journal des années de guerre*, 59–61, entry for September 26, 1914; see Stephen Walsh, *Stravinsky: A Creative Spring, Russia and France, 1882–1934* (New York: Alfred A. Knopf, 1999), 233, 244–45.

[39] A translation of Stravinsky's notes for the second act appears in Craft and Harkins, "Stravinsky's *Svadebka*": 30. Craft mistakenly identifies the chronology of the notes, however, associating them with the final 1923 version of the score. Taruskin restores the heading "Second Act" given by Stravinsky in his notebook on page 7–8; see *Stravinsky and the Russian Traditions*, vol. II: 1340 and n. 40.

[40] Stravinsky was charmed by the possibility that *Les Noces* might contain a line or two by Pushkin. His sketches include references to the songs collected by Pushkin in Kireyevsky's anthology, specifically to pages 54–60 and 48–54; see Vera Stravinsky and Craft, *Pictures and Documents*,

Although the composer included this song among several others having to do with the bride's ritual bath (*bania*) in his sketchbooks, Kireyevsky identified it as a verse sung when the bride returns from the church ceremony. Given its position at the beginning of the fourth tableau, the wedding feast (*krasnïy stol*), it seems doubtful that Stravinsky could have been unaware of its celebratory meaning. If he had been, however, its sound could have motivated its placement. It was duly conflated with Kireyevsky No. 447, in any case, a lively song of praise with a similar imagery (berries) and, as a result, a similar sound sense. The exclamations of joy in this second song are attractive for their sound alone, and are an ideal way, as it must have seemed at the time, to dispel the pervasive atmosphere of lamentation at the close of the third tableau. In the final version of *Les Noces*, lines 1–2 in the earlier verse are separated from lines 3–4 by the interpolation of Kireyevsky No. 447:

> Ai liuli, liuli, liuli! Liushen'ki, ai liuli!
> Iagodka krasna!
> Zemlianichka spela!
> Ai Liushen'ki, Liuli!

> Ai liuli, liuli, liuli! Liushen'ki, ai liuli!
> Pretty [red] berry!
> Ripened strawberry!
> Ai Liushen'ki, Liuli!

As far as the larger organization of *Les Noces* is concerned, inspiration seems to have come early in 1915, and in the form of another verse from Kireyevsky, this one appended as an epigraph to an early draft of the full score:[41]

> Two rivers flow together
> Two matchmakers come together
> They think about the ashblond braid
> How will we unplait this ashblond braid?
> How will we part the braid in two?

Crucial, too, from the standpoint of the scenario as a whole, was Stravinsky's decision to do away with the depictions of the preliminary rituals, the bride

---

619, n. 235. The translations and transliterations of the songs discussed here are derived from Reeder, "Stravinsky's *Les Noces*": 35. "A berry to a berry rolled near!" is on page 54 of Kireyevsky and, like all Pushkin's songs, is from Pskov Province, the location of his father's estate.

[41] Craft and Harkins, "Stravinsky's *Svadebka*": 30. A reproduction of Stravinsky's hand-written copy of these lines, from Kireyevsky no. 999, appears in Vera Stravinsky and Craft, *Pictures and Documents*, pl. 6.

show (*smotrini*) and betrothal (*sgovor*), and to begin, instead, with the bridal shower (*devichnik*), literally on the eve of the wedding itself.[42] Departing from the play and its original sequence of episodes, he drew a large parallel between the Bride's braid (*kosa*) and the Groom's curls (*kundri*). The practice of combing the groom's hair was much less common in Russian folk ritual, and never as significant as the symbolic arrangement of the bride's braid. With the elevation of the groom and the combing of his "locks," however, not only would the first two tableaux be united under a single theme (that of grooming, "At the Bride's" and then "At the Groom's"), but the third – the scene of the Bride's departure – would be provided with an inroad as well. By tradition, the latter had featured a lament of the bride's mother. In line with this new bride/groom symmetry, however, Stravinsky decided to end the tableau with the mothers of both the Bride and Groom lamenting the loss of their children to marriage. Although not rooted in ethnographic reality, "the scene is psychologically sound," as Craft and William Harkins would remark in their introduction to the scenario. Stravinsky "deepened the lament, [bringing] it closer to human truth."[43] The final version of the scenario runs as follows:

Rehearsal Nos.	Scenario
	PART I
0–27	**first tableau: At the Bride's**
	The tableau opens with the soprano solo singing the Bride's *vopl'*. The bridesmaids comb out the Bride's single braid (*kosa*), dividing it into two braids, which are then wound around the Bride's head and covered with a scarf.
27–65	**second tableau: At the Groom's**
	The Groom's curls (*kundri*) are combed, with the groomsmen in attendance. A lament sung by the parents of the Groom follows at Rehearsal Nos. 35–40.

[42] Based on Prokofiev's description, which appeared in *Muzïka* in April 1915, we know that the scenario was close to its final form at this time. According to Prokofiev, *Les Noces* was already conceived as having four tableaux, with the first two scenes described just as they would eventually appear in the final version (although in reversed order: "At the young man's" [*U molodogo*] and "At the young woman's" [*U molodoy*]). Also in place at this time were the "Wedding Table" scene [*Krasnïy stol*] and the ending of the work, in which the newly married couple depart for their bedchamber. V. V. Derzhanovsky, "Za rubezhom: novïye sochineniya Igorya Stravinskogo," *Muzïka* no. 219 (18 April 1915): 262–63. An English translation of this article appears in Taruskin, *Stravinsky and the Russian Traditions*, vol. II: 1319–20.

[43] Craft and Harkins, "Stravinsky's *Svadebka*": 31.

65–87   **third tableau: Seeing off the Bride**

As the Bride departs, the mothers of both Bride and Groom lament the loss of their children (at Rehearsal No. 82). Their lament is a varied repetition of the earlier lament in the second tableau, as sung by the parents of the Groom.

PART II

87–End   **fourth tableau: The Wedding Feast**

In the midst of the celebration (*krasnïy stol*), the marriage bed is prepared and, at Rehearsal No. 130, the newlyweds depart from the feast.

Musical sources in *Les Noces*

One of the earliest musical sources of *Les Noces* dates from July 1913. Stravinsky had been working on *The Nightingale* with his librettist and close friend at the time, Stephan Mitusov. At some point in their collaboration, Mitusov sang two Russian folk songs for the composer, "Ne vesyolaya da kompan'itsa" ("Not a Merry Company") and "Ia vechor v luzhkakh guliala" ("I Wandered in the Meadows in the Evening"). Much later, Stravinsky would identify "Ne vesyolaya da kompan'itsa" as the only "folk-derived" theme in *Les Noces*, going so far as to publish a fragment of the tune (see Example 3.2a). He would also misidentify it as a "proletarian song," recalling the difficulties he had had in transcribing it some fifty years earlier.[44] The inconsistencies in his account have been recorded on several occasions: not only was "Ne vesyolaya da kompan'itsa" published in the Istomin–Dyutsh collection of 1894 (see Example 3.2b), but its profile in that anthology closely approximates its appearance in the fourth tableau of *Les Noces* (see Example 3.2c for the quotation at Rehearsal No. 120). Stravinsky's memory may have failed him, of course, or, as Richard Taruskin has claimed, he may also, at the time of his lengthy neoclassical and serial eras, have wanted to downplay the folkloristic origins of his music.[45] We shall be returning to these themes in Chapter 5.

[44] Istomin and Dyutsh, *Pesni russkogo naroda*. Stravinsky's musical example of the Mitusov song appears in Igor Stravinsky and Robert Craft, *Memories and Commentaries* (Garden City, NY: Doubleday, 1960), 97. Both Mazo and Taruskin mention the song's location in the Istomin and Dyutsh anthology and discuss its musical characteristics. Typical "worker's melodies" originated in the late nineteenth century as part of a developing urban tradition. On the other hand, both the text and the lyric quality of "Ne vesyolaya da kompan'itsa" identify it as a love song (*lyubovnaya*, as classified by Istomin); see Mazo, "Stravinsky's *Les Noces*": 107. Taruskin also includes a facsimile and description of the sketch, which bears the title, "Russian Songs imparted to me by S. S. Mitusov. I. Stravinsky, Ustilug, VII/1913"; see Taruskin, *Stravinsky and the Russian Traditions*, vol. II: 1372–75.

[45] Taruskin, *Stravinsky and the Russian Traditions*, vol. II: 1372.

Example 3.2. The Mitusov song
a) Fragment, as published in Igor Stravinsky and Robert Craft, *Memories and Commentaries* (1960)

b) "Ne vesyolaya da kompan'itsa," as published in the Istomin–Dyutsh Anthology (1894)

c) Quotation of the Mitusov melody in *Les Noces*, fourth tableau

The "Mitusov song" – "Ne vesyolaya da kompan'itsa" – became part of the widely varied collection of sources from which Stravinsky drew inspiration. Initially diverse, all this material was startlingly transformed by the time of the first complete draft of the score in 1917. The process of assimilation – the making of Stravinsky's Russian-period style, in effect – was given the following description by Béla Bartók:

> Stravinsky never mentions the sources of his themes. Neither in his titles nor in footnotes does he ever allude to whether a theme of his is his own invention or whether it is taken from folk music ... This much is certain, [however], that if among the thematic material of Stravinsky's there are some of his own invention (and who can doubt that there are) these are the most faithful and

clever imitations of folk songs. It is also notable that during his "Russian"
period . . . he seldom uses melodies of a closed form consisting of three or four
lines, but short motives of two or three measures, and repeats them "à la
ostinato" . . .[46]

Bartók might have continued his analysis of Stravinsky's "folk" style by turning
to an even smaller musical entity. For Stravinsky's "folk" music is based not so
much on the direct quotation of pre-existing melodies as on the manipulation
of small musical structures. Specifically, his melodies are built from short
melodic units that resemble *popevki* (pl. of *popevka*). The latter term, originally
used to describe identifying gestures in Russian church music, was adopted for
use in studies of folk music during the nineteenth century. In contrast to the
way in which motives are "developed" in nineteenth-century art music,
through the manipulation of pitch and rhythm, *popevki* are relatively "pitch
constant." Examples 3.3a–c show several characteristic folk songs that exhibit
melodic formulations similar to those found in *Les Noces*; they are taken from
collections that would have been familiar to Stravinsky at the time.[47] The short
popevki within each melody are sustained through repetition, juxtaposition,
and, of course, patterns of accentuation. Fundamentally rhythmic in design,
this latter type of invention underlies the mosaic-like character of melody in
Les Noces, the cutting and pasting of small segments, motives, and submotives,
an issue to which we will be directing our attention more specifically in
Chapters 4 and 5.

A sample of Stravinsky's methods – his use of *popevki*, in effect – is
shown in Example 3.4a. Reproduced from the opening four bars of the
second tableau (the scene "At the Groom's," beginning at Rehearsal No.
27), the four bracketed segments are variations (*popevki*) on a single idea,
namely, the pitch D reiterated and embellished by its lower neighbor
C. As we shall see in Chapter 4, each bracketed segment corresponds to a
single line of the text, the means by which, as a general rule, modifications
in the length of these *popevki* were effected. The second and third segments, featuring the rising skip of a fourth, are traceable to the chant
shown in Example 3.4b.

Other sources of melody in *Les Noces* arose no less accidentally.
Descending in a funicular from the mountains of Château d'Oex in
January 1915, Stravinsky found himself in the company of two inebriated
local inhabitants, one of whom sang while the other hiccupped. Amused,
he composed "a hocket imitating this debauched duet, perhaps the only

---

[46] Béla Bartók, "The Influence of Peasant Music on Modern Music," in *Béla Bartók Essays*, ed.
Benjamin Suchoff (Lincoln: University of Nebraska Press, 1992), 343.
[47] The melodies are selected from the Appendix to Mazo, "Stravinsky's *Les Noces*": 137–38.

Example 3.3. Illustrations of *popevki* in Russian folksong
a) N. Rimsky-Korsakov, "Sto russkikh narodnykh pesen," Op. 24, No. 1

b) N. Rimsky-Korsakov, "Sto russkikh narodnykh pesen," Op. 24, No. 88

c) M. Balakirev, "Sbornik russkikh narodnykh pesen," No. 1

real hocket ever written ..."[48] The syncopation of this motive – what would eventually emerge as the "hiccup motive" – found its way, appropriately enough, into countless passages in the fourth tableau, amidst the exuberance of the wedding celebration. Beginning at Rehearsal No. 93, it would unite with the basic melodic pattern of *Les Noces*, the (0 2 5) trichord or "basic cell" (as we shall be calling it), and in the form of a "powerful unifying stroke," as Vera Stravinsky and Craft described it in their 1978 study, *Stravinsky in Pictures and Documents.*[49]

Among Stravinsky's earliest musical sketches for *Les Noces* is a transcription of the bells of St. Paul's Cathedral in London; see the reproduction of this early jotting in Example 3.5a.[50] Only a fragment of this counterpoint appears in the final version of *Les Noces* (at Rehearsal Nos. 18+2 and 73+8; see Examples 3.5b and c), but the sounding of bells became a crucial conceptual element, both a "summons" or "call to participation" at the beginning of the ceremonial act and its eventual "consummation."[51]

From Rehearsal No. 59 to the end of the second tableau, the ringing of bells can be heard in the C-A-C♯/B♭/A-A basso ostinato, sustained for some

[48] Craft and Harkins, "Stravinsky's *Svadebka*": 24. Stravinsky's fondness for his inadvertent find is perhaps best demonstrated by a sketch of the rhythm at Rehearsal No. 127 that he gave as a gift to Vera Sudeikin in September 1921; see *The Salon Album of Vera Sudeikin-Stravinsky*, ed. John E. Bolt (Princeton University Press, 1995), 99.

[49] Vera Stravinsky and Craft, *Pictures and Documents*,151.

[50] Stephen Walsh, *The Music of Stravinsky* (New York: Routledge, Chapman and Hall, 1988), 75–76, 83.

[51] For an account of Stravinsky's response to the bells of St. Paul's Cathedral, see Edwin Evans, *Music and Dance, for Lovers of the Ballet* (London: Herbert Jenkins, [1946]), 89–90. A facsimile of Stravinsky's sketch appears in Vera Stravinsky and Craft, *Pictures and Documents*, 127. In Stravinsky's hand on the sketch: "The bells of St. Paul's in London. Astonishingly beautiful counterpoint such as I have never heard before in my life."

Example 3.4. Stravinsky's use of short melodic fragments

a) *Les Noces*, second tableau, opening block, first four bars

b) *Znamennïy* chant, the fifth *glas*

forty measures in Pianos II and IV. And they can be heard again in the closing pages of the fourth tableau ("the consummation"), beginning with the repetition of the vertical dyad (C♯ B) at Rehearsal No. 133; see Example 5.1e. As part of a stratified texture, fifteen repeats of this two-note chord, played initially by the chimes and bells, are superimposed over a reiterated fragment in the bass solo. And with each of these repeats spaced evenly by eight quarter-note beats (save for a single instance at Rehearsal No. 134+7, where the span is lengthened to eleven beats), the sound of bells tolling becomes quite literal. They do so every four seconds, to be exact, fifteen times per minute, given Stravinsky's metronome marking for the quarter-note beat at 120 BPM. And were it not for the just-noted exception at Rehearsal No. 134+7 (where, in the form of a single 3/4 bar of silence, three quarter-note beats are added to the count), the duration of this final passage of *Les Noces* would amount to exactly one minute.

So entirely consistent is the regularity of this pattern with that of an actual ringing or tolling of church bells, that the irregular beats at Rehearsal No. 134+7 can represent something of a puzzle. They appear to have done so for Pierre Boulez, in any case, a frequent conductor of *Les Noces* during the 1960s and 70s. In a 1968 tale worth recounting here, Boulez not only questioned the correctness and authenticity of the three additional beats, but managed to persuade the composer to do so as well.[52] The infraction

---

[52] See Robert Craft, *An Improbable Life* (Nashville: Vanderbilt University Press, 2002), 281–84. To follow Craft's account of this episode, Boulez, leafing through the score, "talked an inebriated Stravinsky into canceling a bar of silence on the last page of *Les Noces*." The story is also recounted in Stephen Walsh, *Stravinsky: The Second Exile* (New York: Alfred A. Knopf, 2006), 502. For an elegant defense of the irregular beats in question, see Andew Imbrie, "One Measure of Eternity," *Perspectives of New Music* 9, no. 2 (1971): 51–57. According to Imbrie, the flexible

Example 3.5. The bells of St. Paul's Cathedral, London
a) Stravinsky's transcription, London, June, 1914

b) *Les Noces*, first tableau

c) *Les Noces*, third tableau

itself is minute, of course, given the length of the pattern; the single 3/4 bar is the extent by which the total duration of a minute is exceeded. Although swayed at first by Boulez's argument, Stravinsky seems to have reversed himself soon thereafter. A chance to relive something of what might originally have been intended by the extra beats (their ability to provide for a degree of relief from the regularity of the pattern, presumably), may have presented itself at some point. The extra beats were restored later in 1968, in any case, just prior to a performance of *Les Noces* in New York.

Despite the pagan roots of the *svadebnaya igra*, *Les Noces* is "a product of the Russian Church," in which "[i]nvocations to the Virgin and saints are

metrical scheme of the vocal line in these final pages of *Les Noces* is likely to take precedence initially, with the regularity of the bell-like strokes experienced only "subliminally" (56). He predicts a switch to the regularity of the bell-strokes midway through, however, with the listener changing his/her metrical orientation accordingly. Here, Imbrie argues, three beats are added – an extra 3/4 measure, in effect, "one measure of eternity" – as a way of sustaining a sense of timelessness. By breaking away from the regular count of eight quarter-note beats at this point, something of the floating, meterless quality of the music is preserved. "At the exact moment when we are prepared to embrace the 'true' simplicity of the meter of bell-strokes, it eludes us again. The rest of the coda is required to restore our precarious balance" (57).

Example 3.6. a) *Znamennïy* chant, the second *glas*

b) *Les Noces*, second tableau, unaccompanied duet

heard throughout …"[53] Among the sketches for *Les Noces*, a long, unbarred melody may be found, identified by Craft as a fifth-tone *dogmatic* (a prayer to the Virgin) from the *Oktoïkh*, the eight-week cycle of old Russian liturgical [*Znamennïy*] chant.[54] The *popevki* heard at the opening of the second tableau, "At the Groom's," are drawn from this source (see Example 3.4b).

More spiritually resonant here, however, given its culturally embedded religious significance, is the fragment of chant appearing at Rehearsal No. 50 (see Example 3.6a). Following the church rule forbidding the use of instruments during the liturgy, the basses' duet is unaccompanied (Example 3.6b), the only instance of such solo singing in *Les Noces*. The text is unusual as well; it is not a song, but, rather, the *druzhko*'s formulaic spoken request for blessings from the groom's parents to their child.[55] So, too, in contrast to the continuous recycling of most other themes throughout the work, the music here serves only this particular purpose. It is set apart by the comparative purity of its diatonicism and the melismatic contour of its melodic lines. Without doubt, Stravinsky intended to express the underlying sanctity of the proceedings, and was "as close as [he] ever came to a representation of the Orthodox service on the stage."[56]

[53] Stravinsky and Craft, *Expositions and Developments*, 131.

[54] Vera Stravinsky and Craft, *Pictures and Documents*, 149–50; Craft and Harkins, "Stravinsky's *Svadebka*": 27–28. *Znamennïy* chant is derived from the Byzantine, and is based on a system of eight modes or *echoi* (in Russian, *glasy*, pl. of *glas*), each of which possesses a different, characteristic melodic formula.

[55] See Reeder, "Stravinsky's *Les Noces*": 51, n. 40.

[56] Vera Stravinsky and Craft, *Pictures and Documents*, 150.

Only the most profound understanding of Russian folksong could have brought together and united musical sources of such wide-ranging diversity. Remarkable above all in *Les Noces* is Stravinsky's imitation of folk lamentation. Setting the stage during the opening bars, *Les Noces* begins with singing intoned "with short glissandi" in the style of actual lament.[57] These glissandi are the result of a form of embellishment, specifically here, grace notes inflecting the intervals of a major third and perfect fourth. When sung, the gaps in these inflections create a sliding effect, one that is overtly sob-like. Something of the acute emotional distress of the bride is conveyed in this way. The outward symptoms of her distress are mimicked.

No less striking in this regard is the close of the third tableau (Rehearsal Nos. 82 through 87), where the mothers of the Bride and Groom are gathered to bid their farewells. This is the point at which, it will be recalled, Stravinsky "deepened the lament" by allowing both mothers to participate in a final lament before the wedding ceremony.[58] Embellishing the respective melodic lines with grace notes, each mother presents a rendition of her lament in free counterpoint with the other. While rests of varying length help to project an appropriately improvisatory sense of rhythm (see Example 3.7), chromatic inflections of pitch, wholly octatonic in conception (to be discussed in Chapters 4 and 5), reflect a sense of pain and anguish (hushed and mournful at this point, lamentando and pianissimo).

Renard (1915–16)

As a record of the many changes that affected Stravinsky's aesthetic outlook over a ten-year period, the four orchestrations of *Les Noces* are a treasure worth exploring to the fullest.[59] Especially significant is the insight they provide into the influence instrumentation appears to have had on musical style, as well as vice versa. Pieces such as *Pribaoutki*, *Berceuses du chat*, *Renard*, and *The Soldier's Tale* emerged as a supplement, a "diversionary harvest," as we have suggested, offshoots of *Les Noces* and the lengthy period

---

[57] Mazo, "Stravinsky's *Les Noces*": 127. Examples used in this discussion are from this source, 127–36.

[58] Craft and Harkins, "Stravinsky's *Svadebka*": 31.

[59] In Mazo's recent edition of *Les Noces* (London: Chester Music c. 2005), she makes the case for five orchestral versions. Her rationale is based on the discovery of an earlier sketch of the first version in which the ballet begins with the chorus singing about the combing of the bride's hair, rather than with the well-known opening lament. The instrumentation of both versions, however, is the same, and both sketches date from the same early stage in Stravinsky's creative process.

Example 3.7. *Les Noces*, third tableau, concluding lament

of its gestation. All these works would require only a modest instrumental complement of voices and small ensemble. Within them, however, a new instrumental sonority was discovered, a terse, bright, and lean approach that would permanently transform Stravinsky's course. Each of the four known versions of *Les Noces* represents a stage in this process of transformation. Composed over a period extending from *The Rite of Spring* to the cool, post-war objectivism of the *Octet* (1924), each arrangement offers a window into the evolving modernist program that so passionately concerned Stravinsky, Diaghilev, and the Ballets Russes in the years during and immediately following World War I.[60]

Keeping the first orchestration of *Les Noces* in close proximity to the composition of the music, Stravinsky completed an orchestral draft for

---

[60] Stravinsky's many attempts at finding an orchestral "solution" to the problem of *Les Noces* seem at times to have been forgotten by the composer in later life; see Igor Stravinsky and Robert Craft, *Retrospectives and Conclusions* (New York: Alfred A. Knopf, 1969), 118. As time wore on, he grew uncertain about the number and chronology of his many revisions.

seven pages of the first tableau in January 1915.[61] His initial impulse was to reproduce the sound of a Russian peasant band by including balalaikas, guslis (Russian folk psalteries), and guitars. Soon enough, however, and for reasons that were undoubtedly practical, the instruments of this "authentic" conception were replaced by a piano, harp, and two string quintets, one bowed and the other plucked.[62]

It is not known exactly when, in early 1916, Stravinsky set *Les Noces* aside in order to devote himself entirely to *Renard*.[63] What is certain, however, is that the composition of both works was affected dramatically by the composer's discovery of the cimbalom in January of the previous year.[64] In the case of *Renard*, the resonant and somewhat raucous sound of the cimbalom's hammers proved a perfect substitute for the gusli music mentioned in one of the *skazki* (Russian fairy tales) from which *Renard* was assembled. As Stravinsky later recounted, his compositional process began with the setting of this single tale, "The Cat, the Cock, and the Fox."[65] Included as No. 38 in Alexander Afanasyev's vast anthology of *skazki*, the text and its references to the "plink," "plink" of the gusli/cimbalom would evolve into the *pribaoutka* music at Rehearsal No. 62.[66] (We will be taking this up in greater detail in Chapter 6.) Throughout *Renard*, flourishes in the cimbalom – quick scales and arpeggios – function as a kind of instrumental leitmotiv accompanying appearances of Renard the Fox.

Initially, when Stravinsky began composing *Renard*, he seems to have had nothing more sophisticated in mind than a few children's songs or *pribaoutki* (limericks or folk jingles) based upon Afanasyev's collection. The

[61] A plate of the first page of the orchestration of the first tableau, from 1914, appears in Vera Stravinsky and Craft, *Pictures and Documents*, 144.

[62] Stravinsky later remembered the first orchestration as having been written for a "super-*Sacre*"-sized orchestra; see Stravinsky and Craft, *Retrospectives and Conclusions*, 118. Along these same lines, André Schaeffner, who conducted a series of interviews with the composer in 1929–30, reported that *Les Noces*'s first orchestration required 150 players. Schaeffner's account, from his book *Strawinsky* (Paris: Les Editions Rieder, 1931), is reproduced in E. W. White, *Stravinsky: The Composer and His Works* (Berkeley and Los Angeles: University of California Press, 1979), 254.

[63] *Renard* is C. F. Ramuz's French translation of Stravinsky's Russian title, *Baika pro lisu, petukha, kota da baraba* [*The Tale About the Fox, the Cock, the Tomcat, and the Ram*].

[64] Stravinsky had heard the Hungarian cimbalom virtuoso Aladár Rácz and his small string ensemble play at a bar in Geneva. Captivated by Rácz's large peasant dulcimer, he purchased one himself and learned to play it. Rácz described his meeting with Stravinsky in "Igor Stravinsky vu par le cymbaliste Aladár Rácz" in *Feuilles Musicales*. The article is quoted at some length in White, *Stravinsky*, 242.

[65] Stravinsky and Craft, *Expositions and Developments*, 135–36. Taruskin gives a detailed description of the assembly of *Renard*'s libretto in *Stravinsky and the Russian Traditions*, vol. II: 1246–69. The earliest musical notation, which later became the ostinato figure accompanying the Cock's song at Rehearsal Nos. 10 and 42, appears amidst the sketches for *Pribaoutki* made during the summer of 1914. See John Shepard, "The Stravinsky Nachlass: A Provisional Checklist of Music Manuscripts," *MLA Notes* 40 [1983–84]: 719–50.

[66] The numbering used here is from *Narodnïye russkiye skazki* [Russian Folk Tales], ed. M. K. Azadovsky, N. P. Andreyev, and Y. M. Sokolov (Moscow: Academia, 1936–37).

source proved irresistible, however. Overtaken by inspiration, he was soon
compiling, experimenting, and conflating fragments of texts, just as he had
earlier with the verses of the Kireyevsky volume when working on *Les Noces*.
"The Cat, the Cock, and the Fox" served as his point of departure. As an
extensive source of *pribaoutki*, it set the cheerful tone of the music in
motion. In the several variants of this story, the Cock repeatedly falls prey
to Fox's promise of something to eat, a message humorously delivered by
the Fox in patter songs like the one below:

> Cock-a-doodle-doo, little cock
> Golden crest!
> Look out the window
> And I'll give you a pea[67]

Similar to the fairy tales of western Europe, the crucial component – out-
weighing even the conclusion in terms of importance – is the repetition of
dramatic action. In "The Cat, The Cock, and the Fox," the Cock escapes the
Fox in only two of the three renditions recorded by Afanasyev. Familiar with
this narrative device, Stravinsky repeated the Fox's seduction of the Cock in
its entirety, virtually doubling *Renard's* length.

Some of the other *skazki* incorporated into *Renard's* libretto included
"The Fox Confessor" (with "holy mother fox" dressed as a nun), "The Fox
as Mourner," and "Peasant, Bear, and Fox." Working with an ever-
increasing sense of freedom, Stravinsky included an independently composed *pribaoutka*, "Gospodi pomiluy," as a coda.[68] In the improvisatory
spirit of the *skazki* that had served as its source, *Renard* evolved into a new
tale, one that can be summarized as follows:

Rehearsal Nos.	Scenario
1	Allegro. The Cock swaggers on his perch.
11	Enter Renard the fox, dressed as a nun. He tries to seduce the Cock away from the safety of his perch by offering absolution for the Cock's many wives.
19	The Cock jumps into the clutches of Renard (*salto mortale*).
24–41	Con Brio. Enter the Cat and Goat, who save the Cock and then dance.
43	The Cock is back on his perch. Renard returns and tries to tempt the Cock with the promise of something to eat.

---

[67] The English translations in this chapter are taken from Afanasyev, *Russian Fairy Tales*, trans.
Norbert Guterman (New York: Pantheon Books, 1945).
[68] See Taruskin, *Stravinsky and the Russian Traditions*, vol. II: 1267.

52	The Cock again jumps into the clutches of Renard (*salto mortale*). The Cock begs for mercy while being plucked.
62–72	Scherzando. Enter the Cat and Goat, playing a gusli and singing a little *pribaoutka* for Renard, who has retreated into his house.
72–80	The Cat and Goat brandish a knife, pull Renard out of his house and strangle him.
81–90	Cock, Cat and Goat dance. Final *pribaoutka*.

Remarkably, *Renard* contains no direct borrowings of Russian folk tunes. Its "authentic" music is entirely Stravinsky's own, in other words, as is, for that matter, the genre itself, a unique hybrid of folk play, *divertissement*, and ballet. The performance instructions, published in the score, bear this out. The composer's intention was to recreate the atmosphere of a folk street performance, with itinerant players occupying an impromptu space shared with the audience: "The play is acted by clowns, dancers, or acrobats, preferably on a trestle stage placed in front of the orchestra. If performed in a theatre it should be played in front of the curtain ..."[69]

Although *Renard* was finished in August 1916, Stravinsky waited several months before resuming work on *Les Noces*. By the autumn of 1917, however, he had not only completed a short score of *Les Noces*, but had orchestrated much of it as well.[70] The similarities between *Les Noces* and *Renard* are close and numerous, as one might expect, and they include the conflation of Russian folk texts, the uniqueness of genre, and a staging in which all players are visible on stage throughout the production. In terms of instrumentation, however, Stravinsky's second version of *Les Noces* seems more closely related to his "Three Japanese Lyrics" from 1912–13 – from which all doubling of the wind and string parts is omitted – than to the chamber ensemble for *Renard*.[71] The second orchestration of *Les Noces*, following similar lines, was composed as "an orchestra of soloists," the first page of the score specifically prohibiting the doubling of the strings.[72]

[69] *Renard* found its patron late in 1915. In Paris on Christmas day, Stravinsky previewed *Les Noces* and gained a commission for *Renard* from the Princesse de Polignac (sewing-machine heiress Winaretta Singer). The full score manuscript was presented to the princess in September 1916, with the intention that *Renard* would be performed at her home. The performance never materialized, however, and, many years later, Diaghilev claimed possession of Stravinsky's "independent" achievement. The Ballets Russes premiered *Renard* in Paris on May 18, 1922 at the Théâtre National de L'Opéra. Sets and costumes were by Mikhaíl Laryonov. Bronislava Nijinska both choreographed the ballet and danced the role of the fox.

[70] A reconstruction was made by Robert Craft and Ramiro Cortes and premiered in 1973. A recording was released in 1974 by Columbia Records/CBS (M33201).

[71] Derzhanovsky, quoting Prokofiev, mentioned this "extraordinarily interesting" orchestral complement. See note 42.

[72] Stravinsky's date on the score is 29 September/11 October 1917 (Morges). Facsimile pages are reproduced in Vera Stravinsky and Craft, *Pictures and Documents*, pls. 6 and 7.

Unlike *Renard*, too, the scoring here is heavily weighted toward the brass end of the spectrum, perhaps in an attempt to imitate the sound "of a peasant band of *rozhok* players."[73] Twenty-seven winds are required in all, including tuba, keyed bugles, cornets, trombones and the baritone saxophone. Rounding it out was a vocal contingent of four soloists (SATB), a chorus of sixteen voices, percussion, harp, piano, harpsichord, and, of course, cimbalom.

The Soldier's Tale (1918)

In the remaining months of 1917 and into 1918, Stravinsky's progress on *Les Noces* was interrupted by the composition of several shorter pieces, primarily for voice or combination of voices. Then, in September 1918, and partly in response to the economic pressures of war, Stravinsky and his translator at the time, the Swiss novelist C. F. Ramuz, decided to produce *The Soldier's Tale*.[74] Billed initially as a modest mixed-genre touring piece, the forces required for performance were limited to three narrators, two actors, a dancer, and seven instrumentalists. Following *Renard*, and in the tradition of itinerant theater, all players were to remain visible on stage throughout the performance. As with *Renard*, too, the libretto was drawn from Afanasyev's anthology, this time almost exclusively from No. 154, "The Runaway Soldier and the Devil."[75] Entirely new with *The Soldier's Tale*, however, was the relationship between the music and the text. The music was conceived as a "suite" of pieces that could be performed independently from the libretto.

As Ramuz would later recount, the intention early on had been to tell a "story" rather than to present a play.[76] Thus, the libretto for *The Soldier's Tale* unfolds in a strictly narrative fashion and without the textual conflations of *Les Noces* and *Renard*. A fairly straightforward adaptation of "The Runaway Soldier and the Devil," the text was designed to be read (or

---

[73] See Taruskin, *Stravinsky and the Russian Traditions*, vol. II: 1458.

[74] Igor Stravinsky, *An Autobiography*, 61. Stravinsky had first enlisted the help of Charles-Ferdinand Ramuz when translating the libretto of *Renard* into French. In the years directly following *Renard*'s completion, other texts would be translated by Ramuz as well, including those for *Pribaoutki*, *Berceuses du Chat*, and the libretto for *Les Noces*. For details of the collaboration on *The Soldier's Tale*, see Maureen A. Carr, "Igor Stravinsky and Charles-Ferdinand Ramuz: A Study of Their Artistic Collaboration for *Histoire du soldat* (1918)," in *Stravinsky's "Histoire du soldat": A Facsimile of the Sketches*, ed. Maureen A. Carr (Middleton, Wis.: A-R Editions, 2005), 3–19.

[75] Taruskin offers an English translation of the story with titles of the musical interludes interspersed. See *Stravinsky and the Russian Traditions*, vol. II: 1295–97.

[76] Ramuz's comments are taken from a description included in the first draft of the libretto. See Robert Craft, ed., *Stravinsky: Selected Correspondence*, vol. III (New York: Alfred A. Knopf, 1986), 470.

narrated) above or between the individual pieces. The hope had been that both the story and the direct manner of its presentation would attract a widely international – and potentially profitable – audience. The subject matter itself, a somewhat skewed version of the Faust legend, was universally known. Briefly, a soldier falls prey to the devil, who, in the pattern of repetition characteristic of the *skazki*, appears variously as a lepidopterist, a cattle merchant, an old woman (a "procuress"), a violin virtuoso, and, finally, in his true form (with tail and pointed ears).[77]

At the same time, by keeping the music separate from the narration, Stravinsky and Ramuz had hoped to avert some of the difficulties of translation. The need for a "syllable by syllable" translation from the Russian was eliminated. And the content of the story itself was made more flexible. Linguistic regionalisms along with the style of the soldier's uniform could be adjusted to the circumstances of local custom.[78]

But however advantageous from a number of practical angles, the independence of the music from the text in *The Soldier's Tale* proved problematic from a theatrical standpoint. The critical onus here has fallen on the libretto rather than on the musical interludes.[79] Ernest Ansermet, who conducted the first performance in Lausanne, September 28, 1918, immediately singled out the music as the featured player in the collaboration. He would later write that "the score ... for [*The Soldier's Tale*] is really absolute music, the purely musical interest of which remains intact when it is detached from the other elements."[80]

Both the instrumentation and the international flavor mark striking changes in Stravinsky's musical style.[81] The seven instrumentalists – two brass (trombone and cornet), two woodwinds (bassoon and clarinet), two strings (double bass and violin), and percussion – provided for a new balance of timbre and texture. Audiences at the time were startled by the reduction and ultimate rejection of the vast orchestral forces that had served

---

[77] Stravinsky explains that the identity of the "procuress" in early versions of the libretto has changed over time. Initially, she showed the Soldier pictures from her "gallery for hire." She is now more conservatively portrayed as an old woman selling her wares. See Stravinsky and Craft, *Expositions and Developments*, 107.

[78] See Stravinsky and Craft, *Expositions and Developments*, 101–02.

[79] For an account of the negative audience response to the Devil's eventual triumph, see Joan Evans, "'Diabolus triumphans': Stravinsky's *Histoire du soldat* in Weimar and Nazi Germany," in John J. Daverio and John Ogasapian, eds., *The Varieties of Musicology: Essays for Murray Lefkowitz* (Warren, Mich.: Harmonie Park Press, 2000), 177.

[80] See Ernest Ansermet, "*L'Histoire du soldat*," *Chesterian* 10 (Oct. 1920): 291.

[81] According to Stravinsky, the "internationalism" was unintentional. He did acknowledge, however, the influence of the Spanish *pasodoble* in the "Royal March" and American jazz in "Ragtime." The latter piece is particularly striking for its complete lack of "swing." Although Stravinsky had seen the scores to American ragtime, he had never heard a live performance and was, therefore, unimpeded by any sense of the improvisatory nature of the genre. See Stravinsky and Craft, *Expositions and Developments*, 103–05.

Stravinsky's earlier work. Especially important in defining the "characteristic" sound of *The Soldier's Tale* were the violin (fiddle) and the percussion.
Stravinsky identified the violin as representing the Soldier's soul and the
drums the "diablerie."[82] For the violinist, the "stress on motion rather than
emotion" required a style of playing almost mechanistic in its precision.[83]
As for the "drums," they were assigned a role equal in significance to that of
their co-players:

> The role of the batterie [in *The Soldier's Tale*] was another novelty, at least in
> 1918. Percussion sections had long served the orchestra as arsenals and sound-
> prop departments, supplying it with extra colours, articulation, weight. Before
> *The Soldier's Tale*, in which the percussion is a continuing and internally
> consistent element, the "drums" had never really been given their heads.[84]

Played by a single performer, the eight percussion instruments reappear in
the third orchestration of *Les Noces*.

In fact, only six musicians were required for *Les Noces*'s penultimate
version. The dramatic reduction in forces was accomplished by the pianola
(taking over much of the instrumental music), a pair of cimbaloms, a
harmonium, and the aforementioned percussion instruments.[85] To assure
the viability of this unusual instrumental combination, Stravinsky tested out
the individual parts himself.[86] Years later, he would acknowledge the
"polish" and "authentic" quality of this combination of timbres, comparing
it favorably to that of the final score. The latter, although "streamlined,
stronger in volume, and instrumentally more homogeneous," was also
"something of a simplification."[87] This third orchestration, however – and
notwithstanding its sophistication – was abandoned after the completion of
only two tableaux, perhaps because of the difficulty in coordinating its
mechanical and "human" elements.[88]

The definitive orchestral complement for *Les Noces* was conceived in
1921. Stravinsky was suddenly struck by the realization that an orchestra of

---

[82] See Stravinsky and Craft, *Expositions and Developments*, 104.

[83] For a violinist's account of the difficulties posed by Stravinsky's music, see Boris Schwartz,
"Stravinsky, Dushkin, and the Violin," in Jann Pasler, ed., *Confronting Stravinsky* (Berkeley:
University of California Press, 1986), 302–09.

[84] Stravinsky and Craft, *Memories and Commentaries*, 128.

[85] Facsimile pages for this version can be found in Vera Stravinsky and Craft, *Pictures and
Documents*, pl. 7; and *Strawinsky: sein Nachlass, sein Bild* (Basel: Kunstmuseum, 1984), 89.

[86] Stravinsky and Craft, *Memories and Commentaries*, 126.   [87] *Ibid.*, 125–26.

[88] Vera Stravinsky and Craft, *Pictures and Documents*, 155–56. Stravinsky also discussed the
difficulties of synchronization between the live and the mechanical in *An Autobiography*, 104–
05. For an account of his relationship with the pianola, see Rex Lawson, "Stravinsky and the
Pianola," in Jann Pasler, ed., *Confronting Stravinsky* (Berkeley: University of California Press,
1986), 284–301.

four pianos could meet his aesthetic expectations while eliminating the difficulty of synchronizing mechanical instruments with live performers.

Composed mostly in Biarritz in 1922, and later completed in Monaco on April 6, 1923, the vocal part and pianos of this fourth and final version were accompanied by a xylophone, timpani, two crotales (chimes tuned to B♭ and C♯), and a bell. Also included were two side drums (with and without snare), two drums (with and without snare), tambourine, bass drum, cymbals and triangle. With a decade of trial and error behind him, Stravinsky, perhaps half-consciously, had arrived at a percussion orchestra resembling that of a Russian peasant wedding. During the ceremony and celebration of the wedding play, "such instruments as pots and pans – as well as drums, tambourines, and cymbals – were bashed, clapped together, rattled, and rung" as a way of driving away evil spirits.[89] But although the "simplification" of this final arrangement brought the orchestration closer to its folk source, it did so paradoxically with an increased sense of abstraction. Even if the expressive power of the folk melos was never lost, the frame enveloping it had become one of economy, stasis, and impersonality, conditions that would henceforth mark the composer's idiom as a whole.

---

[89] Vera Stravinsky and Craft, *Pictures and Documents*, 156.

4 Meter, motive, and alignment in *Les Noces*: Stravinsky's block and layered structures

Not until early fall, 1914, with Stravinsky immersed in all aspects of the Russian wedding play, did the actual composition of *Les Noces* get under way. Reference has been made (in Chapter 3) to the three-act scenario that had been envisioned early on in the decade-long search for a suitable conceptual and instrumental framework. Incorporating many of the seventeen or so episodes of the original play, the earlier scenario was followed by a scaled-down version in which the idea of a narrative account was gradually replaced by that of a synthesis or crystallization. In particular, the bride-show and betrothal scenes *(smotriní* and *sgovor,* respectively) were eliminated, while the bridal shower or *devichnik,* assigned to Act II in the initial scenario, was moved to the start. Stravinsky's play would begin with the ceremony in full swing, as it were, with a lament on the subject of the Bride and her farewell to maidenhood. This would be symbolized by the parting of her braid.

The final version of the scenario was thus an encapsulation. It sought to evoke – in a moment's time, impressionistically – something of the sense and sensibility of the ancient rituals, much as a snapshot might capture the character as well as the circumstances of a scene recalled from memory. The libretto was formed in the same fashion. Pieced together from "quotations of typical wedding sayings,"[1] the idea here, too, had been to cut and paste, to select in bits and pieces from the Kireyevsky volume of 1,043 wedding songs. Often enough, the verses assembled in this way resembled scraps of conversation, the sorts of lines a shadow narrator of this tale might be imagined as having overheard incidentally in passing from one wedding ceremony to the next. As a form of embodiment, too, a synthesis of what had been passed down through the ages, these same verses represented the "wedding sayings" not of single, individual characters, but of a multitude of brides, grooms, bridesmaids, parents, and guests. To follow what must surely have been Stravinsky's logic at the time, this was a general characterization that in musical terms could best be addressed flexibly rather than in fixed, one-on-one alignments with the vocal soloists. "Individual roles do not exist in *Les Noces,*" the composer remarked in his later commentary

---

[1] Igor Stravinsky and Robert Craft, *Expositions and Developments* (Garden City, NY: Doubleday, 1962), 130.

(one to which reference has already been made in Chapter 3), "only solo voices that impersonate now one type of character and now another."[2]

The idea of a remembrance of past events can seem to be implied here as well, and with special reference to the gaps that such a recollection is likely to entail, the chronologies and match-ups that are apt to be lost in one way or another (who said what to whom, for example). The conception is colored by the suggestion of a flashback, in other words, of scenes caught in the act.[3] Ordered and disciplined, the arrangements of a bygone era, reflective of a sense of belief and community, are recalled not only incompletely but also with a mixture of regret, awe, and enchantment. The vision is less that of a primitive authority or "murderous collective," as Stravinsky's detractors have claimed,[4] than that of a faith and certainty lost and incapable of being retrieved.

To a remarkable degree, too, the foregoing can be shown to have had its precedents in the practices that, over the centuries in peasant Russia, surrounded the actual performances of the ritual play. The tradition of contracting professional singers, weepers, and "criers" for the staging of many of the episodes meant that, in any given enactment of the *devichnik*, the real bride is likely to have been represented by a form of characterization, someone who had been hired to impersonate her concerns and feelings. In much the same way that, in Stravinsky's play, "individual roles" were replaced by character types who were not identified consistently with specific vocal soloists, wedding parties were separated from the rituals themselves and their verses, with the latter sung and acted out by professionals who could be relied upon to produce a faithful account of the traditional sequence of events. Indeed, as the references in these pages to the idea of a ritual play have sought to make clear, Stravinsky's play was a play once removed. Fashioned from ritual acts which had themselves become a form of theater, the separation between individual characters

---

[2] *Ibid.*, 131. "Thus the soprano in the opening scene is not the Bride, but merely a bride's voice; the same voice is associated with the goose in the last scene. Similarly, the Groom's words are sung by a tenor in the grooming scene, but by a bass at the end; and the two unaccompanied bass voices in the second scene, however much their music may suggest the actual reading of the marriage service, are not to be identified with two priests. Even the proper names in the text such as Palagai or Saveliushka belong to no one in particular. They were chosen for their sound, their syllables, and their Russian typicality."

[3] *Ibid.*, 133. The spectacle itself contributes to this impression of past events recalled as a living part of the present. In the collage-like construction that served early on (as early as 1914, in fact) as an essential part of the drama, the chorus, vocal soloists, and instrumentalists were assigned to the stage. In contemporary dress and set apart from the dancers in this way, the musicians were placed in direct juxtaposition with the ritual enactment. As Stravinsky acknowledged several decades after the premiere of *Les Noces*, "my original idea was that the whole company of musicians and dancers should be together on the stage as equal participants." Some of these points were mentioned earlier, in Chapter 3.

[4] See Theodor W. Adorno, "Stravinsky: A Dialectical Portrait," in Theodor W. Adorno, *Quasi una Fantasia: Essays on Modern Music*, trans. Rodney Livingstone (London: Verso, 1998), 149.

and character types, and between the personal feelings of the former and impersonal play-acting, had for centuries been an integral part of the festivities.

Yet the composer's attraction to the folk texts of Kireyevsky's anthology could not have been sentimental alone. It could not have been the result solely of his homesickness, in other words of the circumstances of his exile in Switzerland during the war years. Nor could it have been entirely a matter of the sounds and syllables of Russian popular verse, the way in which, as we shall see in Chapter 6, the flexible accents that had traditionally been a part of the singing of that verse could be made to accommodate the displaced accents of his musical idiom. What seems to have excited him first and foremost was the particular expressive character of ritual and ritual performance. The idea of a tradition grown remorseless in its hold, inelastic in its requirement of a simple and direct repetition of a creed, is what seems to have whetted his appetite. Shaped "with the gravity and cool" befitting a certain age and character,[5] ritual acts left little allowance for personal expression. And it was undoubtedly here that the most sympathetic of chords was struck. The demands for strictness in the observance of an ancient rite of passage could be met in Stravinsky's music not only by a repetition that was often literal and relentless (stubborn and unyielding, as his critics have often complained), but also, in its performance, by the need for a strict, metronomic application of the beat. For reasons touched upon in our introductory chapter, the conventions of expressive timing and nuance had to be kept to a minimum. This included much of what by way of traditional practice had been left to the discretion of the performer. Reduced by such means was a sense of the personal, the emotion that had traditionally been stirred by expressive nuance.

In the confrontation between individual characters and impersonal forces (or truths) of an unforgiving nature, the limitations of the former are often put to the test. In Stravinsky's texts and scenarios, an individual's vanities are often exposed, his/her pride humbled in one way or another. The emphasis on rock-like faith is also an emphasis on tradition, belonging, and connectedness, not necessarily on the individual personality ("charisma"). As many have observed, the message is "anti-psychological" in these respects.[6] The

---

[5] Jeffrey Mark, "The Fundamental Qualities of Folk Music," *Music and Letters* 10 (1929): 289. Mark's descriptions of folk song and the nature of its appeal are discussed at greater length in Richard Taruskin, *Stravinsky and The Russian Traditions: A Biography of the Works Through "Mavra,"* 2 vols. (Berkeley: University of California Press, 1996), vol. II: 1323.

[6] In Theodor W. Adorno, *Philosophy of Modern Music*, trans. Anne G. Mitchell and Wesley V. Bloomster (New York: Seabury Press, 1973), Stravinsky's music is imagined as embodying an "anti-psychological rage." The repetitive, ritualistic features of his music are "primitive" and pre-individual, according to Adorno, matters to which we shall be turning more specifically in Chapter 10. See, too, Richard Taruskin, *Defining Russia Musically: Historical and Hermeneutical*

individual is urged to look outward rather than within. And this is as much a part of *Les Noces* as it would later be of neoclassical endeavors such as *Oedipus Rex* (1928) and the *Symphony of Psalms* (1930), and of serial works such as *The Flood* (1962) and the *Requiem Canticles* (1966).

The separations mentioned above between character and character type, and between personal feelings and the feelings to which the rituals themselves make reference, are integral to Stravinsky's play. In the opening of the first tableau (see Example 4.1), the Bride weeps not out of heartfelt inclination, necessarily, but out of personal and social obligation. Weighted down by tradition, family, and society, she weeps "because, ritualistically, she *must* weep," as Stravinsky expressed it.[7] Similarly, following the *devichnik* and the bride's departure with the wedding train, the bride must never weep. Here, the slightest sob would have constituted an affront to the groom's parents and family.[8]

And such, too, are the details with which Stravinsky's score is often intimately in tune. In the soprano's three-note melodic motive that opens the first tableau, the grace-note F♯, sliding glissando-like into the motive's lower D, allows for the suggestion of a gasp or sob. In imitation of the *plach*, the traditional formal lament, notes of this kind were omitted from the transformation of the motive in the wedding feast of the fourth tableau. This was owing to their association with the *plach*, with the lamentation of the opening blocks and their subsequent restatements throughout the first tableau (see the blocks labeled A, B, and C in Example 4.1). Any suggestion of lament would have been inconsistent with the celebratory context of the *krasnïy stol*.

Indeed, from a more strictly musical standpoint, the character of the repetition of the (E D B) trichord is ritualistic. With E as the point of departure and return, melody in the opening block of *Les Noces* consists of the reiteration of the three pitches, E, D, and B, with F♯ sounded as a grace note to D.[9] The confinement of melody to these three or four pitches extends to subsequent

---

Essays (Princeton University Press, 1997), 383. *The Rite of Spring* and its scenario are cited for their absence of compassion and a sense of the individual (their "anti-humanism," in effect), their "denial of psychology." Many of Taruskin's concerns in this regard mirror Adorno's.

[7] Stravinsky and Craft, *Expositions and Developments*, 131–32: "The Bride weeps in the first scene, not necessarily because of real sorrow at her prospective loss of virginity, but because, ritualistically, she *must* weep."

[8] See Y. M. Sokolov, *Russian Folklore*, trans. Catherine Ruth Smith (New York: Macmillan, 1950), 211–13.

[9] Sounded in Piano III against the E in the soprano, the D♯ on the initial downbeat of *Les Noces* is chromatic and, as such, incidental to the main (diatonic) forces at work, which include the E pitch-class priority, the (E D B) trichord, and the grace-note F♯. Although D♯ prefigures the D♯ at Rehearsal No. 2 and, later in the lament at Rehearsal No. 35 in the second tableau, the intervention of E♭ and octatonic relations, its use is coloristic here at the outset of *Les Noces*, a way of invoking something of the harsh, off-key sounds of "primitive," peasant instruments. Note, too, that in comparison to the sustained Es and Ds in the opening block, D♯ is cut off abruptly as a sixteenth note.

Example 4.1. *Les Noces*, first tableau, blocks A, B, and C

restatements of block A as well. Within each of these restatements, returns to E are *always* preceded by the D. At the same time, D, succeeded by E in this fashion, is *always* inflected by the grace note F♯, and is *always* doubled and accented by Pianos I and III and the xylophone.

Successive taps on the cymbal (wooden mallet) are no less systematic (again, see Example 4.1). The time-spans between these taps number seven,

Example 4.1. (contd.)

six, five, four, three and two eighth-note beats, respectively, with each span marked by the reduction of a single eighth-note beat. In this way, the pattern of repetition in the cymbal unfolds as a separate layer, independently of the repetition in the vocal and instrumental parts. A large-scale stratification may be inferred, the sort of layering alluded to in the Introduction.

Crucially, too, the vocal and instrumental parts in blocks A and B are *never* exchanged in an imitative dialogue, but are fixed in register as well as in part. No "conversation" may be detected on the part of the (E D B) motive, no imitative interaction between the parts or instruments. Nor are there any transpositions in subsequent restatements of these blocks.

Indeed, the system, hardness, and inertness identified with Stravinsky's music as a whole can seem to have reached an early prime in these opening bars of *Les Noces*. (An "icy comedy" is how *Les Noces* was described early on;[10] Nicholai Myaskovsky, writing to Sergei Prokofiev in 1924, pronounced it "prickly and aesthetic.")[11] From start to finish, vertical or "harmonic" coincidence is fixed with little or no sense of movement or progress. Putting aside the pitchless taps on the cymbal (the only source here of a form of stratification), "harmony" midway through this block is little different from what it is at the beginning or at the conclusion.

At the same time, however, all is not as it might at first appear. Against the intensely static implications of the repetition, a number of forces do shift flexibly. As Stravinsky's rapidly changing bar lines make clear, returns to E as the point of departure are irregularly spaced. And what this means is that, in relation to any steady levels of metrical pulsation that may be inferred above and beyond the notated irregularity, the alignment of these returns will shift. And herein lies the heart of the invention. As pitch, articulation and instrumental assignment are held constant, the metrical alignment of the reiterated (E D B) trichord and its embedded segments will be displaced.

Moreover, if a degree of give-and-take may be sensed on the part of at least one musical dimension, a similar degree may be inferred from Stravinsky's adaptation of the original play. From what is known of the early performing practices of the wedding ceremony, the separations between character and character type and between genuine feeling and play-acting were not cut and dried. One of the aims of the wedding rituals, even when enacted by hired professionals, was to awaken within both the bride and the other participants something of the "specific emotions and thoughts" to which reference was being made.[12] Genuine feeling and the feelings demanded by the ceremonial traditions were supposed to overlap. And this is what ritual is, of course, not public exercise alone, but public exercise mixed with the personal. It involves the expression, by means necessarily public or community-based, of what are presumed to be the "emotions and thoughts" of an individual. Communication with the outside world is guaranteed, while a buffer is afforded against the perils of an individual's isolation. The emphasis, although on commiseration and

---

[10] Levinson, quoted in Richard Taruskin, *Stravinsky and the Russian Traditions*: Vol. II: 1322.

[11] Letter to Sergei Prokofiev, April 7, 1924; in Kozlova and Yatseno, eds., *Prokof'yev i Myaskovskiy: Perepiska*, 190. Quoted in Taruskin, *Stravinsky and the Russian Traditions*, vol. II: 1323.

[12] Sokolov, *Russian Folklore*, 213.

bonding, comes not wholly at the expense of the concerns of the individual, in other words. Ritual acts as a go-between in this regard, a way of easing the public strain of a personal remorse, easing as well the difficulties of the community in relating to that remorse. The proxy performances associated with the wedding rituals were thus not entirely stereotypical. From what may be gathered from the evidence, formulas were combined with improvisation, with the latter intended as a more immediate reflection of the bride's true feelings. By such means, the stock in trade merged with the personal. And successful performances were not only "emotionally infectious" (beckoning the participants in the appropriate way),[13] but designed as a combination of the communal and the individual.

Inflecting the opening pages of *Les Noces*, the grace-note F♯ is a written part of Stravinsky's score. The hint it gives of a sob is integral to the composer's larger conception. And so, too, in the first line of the text, is the stutter in the setting of the Russian word *kosal*, meaning "braid." The isolated repetition of the first syllable of this word produces an effect similar to that of the grace-note F♯, namely, that of a gasp or sob. And this, too, is integral. The motivation is not only poetic, but musical as well, an aspect of structure and musical understanding,

And yet the effect is also spontaneous and unrehearsed. Even in the strictest, most exacting performances of *Les Noces*, the experience of the individual bride is apt not to be lost. The grace-notes and stutter motives are still likely to be heard and understood as reflective of feeling. And much of this has been overlooked by the harshest detractors of Stravinsky's music, critics who would equate the repetitive, percussive, and metronomic features of pieces such as *Les Noces* (the "mechanical") not only with ritual and ritual action, but with a collective will as well, a primitive, autocratic, and "anti-humanistic" voice standing in opposition to the interests of the solo person.[14] We shall be returning to these issues in Chapter 10.

Metrical displacement in the first tableau

Labeled A, B, and C in Example 4.1, the opening three blocks of the first tableau are distinguished from one another by their tempos and their heard or concealed (as opposed to notated) meters. While the eighth-note beat is assigned the metronome marking of 80 BPM in block A, it is assigned the marking of 160 BPM in block B; in block C, the dotted quarter-note beat receives the marking of 90 BPM. Blocks A and B are

[13] *Ibid.*, 214.   [14] Adorno, "Stravinsky: A Dialectical Portrait," 147.

quoted in their entirety in Example 4.1, while block C is cited only in part. Included as well is a portion of the return of block A at Rehearsal No. 4.

The two successive 3/8 measures that begin and end block A at mm. 1–2 and 9–10 accommodate the same complete neighbor-note motion, namely, E-(D-E). In the latter, the pitch E is inflected by D, its lower neighbor note, while the segment D-E, separated from the initial E by two eighth-note beats, is a submotive. Most eventful from a motivic standpoint in both blocks A and B is indeed the latter submotive. Marked off by brackets below the stave of the soprano line in Example 4.1, D-E is a part of E-(D-E) and of subsequent extensions of this motive as well. Returns to E invariably come by way of D, while, in block A, the succession is stressed by octave doublings in Piano I and III.

More to the point, D-E is always barred as an over-the-barline succession. Irrespective of the notated irregularity, D-E always assumes the same metrical alignment. Hence, just as with the lengthier E-(D-E) motive, the score would seem to latch on to a fixed element or constancy, here in the form of the smaller but more pervasive D-E segment. In addition, E, as the registrally fixed pitch of departure and return, always falls on the first beats of the shifting bar lines. Indeed, as can readily be seen, the notated irregularity of block A is in large part determined by these metrically fixed alignments; the latter tend to regulate the irregularity, as it were. The shifting bar lines seek, at least in part, to preserve fixed or parallel alignments for E-(D-E), D-E, and the single pitch E.

A summary of these conclusions appears in Examples 4.2a, b, and c: two analytical rebarrings in Examples 4.2a and b demonstrate just how regular the notated irregularity is. Observe how the shifting meter revolves around the aforementioned fixed components, and, in particular, the over-the-barline alignment of D-E. Indeed, according to Examples 4.2a and b, block A contains only three motivically defined metrical units: a 3/8 bar for E-(D-E), another 3/8 bar for the dotted quarter-note E, and a 5/8 bar for E-D-B-(D-E). And if we omit the dotted quarter-note, the scheme reduces to only two such units: E-(D-E) and an extension of this motive in the form of E-D-B-(D-E). (In the fifth bar of the analytical rebarrings of Examples 4.2a and b, the dot of the quarter-note must yield to D as an eighth-note [marked by parentheses] to allow for a complete motivic correlation.) So, too, there are only 3/8 and 5/8 measures or "phrases"; four 3/8 measures with a total of twelve eighth-note beats, and three 5/8 measures for a total of fifteen beats. (The implications of three as a multiple in each case will be discussed below.) And since two 3/8 measures for the E-(D-E) motive serve as a point of departure and return for the block as a whole, the 5/8 measures are

Example 4.2. *Les Noces*, first tableau, block A, motivic segmentations

recognized as *extensions* of the latter; each 5/8 measure delays, by two beats, the return of D to E.

Up to this point the logic of the irregular barring in block A has been pursued solely from the standpoint of metrically fixed elements. What may be termed the opposite of fixed alignment is *displacement*, a modification of accents, specifically, *metrical* accents. For, as can readily be seen from the notated bar line and the motivic rebarrings of Examples 4.2a and b, displacement is not here graphically a part of the invention. On the contrary, and as suggested, each motive assumes, in relation to the shifting notated meter, a fixed location: E-(D-E) is barred as a 3/8 measure, D-E as an over-the-barline succession, while E falls on the downbeats of the measures in question.

Standing in direct opposition to these fixed arrangements, however, are the highly irregular spans separating successive repeats of the various motives. Bracketed above the stave in Example 4.2d, the spans defined by the principal D-E motive and its repeats number five, eight, five, three, and four eighth-note beats; they are underscored not only by the octave doublings accompanying the initial D of the D-E motive (in Pianos I and III), but also by a punctuating D in the xylophone. The full count for block A is twenty-seven eighth-note beats, where, once again, the number three is a multiple with implications as far as the meter is concerned.

In turn, when set against an inferred metrical periodicity, the irregularity of the spans between repeats of the D-E segment will mean that the latter will be displaced. And the implications here are just the opposite of what may be notationally evident. Block A may be barred conservatively. As

Example 4.3. *Les Noces*, first tableau; block A, alternative barring

a) notated (radical)

b) rebarred (conservative)

the 1–2–3 brackets affixed to the staves in Example 4.1 indicate, a 3/8 meter may be inferred from the E-(D-E) motive of the opening two measures and imposed on the block as a whole. Example 4.3a reproduces the radical notation of Stravinsky's score (soprano part alone), while Example 4.3b shows the conservative rebarring.[15]

Thus, in the opening two measures of *Les Noces*, the stressed D-E unit assumes its over-the-barline, upbeat-downbeat placement. But subsequent repeats contradict this identity. In the 3/8 barring of Example 4.3b, the D in this succession falls on the second beat at m. 3, and then on the first beat at m. 6. Hence a patterned cycle of displacement is revealed. The D of the D-E succession is introduced on the third beat, is subsequently displaced to the second and first beats, and then, in the completion of the cycle, is displaced yet another notch back to the original third beat. At this latter point, D-E resumes its over-the-barline alignment in conjunction with the return of the E-(D-E) motive in the final bars of the block. At the same time, the 3/8 meter emerges "on target" with the notated irregularity. The two conflicting meters are aligned as block A draws to a close. And this is likely to intensify the listener's "feel" of the 3/8 meter, along with the displacements which, as we have indicated, depend for their apprehension on this "feel."

Similar conclusions may be drawn from the material of block B; the radical notation appears in Example 4.4a, the conservative rebarring in Example 4.4b. Here, however, the periodicity is duple rather than triple. Moreover, the foreground irregularity comes by way of a subtactus unit, while in block A it surfaces by way of the tactus. In other words, while Stravinsky doubles the metronome marking for the eighth-note beat from 80 to 160 BPM,

[15] Analytical rebarrings of Stravinsky's music, designed for the most part to reveal the hidden periodicity beneath the notated irregularity, were first introduced by Leonard Meyer in his discussion of the opening "Soldier's March" in *The Soldier's Tale*; see Leonard B. Meyer, *Emotion and Meaning in Music* (University of Chicago Press, 1956), 120. They have since been applied for roughly the same purposes in Pieter C. van den Toorn, *The Music of Igor Stravinsky* (New Haven: Yale University Press, 1983), and Pieter C. van den Toorn, *Stravinsky and "The Rite of Spring": The Beginnings of a Musical Language* (Berkeley: University of California Press, 1987), 71–93.

Example 4.4. *Les Noces*, first tableau, block B, alternative barring

a) notated (radical)

Ve   chor -   te - bia Ko - syn - ka   Ma -   tu - shka

b) rebarred (conservative)

a) notated (contd.)

plia - la,___   Ma - tu - shka plia - la

b) rebarred (contd.)

the listener is far more apt to hold on to the marking of 80, which becomes the marking for the quarter-note beat (as the tactus). And with the eighth-note beat relegated to a subtactus unit, the 2/4 meter becomes a good deal more evident in block B than the 3/8 meter is in block A.

Crucial to the quarter-note beat and the 2/4 meter in block B are the returns to the intoning pitch E. As can be seen by the rebarring of the first four measures of block B (Example 4.4b), returns to E mark the quarter-note beat and, in the first and third measures, the half-note beat or bar line as well. The accentuation is agogic as well as periodic. Decisive is the eventual intersection of the two conflicting metrical structures as block B draws to a close. The steady 2/4 meter arrives "on target" with the notated irregularity, a circumstance which, just as with the concluding measures of block A, is likely to strengthen the listener's sense of the concealed meter.

Moreover, if a continuous tactus and the "targeting" of an underlying meter can make for a smooth transition between blocks A and B, they can do so between blocks B and C as well. As block C follows block B (see Example 4.1), the dotted quarter-note beat assumes the metronome marking of 80 BPM, which in turn stipulates a triple division of the retained tactus. And while, according to Stravinsky's notated irregularity, the heavily accented (F♯-E♯)-E figure falls on the downbeat of the first measure, the F♯-E♯ segment of this figure is far more likely to be heard and understood as a stressed upbeat to the reciting pitch E. Not only does the conservative

Example 4.5. *Les Noces*, first tableau, block C, alternative barring

a) notated (radical)

Che - su po-che-su Nas - ta - si-nu ko-su   Che - su po-che-su Ti-mo   fe ev-nu ru- sa,   a   esh___

b) rebarred (conservative)

rebarring of Example 4.5b favor such a reading, but, both in blocks A and B, F♯ is inflected as a grace note to the heavily accented D, with the latter appearing as an upbeat to E as the point of departure and return. (In the rebarred version of block A, Example 4.3b, the cycle of displacement begins and ends with D as an upbeat to the E.)

To reiterate: both the earlier D of the reiterated D-E motive in blocks A and B and this present F♯-E♯ segment are accented neighbor-note inflections to the E. And they are likely to be matched as such by the listener, who is also likely to retain something of the upbeat with which, at least initially in blocks A and B, the D of the D-E unit is identified. The 2/4 meter of the conservative version of block B favors this alternative, since, as is shown in Examples 4.1 and 4.5a, an extension following the repeat sign emerges at block C with an extra eighth-note beat to spare.

Further along in block C, the invention follows a familiar path. Subsequent repeats of the punctuating (F♯-E♯)-E figure are spaced irregularly, resulting, as can be seen by the rebarred version of Example 4.5b, in a series of metrical displacements. Introduced on the sixth eighth-note beat of a 6/8 measure, the figure is displaced to the fifth beat, where it is repeated four times. It is then displaced to the first eighth-note beat, before resuming its initial placement on the sixth beat. If the dotted quarter-note beat (as the tactus) is taken as the gauge rather than the dotted half-note beat or the 6/8 bar line, a patterned cycle of displacement results, one which starts on the third eighth-note beat of the dotted quarter-note, is displaced to the second and first eighth-note beats, respectively, and then back to its initial placement on the third eighth-note beat. Significantly, the rebarred 6/8 version of block C arrives "on target" with the notated irregularity and the somewhat modified restatement of block A at Rehearsal No. 4.

At the same time, the actual *source* of the irregular spans marked off by the (F♯-E♯)-E figure and its repeats may be traced to the lines of Stravinsky's text. For the irregular spans in the music and the varying lengths of these lines coincide. While each line of the text begins with a punctuation of the (F♯-E♯)-E figure and a snare-drum roll (the latter is not shown in Example

4.5a), it ends with a single sound, namely, *u*, the marker for first-person present verb form and feminine direct objects. The first four lines of the text, coupled with an English translation, are as follows:

> Ch'e-su, po-ch'e-su Na-sta-s'i-nu ko-su,
> I comb, I shall comb, Natasha's braid
>
> Ch'e-su, po-ch'e-su Ti-mo-fe-ev-nu ara-su,
> I comb, I shall comb Timofeevna's curls
>
> ai-ehch'o po-ch'e-su,
> and still I shall comb,
>
> a-i kosu, za-pl'e-tu
> and even braid, I will plait

Sung by a chorus of sopranos and altos (bridesmaids), the verses accompany the combing out of the Bride's maiden braid. The eighth-note motion in block C is also a form of borrowing, an imitation of another form of lament, as we have noted in the preceding chapter (see Example 3.1a), a rapid form of syllabification termed *prichitaniye* .

Remarkably, too, the irregular spans in block C were underscored by Bronislava Nijinska's original choreography. To judge from the 1990 reconstruction of her designs by the Paris Opera Ballet,[16] repeats of the (F♯-E♯)-E figure were accompanied by a lifting of the foot (a *battement dégagé* in second position), while the *prichitaniye*-like chanting on E was danced on pointe. Danced accents thus accompanied the musical accents of displacement. (Unlike many early modernists, Nijinska used pointe, although with the idea of affecting a sense of heaviness rather than the traditional lightness. Her pointes in *Les Noces* were hard and grounded, and had sought to convey an atmosphere of earthiness, of massed bodies "weighted by centuries of toil.")[17]

Crucially, restatements of block C at Rehearsal Nos. 7 and 24 were choreographed in an identical manner. Consistent with the repetition of pitch, rhythm, and instrumentation at these points, Nijinska's dance movements were reproduced as well. Underscored visually by such means was thus the effect of a juxtaposition, of the separation of block C from the blocks preceding and succeeding it.

In conclusion, while a single, uninterrupted tactus with the marking of 80 BPM unites blocks A, B, and C in the first tableau, separate 3/8, 2/4, and 6/8 meters may be inferred alongside the notated irregularity. In addition to

---

[16] See the video-recording *Paris Dances Diaghilev* (Paris: Elektra Nonsuch Dance Collections, 1990).

[17] Lynn Garafola, *Diaghilev's Ballets Russes* (New York: Oxford University Press, 1989), 126.

these concealed meters, the three blocks differ in their pitch structures. As we shall see in Chapter 5, while block A is diatonic in its referential implications, block B is overtly octatonic.

The distinctions in content between blocks A, B, and C remain fixed at subsequent restatements of these blocks. At Rehearsal No. 8+2 (not shown in Example 4.1), block A reappears sharply curtailed and cut off from blocks B and C. Yet, in pitch, rhythm, and instrumentation, the restatement is virtually unchanged from the initial statement. And this is true as well of the restatement of block C at the end of the first tableau. Although lengthened somewhat and separated from blocks A and B, block C is unchanged content-wise.

In turn, these fixed contents are counterbalanced not only by the slight variations that can arise from changes in the text, but also by adjustments in length, ordering, and alignment. At their subsequent restatements, the three blocks float free of their initial order, a circumstance that, for the listener, is likely to enhance the sense of their independence of each other, of their being placed in juxtaposition rather than as part of a more continuous flow. Here, the idea of a cutting and pasting of blocks can suggest itself, along with that of a montage and the discontinuities implied by this concept. Wider topics of this kind will be the focus of our discussion of the *Symphonies of Wind Instruments* in Chapter 8.

Block structures in the second tableau

The remaining three tableaux of *Les Noces* are block structures similar to the one surveyed above. Intended for the Groom and his party (scored for two tenors and basses), the opening of the second tableau was conceived in counterpoint to the bridal lament of the first. Featured is the other side of the bride/groom parallel, one of the many ideas that, accompanied by epigraphs, appear to have guided the large-scale construction of *Les Noces*. The bridal concerns of the first tableau ("at the Bride's") are answered by those of the groom in the second ("at the Groom's").

To some extent, too, the bride/groom parallel is musical as well as dramatic. The initial blocks of the second tableau are as abrupt in their juxtapositions as are those of the first. The first four measures of the opening block, condensed in Example 4.6a, are restated at Rehearsal Nos. 30, 33, and 44 (Examples 4.6b–d); the initial statement at Rehearsal No. 27 continues for some six measures, while subsequent restatements at Rehearsal Nos. 30 and 33 are confined to the initial four measures. Musically, the scheme may be grasped quite readily. Two motivic segments, bracketed and labeled a and b in Examples 4.6a–d, may be inferred from the repetition in both the initial statement and in subsequent restatements. Both segments begin with the pitch D reiterated and embellished by C, the sort of intonation with lower neighbor-note inflection (usually a whole tone apart) that characterizes much of the melodic invention in *Les Noces* (indeed, works of the Russian period generally). But while both segments begin with the recitation and inflection of segment a, segment b concludes with an upward leap of a fourth, C–F, followed by a stepwise descent back to the recitation-pitch D. The shape of this leap may be traced not only to authentic folk songs, but, as we have suggested in Chapter 3, to *Znamenniy* chant as well.[18]

Moreover, the accompanying texts, with their frequent allusions to the Groom's "curls" or "locks" *(kudri)*, are indicative of yet another idea that seems to have shaped the early composition of *Les Noces*, namely, the tress/curls parallel. The Groom's locks match the Bridal tress of the first tableau. And, here again, the conception of the parallel is musical as well as dramatic and poetic. Segment a, the intonation with lower neighbor-note inflection, is a variation of the bridal lament of the first tableau; more specifically, D-D-D-C-D in the opening measures of the second tableau relates to E-(D-E) in the opening bars of the first, where the pitch recitation of E is inflected by D as the lower neighbor note. At the same time, however, segment a in the second tableau is assigned to a chorus of tenors, while the earlier lament was assigned to the soprano solo. In turn, segment b, which begins as if it were a repeat of segment a, adds the new motivic shape C-F that will become identified with the Groom and the combing of his locks.

Often, too, the repetition of the two motives a and b is modified slightly, both within the initial statement and in moving from one restatement to the next. And the modification is additive rather than elaborational. Eighth-note beats are added to or subtracted from the initial repeats. Thus, the statement at Rehearsal No. 27 consists of the motivic succession $a_6 + b_7 + b_6 + a_5$, where the repeat of segment a is shortened from a_6 to a_5, and the repeat of segment b, from b_7 to b_6. (The subscripts in these designations refer to the encompassed number of eighth-note beats.) Crucially, then, the repetition of these motives mirrors the larger block structure. What happens to the block of which motives a and b are a part happens to the motives as well. They, too, when repeated, are subjected to a form of lengthening, shortening, and/or re-ordering. And the juxtaposition that has thus far been linked solely to the behavior of blocks may be linked to that of motives as well. The process is operative at more than one level of grouping structure.

So, too, in subsequent restatements of the initial block at Rehearsal No. 27, the initial order of the segments is reshuffled. At Rehearsal No. 30

---

[18] See Examples 3.4a and b. In Chapter 3 we compared the four segments of the opening block of the second tableau to the use of *popevki* in Russian folk songs and liturgical chant.

Example 4.6. *Les Noces*, second tableau, opening block, subsequent restatements

(see Example 4.6b), the restatement begins not with segment a₆, but with the succession of segments b₇+b₅. Coupled with these reorderings are a number of consistencies, however. All four statements and restatements conclude with segment a5, while all four include the succession b₇+b₆ (or b₅). (In the abbreviated outline of the four statements in Figure 4.1, brackets enclose the retained successions.)

In addition, modifications in the repetition of the two segments reflect the lines of Stravinsky's text. In a scheme identical to that introduced by block C in the first tableau, the segmentation reflects the varying lengths or syllable counts of these lines. With the first four lines of the initial statement, the first and last syllables of each line are stressed, with the poetic meter realigned accordingly. Figure 4.2 includes a syllabified transliteration along with a

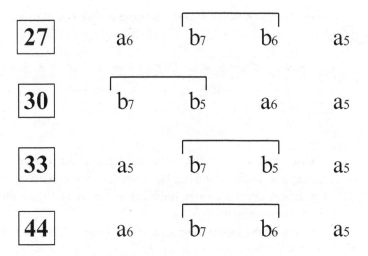

Figure 4.1. *Les Noces*, second tableau, opening block and subsequent restatements; reshuffling of motives a and b

Prechistaia Mat	a6	5 syllables
Oh, purest Mother		+ 8th-note rest
khodi, khodi k nam u khát,	b7	7 syllables
come, come, to our hut,		
svakhe pomogát	b6	5 syllables
to help the matchmaker		+ 8th-note rest
kúdri rashesát,	a5	5 syllables
comb out the curls,		

Figure 4.2. *Les Noces*, second tableau, block A, opening four lines

word-for-word English translation; the syllable count of each line is included on the right-hand side.

Similar to block C in the first tableau, too, is the short snare-drum roll that announces the beginning of each line. At the same time, each line ends with the same Russian sound, namely, *at'*, most often the palatalized marker of an infinitive verb. The phonetic markings themselves are sufficient to guarantee a clear reading of the four-fold division of the text. At Rehearsal No. 33 (see Example 4.6c), the opening four measures are restated verbatim, but without the original eighth-note rests (the punctuation marks at the end of segments a_6 and b_6 (1), in other words).

Example 4.7. *Les Noces*, second tableau, opening block, alternative segmentations

Often enough, too, the varying lengths of Stravinsky's lines of poetry correspond to the changing bar lines. Yet the exceptions to this rule are significant, and they carry implications so far as the second tableau as a whole is concerned.

Consider the initial statement of the opening block at Rehearsal No. 27. Bracketed above the stave in Example 4.7 is the segmental succession $a_6+b_7+b_6(1)+a_5$, with the four individual segments corresponding to the four lines of Stravinsky's text. Bracketed below in this example are the segments of Stravinsky's bar lines. And of concern here is less the ambiguity of these competing segmentations (the fact that the shifting lines of poetry are often out of phase with the notated meter), than the rationale behind the shifting bar lines. Thus, segment b_7, bracketed above the stave in Example 4.7 and representing the second line of the text, straddles the bar line between the second and third measures. It forces the succeeding segment $b_6(1)$ to begin on the second eighth-note beat of the third measure. And the entrance of segment $b_6(1)$ is marked not only by an accent at this point, but by the snare-drum roll as well, the same roll that marks the entrances of the other three segments. Indeed, the motivic segmentation bracketed above the stave in Example 4.7 would seem to be the one most likely to prevail in a straightforward reading of this statement, given not only the lines of Stravinsky's text but also these added musical factors.

Yet the bar lines bracketed below in Example 4.7 are a segmentation as well. They, too, carry motivic implications, beginning with segment b_5 of the third measure, a variant of motive $b_6(2)$ which it follows, and a displacement as well. In this alternative reading, the initial pitch D on the downbeat of the third measure is the start of segment b_5, not the end of segment b_7. And the overlapping of these motivic variants adds to the complexity of the statement: *four different versions of motive b are introduced within the first three bars*, b_5, b_7, and two versions of b_6, namely, $b_6(1)$ and $b_6(2)$. And were we to include on this list motive a as the source of motive b, the number of variants would double. At the same time, this inclusion of additional variants would not be to question, at a more determinate level of grouping, the integrity of motive a as it relates to motive b. Following the repeat of motive a in the fourth measure of the opening block (see Example 4.7), its status as a separate motive is likely to be secured in the mind of the listener. Only, the origin of motive b as an *extension* of motive a is no less likely to figure in the listener's perception of these motivic relationships.

Significantly, too, the modification of motives a and b consists not of a traditional harmonic or melodic elaboration, but of a cutting and pasting, as we have noted already, an addition or subtraction of eighth-note beats that ends occasionally with a form of metrical displacement. The congestion of variants resulting from this process, although concealed by a surface that can seem bluntly repetitive at times, is astonishing.

In sum, if the bar lines in Example 4.7 are considered separately from the lines of the text, segment $b_6(2)$ begins with three repeated Ds while segment b_5 begins with only two. And the subtracted eighth-note beat in the repetition of these Ds displaces segment b_5 in relation to $b_6(2)$. Shifted from the third to the second eighth-note beat of the 3/4 and 5/8 measures, the D-C-F-E-(D) segment of motive b arrives an eighth-note beat "too soon." From the standpoint of the tactus, it falls first on and then off the quarter-note beat. And the mismatch will be sensed as long as the quarter-note beat is sustained beyond the first beat of the third measure (beyond the repeated Ds, in other words). Segments $b_6(2)$ and b_5 cannot be aligned in a fashion that is metrically parallel, and the thwarting of the listener's expectations in this regard (expectations of metrical parallelism, raised in turn by the repeated Ds of segment b_5) is likely to disrupt his/her metrical bearings. More specifically, the listener's sense of the quarter-note and dotted half-note beats, likely to have been activated by segments a_6 and $b_6(2)$ of the initial two 3/4 bars, is apt to be disrupted.

The reader will note, too, that Stravinsky's accompanying text is not unaffected by these manipulations. If there are displacements as well as relocations of motives and lengthier successions of segments, then there will also be changes in the alignment of repeated phrases, words, and syllables. In Example 4.6b, the bracketed succession b_7+b_5 is accompanied by a repetition of the phrase "khodi k nam u khát." And since motive b_5 is a displacement of b_7, the repetition of this phrase will be displaced as well; its final and accented syllable in "u khát" will occur first on and then off the quarter-note beat.[19] We will be addressing text-setting issues of this kind more closely in Chapter 6.

---

[19] In connection with the text-setting in this initial block and its subsequent restatements in the second tableau, see the revealing commentary in Chandler Carter, "*The Rake's Progress* and Stravinsky's Return: the Composer's Evolving Approach to Setting Text," *Journal of the American Musicological Society* 63, no. 3 (2010) 555–56. As with Example 4.8c in this chapter, Carter offers a conservative rebarring of this material in 3/4.

Moreover, in the initial statement and subsequent restatements of the opening block, segment b_5 emerges as a metrical troublemaker (see Example 4.7). Its five eighth-note beats, missing the 3/4 bar line by a single eighth-note beat, are likely to catch the listener off guard, causing him/her to lose his/her sense of the quarter-note beat. Listeners may seek to align segment b_5 in a metrically parallel fashion (an alignment that is not possible beyond the repeated Ds, as we have suggested), or they may seek to hear b_5 conservatively as a displacement of $b_6(2)$ (with the quarter-note beat and possibly even the full 3/4 meter sustained as a background). Either way, however, it is the conflict of these options that underlies the play of this initial block, the point that is sustained from one restatement to the next. Implications of meter and alignment are raised and then thwarted. Simple and direct in outward appearance, the opening measures are more readily the ignition of a form of musical intrigue, one extending through the whole of the second tableau. Reappearances of segment b_5 constantly act to disrupt the 3/4 meter and to renew a sense of suspense and anticipation.[20]

Examples 4.8a–c map out three possible readings of the initial statement at Rehearsal No. 27. Stravinsky's notated meter is reproduced in the first of these readings, Example 4.8a, while, in Example 4.8b, the statement is rebarred analytically in order to align the repeats of segments a and b in a parallel fashion. In Example 4.8b, all appearances of motives a and b fall on the downbeats of the given bar lines. From the standpoint of the listener, a sense of the quarter-note beat and the 3/4 meter is interrupted in the third measure, following the repeated Ds of segment b_5. Segments $b_6(2)$ and b_5 cannot be aligned properly, and the interruption of the meter lasts until the entrance of segment a_5 in the fourth measure, at which point another attempt is made at parallelism, with the listener's metrical bearings restored in the process. Quickly enough, however, these restored bearings are likely to be challenged

---

[20] For a slightly different metrical reading of block A and its restatements in the second tableau, see Gretchen Horlacher, "Metric Irregularity in *Les Noces*: The Problem of Periodicity," *Journal of Music Theory* 39, no. 2 (1995): 285–310. Many of Horlacher's concerns overlap with this present analysis, such as her treatment of displacement and metrical parallelism, the problem of either "assigning a new metric identity to a motive in order to continue counting periodically" (displacement), or of breaking with the latter "in order to preserve the motive's metric identity" (metrical parallelism) (289). She also addresses the issue of added or subtracted beats at a given level of pulsation, and the degree to which, with a regular recurrence of such additions or subtractions, a meter might be sustained. On the other hand, she ignores the competing motivic segments as defined by the lines of Stravinsky's text (those outlined by the brackets above the quotation in Example 4.7). And in rebarring this material with a 3/4 meter, she does so from start to finish for the whole of block A and its restatements, continuously and without interruption. As indicated in Example 4.7, however, the metrical bearings of the listener are more likely to be disrupted (or at least challenged) at some point by the non-parallelism of segment b_5 and its repeats.

Example 4.8. *Les Noces*, second tableau, opening block, alternative barrings

a) notated

b) rebarred (radical)

c) rebarred (conservative)

d) rebarred (with displacements deleted)

by the shortening of segment a_6 to a_5. As it appears in Example 4.8b, meter throughout is driven by these considerations of motivic parallelism.

In contrast, the conservative reading of Example 4.8c reduces the opening block still further by replacing the irregular barring with a steady 3/4 meter; in Example 4.8d the displacements of motives a and b are eliminated altogether. Thus, as the brackets below the stave in Example 4.8d indicate, repeats of the two motives are not modified; their lengths are not altered by a subtraction or addition of eighth-note beats. Laid bare by such means is something of the nature of Stravinsky's invention, the "straight," unadorned models against which the changes in the length and metrical alignment of motives a and b can be imagined as having been implemented.

Layered structures in the second tableau

In a climactic block later at Rehearsal Nos. 59–61 in the second tableau, segment b_5 and its irregular 5/8 measure are again exposed as metrical troublemakers. A product of Stravinsky's shifting bar lines, segment b_5 is overshadowed in the opening block by segments b_7 and b_6 and the lines of the text. Detaching itself from that earlier context, however, segment b_5 is placed in juxtaposition to a new 6/8 (or 3/4) bar of contrasting material and instrumental figuration (see the brackets above and below the stave of the

Example 4.9. *Les Noces*, second tableau, climactic section

Collections II and I

opening measure in Example 4.9). Another block is formed in the process, a mini-structure within the larger block structure of the second tableau as a whole. Five repeats of segment b_5 (or b_6) follow, each of these succeeded by the contrasting segment c_6.

At the same time, the alternation between motives b_5 (or b_6) and c_6 is superimposed over a basso ostinato. Consisting of a conflicting period of four quarter-note beats, the ostinato forms a second layer. And while, from the standpoint of the vocal and instrumental forces that are brought to bear, the first layer (the alternating motives b_5 (or b_6) and c_6) greatly outweighs the second, the steady 3/4 meter that may be heard and inferred throughout this section is a *composite*, a product of both layers.[21] (See the 1–2–3 brackets above the stave in Example 4.9.) While the 3/4 bar line derives from Stravinsky's notated 6/8 meter (changed to 3/4 at Rehearsal No. 60+1, however), the quarter-note beat, the likely tactus with a marking of 120 BPM, derives from the ostinato pattern of four quarter-note beats.

An account of the climactic section appears in Example 4.9. Crucial here again is the listener's ability to infer a steady meter and to retrieve it in the event of a disruption (which may last no longer than a second or so). At the same time, the listener's expectations in this regard are likely to have crystallized earlier (however much repeats of segment b_5 may have worked to subvert any such crystallization). More specifically, segment b_5 or (b_6) at Rehearsal No. 59, although detached from the remaining segments of the initial block, is likely to be heard in relation to that earlier point of departure. To some degree at least, the segments that precede it at Rehearsal No. 27 (segments a_6 and $b_6(2)$) and the steady 3/4 meter that may be inferred from this initial succession are still likely to figure in the listener's perception at Rehearsal No. 59 (see the brackets below the staves in Example 4.9).

The difference, however, is that the conditions that may have triggered a disruption of the 3/4 meter earlier at Rehearsal No. 27 and at subsequent restatements of the initial block are no longer present. At Rehearsal No. 59, segment b_5 is not followed by a repetition of motive a on the second quarter-note beat of the succeeding measure (as it is at rehearsal No. 27). And the repetition of motive a does not leave motive b with an irregular count of seven eighth-note beats, with motive a misaligned and

---

[21] On the matter of a composite meter, see Justin London, *Hearing in Time: Psychological Aspects of Musical Meter* (Oxford University Press, 2004), 84. Confronted with two conflicting, regularly recurring patterns of accents, listeners generally focus on one while ignoring the metrical implications of the other. Alternatively, however, they may "extract a composite pattern" from elements of the two conflicting streams.

the meter quite possibly disrupted as a result; see Example 4.7. Instead, segment b_5 is left with a regular count of six eighth-note beats. It is followed by a new motive, motive c_6, whose initial quarter-note beat (or initial dotted quarter-note beat, following the 6/8 signature) can fall just as easily on the second eighth-note beat of the succeeding measure as it can on the first.

Motive c_6 has no prior history of alignment, in other words, so that the listener's expectations can be relatively unsettled at this point. In effect, segment b_5 need not be read as notated. The first eighth-note beat of the succeeding measure can be made to even out the five eighth-note beats, with segment b_5 becoming b_6 and motive c_6 entering on the second eighth-note beat (see the brackets above the stave in Example 4.9). And although this interpretation of the meter is at odds with the lines of Stravinsky's text (the latter constituting the basis for the notated irregular 5/8 and 6/8 bars), it can be pursued with little resistance through the entirety of the block. The 3/4 meter is interrupted only by the irregular 2/4 bar just prior to Rehearsal No. 60, where, however, the deleted quarter-note beat is likely to be treated radically, with the listener immediately realigning him/herself to the 3/4 meter with motive c_6 in the following measure.

Only at the very end of the section is there anything like a resolution to the dislocation caused by Stravinsky's irregular bar lines and the inferred 3/4 meter. At Rehearsal No. 60+1, an eighth-note beat is subtracted from motive c_6. As a result, in the following bar, segment b_5 (or b_6) arrives an eighth-note beat "too soon," falling off rather than on the quarter-note beat of the continuing 3/4 meter. And although the notated bar line accommodates the subtraction (an irregular 5/8 measure is inserted in a fashion parallel to the 5/8 measure at Rehearsal No. 59), the 3/4 meter may continue uninterrupted and with little resistance. The climactic point of arrival of the block as a whole coincides with the displacement of motives b_5 (or b_6) and c_6. At the same time, an immediate repeat of motive c_6, realigned off the quarter-note beat, serves to confirm the reversal. (The reader will note, however, that the "targeting" of the 3/4 meter at Rehearsal No. 60+3 is only partial. Only the quarter-note beat and not the 3/4 bar line or dotted half-note beat arrives "on target" with Stravinsky's shifting bar lines.)

Adding to the sense of arrival at Rehearsal No. 60+3 is the flurry of scales in Pianos II and III, and the xylophone (see Example 4.9). Substituting for the ascending diatonic scales that had accompanied motive c_6 for much of this section, the scales are octatonic for the most part, accountable to Collections I and II. More specifically, tritone-related (0 2 3 5) Dorian tetrachords are outlined on the quarter-note beat. And they are outlined in this fashion for both Collections I and II, the one being superimposed over the other.

In effect, a form of octatonic-diatonic interaction may be inferred from the closing bars of this section. Linked to the octatonic is segment b_5 (or b_6), whose (G F E D) tetrachord is shared by Collection I. Similarly, Collection II's (D C B A) tetrachord overlaps with the ascending A-scale or A-scales that accompany motive c_6 up to this point. The perfect fifth separating the two octatonic scales is a form of connection as well, shared by the accompanying parts of segment b_5 (or b_6).

As a form of imitation, the octatonic scales at Rehearsal No. 60+3 are decorative rather than substantive, a way of adding color (or discolor, as the case may be) to the diatonic foundation of this music. Stravinsky's intentions may well have been to invoke the sound of an authentic peasant band at this point, by mimicking the rattling, slightly off-key effect of coarse, partially home-made instruments. As we shall see in Chapter 5, simulations of this kind may be inferred elsewhere in *Les Noces*, most notably in a passage of transition in the third tableau and then again in the opening blocks of the fourth.

Additional layered structures

Earlier, in Chapter 3, we cited the multi-layered textures in Russian folk rituals as a possible source of some of the stratification in *Les Noces*. Typical of many wedding episodes are textures in which the various inflections associated with lament and, above all, the *vopl'*, are superimposed over choruses with more song-like or syllabic phrases. The result is a conversation of sorts, with each protagonist represented by a separate layer. In practice, the material can move back and forth antiphonally or be combined in the form of a superimposition (see Example 3.1a). Our impression is that something similar may well have been intended by the stratification at Rehearsal Nos. 36–40 in the second tableau, a lament featuring the parents of the Groom (see Example 4.10). Retained by this new block is the idea of a pitch-recitation embellished by a lower neighbor note a whole-step apart. The tone is again one of commiseration, marked by a return to the grace-notes of the first tableau.

Three separate layers may be inferred at Rehearsal Nos. 35–40: a vocal fragment initially spanning ten quarter-note beats (five 2/4 bars), an ostinato spanning a single quarter-note beat (the A–B♭ reiteration in Pianos I and III), and a punctuating chord spanning three such beats. Modifications in the repetition of the vocal fragment are extensive. Beginning already at Rehearsal No. 37, repeats of this fragment are often cut short, with the initial span of ten quarter-note beats undermined as a result. Yet the remaining two layers of instrumental accompaniment are true ostinatos. The fragments and chords in

Example 4.10. *Les Noces*, second tableau, lament, layered structure

Collection III

Pianos I and III and in Pianos II and IV, respectively, repeat at regular intervals throughout. And so the invention would seem to consist of a tightly-knit system of independently revolving parts, of the shifts in alignment that result from these parts, and of the harmonic and metrical implications that may in turn be inferred from these shifts in alignment. Points of intersection are of consequence as well. Regular recurrences of such points imply higher-level metrical structures.

As the likely tactus with a marking of 104 BPM, the quarter-note beat is underscored by all three layers. In contrast, returns to E♭, as the initial point

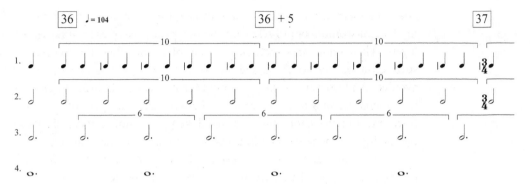

Figure 4.3. *Les Noces*, second tableau, lament; layered structure, levels of pulsation

of departure in the vocal fragment, mark off the half-note beat or bar line. The latter is obscured at times, to be sure, by the persistence of the punctuating chord and its dotted half-note beat. Much of the play of this passage of lament rests accordingly, that is, with a 2/4 bar line established and then lost temporarily.

Two of the three layers are thus in conflict, entrances of the vocal fragment (the notated 2/4 meter that may be inferred from these entrances), and the chord-punctuation in Pianos II and IV (the dotted half-note beat that may in turn be inferred from these punctuations). Shared as a common denominator is the quarter-note beat, exposed and underscored by the ostinato in Pianos I and III. And the conflict itself is hemiola-like and hypermetrical. In Figure 4.3, the quarter-note beats at an initial level of pulsation (1) are interpreted at three successive levels by (2) the bar line or half-note beat, (3) the conflicting dotted half-note beat, and (4) the dotted whole-note beat. Points of intersection between the second and third levels imply the fourth, the dotted whole-note beat, which encloses the twos and threes of the hemiola. In turn, the implied dotted whole-note beat conflicts with the spans of ten quarter-note beats (or five 2/4 measures) of the vocal fragment.

Another complication at the outset of the lament lies with the timing of the punctuation in Pianos II and IV, which begins not on the first but on the second quarter-note beat of the 2/4 bar line. The reasoning behind this placement may be traced to the downbeat at Rehearsal No. 36+5. There, the intersection of half and dotted half-note beats coincides with the initial repeat of the complete vocal fragment and its span of ten quarter-note beats (see Figure 4.3). Stravinsky's intention may well have been to reinforce this lengthy span at just this juncture. For, apart from the downbeat further along at Rehearsal No. 39+2, there are no other coincidences of this kind between the chord-punctuation in Pianos II and IV and the entrances of the vocal fragment and its lengthy span. In fact, the essential musical point in the lament would seem to rest with the independence of each of these two layers. Throughout this section, for example, more than two repeats in succession of the vocal fragment's span of ten quarter-note beats are avoided. And they are avoided, it would seem, precisely in order to prevent the emergence of a form of regularity between the entrances of the vocal fragment and the chord-punctuation. Likely to manifest itself via these conflicting components is an impression of separation and isolation.

In psychological terms, the idea would seem to be that the listener, holding on to one of the two interpretations of the tactus at the second and third levels in Figure 4.3, feels the other dimly as a threat. Although his/her metrical orientation may be overturned at some point, the two interpretations cannot be attended to simultaneously. Perceptual matters of this kind were discussed briefly in Chapter 1.

Conflicts involving hemiolas are not unique to Stravinsky's music, of course. They may be found often enough in eighteenth- and nineteenth-century music, although not ordinarily with the sort of persistence marking their appearance here. Especially at the level of the bar line and just below, earlier conflicts are brief and tend to be resolved in some fashion. A point of intersection between the triple and duple layers, marked structurally in melodic and harmonic terms, brings the conflict to a close. (In conjunction with Examples 1.5a, 1.6, and 1.7, see our earlier discussion of the role of displacement in traditional hemiola patterns.) Here, however, the conflict extends through the entirety of the passage in question. And instead of resolving, the two conflicting layers are brought to an abrupt halt at Rehearsal No. 40.

In poetic terms, the absence of a form of resolution in the lament can suggest the presence of something stiff and unyielding. Indeed, the persistence of the chord-punctuation can seem to imply a form of indifference. The pleas of the parents of the Groom, coming by way of the vocal fragment and the greater fluidity of its entrances ("To whom will these curls pass?"), are answered by the striking of a single chord, fourteen times. Lacking variation in its time-spans, pitches, instrumentation, and articulation, the punctuation can seem to point to the unbending character of the forces allied against the parents and their hushed pleas. In the same way that, in musical terms, the dotted half-note beat remains unaffected (objectively speaking) by the continuation of the 2/4 meter, dramatically, the course of events initiated by the betrothal is incapable of being swayed by the entreaties of the two parents. The relentlessness of the repetition in Pianos II and IV echos the resistance of the ritual action to any form of intervention on the part of the parents.

At the same time, the musically static implications of the stratification are not matters of metrical alignment and duration alone. The confinement of the

Example 4.11. *Les Noces*, second tableau, lament, embedded (0 2 5)s

various reiterated fragments to a system of gears locked and rotating in place is matched by their confinement to a single transposition of the octatonic set, namely, Collection III. (A single fragment at Rehearsal No. 36+5 – indeed, a single pitch, the B in this fragment – lies outside the given transposition.) All three parts are confined accordingly, subject to the symmetries of Collection III and to the redundancies in interval-class content.

The vocal fragment, wholly octatonic and entering initially on E♭, is subsequently transposed along the minor-third cycle from E♭ to C and A (see Example 4.10). If this fragment's initial whole-step reiteration E♭-D♭ and its subsequent transpositions to (C-B♭) and (A-G) are linked in the form of a chain, more specific symmetries are revealed, in particular, those with C-B♭ and D♭-C-B♭-A as their axes. At Rehearsal Nos. 35–40, A-B♭ is underscored by the ostinato in Pianos II and IV, while D♭/C is a part of the punctuating chord in Pianos II and IV. And this, too, can suggest separately revolving parts. No less than the shifting alignments of these parts, the vocal fragment and its transpositions are locked in from a pitch-relational standpoint.

Indeed, inundated with forms of the (0 2 5) trichord, the vocal fragment is also richly motivic. Boxed in Example 4.11 are the most obvious of these forms, namely (E♭ D♭ B♭), which includes the grace-note B♭, and, following the outline of the C-major triad, F♯-E-C♯. Striking here as well is the persistence of the minor-third gap, a motivic detail that will concern us more specifically in Chapter 5.

Conclusions

Juxtaposition and stratification are all-encompassing. All dimensions of musical discourse are implicated by these processes, including melody, harmony (vertical coincidence), meter, duration, timbre, and instrumentation. The sharp contrasts that can set one block off against another are often matters not of pitch alone (melody and harmony), but of register, dynamics, and instrumentation as well. Clear-cut distinctions can be crucial to the idea of a juxtaposition, whether the entities being juxtaposed are motives or blocks. As we have noted, the process may implicate more than one level of grouping structure, the level of the motive as well as that of the block.

In the climactic block of the second tableau (see Example 4.9), the two motives b_5 (or b_6) and c_6 alternate with one another in the manner of a juxtaposition. While motive b is scored for tenors and basses, motive c is scored for four soloists and a full chorus. These contrasting forces are fixed from one repeat to the next, notwithstanding the changes in the lengths and metrical alignments of the two motives. Indeed, the stability in content serves as a foil for the modifications in length and placement.

Internally, lengthier blocks are often made up of motivic successions similar to the one examined above in connection with the opening block of the second tableau. When repeated, the motives within these successions may be lengthened, shortened, reshuffled, or deleted altogether, adjustments which can cause the larger blocks of which they are a part to be modified in a similar fashion. The element of development peculiar to Stravinsky's block structures may be located accordingly. For the same modifications can also cause the repeated motives and blocks to shift (be displaced) in relation to an established meter.

Crucially, the accompanying parts of a typical block are synchronized. They move in step with the main motive or succession of motives, according to the spans defined by one or the other of these alternatives. A consequence of this synchronization is that *the alignment of these parts never shifts, but remains fixed*. This is in contrast to the fragments and chords of a layered structure or stratification, obviously, which repeat according to varying spans. Here, *alignment shifts between the parts as well as in relation to the meter*. And the registral, dynamic, and instrumental contrasts that can exist vertically between the individual blocks of a block structure can exist horizontally between the superimposed layers of a layered structure. The separations are defined horizontally, in other words, as the need for each block to stand out against the others is replaced by the need for each layer to do so.

Layered textures may appear either as single blocks within larger formations or as whole pieces, tableaux, or movements. The first of the *Three Pieces for String Quartet* is a stratification in its entirety, as are many of the dance movements of *The Rite of Spring*. The typical grouping hierarchy in works of the Russian period runs as follows:

1. work
2. tableau, movement, piece
3. section
4. block
5. motive, fragment

No doubt, processes of juxtaposition and stratification can overlap at times, with blocks and sections partaking of both. Such is the case with the just-noted climactic block in the second tableau, where the juxtaposed motives b_5 (or b_6) and c_6 are a separate layer superimposed over another layer in the bass. So, too, in the first tableau, block A is clearly a mixture of sorts. Although the tableau itself is a block structure, internally, the single block A and its subsequent restatements are not so easily defined. Reiterated pitches and fragments in the four pianos and xylophone share the same spans; they are synchronized with the main line of the soprano solo and the repetition of the embedded D-E motive. (See the brackets below the stave of the soprano line in Example 4.1.) And synchronization of this kind is ordinarily the case with the individual blocks of a large-scale structure. Parts are fixed in their alignment; they proceed en masse, so to speak, and with the invention thus dependent on adjustments in the length and order of the blocks from one restatement to the next.

Exceptional with block A in the first tableau, however, is the succession of taps on the cymbal (see Example 4.1). As we have noted already, the pattern of repetition defined by these taps, although systematic in and of itself, is not aligned with that of the remaining parts. And so a measure of stratification is introduced at this point. Features identified with both types of structure, block and layered, are engaged. And the two types are perhaps best viewed in this light, that is, as extremes in a spectrum that can admit a wide range of variation.

5 Melody and harmony in *Les Noces*

Much of the melodic material of *Les Noces* consists not of melodies or themes, properly speaking, but of fragments and motives. The short, fragmentary character of this material, a feature of Stravinsky's Russian-period works generally, is symptomatic of the processes discussed in Chapter 4. Within a given block or stratified texture, fragments are not introduced as thematic parts, segments of larger shapes which are subsequently detached and subjected to a development along Classical lines; rather, they are sliced up into even smaller units (or "cells") and repeated ostinato-wise, assuming a mosaic-like appearance. If the repetition of these fragments is metrically uneven or irregular, a form of displacement will result. And displacement, the reader will recall, is an integral part of both block and layered structures.[1]

Generally of limited range, the fragments and motives of *Les Noces* number from two to five pitches. As a rule, they are open-ended and without cadential expression, inviting the immediate and often continuous repetition discussed in earlier chapters. At the same time, open-endedness is tied to a diatonicism that is distinctly modal and often Dorian, with many of the fragments outlining Dorian tetrachords. Typically, too, the latter are gapped in the manner indicated previously. The principal fragment of the opening blocks of *Les Noces*, (E D B), lacks a C♯, and the incompleteness of this outline persists in many subsequent articulations.

In fact, when (0 2 5) incomplete in this fashion, the Dorian tetrachord assumes the earmarks of a melodic cell or "basic motive." Inversions surface in this light, that is, as departures from the parent or untransformed form. At the same time, the encircling interval of 5, the fourth, is critically identifying, and is nearly always present in these terms (without interval complementation, in other words). Minor-third gaps pervade lengthier segments as well, with the latter acquiring a pentatonic or "anhemitonic" character. Subject to a repetition that is often relentless, the gaps are made all the more conspicuous. The repetition intensifies the sense of what is being omitted, which, for the most part, are semitones and the potential of

---

[1] The alignment of two or more stratified motives or chords can shift in two ways, as we have noted in Chapter 1, between the motives and chords themselves and as each relates to the meter. See the lament at Rehearsal Nos. 35–40 in *Les Noces*, a single block of stratification within the block structure of the second tableau as a whole.

these "tones" for creating a sense of movement by way of the leading-tone function. While the reduction in interval-class content would have made for a somewhat static framework in any case, the particular gaps in question intensify the archaic or "primitive" character of the folk element.

Reproduced in Example 5.1a–e are varied appearances of the (0 2 5) melodic cell, each with a different contour and rhythmic profile. Starting with the opening fragment (E D B) of the first tableau (Example 5.1a), this may be compared, in Example 5.1b, to a similar segment at Rehearsal No. 9 (motive x, as we shall be labeling it), and, in Example 5.1c, to the syncopated "hiccup motive" as it first appears at Rehearsal Nos. 91 and 92 in the fourth tableau.[2] The syncopation of the "hiccup motive" reappears at Rehearsal No. 92 (see Example 5.1d). Transposed to (E♭ D♭ B♭), it surfaces as a form of accompaniment at this point, doing so in two halves or two bars, with the second of these bars consisting of the displaced repeat of the first (the actual syncopation or "hiccup").

The culminating pages of *Les Noces* feature a further transposition of the (0 2 5) melodic cell, this time to (C♯ B G♯). Shown in Example 5.1e, the mood here is solemn and apotheosis-like, the setting not unlike that at the conclusion of *The Firebird* and, later, pieces such as the *Symphonies of Wind Instruments* (1920), the *Octet* (1924), *Apollo Musagetes* (1928), and the *Symphony of Psalms* (1930). A plateau is reached at the close of these works, a stoppage of harmonic rhythm, in which a featured motive, repeated again and again as a refrain, alternates with another short block or chord in anticipation of a final cut-off.[3]

A layered structure may also be inferred from the concluding bars of the fourth tableau at Rehearsal Nos. 133–35 (see Example 5.1e). Here, periodic strikings of a single two-note chord (C♯ B) in the chimes, bells and pianos are superimposed over varying repeats of the (C♯ B G♯) motive in the bass solo. While repeats of the single chord are spaced regularly by eight quarter-note beats, those of the motive are spaced irregularly. (An exception to the

---

[2] The story of the "hiccup motive" was recounted briefly in Chapter 3; see Robert Craft with William Harkins, "Stravinsky's *Svadebka*: An Introduction," *New York Review of Books*, December 14, 1972: 24. Or see Vera Stravinsky and Robert Craft, *Stravinsky in Pictures and Documents* (New York: Simon and Schuster, 1978), 151. A "brilliant unifying stroke" is how Vera Stravinsky and Craft describe the transformation of the (0 2 5) trichord by the syncopation of the "hiccup motive."

[3] The "Apothéose" at the conclusion of *Apollo* is discussed in a somewhat similar fashion in Arnold Whittall, "Stravinsky in Context," in Jonathan Cross, ed., *The Cambridge Companion to Stravinsky* (Cambridge University Press, 2003), 51–54. The "solemn, processional" quality of the "Apothéose" in *Apollo* is compared to the endings of *The Firebird* and *Les Noces*, each of these indicative, as Whittall would have it, of "Stravinsky's uniquely 'cool' spirit of tragic vulnerability and loss." See, too, and again in connection with *Apollo's* conclusion, the reference to "mysterious, other worldly purity" in Stephen Walsh, *Stravinsky: A Creative Spring, Russia and France, 1882–1934* (New York: Knopf, 1999), 500.

Example 5.1. *Les Noces*, (0 2 5) melodic cell, transformations

a) opening lament

b) motive x

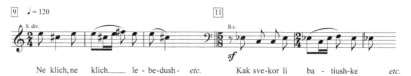

c) hiccup motive

d) hiccup motive

e) hiccup motive

rule occurs at Rehearsal No. 134+7, where the span between repeats of the chord totals eleven eighth-note beats. As we have indicated already in Chapter 3, successive soundings of the (C♯ B) chord, fifteen in all, are strongly suggestive of the ringing of church bells.)[4] The vertical alignment of the two layers shifts as a result of the varying spans, harmonically and metrically, with each layer acquiring a degree of independence, and the setting itself a stratified, superimposed quality.

The repeat structures underlying the two final versions of the basic motive in Examples 5.1d and e are also characteristic of Stravinsky's invention, matters to which we shall also be turning in due course (see, especially, Chapter 8). Of concern here, however, is the long-term progress of the (0 2 5) motive or "basic cell," the extraordinary transformation of its character, theatrically as well as musically dramatic. Crucial is the origin of the syncopation and its "hiccup" effect. Conceived initially as a way of mimicking the singing and shouting of guests inebriated and suffering from bouts of the hiccups (see Example 5.1c), the syncopation and the displacement of the motive color all subsequent appearances, including those featured in the apotheosis of the concluding bars. Here, as we have suggested, the mood shifts abruptly from one of drunken revelry to one of solemn and quiet reflection.

Melody and the folk element

Many of the characteristics of melody surveyed above may be attributed to Russian folk or church music. Mention was made in Chapter 3 of a number of direct borrowings, among these, "Ne vesyolaya da kompan'itsa" ("Not a Merry Company"). Transcribed by the composer with the assistance of his friend and collaborator at the time, Stepan Mitusov (see Examples 3.2a and b), appearances of the "Mitusov song" in the fourth tableau are exceptional in *Les Noces*. They are the only instances in which a borrowed melody is quoted in its entirety.

---

[4] For an explanation for the eleven quarter-note beats of Rehearsal No. 134+7 (the addition of three beats at this point, an extra 3/4 measure), see Andrew Imbrie, "One Measure of Eternity," *Perspectives of New Music* 9, no. 2 (1971): 51–57. Imbrie attributes this single irregularity in the bell-like repetition of the two-note chord to something quite purposeful, namely, Stravinsky's attempt to sustain the sense in this music of a suspension of time. Just at the point at which the listener's perception of meter is likely to switch from the flexibility of the vocal line to the regularity of the repeated two-note chord, three beats are added in an effort to prevent this from happening. The irregularity preserves something of the floating, meterless quality of the passage. "At the exact moment when we are prepared to embrace the 'time' simplicity of the meter of bell-strokes, it eludes us again. The rest of the coda is required to restore our precarious balance" (57). See note 52 in Chapter 3.

More typical of the melodic invention in *Les Noces* are the individual segments a and b of the opening block of the second tableau. Traced in Chapter 4 (see, especially, Example 4.7), the melodic leap C-F, identified with the Groom, is derived in large part from *Znamenniy* chant. Yet it is not a theme or a melody, but, rather, a segment of a segment, the closing figure of segment b. In addition, innumerable fragments, not traceable to specific sources at all, are apparently folk-like rather than folk-derived. They are products not of borrowing but of *simulation* ("fabrication," as Stravinsky described it).[5] Many seem to have been composed as "faithful and clever imitations of folk songs", to follow Béla Bartók's early account of Stravinsky's methods.[6] And this would seem to be the case not only in *Les Noces*, but in other late Russian-period works as well, including the *Three Pieces for String Quartet* (1914), *Renard* (1916), *The Soldier's Tale* (1918), and the *Symphonies of Wind Instruments* (1920).

In sum, Stravinsky's uniquely designed Russian-period style was served often enough not by the genuine article, but by more intrinsically (or "organically") developed material, melodic parts whose origins lay more immediately with the compositional processes at hand.[7] Such parts were the product of a musical consciousness steeped in Russian folk idioms, to be sure, but perhaps more particularly in the uses to which those idioms could be put, the ways they could be made to serve rhythmic and metrical practices already fully a part of Stravinsky's style. And the further the composer traveled from his point of departure in the form of the three early ballets (*The Firebird, Petrushka*, and *The Rite of Spring*), the more problematic does the explicit borrowing of authentic folk songs and the process of assimilation appear to have become. "If any of these [Russian-period] pieces *sounds* like aboriginal folk music," Stravinsky would later remark, "it may be because my powers of fabrication were able to tap some unconscious 'folk' memory."[8]

The path from *The Firebird* (1910) to the later Russian-period pieces is clear enough in this regard. The complete and quite explicit settings of Russian folk songs in the earlier ballet (often reminiscent of the settings in

[5] See Igor Stravinsky and Robert Craft, *Memories and Commentaries* (Berkeley: University of California Press, 1981), 98. Original publication, 1960.
[6] Béla Bartók, *Béla Bartók Essays*, ed. Benjamin Suchoff (Lincoln: University of Nebraska Press, 1992), 343.
[7] Much the same can be said of Leoš Janáček's melodic style. In Janáček's opera *Jenufa*, for example, the melodic content, although consisting occasionally of explicit folk-song borrowings, is more readily folk-sounding, a product of the composer's internalization of various general and specific features of Moravian folk melodies. See the brief discussion of this in Geoffrey O'Brien, "Nightmare on the Prairie," *New York Review of Books*, September 21, 2006: 35–37.
[8] Stravinsky and Craft, *Memories and Commentaries*, 98.

Rimsky-Korsakov's operas and symphonic poems) are succeeded by the much shorter fragments and motives of the later works.

More specifically, the dissection, reordering, and interpolation of these shorter fragments constitutes a form of cutting and pasting touched upon already. The technique of juxtaposition is both local and global in scope, having as much to do with the treatment of these short melodic fragments as with larger blocks of material. On the smallest of scales, it involves the division and juxtaposition of fragments and motives, as with the manipulation of segments a and b in the opening block of the second tableau of *Les Noces* (see Example 4.7).

In his lengthy polemic against "folkloristic symphonies," Arnold Schoenberg argued against the use of borrowed folk or popular material, suggesting that such material could not be assimilated properly by the constructed artwork.[9] In Schoenberg's view, the two sides of this equation could not be made to cohere. And the problem lay with the mode of conception. Borrowed folk melodies were conceived outside the compositional process. They came whole and ready made, implying not some further development, but qualities that were capable of being appreciated and savored for what they already were. An aesthetic purpose had been realized in full, in other words, and short of merely repeating that purpose in various settings or arrangements, little could be added.

In effect, bits and pieces of a borrowed folk melody could not be chiseled off and submitted to a developing variation, the traditional and Classical means by which, according to Schoenberg, motivic parts were worked into the body of a work and made whole and "organic," individual and contextual.[10] And attempts to work them in this way, to treat them as if they had in fact sprung from the compositional process itself, were doomed to

[9] See Arnold Schoenberg, *Style and Idea: Selected Writings of Arnold Schoenberg*, ed. Leonard Stein, trans. Leo Black (Berkeley: University of California Press, 1985): "Folkloristic Symphonies" (1947), 164–65: "Structurally, there never remains in popular tunes an unsolved problem, the consequences of which will show up only later ... There is nothing in them that asks for expansion ... A motive, in contrast to this, is incomplete and depends on continuations; explanations, clarifications, conclusions, consequences, etc ... In artistically superior compositions of this kind, the 'motive of the variation' is derived through 'developing variations' of basic features of the theme." For a still earlier critique of what Schoenberg called "folklorists" and "quasi-tonalists," see the Foreword to his *Drei Satiren*, Op. 38, a translation of which may be found in Scott Messing, *Neoclassicism in Music: From the Genesis of the Concept through the Schoenberg/Stravinsky Polemic* (University of Rochester Press, 1996), 144. Interestingly, Schoenberg appears not always to have been averse to the borrowing of popular tunes in contexts of developing variation and the Classical style. The variation movement in his Suite, Op. 29, a piece interrupted for the *Drei Satiren*, is based on a borrowed German folk song, namely, "Ännchen von Tharau." The song appears entangled in a web of figures and motives, within which it is not only encased (often submerged), but to which it contributes as well.

[10] Typically, Schoenberg defined the Classical style in thematic–motivic terms, according to the principle of "developing variation." See note 25 in Chapter 1.

failure. They could not but lead to an acute form of artificiality, something forced and labored. And the character of the borrowed material, which had in all likelihood prompted the borrowing in the first place, would be lost in the process.

But this argument fails where Stravinsky's methods are considered more specifically. The "folkloristic" in pieces such as *Les Noces* and *Renard* has far less to do with the incorporation of Russian folk songs borrowed whole than with the manipulation of short, open-ended, fragments traceable often enough to Stravinsky's own "powers of fabrication." This is not to deny the few instances of direct and explicit borrowing, but only to suggest that such borrowing figures as but one of the many ways in which the folk element was exploited.

At the same time, Stravinsky's reference to his own "powers of fabrication" carries implications extending beyond the Russian period. Direct borrowings are present in neoclassical works as well, in the *Jeu de Cartes* (1935), for example, in the "Dumbarton Oaks" Concerto in E-flat (1938), and in *The Rake's Progress* (1951). Quotations from Rossini's *The Barber of Seville* appear in the *Presto* section of "Deal III" in *Jeu de Cartes*, from Bach's Brandenburg Concerto No. 1 in the first movement of the concerto, and from Mozart's *Così fan Tutte* in the opening of *The Rake's Progress*. Here, too, however, the quotation is overshadowed by the invention. (In the opening pages of Act I in *The Rake's Progress*, the one-measure motive that appears ostinato-like in various transposed forms throughout could have been lifted from any one of Mozart's operas, so entirely idiomatic is it from a melodic standpoint.) And the direct connection that can be drawn in this way between the authentic Russian folk idioms that lie in the background of the Russian period and the Baroque and Classical conventions that underlie neoclassicism can seem very much to the point. The actual materials may differ in origin and character, yet the two orientations of which they are a part share a compositional process. "What I love I wish to make my own," Stravinsky remarked in one of his "conversations" with Robert Craft; "I am probably describing a rare form of kleptomania."[11] His instinct was "to repeat in [his] own accent."[12]

And so, for Stravinsky, the issue of melody may well have been a sensitive and complicated one. In the small-scale cutting and pasting of fragments another sort of melody was required, one different in kind from that which

[11] Stravinsky and Craft, *Memories and Commentaries*, 110.

[12] See Igor Stravinsky and Robert Craft, *Expositions and Developments* (Garden City, NY: Doubleday, 1962), 128. In connection with the "recomposition" of Pergolesi's music in *Pulcinella* (1919), Stravinsky remarked in retrospect that his best option at the time had consisted not of committing a forgery but of repeating this music "in my own accent."

had characterized the music of his predecessors. Greater pliancy was required, the ability of a melody to submit to the processes of division, repetition, and metrical displacement detailed here and in previous chapters. And what critics condemned early on as a "lack of melody" in Stravinsky's music can therefore be described more accurately as the absence of a particular kind of melody,[13] the sorts of themes or "beautiful melodies" made famous in the music of composers such as Tchaikovsky and Rachmaninov. The same critics ridiculed the "lack of a melodic faculty" on Stravinsky's part, the composer's apparent inability to chisel a melodic substance of his own.[14]

Unfortunately, too, Stravinsky's own scattered accounts of the role of borrowed folk material in his music are replete with errors and omissions. On several occasions he seems to have forgotten the circumstances attending the conception of some of the works in question.[15] Sensitive to the criticism of his detractors, he may also have wished to downplay the extent of his early (as well as late) reliance on borrowed material. The neoclassical about-face of the early 1920s may have played a role as well. Abrupt and radical in character, the "change of life" at this time may have left the composer eager to advertise the new at the expense of the old and the folkloristic.[16] (He would later claim that much of the neoclassical ballet *Apollo* had been composed with the idea of pursuing a longer melodic line, one that was purged of the fragmentary, folk-like character of his earlier works.)[17] There are broad aesthetic issues, in other words, as the early preoccupation with folklorism gave way to a concern for the work itself ("the thing made," as Stravinsky later termed it).[18] By the early 1920s, Stravinsky's gravitation toward a brand of formalist aesthetics had been taking place for the better part of a decade.

---

[13] See the discussion of this in Pierre Boulez, "Stravinsky Remains," in Pierre Boulez, *Stocktakings from an Apprenticeship*, trans. Stephen Walsh (Oxford University Press, 1991), 106–07. Boulez traces the early criticism of what he calls the "lack of melody" in Stravinsky's music to the various gapped, folkloristic features in pieces such as *The Rite of Spring* and *Les Noces*. His conclusion, however, is that "it is not a question of a lack of melody so much as a certain quality of melody – a certain archaizing tendency from a tonal point of view."

[14] See Constant Lambert, *Music Ho! A Study of Music in Decline*. 3rd edn. (London: Faber and Faber, 1966), 91. Toward the end of the nineteenth century, similar complaints were leveled against the music of Stravinsky's teacher, Rimsky-Korsakov, and to the effect that it, too, lacked melody and had relied too heavily on the borrowing and arranging of folk tunes. This may also have contributed to Stravinsky's angst about melody and the nature of its role in his music. See Gerald Abraham, *Studies in Russian Music* (London: William Reeves, 1935), 64.

[15] See Stravinsky and Craft, *Memories and Commentaries*, 97–98.

[16] For Stravinsky's own acknowledgement of his various stylistic "changes of life" (as he called them), see Igor Stravinsky and Robert Craft, *Themes and Episodes* (New York: Knopf, 1966), 23.

[17] See Igor Stravinsky and Robert Craft, *Dialogues and a Diary* (Garden City, NY: Doubleday, 1963), 17. "In *Apollo* I tried to discover a melodism free of folk-lore," he later recalled.

[18] Igor Stravinsky and Robert Craft, *Retrospectives and Conclusions* (New York: Knopf, 1969), 48.

A wealth of factors may have entered his reasoning, in fact, even if the errors of his remarks on the subject of the folkloristic are not thereby wholly explained. As late as 1960, he would contend, as he had earlier in the century,[19] that the direct borrowing in *The Rite of Spring* and *Les Noces* had been confined to a single instance in each case, to the opening melody in the bassoon in the case of *The Rite of Spring*, and to the "Mitusov song" in the fourth tableau of *Les Noces*.[20] Yet, as has now been amply documented, a study by Lawrence Morton in 1978 cited four additional tunes with obvious ties to subsequent dance movements in *The Rite of Spring*.[21] These tunes were spotted in the anthology of Lithuanian folk songs from which the opening bassoon melody had been abstracted.[22] And this was followed by Richard Taruskin's pathbreaking study of "Russian Folk Melodies in *The Rite of Spring*," in which several more tunes were cited, although in additional anthologies and with ties to *The Rite of Spring* less obvious than those that had been cited by Morton.[23]

A certain ambiguity is thus likely to attach itself to the above assertion regarding the folk or church-related origins of much of the melodic content of *Les Noces*. There are cases of direct borrowing, to be sure, cases traceable at least in part to authentic sources. Yet much of the material seems to have been conceived in the manner indicated by the composer, that is, as a form of improvisation *à la manière de*, a simulation in which, from the start of the compositional process, bits and pieces of folk music, tapped sometimes from the composer's "unconscious folk memory," meshed with the ways and means of his own stylistic devices. And from what we know of the approach, it could not have differed all that much from the way in which neoclassical works were conceived. Beneath the surface of these two orientations, the Russian folk idioms that had served the earlier Russian period were replaced by the Baroque and Classical materials that would serve the later neoclassical one. And in a final "change of life" during the early 1950s,[24] the Classical materials would be replaced by a number of serial

---

[19] The contention that Stravinsky's folksong borrowing in *The Rite of Spring* had been confined to a single instance, namely, the opening melody in the bassoon, is reiterated in André Schaeffner, *Strawinsky* (Paris: Rieder, 1931). Schaeffner relied heavily on a series of interviews with the composer himself in compiling the background material for his biography.

[20] See Stravinsky and Craft, *Memories and Commentaries*, 97.

[21] See Lawrence Morton, "Footnotes to Stravinsky Studies: *Le Sacré du Printemps*," *Tempo* 128 (1979): 9–16.

[22] Anton Juszkiewicz, *Litauische Volks-Weisen* (Kracow, Verlag der Polnischen Akademie der Wisserschaften, 1900).

[23] Richard Taruskin, "Russian Folk Melodies in *The Rite of Spring*," *Journal of the American Musicological Society* 33, no. 3 (1980): 512–13. Or see Taruskin, *Stravinsky and The Russian Traditions: A Biography of the Works Through "Mavra,"* 2 vols. (Berkeley: University of California Press, 1996), vol. II: 906–33.

[24] See Stravinsky and Craft, *Themes and Episodes*, 23.

Example 5.2. Anton Juszkiewicz, *Litauische Volks-Weisen,* folk songs with (0 2 3 5) outlines

a) No. 787

b) No. 34

c) No. 1,553

approaches, among these, perhaps most conspicuously, those of Anton Webern.

Another look at the (0 2 3 5) Dorian tetrachord can further illuminate the nature of these exchanges. Quite apart from the tetrachord's role in *Les Noces,* it may be found in Russian and Lithuanian folk songs, above all, evidently, in "seasonal songs" or *kalendarniye pesni;* the three melodies quoted in Example 5.2 are from the collection of Lithuanian songs mentioned above in connection with *The Rite of Spring.*[25] The same tetrachord

---

[25] See the discussion of these "seasonal songs" in Taruskin, *Stravinsky and The Russian Traditions,* 914–23. Taruskin lays particular stress on Russian "springtime songs" or *vesnyanki* as sources of the (0 2 3 5) melodic tetrachord in *The Rite of Spring.* Of the three Lithuanian folk songs quoted in Example 5.2, No. 787 from the Juszkiewicz anthology is a possible source of the fragment introduced at Rehearsal No. 19 in *The Rite of Spring,* while No. 34 may have led to phrase B of the opening melody in the bassoon (in contour and in pitch-specific terms as well; see Example 5.11). In turn, phrase B anticipates the Db-Bb-Eb-Bb ostinato of the "Danses des Adolescentes." Motivic connections of this kind, triggered by the (0 2 5) melodic "cell" and the (0 2 3 5) Dorian tetrachord in Part I of *The Rite,* are traced here in Example 5.12a–f. For further discussion of these and other possible borrowings from the Juszkiewicz collection, see Taruskin, *Stravinsky and The Russian Traditions,* 895–906.

may also be (0 2 5) or (0 3 5) incomplete in its articulation. In fact, there are general references to trichords in the anthologies consulted by the composer at the time of the conception of *Les Noces*. In Dahl's *Dictionary of the Russian Language*, for example, descriptions of funeral laments, some of these indistinguishable from those of the bridal laments (with *lamentation* the key melodic category here), refer to "a single monotonous motive, the repetition of three tones."[26]

At the same time, however, sources of this kind can be stretched only so far. The role of the (0 2 3 5) tetrachord in *Les Noces*, complete or (0 2 5) incomplete, has as much to do with techniques of juxtaposition and stratification and with the evolution of Stravinsky's Russian-period style as it does with these incidental and often loosely defined ties to specific folk sources. In the opening blocks of *Les Noces*, for example, repeats of the (E D B) trichord and its embedded D-E segment are as much a product of the composer's instinct to displace metrically and to pattern and target a series of displacements as they are of the chants and wedding songs transcribed in, say, the Istomin-Liapunov collection of 1898. And the need for analytical, historical, and critical contexts to highlight the compositional process can often be met as effectively with the remaining works of the Russian period as it can by the relevant folk sources.[27]

On a broader scale, too, the need for analytical foils can be met not only by the music of Stravinsky's immediate predecessors in Russia (by the music of his teacher, Rimsky-Korsakov, for example), but by the works of his contemporaries as well. Outlines of (0 2 3 5) tetrachords may be found not only in Russian and Lithuanian folk songs, but in the folk-song repertories of Eastern European countries more generally, including those of Hungary. They appear in Bartók's music, for example, and in contexts which are otherwise folk-like in character. And they are sometimes octatonically conceived as well, as with the fugal subject in Bartók's Third String Quartet (see Example 5.3), or the tritone-related (0 2 3 5)s that are superimposed in "Diminished Fifths," No. 101 in Bartók's *Mikrokosmos* (see Example 5.4). Compare the tritone-related tetrachords in Example 5.4 with those at Rehearsal No. 11 in *Les Noces* (see Example 2.3) or with those at Rehearsal No. 64 in *The Rite of Spring* (Example 5.5). The delineation of these tetrachords, (B A G♯ F♯)(F E♭ (D) C) in *Les Noces*, becomes

---

[26] See the earlier discussion of Dahl's entries in Taruskin, *Stravinsky and The Russian Traditions*, vol. II: 1326.

[27] Indeed, the need for additional contexts can often be met quite effectively by works of the neoclassical and serial eras as well. For example, the twelve-tone row of Stravinsky's last published work, *The Owl and The Pussycat* (1966), is very nearly *derived* from the standpoint of the (0 2 5) trichord. Three of its four trichords are (0 2 5)s, the fourth being a form of (0 1 4).

Example 5.3. Bartók, Third String Quartet, octatonic fugal subject with (0 2 3 5) segments

(G F E D)(C♯ (B) A♯ G♯) in *The Rite of Spring.* (For the reasons already outlined in the introduction, the pitch-lettering in these analytical designations *descends*. Individual pitches in parentheses, missing from the actual articulation, underscore the minor-third gaps alluded to above.) While the construction in these three examples differs in its detail, above all in motivic contour, rhythm, and vertical alignment, the segmentation in the large remains very much the same. Featured is a superimposition of tritone-related (0 2 3 5) tetrachords.

Often, too, the (0 2 3 5) tetrachords in Bartók's music are gapped in the manner indicated above: compare, in Example 5.6a, the D-G-E melodic contour in Bartók's Third String Quartet (second violin and viola) to the F-B♭-G outline in the English horn at Rehearsal No. 7 in *The Rite of Spring* (see Example 5.6b). The folk resonance in these passages, archaic or "primitive" in character, can seem quite similar. In Example 5.6b from *The Rite of Spring*, successive appearances of the F-B♭-G fragment throughout the Introduction are fixed instrumentally as well as registrally, confined not only to a single instrument, the English horn, but to a single mode of attack as well. This, too, can seem rustic or "archaic" in its effect, as if the limitations of range and the gapped character of the articulation had come as a result of a "primitively" defective means of transmission.

Example 5.4. Bartók, *Mikrokosmos*, "Diminished Fifths," No. 101: tritone-related (0 2 3 5) tetrachords

Example 5.5. *The Rite of Spring*, "Ritual of the Rival Tribes," tritone-related (0 2 3 5) tetrachords, complete and (0 3 5) incomplete

Example 5.6a. Bartók, Third String Quartet, (0 (2) 3 5) gapped tetrachords (2nd violin, viola)

Example 5.6b. *The Rite of Spring*, Introduction, (0 (2) 3 5) gapped tetrachord (E. hn.)

Collection I

Example 5.7. Bartók, Third String Quartet, tritone-related (0 (2) 3 5) gapped tetrachords, ostinatos

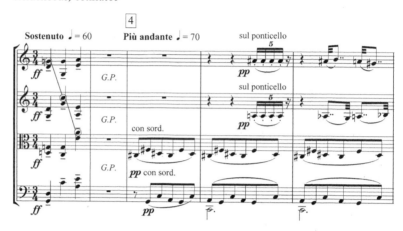

Example 5.8. Bartók, Violin Concerto, I, opening

Finally, the excerpt cited in Example 5.7 is from the opening pages of Bartók's Third String Quartet; the tritone-related (0 3 5)s are superimposed in the form of an ostinato. Included in Example 5.8 is an excerpt from the opening of Bartók's Violin Concerto (1938). Critical here are the minor-third gaps, above all, the B-F♯-A outline in the lower strings, pizzicato. The Dorian scale may be inferred, impaired somewhat by the D♯ in the accompanying chords: (B A G♯ F♯)(E D C♯ B), in descending formation. Indeed, often impaired in this way by a conflicting major third, the D-scale figures prominently in the Hungarian folksong repertory referred to by Bartók as "New Style."[28] Hungarian gypsy music is invoked in a number of ways as

---

[28] See Béla Bartók, *The Hungarian Folk Song*, ed. Benjamin Suchoff (Albany: State University of New York Press, 1981), 37–38. Cited in David E. Schneider, "A Context for Béla Bartók on the Eve of World War II: The Violin Concerto (1938)," *repercussions* (1996): 50.

well. In particular, the tempo and form of accompaniment in the opening pages of the Violin Concerto (see the strings, pizzicato) are derived in part from a repertory of conscription songs known as *verbunkos*.[29]

The suggestion here is not that the distinguishing features of Stravinsky's early music and of the Russian folk idioms that underlie it are unimportant or negligible. The point, rather, is that traits of Russian popular music in *Les Noces* and other works of the Russian period can often be found in other folksong repertories. And the general sense of a folk idiom that overlapping of this kind is likely to produce (the cultivation of a sense of the folk-like or "folkish" on the part of the listener) can be critical to an appreciation of works such as *The Rite of Spring* and *Les Noces*. This is likely to be especially true of listeners with little or no familiarity with the scenarios or the Russian background of these works.[30]

In Carl Orff's *Music for Children*, such a general sense of a folk reference can again seem very much to the point. The overall design of Orff's collection of songs is practical as well as pedagogical. Orff proceeds from the simplest and most elementary unisons and octaves to more complex melodic configurations. Yet the (0 2 5) trichords featured in the fourth song, a nursery rhyme entitled "Bell Horses" (see Example 5.9), clearly invoke an archaic folk element as well.[31]

Claims of this kind are easily disputed, of course: the idea of a general folk reference and the significance that may be attached to Stravinsky's compositional processes, his "powers of fabrication." Folklorists could claim that the expressive quality of *Les Noces*, the incisive, ritual-like character of the repetition, for example, is not Stravinsky's alone (did not originate with the composer), but is Russian through and through, and is traceable to the composer's familiarity with and close study of Russian folk verse and song.

---

[29] See Schneider, "A Context for Béla Bartók," 53–65.

[30] The case for a general folk resonance – near-universal qualities in folk song and its performance – is made by, among others, Leoš Janáček. See Mirka Zemanova, ed. and trans., *Janáček's Uncollected Essays on Music* (New York: Rizzoli International, 1989), 60. "Without knowing beforehand whether a folk song is Czech, English, or French," Janáček averred, "I would be unable to identify it as one or the other. Folk song has one spirit, because it possesses the pure man, with God's own culture, and not one grafted upon him." For further discussion, see Jonathan Pearl, *The Music of Language: The Notebooks of Leoš Janáček*, Ph.D. diss., University of California at Santa Barbara, 2005.

[31] Orff's "Bell Horses" might be compared to another set of nursery rhymes, namely, Stravinsky's *Trois Histoires pour enfants* (1917). The first of these *Histoires*, "Tilimbom," begins with a similar reiteration of the (0 2 5) trichord, specifically, the melodic outline D-A-C. It should be noted in this connection, however, that contexts and repertories exploiting the (0 2 5) trichord or the gapped character of the pentatonic scale need not be folk-like in character. For a discussion of the uses of the (0 2 5) trichord and various gapped scales in Mahler's music, see Stephen Hefling, "The Composition of Mahler's 'Ich bin der Welt abhanden gekommen'," in *Gustav Mahler*, ed. Hermann Danuser (Darmstadt: Wissenschaftlichen Buchgesellschaft, 1992), 96–158. Uses of the (0 2 5) trichord in popular tunes of the Tin Pan Alley tradition are discussed in David Carson Berry, "The Structural Roles of Pentatonicism in Tin Pan Alley Songs," paper delivered at the annual meeting of the Society for Music Theory (SMT), University of Wisconsin, Madison, 2003.

Example 5.9. Carl Orff, *Music for Children*, No. 7, "Bell Horses"

A discovery rather than an invention in this respect, the quality is something that is transmitted by the composer, who in turn assumes the role of a vessel or medium. (Historians have argued that, even if the folk-like or popular traits widely associated with a particular national character are found upon closer inspection to be international in origin and scope, the national association would remain an "aesthetic fact" in need of recognition and study by scholars.[32] The fact that Stravinsky's (0 2 (3) 5)s and short, repetitive melodic fragments are indicative of folk categories other than

---

[32] Carl Dahlhaus, *Between Romanticism and Modernism*, trans. Mary Whittall (Berkeley: University of California Press, 1980), "Nationalism and Music," 86: "if a composer intended a

Russian does not invalidate their association with Russia or the Russian folk past. What counts, evidently, is the larger context of these associations, not the small traits that can be abstracted and isolated analytically.)

But the task of disentangling entrenched musical features and qualities of this kind lies beyond the conceptual framework that has here been brought to bear. In terms as intangible as these, competing claims about the origin of *Les Noces* and of Stravinsky's Russian-period style more generally are not readily susceptible to resolution. On a more practical level, various kinds of borrowings can be cited: the Mitusov song, gapped (0 2 3 5) tetrachords, simulations, and the like. The technique of repeating and rearranging small fragments and motives (often tiny segments, as we have seen) may have originated with the use of *popevki* in Russian folk songs and liturgical chant (see Examples 3.3 and 3.4a), while a number of more specific inflections may have stemmed from the three categories of ritual lament surveyed in Chapter 3 (see Examples 3.1a and b). Yet, as in earlier chapters, we subscribe to the idea of an overlapping of feature shared between Stravinsky and his sources, not necessarily to competition between disparate or conflicting ones. Sensed affinities are what seem to have drawn Stravinsky to Russian folk verse, songs, rhythms, and accents, sensibilities that were felt to be compatible in one way or another, capable of being placed at the service of his own devices. And if, in the form of *Les Noces*, something genuinely Russian was created as a result of this symbiosis, then we can only assume the creation to have had as much to do with Stravinsky's imagination, his insights and interpretations, musical and otherwise, as with the folk sources that lay at his disposal. At the deepest level of sense and sensibility, the two sides of the interplay are inextricable. A particular feature or quality cannot be singled out and assigned to Stravinsky's folk sources without being assigned to the composer as well.

Preliminary remarks; a *Tonnetz* for *Les Noces*

Reproduced in Example 5.10 is the Lithuanian folk song from which the opening of *The Rite of Spring* is derived. Stravinsky's adaptation, scored for

piece of music to be national in character and the hearers believe it to be so, that is something which the historian must accept as an aesthetic fact, even if stylistic analysis – the attempt to "verify" the aesthetic premise by reference to musical features – fails to produce any evidence." While some folk idioms are "regional or even local in character and coloring, some traits which were felt to be specifically national in the nineteenth century actually stretch far across national boundaries. This is a fact which remained concealed because the study of folk music was carried out only on a national level. But to write off the nationalist interpretation of folk music as an aesthetic error which is now being set right by empirical research would also be a mistake: a misuse of the categories. Aesthetically it is perfectly legitimate to call bagpipe drones and sharpened fourths typically Polish when they occur in Chopin and typically Norwegian when they occur in Grieg."

Example 5.10. Anton Juszkiewicz, *Litauische Volks-Weisen*, source of *The Rite of Spring*, Introduction, opening bassoon melody

solo bassoon, appears in Example 5.11. Vertical bars mark off the melody's four phrases, while, just below the stave, beams connecting a number of stemmed notes highlight the underlying pitch-motions. The analytical reduction exposes both the repetitive character of the melody and its elaborational structure.

Each of the melody's four phrases consists of a return to the pitch C and a descending passing motion C-B-A, a "linear progression" spanning a minor third. In phrases A, A1, and A2, the passing tone B is "prolonged" by way of an (E G B) triadic outline. The "prolongation" is missing in phrase B, where the motion C-B-A is followed by the descending fourth, D-A. Crucial here is not only the (D C B A) tetrachord that results from this linkage, but also the particular manner of its articulation, the C-B-A/D-A pitch-interval ordering or contour. The repetition of the first of these two segments, C-B-A, is also of consequence as a thematic feature.

In its overall rhythmic shape, the melody relates only rather weakly to the melodic life of *The Rite of Spring*. As a whole, it bears scant resemblance to the vast array of themes, motives, and fragments that follow in subsequent dance movements. In skeletal form, however, as outlined below the quotation in Example 5.11, something of its role at the head of a host of motivic networks may be gleaned.

Thus, the C-B-A/D-A outline of phrase B anticipates the Db-Bb/Eb-Bb ostinato that enters at the end of the Introduction, a transposition up a semitone (see Examples 5.12a and 5.12b). Running through nearly the entirety of the succeeding "Danses des Adolescentes," the ostinato's tetrachord is (0 2 5) incomplete, gapped in terms of (Eb Db (C) Bb). Yet its prefigurement by phrase B in the opening bars of the Introduction is underscored in a number of ways: the ostinato retains not only the pitch-interval ordering or contour of phrase B, but, obviously, by way of the repetition of the minor third spanning the initial motivic segment C-B-A, its repetitive features as well.

Example 5.11. *The Rite of Spring*, Introduction, opening bassoon melody

Indeed, the emergence of the ostinato out of phrase B is likely to be felt quite unmistakably by the listener. In a motivic connection of this kind, one that is sustained as part of a train of such connections, the significance of a given variant is felt to be derived at least in part from its point of departure (the opening melody in the bassoon). At the same time, listeners are likely to focus automatically on the *differences* that are projected, not necessarily on any variant taken singly and placed in a studied adjacency with its prior and succeeding variants; what seems to count is the *relationship* that is formed.[33] In the process, the variant, here in the form of the ostinato, acquires a sense of motivation, a sense of having been led from the earlier idea as part of a single, overreaching train of thought. Growth may be sensed as well, and notwithstanding the repetitive, pitch-relational features that would seem to imply just the opposite, namely stasis. The repeat of the melody in full at Rehearsal No. 11, seven bars before the entrance of the ostinato, is likely to sharpen the listener's sense of the connection between the earlier phrase B and the ostinato pattern.

At Rehearsal No. 13 (see Example 5.12c), the ostinato's pitches E♭, D♭, and B♭ are aligned to a dominant seventh on E♭, the upper half of the notorious "Augurs of Spring" chord. Retained at this point is the register and grouping of the three pitches; the $^6_5$ first inversion of the dominant seventh is critical in this respect. The (0 2 3 5) melody at Rehearsal No. 28+4 is wholly diatonic, accountable to the D-scale on E♭ (see Example 5.12d), while the configuration that follows at Rehearsal No. 37 is octatonic (see Example 5.12e). The final (0 2 3 5) tetrachordal fragment shown in Example 5.12f is the principal fragment of the "Dance of the Earth." In triplet figures, its D♭-C-B♭/E♭-B♭ contour preserves in full the original outline of phrase B.

---

[33] For further comment on the psychological processes underlying the listener's recognition of motivic connections of this kind, see Carl Dahlhaus, *Esthetics of Music*, trans. William W. Austin (Cambridge University Press, 1982), 76–77.

Example 5.12. *The Rite of Spring*, phrase B, motivic connections

a)

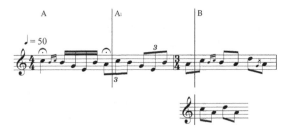

b)

c)

d)

e)

f)

Stretching through the whole of Part I of *The Rite of Spring*, the trail of motivic transformations plotted in Example 5.12 is one of many. The alterations themselves are but a fraction of what a more systematic approach might have yielded.[34] The (0 2 3 5) tetrachord, common to the octatonic and diatonic sets, serves as a basic cell or "common denominator," a piece of vocabulary that is very nearly continuously operative in *The Rite* from one dance movement to the next. When (0 2 5) incomplete or gapped, it may be attached to the dominant seventh chord, and along the lines indicated in connection with the three pitches of the Db-Bb/Eb-Bb ostinato. The referential implications of this attachment are invariably octatonic.

Much of the foregoing applies to *Les Noces* as well, although with a change in focus. While *The Rite of Spring* is ostensibly octatonic or octatonic–diatonic, *Les Noces* is just the opposite. Octatonic relations tend to intrude occasionally on an established diatonic framework. And they tend to do so in response to two types of dramatic action: either they accompany a form of lament or, just the opposite, animated celebration and boisterousness. In the first of these categories (see Examples 3.7 and 4.10), they inflect the diatonic base with a form of chromaticism, accompanied by the swooping grace-notes described in Chapters 3 and 4. In the second category their use is more decorative, reflective of another form of *simulation*. They can seem to represent the composer's attempt to simulate a peasant ensemble, one with coarse, "primitive" instruments. As it happens, however, the simulation itself is in no way inconsistent with structure or "system." In the opening blocks of the fourth tableau, it coincides with subtle and highly elaborate ways of combining and superimposing transpositions of the octatonic set.

The diatonic framework itself is modal in conception, as we have remarked, and often Dorian as well. In the opening two blocks of *Les Noces* (blocks A and B, as we have labeled them in Chapter 4), the (0 2 3 5) tetrachord, (0 2 5) incomplete in terms of (E D B), is both the principal melodic fragment and the connecting link between the diatonic and the octatonic. In block A, (E D B) tilts toward the diatonic side of the referential exchange, however slightly, by way of the embellishing grace-note F♯.[35] With the start of block B at Rehearsal No. 1, however, the orientation is

---

[34] See the more extensive study of these motivic connections in Pieter C. van den Toorn, *Stravinsky and "The Rite of Spring": The Beginnings of a Musical Language* (Berkeley: University of California Press, 1987), 140–43, 48–86.

[35] The D♯ sounded in Pianos I and II on the first downbeat of Block A (see Example 4.1) is chromatic and incidental to the D-E unit, the pitch-class priority of E, the (E D B) trichord, and its grace note F♯. D♯ prefigures a number of subsequent relationships, however, including the intervention of Eb and octatonic relations in the lament at Rehearsal Nos. 35–40 in the second tableau. Notice that D♯ is cut off as a sixteenth note in relation to the sustained Es and, further along, the sustained Ds of the all-important D-E motive. See note 9 in Chapter 4.

block A	(E	D	(C♯)	B)	((A)	(G)	F♯	E)
	(0	2	3	5)	(7	9	10	0)

block B	(E	D	(C♯)	B)	((A)	(G)	F♯	E)
Reh. 1	(0	2	3	5)	(7	9	10	0)

	(E	D	(C♯)	B)	(B♭	(A♭)	(G)	F)
	(0	2	3	5)	(6	8	9	11)

Collection I

Figure 5.1. *Les Noces*, blocks A and B, octatonic–diatonic interaction

octatonic with the entrance of the pitches B♭ and F. Retained as the common link, (E D B) undergoes a transformation. Initially diatonic, it is octatonic at Rehearsal No. 1.

The transaction is summarized in Figure 5.1. First in pitch letters and then in pitch numbers, adjoining (0 2 (3) 5) tetrachords are first fifth-related, diatonic in terms of the Dorian scale, and then tritone-related in terms of the octatonic set. Separated diatonically by a whole-step, they are separated octatonically by a semitone. And in moving from a diatonic framework to the octatonic Collection I framework at Rehearsal No. 1, B♭ and F, pitch numbers 6 and 11 in relation to E as pitch number 0 (the tritone and the 0–11 or major-seventh span), signal the intervention of octatonic relations. (E carries implications of pitch-class priority throughout much of the first tableau; in the opening blocks, its reiteration as a melodic point of departure and return is crucial in this regard.)

At the same time, the transaction is survived by F♯ as the embellishing grace note to the D. The octatonicism at Rehearsal No. 1 is slightly impaired, in other words, with a "diatonic F♯" clashing occasionally with the "octatonic F." The specifics of these relations, octatonic–diatonic rather than merely octatonic, go to the heart of the matter where pitch relations in *Les Noces* and in other Russian-period pieces are concerned. In works such as *Petrushka*, *The Rite of Spring*, *Renard*, and *The Soldier's Tale*, they capture much of what is broadly typical of the period.[36]

---

[36] *Les Noces* ends in much the same fashion that it begins, namely, with a mixed octatonic (Collection I)–diatonic setting. However, instead of a "diatonic F♯" inflecting the (E D B) trichord in blocks A and B of the first tableau, an octatonic figure (E-D)-C♯ inflects (C♯ B G♯) at the close of the fourth (see Example 5.1e). The superimposed (C♯ B) two-note chord in the closing measures of *Les Noces* verticalizes (C♯ B) of the (C♯ B G♯) trichord, and is a transposition of the D-E motive repeated over the bar line throughout blocks A and B in the first tableau.

Even at this early stage of the analysis, however, the formulation is not without complication. To account for the grace-note F♯ in the opening block, the (A G F♯ E) tetrachord was inferred (see Figure 5.1), an extension that completed the Dorian scale in terms of (E D (C♯) B) ((A) (G) F♯ E). No less credibly, however, (B (A) (G♯) F♯) could have been inferred, with the Dorian scale completed above rather than below the (E D (C♯) B) unit. And subsequent events would seem to confirm this latter option.

At Rehearsal No. 9, another fragment is introduced, this time in the chorus (see Example 5.13). Reiterated ostinato-wise throughout much of the remainder of the first tableau and the bulk of the third, this new motive (motive x, as we have labeled it) is another (0 2 5) incomplete or gapped tetrachord, here in terms of (F♯ E C♯). Joined by a persistent D in the accompaniment, however, it would at first seem to imply a continuation of the earlier (E D (C♯) B) unit. Later at Rehearsal No. 10, a whole-tone fragment with D♯ intervenes (again, see Example 5.13): in the tenor solo, (D♯ C♯ B A) is either a whole-tone segment or the central segment of another Dorian scale, (F♯ E D♯ C♯)(B A G♯ F♯).

Following a 5/8 bar of transition before Rehearsal No. 11, motive x returns in the bass solo, transposed to (F E♭ C). Appearing several times throughout the first and third tableaux, the transition, a descending step-wise succession of six triads, will be discussed presently. Relevant here, however, is the top line of this transition, a hexachordal scale implying a gapped Dorian scale in terms of F♯-E-D♯-C♯-B-A-(G♯)-F♯. Joined by earlier tetrachordal articulations, including (E D C♯ B) and (B A G♯ F♯), this new scale yields a chain of three fifth-related (0 2 3 5)s, (F♯ E D♯ C♯), (B A G♯ F♯), and (E D C♯ B). And in moving from this diatonic chain to the octatonicism at Rehearsal No.11, (B A G♯ F♯) survives as the connecting link. Motive x, transposed to (F E♭ C) in the bass solo, signals the intervention of octatonic relations (see Example 5.13).

As we have seen earlier in Example 2.3, however, the octatonicism at Rehearsal No. 11 entails a degree of interference. In the accompanying piano parts, the pitch B♭ lies outside the octatonic transposition in question, namely, Collection II. And at Rehearsal No. 11+3, another transposition of motive x, (E D B) in the soprano solo, is superimposed over the octatonic component. Thus, while (B A G♯ F♯) and (E D B) yield a gapped Dorian scale in the accompanying piano parts and soprano solo, (B A G♯ F♯) and (F E♭ C) form a gapped octatonic scale. As illustrated with pitch letters in Figure 5.2, the diatonic layers are superimposed over the octatonic ones at this point, with the result a form of octatonic–diatonic interaction involving the D-scale on B and Collection II. (B A G♯ F♯) prevails as the shared connecting link at this juncture. The outline itself stretches from the opening of *Les Noces* to the referential interaction at Rehearsal No. 11.

Example 5.13. *Les Noces*, first tableau

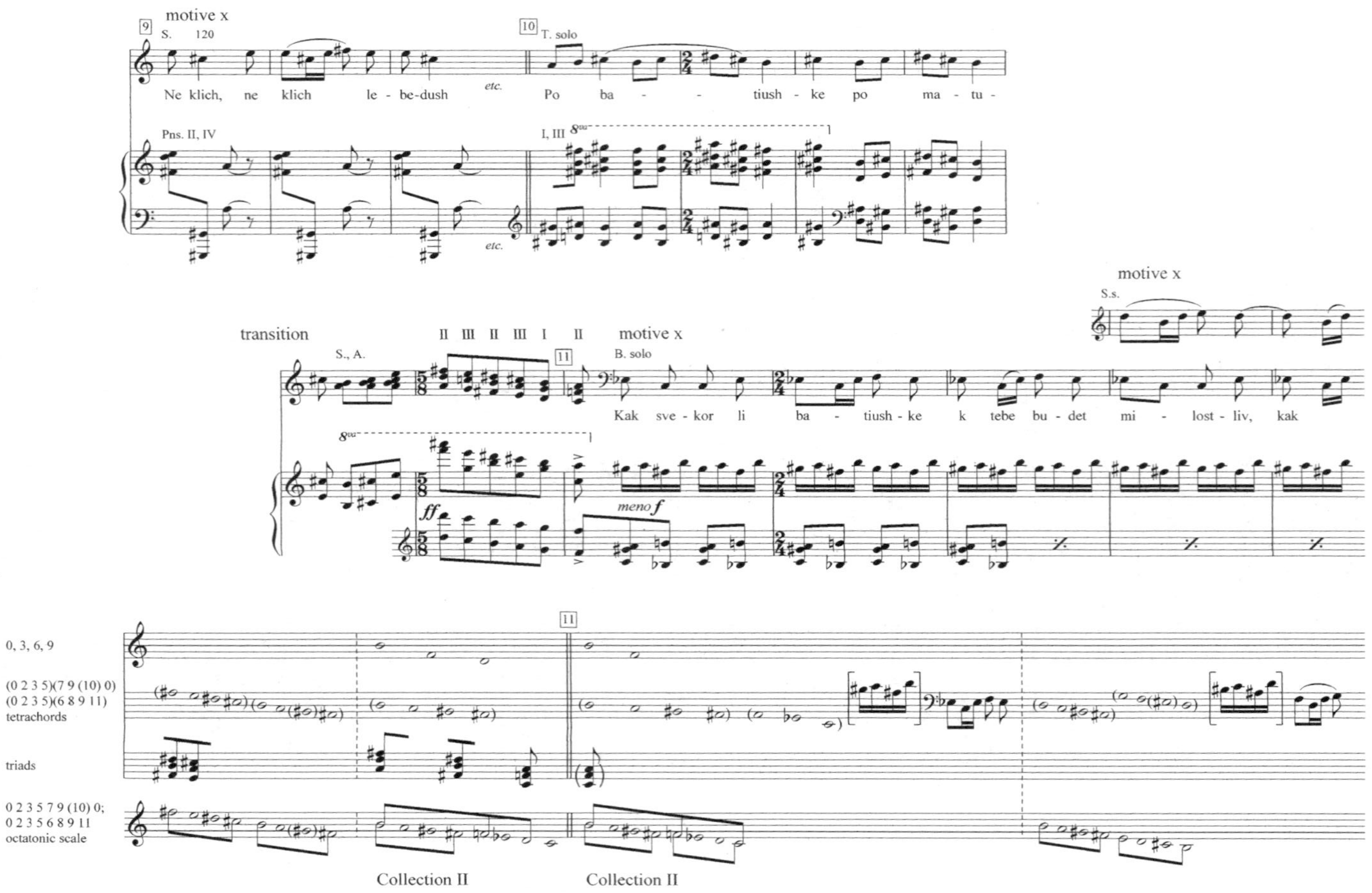

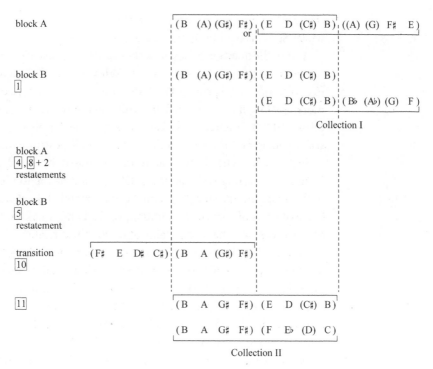

Figure 5.2. *Les Noces*, opening blocks, (0 2 (3) 5) tetrachords, octatonic–diatonic interaction

Of course, not all blocks and sections in *Les Noces* lend themselves readily to an account by way of scales or scalar orderings. Most passages can be identified along diatonic and/or octatonic lines, to be sure, but the incompleteness of the articulation, especially where the diatonic set is concerned, can pose problems in this regard. This is as true of the Dorian mode as it is of the other diatonic orderings, notwithstanding the adjoining (0 2 3 5) tetrachords of the D-scale, a symmetrical formation that would seem to follow quite readily from the (0 2 3 5) tetrachordal emphasis of *Les Noces*. Moreover, the issue of pitch-class priority, to the extent that such priority can be heard and understood to assert itself by means of reiteration, phenomenal accents, and persistence (by means of the *survival* of a given entity from one block to the next), can sometimes seem beside the point as well. The matter concerns not articulation alone but fundamental characteristics as well. The sorts of priorities among pitch classes identified with tonal processes and the major or C-scale ordering of the diatonic set do not obtain in settings where the symmetries of the (0 2 3 5) tetrachord and those of the various Dorian and octatonic orderings prevail. In Stravinsky's music, a stratification of reiterating tetrachords or triads, often (0, 3, 6, 9) related, is likely to add to the sense of standstill among the competing entities or pitch classes, the "polarity" to which Stravinsky himself referred in this connection.[37]

And so the question arises: in seeking a wider, global view of *Les Noces*, can we circumvent some of these issues? With the (0 2 3 5) tetrachord and its (0 2 5) subset as the principal melodic units of vocabulary, can we retreat to a more abstract model, one which, while retaining the diatonic idea of fifth-related (0 2 3 5) tetrachords, can sidestep issues of pitch-class priority and scalar demarcation? Can something of the whole be captured by such means?

Such an analytic-theoretical retreat is posed by the Master Chart of Figure 5.3. Starting with the (F♯ E D♯ C♯) unit at the top left-hand corner of this diagram, the (0 2 3 5) tetrachord is extended downward through the circle of fifths or 7-cycle. In addition, vertical lines mark off the intersection of this cycle with the three chains of minor-third related (0 2 3 5)s. Each of these latter 3-cycles is shown to "contain" four interlocking (0 2 3 5)s which together imply one of the three content-distinguishable octatonic transpositions, labeled I, II, and III. The descending cycle of fifth-related (0 2 3 5)s is thus read horizontally from left to right across Figure 5.3 (see the encircling arrow), while the descending minor-third related (0 2 3 5)s are read vertically. The four cycles of major-third related (0 2 3 5)s that appear diagonally across the vertical lines are of no particular concern to pitch relations in *Les Noces*. However, the lines drawn diagonally within the initial Collection III column refer to the (0 1 3 4) tetrachord, another subset of the octatonic set. Prevalent in neoclassical and even in serial works as a cohesive melodic factor, the (0 1 3 4) tetrachord figures hardly at all in *Les Noces*, however, or indeed in Russian-period works more generally.

In Figure 5.3, we venture about as close as we can to the construction of a pitch-relational "system" for *Les Noces*. As with all abstractions of a high order, the problem is one of maintaining meaningful contact with the concrete point of departure. Not all blocks and sections can be shown to comply readily with the resultant format, even in the first tableau. And there are melodies and fragments which are not Dorian in shape or content, even if minor-third gaps and the pentatonic character of these gaps remain immediately identifying features. Examined closely in Chapter 4 (see Examples 4.6a–d), the two segments a and b of the opening block of the second tableau are a case in point. Associated with the character of the

---

[37] See Igor Stravinsky, *Poetics of Music in the Form of Six Lessons*, trans. Arthur Knodel and Ingolf Dahl (New York: Vintage, 1956). 39–44. The relevance of the notion of "polarity" to octatonic pitch relations in Stravinsky's music is pursued in Arthur Berger, "Problems of Pitch Organization in Stravinsky," in Benjamin Boretz and Edward T. Cone, eds., *Perspectives on Schoenberg and Stravinsky* (New York: W. W. Norton, 1972), 137–38. See, also, Pieter C. van den Toorn, *The Music of Igor Stravinsky* (New Haven: Yale University Press, 1983), 51–52, 61–64.

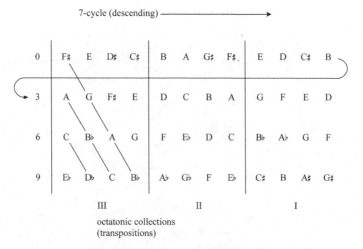

Figure 5.3. Master chart, (0 2 3 5) tetrachords, intersecting 7- and 3-cycles

Groom and the curling of his "locks" or *kudri*, these segments are not Dorian from the standpoint of the (0 2 3 5) tetrachord or the Dorian scale. Instead, the A-scale on D would seem to be implicated as a referential ordering, owing not only to the reiterated D as the likely pitch-class of priority, but also to a persistent B♭ in the accompanying parts.

At the same time, questions of order or succession are largely ignored. Figure 5.3 is atemporal in this regard. "Less real than imaginary," as one observer has described the impression left by Hugo Riemann's tables of large-scale pitch relations (*Tonnetze*),[38] the simplified network pictured here is inevitably a "conceptual grid," a "vast abstraction from musical experience."[39] Given the diatonic and octatonic sets as underlying assumptions of this music (categories of *reference* where content and scalar ordering are concerned), the intersection of these sets and orderings is represented graphically by means of the (0 2 3 5) tetrachord. The representation comes in the form of a *resource*; what may be inferred more specifically in connection with *Les Noces* are

[38] The idea of the *Tonnetz*, an all-embracing chart of tonal relations, may be traced to the writings of Hugo Riemann and other music theorists of the nineteenth and early twentieth centuries; see, especially, Hugo Riemann, "Ideen zu einer 'Lehre von den Tonvorstellungen'," *Jahrbuch der Musikbibliothek Peters*, 1914–15. And see the excellent translation of the latter with commentary in Robert W. Wason and Elizabeth West Marvin, "Ideas for a Study 'On the Imagination of Tone'," *Journal of Music Theory* (1992): 81–117. At the same time, however, Figures 5.3, 5.4, 5.5, 5.6, and 5.7 in this present chapter stem from more recent developments in neo-Riemannian theory; see, for example, Brian Hyer, "Reimag(in)ing Riemann," *Journal of Music Theory* 39 (1995): 101–38, and Richard Cohn, "Neo-Riemannian Operations, Parsimonious Trichords, and their *Tonnetz* Representations," *Journal of Music Theory* 41 (1997): 1–66. The obvious distinction of these present, simplified models rests with the unit of vocabulary itself, which is not the triad, but the (0 2 3 5) tetrachord.

[39] See Hyer, *Reimag(in)ing Riemann*, 101–02.

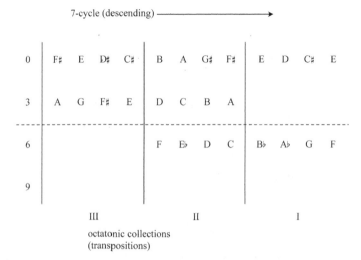

Figure 5.4. *Les Noces*, first tableau, intersecting 7- and 3-cycles

pockets of concentration, chains of three or more (0 2 3 5)s from within the completed 7-cycle.

Thus, in the first tableau, a string of five (0 2 (3) 5) tetrachords predominates on the diatonic side of the referential coin; see the dotted line drawn horizontally across the modified chart in Figure 5.4. Irrespective of order, in other words, five (0 2 (3) 5)s linked along the 7-cycle may be inferred from the blocks and sections of the first tableau, each of these committed diatonically in one way or another. Below the dotted line in Figure 5.4, the (F E♭ (D) C) and (B♭ (A♭) (G) F) tetrachords are tied more specifically to the octatonic intervention at Rehearsal Nos. 1 and 11.

So, too, in this same connection, in the lengthy passage of lament at Rehearsal Nos.35–40 in the second tableau, as examined briefly in Chapter 4 (see Example 4.10), the octatonic engagement proceeds vertically up the Collection III column; introduced in terms of (E♭ D♭ B♭) in the bass solo, the vocal fragment's initial (0 2 5) is subsequently transposed to (C B♭ G) and (A G E). Octatonic relations proceed vertically up or down one of the three transpositional columns in Figure 5.3, while diatonic relations proceed horizontally.

Much of the material in the fourth tableau may be isolated even more dramatically. The three (0 2 3 5) tetrachords of the fourth and final horizontal line of Figure 5.3, (0 2 3 5)s specifically *not* engaged in the first tableau, are heavily engaged in the fourth. This engagement involves, above all, the (D♭ C♭ B♭ A♭) tetrachord, the final link in the complete cycle of twelve fifth-related (0 2 3 5)s. Touched upon already in connection with

Example 5.1e, the latter tetrachord figures at the outset of the fourth tableau and, enharmonically in terms of (C♯ B (A♯) G♯), heavily at the close as well.

The point of the *Tonnetz* sketched in Figure 5.5 lies, once again, with the intersection of the 7-cycle and the 2–1 ordering of the octatonic scale. Moving horizontally from left to right, an ascending 7-cycle intersects with the 3-cycles, which are read vertically. Whole tones or 2-cycles are featured along the northeast-to-southwest diagonal. Each pitch-designation in this display can stand for a single (0 2 3 5) tetrachord, the unit of vocabulary, which is read in descending order; in the second horizontal line from the top, for example, the encircled pitch E can stand for (E D C♯ B). At the same time, however, (0 2 3 5)s, (0 2 5)s, and (0 3 5)s are encased within the network itself, as can be seen by the solid and dotted lines and the resultant squares, parallelograms, and triangles. Beginning initially with (E D C♯ B), (E D B) and (E C♯ B), double triangles (parallelograms) mark off complete (0 2 3 5)s while single triangles mark off (0 2 5)s and (0 3 5)s. At the bottom of the diagram, pairs of 3-cycles are bracketed and identified by Roman numerals, showing the given octatonic collections (or transpositions).

More specifically still, the (0 2 5)s and (0 3 5)s in Figure 5.5 are distinguished from one another by their westward and eastward-pointing triangles, respectively. The two are inversionally related, and may be compared in this respect to the parallel relationship (or P) between major and minor triads. Thus, in moving from (E D B) to (E C♯ B) (see the arrow pointing southwest in Figure 5.5), the boundary pitches E and B are retained as common tones, while the middle pitch shifts by semitone, D to C♯. In Riemannian terms, the arrows pointing northwest and northeast signify transformations analogous to those defined by the relative (R) and *Leittonwechsel* (L), respectively.[40]

We should caution, however, that, as are shown in Figure 5.5, the P, R, and L operations and the parsimonious voice-leading implied by these operations are relevant scarcely at all to the octatonic or octatonic–diatonic passages in Russian-period works such as *The Rite of Spring, Les Noces,* and *Renard.*[41] Not only is the minor form of the (0 2 5) basic

---

[40] Figure 5.5, featuring (0 2 3 5) tetrachords and (0 2 5/0 3 5) trichords, is modeled after the triadic *Tonnetze* in Cohn, "Neo-Riemannian Operations," 14–15.

[41] By *parsimony* is meant a smooth type of voice leading in which the two common tones between third-related or parallel triads are sustained as such, while the third tone moves by semitone or tone. See the discussion of "maximally smooth" voice leading of this kind in Cohn, "Neo-Riemannian Operations," 1–7. Our point here, however, is that, when moving octatonically in Stravinsky's music from, say, (E D B) to (C♯ B G♯), the minor form of the first of these trichords, (E C♯ B), which would mirror this type of voice leading, is usually missing (see Figure 5.5). Analogously, when moving triadically from, say, (E G♯ B) to (G B D), (E G B) is most often absent (see Figure 5.7). By contrast, a *parsimonious graph* is one in which the

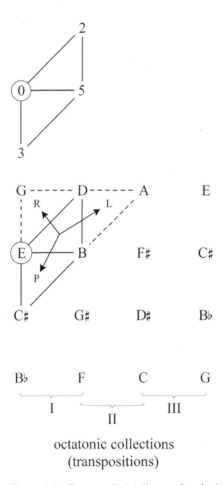

octatonic collections
(transpositions)

Figure 5.5. *Tonnetz*, (0 2 3 5) tetrachords, (0 2 5/0 3 5) trichordal subsets; *Les Noces*, octatonic–diatonic interaction

cell, (0 3 5), most often missing from such passages, but the relevant (0 2 5)s tend to be transposed quite literally along one of the 3-cycles, the (0, 3, 6, 9) partitioning elements of Collection I, II, or III, with the latter underscored as a result.

More pertinent to the particulars of octatonic–diatonic interaction in *Les Noces* is the global perspective outlined by the shaded triangles in Figure 5.6, according to which *Les Noces* begins with (E D B) in the first tableau and ends with (C♯ B G♯) at the conclusion of the fourth. ((E D B) is featured at subsequent restatements of blocks A and B as well, of course,

common tones linking, say, (E D B), (C♯ B G♯) and (F♯ E C♯) are located at the vertices of the graphic shapes representing those trichords (see Figure 5.6). They are represented as points of overlap.

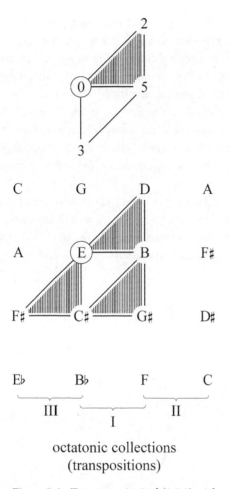

octatonic collections
(transpositions)

Figure 5.6. *Tonnetz*, principal (0 2 5) trichords (shaded triangles); *Les Noces*, global perspective

and heavily again at Rehearsal Nos. 68–74 in the third tableau.) These minor third-related (0 2 5)s, (E D B) and (C♯ B G♯), are octatonic (Collection I), as can be seen by their appearance along the relevant 3-cycles in Figure 5.6. At the same time, (E D B) is succeeded by motive x in terms of (F♯ E C♯) at Rehearsal Nos. 9 and 20, where the common tone E is sustained registrally. An aspect of smooth voice-leading, the retention of this common tone allows the transposition up a whole step to be exposed that much more readily. ((F♯ E C♯) is featured at Rehearsal Nos. 14–21 in the first tableau, and reappears at Nos. 70–77 in the third as well. It is paired with (C♯ B G♯) at Nos. 75–77.)

The larger point, however, is that these principal renditions of the basic cell in Figure 5.6 are (0 2 5)s. Just as with the vast majority of such renditions in *Les Noces* (indeed, in *The Rite of Spring* as well), they are the westward-pointing triangles in Figure 5.6, not the eastward-pointing ones. And this is true of the major triad as well, as plotted along the 7- and 3-cycles of the triadic *Tonnetz* sketched in Figure 5.7, along the horizontal and vertical axes, respectively. Here, too, in octatonic contexts of the Russian period, the minor triad is evident scarcely at all as an intermediary between transpositions of the major triad or dominant seventh along one of the minor-third cycles.

More generally, too, as they affect the analytical application of these various charts and *Tonnetze* to *Les Noces* and other works of Stravinsky's Russian period, the sorts of patterned chains that have resulted from the application of neo-Riemannian operations to selected passages in the works

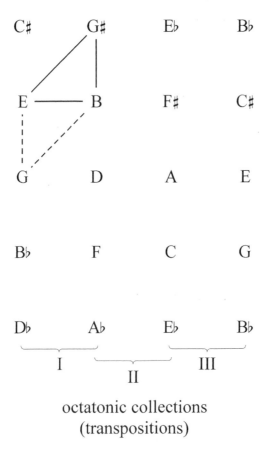

octatonic collections
(transpositions)

Figure 5.7. *Tonnetz*, triads; octatonic–diatonic interaction

of composers such as Wagner and Liszt are not ordinarily available here.[42] This is because the idea of a steady, bar-by-bar *progression* of (0 2 (3) 5)s, triads, and dominant sevenths is consistently negated by the registrally fixed points at which such units are repeated and statically superimposed. Although harmonic change and even progress is possible between larger blocks of material, such is not ordinarily the case on a more local basis. In reading up or down one of the minor-third chains in Figures 5.6 and 5.7, the octatonically related (0 2 (3) 5)s and triads tend to oscillate or become bunched together in practice, and hence not to succeed one another as part of a regular pattern of progression.

And quite apart from the question of vocabulary, different transpositional paths and forms of set-class intersection have been emphasized by neo-Riemannian theory and analysis. With the triad as the unit of vocabulary, Richard Cohn's charts have featured the major-third or 4-cycle and its intersection with set class 6–20. In this way, to follow Cohn's argument, triadic yet non-tonal passages in nineteenth-century music are made to relate to the atonal universe of the twentieth.[43] Here, of course, with a more explicit view toward *Les Noces* and other works of Stravinsky's Russian period, it is the minor-third or 3-cycle and its intersection with the octatonic set, set class 8–28, that are underscored.

Complete and incomplete chains of minor third-related triads and dominant sevenths, local or more regional in character, abound in the music of Liszt and Wagner, of course, while, in that of Stravinsky's Russian predecessors, the 4-cycle is not absent altogether. (See, in connection with the latter, the major third-related triads or set class 6–20 at the opening of Rimsky-Korsakov's "Antar" Symphony No. 2.) As a transpositional path in Stravinsky's Russian-period works and in many neoclassical ones as well, however, the minor-third cycle prevails very nearly to the exclusion of the 4-cycle.

Octatonic–diatonic interaction in the first and third tableaux

The passage of transition alluded to in our discussion above of the opening blocks of *Les Noces* occurs five times throughout the first and third tableaux; at Rehearsal Nos. 10+4, 16+1, 17+1, and 20+3 in the first, and at No. 67+5 in

---

[42] See, for example, Hyer, "Reimag(in)ing Riemann," 111–13. A complete chain of chromatic third relations, interpreted in neo-Riemannian fashion as a chain of P and L relations (with the parallel relation preceding the *Leittonwechsel*), is inferred from a passage in Wagner's *Die Walküre*, Act III, Scene 3. Or see, in David Lewin, "Rehearings: Wagner, *The Ring* and *Parsifal*," *19th Century Music* 15, no. 1 (1992): 56–57, the patterned chain of alternating P and L relations, as inferred from a variant of the Communion theme in Wagner's *Parsifal*, Act I.

[43] See Richard Cohn, "Maximally Smooth Cycles, Hexatonic Systems, and the Analysis of Late-Romantic Triadic Progressions," *Music Analysis* 15, no. 1 (1996): 9–40.

the third. In the three occurrences furnished by the quotations in Examples 5.13, 5.14, and 5.16 (Nos. 16+1 and 17+1 in the first tableau are omitted), the passage serves to unite a diatonic block at Nos. 9, 20, and 65 (where motive x in terms of (F♯ E C♯) in the vocal parts is the (0 2 5) basic cell) with a variety of octatonic (Collection II) or octatonic (Collection II)–diatonic settings at Rehearsal Nos. 11, 21, and 68. At Rehearsal No. 11 in the first tableau, for example, the octatonic (Collection II) component consists of the tritone-related (0 2 (3) 5) tetrachords (B A G♯ F♯) and (F E♭ (D) C); (B A G♯ F♯) serves as the connecting link to the diatonic component in the soprano solo and accompanying piano parts. The interaction, summarized in Figure 5.2, comes at the end of a trail of such relations.

So, too, the transition at Rehearsal No. 10+4 partakes of both sides of the referential interaction, the diatonic from which it departs and the octatonic–diatonic to which it leads (see Example 5.13). Harmonically, six major triads in second inversion descend in stepwise succession. Yet the rationale for this succession is linear as well as harmonic. The hexachordal scale mentioned above, F♯-E-D♯-C♯-B-A, is actually one of three superimposed hexachords, each of these an instance of the same type, namely (0 2 3 5 7 9). The motivation is securely fastened in these terms.

Of course, the (0 2 3 5 7 9) hexachord could be viewed alternatively as a six-note subset of the Dorian scale. Such a conception leaves the lower of the D-scale's two (0 2 3 5) tetrachords incomplete, gapped in the by now familiar manner: (F♯ E D♯ C♯)(B A (G♯) F♯). And this would underscore, in analytic-theoretical terms once again, the incompleteness of the articulation in *Les Noces*, the fundamentally gapped, pentatonic, or "anhemitonic" character of the melodic invention along with the archaic nature of the folk element.

Yet the (0 2 3 5 7 9) hexachord harbors a subset structure of its own, a vocabulary of triads and (0 2 3 5) tetrachords that can assert itself as a cohesive frame of reference even in contexts where, by means of a closing of the relevant minor-third gaps, a seventh pitch class does impose itself. Such contexts are characterized in the main by reiterating, and often oscillating, back-and-forth motions. They include not only the transition and its restatements, but, as we shall see, a number of lengthy blocks in the first and third tableaux as well.

Thus, while the (F♯ E D♯ C♯ B A) hexachord presides on top of the succession of triads (or is central to the activity, especially when, at Rehearsal Nos. 10 and 67, the preceding tenor fragment is included), the transition actually contains three superimposed (0 2 3 5 7 9) hexachords: (F♯ E D♯ C♯ B A), (D C B A G F), and (A G F♯ E D C), reading down from top to bottom. (See Example 5.15.) Each of these superimposed (0 2 3 5 7 9) hexachords is represented by its two major triads, a whole step apart: The

Example 5.14. *Les Noces*, third tableau

(B D♯ F♯) and (A C♯ E) triads represent (F♯ E D♯ C♯ B A), (G B D) and (F A C)
represent (D C B A G F), while (D F♯ A) and (C E G) represent (A G F♯ E D
C). A total of six triads are engaged in this way, each in second inversion. So,
too, each pair of triads *exhausts* the particular (0 2 3 5 7 9) hexachord of which
it is a member; each pair *partitions* the relevant hexachord in this way. And in
the octatonic–diatonic blocks that follow the transitional succession at
Rehearsal Nos. 11, 21, and 68, the six triads could have implicated any one
of the three octatonic transpositions. In fact, Collection III seems favored in
this respect, owing to the (F♯ E D♯ C♯) and (A G F♯ E) "upper" (0 2 3 5)
tetrachords of (F♯ E D♯ C♯ B A) and (A G F♯ E D C). But Collection I is also
implicated, first by the (G F D) trichord and then by the (G B D) triad of the

Example 5.14. (contd.)

(D C B A G F) hexachord; and, subsequently at No.18 (not shown here), the transition does proceed to a Collection I passage.

Note that above the actual quotation of the transition in Examples 5.13, 5.14, 5.15, and 5.16, the three collections (transpositions) are identified by Roman numerals. Crucial here is the alternation between Collections II and III; only the Collection I triad (G B D) upsets this pattern. As we shall see, rapid alternations of this kind between two of the three octatonic collections are featured regularly in the instrumental accompaniment of the fourth tableau; with a point of departure established early on, the implications were stretched further in the fourth. In addition, at Rehearsal No. 67+6 (see Example 5.14), the transition is accompanied in Pianos I, II, and III by

Example 5.14. (contd.)

an *ascending* scale of second-inversion major triads. Although clashing with the triads of the descending succession, these new triads adhere to the given octatonic collections. They are subsets of the transpositions (see the Roman numerals in Example 5.14), and manage, in this way, to preserve the octatonic sound at each eighth-note beat. Vertically speaking, the clashing of the superimposed triads is entirely octatonic, in other words, with each of the resultant "chords" conceived with reference to a single collection.

At the same time, within the system of alternation established for the transition, the new triads at Rehearsal No. 67+6 offer a heightened form of dissonance, one that is coloristic in character. More specifically, the sound of these rapidly clashing triads can suggest the rattling, off-pitch sound of

Example 5.14. (contd.)

Example 5.15. *Les Noces*, transition, (0 2 3 5 7 9) hexachords

Example 5.16. *Les Noces*, first tableau

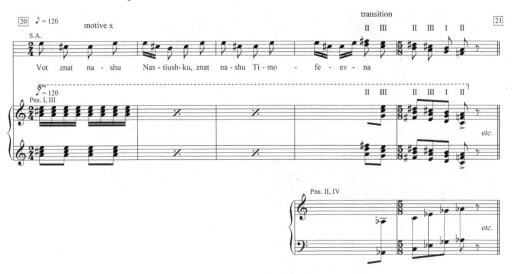

"primitive," peasant instruments, the sorts of bands that may well have lain in the back of Stravinsky's mind at the time.

And so the question arises at Rehearsal Nos. 11, 21, and 68: Why Collection II? Why should Collection II have followed the transition in three out of its five occurrences? The answer would seem to rest with the triadic articulation of the three superimposed (0 2 3 5 7 9) hexachords, the succession of six second-inversion major triads rooted on D, C, B, A, G, and F, along with the triads of the accompanying ascending scale at Rehearsal No. 67+6. Thus, three of the original six triads, (B D♯ F♯), (D F♯ A), and (F A C), refer to Collection II. And the triadic succession is flanked by Collection II's tritone-related triads, (B D♯ F♯) and (F A C). Moreover, that Stravinsky was conscious of this transitional commitment to Collection II seems evident in the (near) repeat of the transition at Nos. 17+5 and 20+3 (see Example 5.16): A dominant seventh on A♭ is outlined in Piano IV to complete a (B, A♭, F, D) symmetrically-defined partitioning of this collection in terms of its triads and dominant sevenths.

Consequently, the passage of transition is interpreted as an interaction between Collection II and the (F♯ E D♯ C♯ B A) hexachord, with the connecting link discernible in terms not only of (B A F♯), but also of the (B D♯ F♯) triad. (See the dotted line in the analytical notation accompanying Examples 5.13 and 5.14.)

Still, the octatonic setting at Rehearsal Nos. 68–70 in the third tableau (see Example 5.14) merits further consideration. For while the instrumental

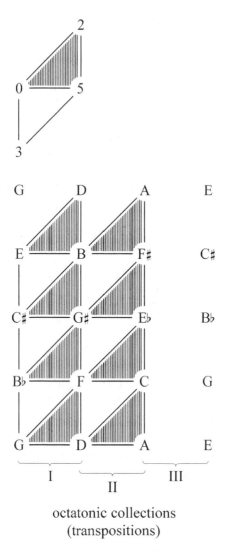

octatonic collections
(transpositions)

Figure 5.8. *Tonnetz*, (0 2 5) trichords (shaded triangles), octatonic Collections I and II; *Les Noces*, third tableau, Reh. Nos. 68–70

component at Nos. 68–70 refers to Collection II (the G♯-F-B-D basso ostinato of Piano IV articulates the (B, G♯, F, D) symmetrically-defined partitioning elements of Collection II, the roots of the reiterating dominant sevenths in Pianos I and III), the vocal ensemble introduces a succession of (0 2 5) trichords at E, C♯, B♭, and G. These (0 2 5)s are transpositions of motive x. Introduced diatonically at Rehearsal Nos. 9, 14, 20, and 65 in terms of (F♯ E C♯), motive x is here confined to a single octatonic transposition. And while pitch numbers 2 and 5 of these (0 2 5)s are accountable to Collection II – and are, indeed, metrically accented in this particular version of the basic motive – pitch number 0 as E, C♯, B♭, and G lies *outside* Collection II. In fact, this vocal (E, C♯, B♭, G) symmetrically-defined succession of (0 2 5)s is, in its entirety, an (0 2 5) tetrachordal partitioning of Collection I. The succession is introduced in terms of (E D B) in the bass solo at No. 68, and is subsequently transposed to (C♯ B G♯) in the soprano at No. 68+2, (B♭ A♭ F) in the bass at No. 69+2, and (G F D) in the soprano at No. 69+4. And so the octatonic block at Nos. 68–70 refers to *both* Collections II and I. Along with the tremolo in Piano II, the (B, A♭, F, D) symmetrically-defined dominant sevenths in Pianos I and III implicate Collection II, while the (E, C♯, B♭, G) symmetrically-defined succession of (0 2 5)s in the vocal parts implicates Collection I.

Moreover, the G♯-F-B-D basso ostinato of Piano IV is the link connecting these two octatonic transpositions. Reproduced in Figure 5.8 is the earlier *Tonnetz* of Figure 5.5, extended somewhat in order to accommodate this present collectional interaction. Two rows of shaded, westward-pointing triangles are shown descending along the vertical axis, the first of these representing the vocal component, the succession of (0 2 5)s at E, C♯, B♭, and G, accountable to Collection I, and the second representing the instrumental contribution in Pianos I and III, the (0 2 5)s of the (0 2 5 8) dominant sevenths at B, G♯, F, and D, accountable to Collection II. Splitting the two rows is the B-G♯-F-D minor-third chain, the diminished seventh shared by Collections I and II. Also useful in this context is the hyper-octatonic network plotted in Figure 2.1. Moving from the first to the second of the three circles in this regional diagram, the lower case letters of the first circle become the upper case letters of the second. (A parsimonious graph of the dominant seventh traversing the 3- and 7-cycles would require a three-dimensional *Tonnetz*.)[44] Partially parsimonious, the graph of Figure 5.9 shows the two diminished sevenths of Collection II along the horizontal axis, with A-F♯-D♯-C running down the middle and flanked on each side by B, G♯, F, and D, the roots of the four dominant-seventh chords. The latter are represented by the alternating blank and shaded triangles.

---

[44] See the following four papers in the *Journal of Music Theory* 42 , no. 2 (1998), a special issue devoted to neo-Riemannian theory: Adrian Childs, "Moving Beyond Neo-Riemannian Triads: Exploring a Transformational Model for Seventh Chords," 181–94; Edward Gollin, "Some Aspects of Three-Dimensional *Tonnetze*," 195–206; Stephen Soderberg, "The T-Hex Constellation," 207–18, and Jack Douthett and Peter Steinbach, "Parsimonious Graphs: A Study in Parsimony, Contextual Transformations, and Modes of Limited Transposition," 241–64. Each of these papers deals with the minor seventh and half-diminished seventh chords as well as the dominant seventh.

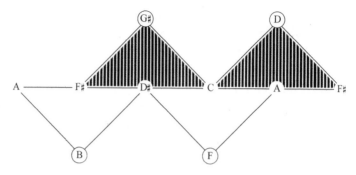

Figure 5.9. *Les Noces*, octatonic Collection II, dominant sevenths

Significantly, too, as the analytical portion of Example 5.14 makes clear, the block at Rehearsal Nos. 68–70 moves very smoothly into the Collection I block at Nos. 70–72, where the G♯-F-B-D basso ostinato in Piano IV may persevere as the shared diminished seventh chord between Collections II and I. Indeed, pausing for a moment, we might consider how impressively the block at Nos. 68–70 demonstrates the conditions of balance, harmonic stasis, "polarity," and deadlock associated with the symmetry of the octatonic set and its engagement in *Les Noces* and in Stravinsky's music more generally. The poised equilibrium exhibited by the varying rhythmic periods is exquisite, a triumph of the octatonic imagination. Few passages in Russian-period works can match the invention here, the subtle play of symmetrical confinement that unfolds through a superimposition of fragments whose entrances, spaced irregularly in relation to each other and the 2/4 meter, effect a vertical (or "harmonic") coincidence that is constantly changing. In this respect, the block is a stratification. The steady rhythmic period of four quarter-note beats in Piano IV stands in opposition to the irregularly spaced entrances of the dominant sevenths in Pianos I and III.

Even the G♯-F-B-D basso ostinato, the principal means of support for the 2/4 meter, is qualified in unusual ways. Far from straightforward, it, too, harbors a complication. For it consists not of a single layer, but, remarkably here, of a form of stratification of its own. Since the last two quarter notes of the pattern are tied as a half note, only three of its four pitches are included. As can be seen by the brackets below the stave for Piano IV in Example 5.17, a fifth beat is required to accommodate the fourth pitch, a D. From within the same ostinato, then, two separate layers may be inferred, two systems of repetition, the one defined by duration, the other by pitch. Both systems are traced in their entirety in Example 5.17, by way of the brackets above and below the stave; only after sixteen beats is there a point of intersection

Example 5.17. *Les Noces*, third tableau, basso ostinato; patterns defined by a) duration and b) pitch

between the two. And here, too, as an added complication, a high degree of independence may be inferred. Thus, the resultant points of intersection at Rehearsal Nos. 69+1, 70, 71, and just prior to 72 fail to coincide with points exhibiting a comparable significance in the remaining fragments in Pianos I, II, III, and the vocal parts.

At the same time, support for the 2/4 meter can be traced to a variety of sources, of which the G♯-F-B-D basso ostinato, as defined in terms of duration, is but one. At least initially, the reiterating dominant sevenths in Pianos I and III are also a means of support. Entering on the downbeat at Rehearsal No. 68+3 (see Example 5.14), the pattern of this reiteration consists of an eighth note and two sixteenths, followed, on the second beat, by two eighths. And with each downbeat marked by a return to the same (B A F♯ D♯) dominant seventh, the 2/4 meter is powerfully reinforced. Soon enough, however, a form of displacement intervenes. Although not shown in Example 5.14, entrances of this dominant seventh fragment at Rehearsal No. 69+5 are shifted from the first to the second quarter-note beat of the 2/4 bar line; the initial span of ten quarter-note beats is followed by an irregular span of seven beats. Consistent with Stravinsky's displacement schemes more generally, what begins as a form of support ends by becoming a source of disruption and upheaval. For the listener, the displacement is likely to be disruptive of the half-note beat and hence of the 2/4 design itself. As the likely tactus, the quarter-note beat may continue unimpeded.

Finally, in the concluding blocks of the third tableau at Rehearsal Nos. 78–87, the (A G F♯ E D C) diatonic hexachord may be inferred as central to the articulation. A closing of its minor-third gap, C–A, may render the surroundings fully diatonic with a B as pitch number 10 (tending to implicate the D-scale on A, but with this hexachord's partitioning formulae intact), or signal the intervention of octatonic relations with a "chromatic" B♭ as pitch number 11. Alternatively, a "chromatic" E♭ as pitch number 6 could signal such an intervention.

Thus, at Nos. 78–80 (see Example 5.14), the reiterating G-F♯-E-D-A-(G) fragment in Pianos I and III and the vocal ensemble refer to the (A G F♯ E D C) hexachord. As earlier at Nos. 68–70, Collection II's dominant sevenths on B, F, and D intervene off-the-beat (here in Pianos II and IV, *sforzando*), so that the block refers to both the (A G F♯ E D C) hexachord and the octatonic Collection II. Then, in the following block at No. 80, the G-F♯-E-D-A-(G) fragment is harmonized in terms of the (A G F♯E D C) hexachord's two major triads, (D F♯ A) and (C E G). This (D F♯ A)-(C E G) harmonization is superimposed on a third triad, (A C E) in Piano IV. (As mentioned earlier, the (0 2 3 5 7 9) hexachord yields three triads as subsets; (A G F♯ E D C), yields the whole step-related major triads (D F♯ A) and (C E G), and the minor triad, (A C E).)

Then, at No. 82, the "diatonic B" in the vocal parts as pitch number 10 is replaced by an "octatonic B♭" as the chromatic pitch number 11 in the octatonic scale's 2–1 ordering; and the (A G F♯ E D C) diatonic framework of Rehearsal Nos. 78–82 gives way to a fully committed octatonic Collection III framework at Nos. 82–87. In this final move, A and the (A G F♯ E) tetrachord prevail as shared, between-block (and between-reference) con-necting links. So, too, in this lengthy concluding block of the third tableau (which celebrates the departure of the Bride), the two mothers of the Bride and Bridegroom gather in hushed lament (lamentando and *p*, subito), murmuring their mournful farewells (see Example 3.7). A variant of the earlier lament of the parents of the Groom (see Example 4.10), the one here is sung to an A-G-F♯-A♯-C♯-C-B♭-G-(A) fragment, which, wholly octatonic and accountable to Collection III, is systematically transposed to the remaining (0, 3, 6, 9) symmetrically defined partitioning elements of Collection III.

But the entire concluding section of the third tableau at Nos. 78–87 exemplifies the ways in which, as detailed earlier in this chapter, ostensibly

diatonic settings are intruded upon by octatonic relations: the D-scale or
(0 2 3 5 7 9) hexachord, through their two complete or incomplete (0 2 3 5)
(7 9 (10) 0) tetrachords, may implicate two of the three octatonic collections
in octatonic–diatonic interaction. At Rehearsal Nos. 78–80, the lower (D C
A) unit of the (A G F♯ E)(D C A) hexachord implicates Collection II in
terms of this collection's dominant sevenths at B, F, and D, while the upper
(A G F♯ E) tetrachord implicates Collection III at Nos. 80–87 by means
initially of an "intruding" pitch number 11, the B♭.[45]

Interactions in the fourth tableau

Magical above all in the fourth tableau are the continuing transformations of
the basic motive, the (0 2 3 5) tetrachord and its (0 2 5) gapped, trichordal
form. Some of these transformations are traced in Examples 5.18a–b, and
5.19a–f. Beginning with the repeat structure of the opening fragment (Example
5.18a) and ending with the culminating block at Rehearsal Nos. 133–35
(Example 5.19f), the list includes several restatements as well. In all, eight
different versions of the basic motive are stated in chronological order.

The opening fragment, (E♭ D♭ C♭ B♭) in the chorus (see Example 5.18a), is
not a Dorian tetrachord. However, D♭, as the point of departure and return, is
clearly the pitch class of priority, in relation to which E♭ is the inflection. And
just as E♭ corresponds to the grace note F♯ in the opening two blocks of the first
tableau, so, too, the (D♭ C♭) simultaneity on the downbeat of this opening block
of the fourth tableau corresponds to the earlier stressed D-E segment and its
repeats. (Enharmonically in terms of (C♯ B), (D♭ C♭) will return as the
reiterated, concluding simultaneity of *Les Noces*.) A♭, the crucial fourth-
defining pitch vis-à-vis D♭ and the (D♭ C♭ B♭ A♭) tetrachord, is introduced
in the contrasting block that follows at Rehearsal No. 87+4 (see Example 5.18b).
In the soprano solo, a B♭-A♭-D♭ outline features the (D♭ (C♭) B♭ A♭) unit, a
gapped (0 (2) 3 5) tetrachord structurally different from the (0 2 (3) 5)s
encountered most often not only in *Les Noces* but in works of the Russian
period generally. Here, the minor-third gap appears on the top of the tetrachord
rather than on the bottom – in essence, an inversion of the standard form.

The syncopation of the "hiccup motive" introduced at Rehearsal Nos. 91
and 92 (see Examples 5.19a and 5.19b, respectively) accompanies nearly all
subsequent versions of the basic motive. Its origin has been related in earlier
chapters. Returning home on an evening in April, 1916, Stravinsky was struck
by the singing of two inebriated co-passengers on a funicular. Alert to the

---

[45] See the analytical sketches or "summaries" of some of these relationships in van den Toorn, *The
Music of Igor Stravinsky*, 174.

Example 5.18. *Les Noces*, fourth tableau

a) opening block

b) contrasting block

effect of syncopation (a consequence, evidently, of a case of the hiccups on the part of his co-passengers), he moved quickly with the idea of accompanying some of the celebratory texts of the fourth tableau with a similar effect, one capable of capturing something of the inebriation as well as the stumbling character of the wedding guests. Starting with the "hiccup motive" itself at Rehearsal Nos. 91 and 92, a form of syncopation found its way into countless subsequent versions of the basic motive. And it did so along lines that could not have been more characteristic of Stravinsky's methods.

Thus, in the motivic successions at Rehearsal Nos. 91 and 92 (see Example 5.19a and b), the syncopation is conceived as part of a larger pattern of metrical displacement. The bar lines in these successions are paired in twos; motives fall first off (the syncopation) and then on the quarter-note beat (the displacement of the syncopation). Double repeat structures result from the repetition of this pattern, specifically $(A_4+B_3)+(A_4+B_3)$, where the letters A and B stand for the first and second measures of a pair of bar lines, respectively, and the subscript numbers refer to the encompassed number of quarter-note beats. (See the brackets in Examples 5.18a and 5.19a–f.) In a

Example 5.19. *Les Noces*, fourth tableau, the hiccup motive and its transformations:
A = off the quarter-note beat, B = on the quarter-note beat

a)

c) with material of the opening block superimposed

single pair of bar lines, measure B consists of a displaced repeat of the motive of measure A. And although this scheme would often be reversed in future years, with the syncopation coming as a subsequent displacement of the initial motive, it is one to which Stravinsky would turn again and again in the construction of thematic shapes in pieces of both the Russian and neoclassical eras. As we shall see in Chapter 8, it is one for which a wealth of anticipation may be cited as well, close and important precedents above all in the music of Debussy and Rimsky-Korsakov. If the displacement is eliminated from the scheme (in effect, that which renders it Stravinskian in character), something like an a+a archetype is left standing, a melodic repeat

Example 5.19. (contd.)

d) with displacement sequence A + B reversed

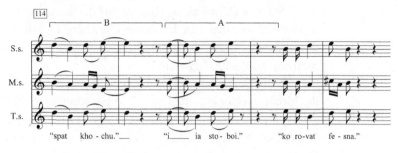

e)

f)

structure that can be found replicated in the music of a great many styles, historical periods, and even cultures.[46]

Typically in Stravinsky's music, the scheme is reversed, as we have suggested, with the syncopation realized as a displacement of an initial motive or configuration. Measure A follows measure B, in other words. Such is the case with the hiccup motive as well, in fact, at least as far as its later appearances in the fourth tableau are concerned: in Examples 5.19d

---

[46] See the discussion of the a+a+b melodic formula in Eugene Narmour, "The Top-Down and Bottom-Up Systems of Musical Implication: Building on Meyer's Theory of Emotional Syntax," *Music Perception* 9, no. 1 (1991): 8–11.

and f, measure A, the syncopated version of the motive, follows as a
displacement of measure B. The two-measure pattern as a whole is also
displaced by such means, A_4+B_3, not just the single motive. And this, too, is
a complication that can be found elsewhere in Stravinsky's settings of
displacement, above all, as we shall see in Chapter 6, with a number of
motives and themes in *Renard*.

In terms of pitch relations generally, subsequent appearances of
the hiccup motive are often (0 2 3 5) tetrachordal or (0 2 5) trichordal in
design; transformations, in the latter case, of the basic cell. At Rehearsal
No. 91 (see Example 5.19a), the (G F E D) tetrachord is formed by the union
of measure A and its repeat; it is made octatonic by virtue of the tritone-
related pitch A♭ in measure B, octatonic in terms of Collection I, more
specifically that particular transposition featured not only in the accompaniment at Rehearsal No. 91, but throughout much of the fourth tableau
as well.

Crucially, the 4/4+3/4 repeat structures at Rehearsal Nos. 91, 92 and
93 mirror those of the opening fragment in the chorus. All are variations on
the same 4/4 + 3/4 metrical scheme, the motivation for which may
have sprung initially from the hiccup motive rather than from the opening
fragment. Such a point of departure for the fourth tableau is in keeping
with the significance the composer seems to have attached to the idea
of the syncopated hiccup, even if the extant sketches are not entirely
conclusive on this point. More specifically, the hiccup motive, D♭-B♭-D♭-
E♭ in Piano I at Rehearsal No. 93 (see Example 5.19c), spans seven eighth-
note beats. Its displaced repeat, falling on the downbeat of the following
measure, arrives an eighth-note beat "too soon." The displacement and
resultant compression account in part for the shortening of the second
measure from four to three quarter-note beats. At the same time, the
doubling of the entire structure may also have been a part of the initial
conception. And with the hiccup motive and its displaced repeat followed
immediately by a repetition, a logical consequence would have been the
elimination of the hypothetical fourth quarter-note beat from the second
measure.

Noteworthy here as well is the original choreography and the role it
appears to have assumed in delineating these structures. From what
may be gathered from the 1990 revival of Bronislava Nijinska's
designs,[47] the latter were constructivist in character, tending to underscore the block-like quality of the music. And nowhere is this more

---

[47] Reference here is to the videorecording *Paris Dances Diaghilev* (Paris: Elektra Nonesuch Dance
Collections, 1990).

apparent than with the opening 4/4 + 3/4 blocks and their subsequent restatements in the fourth tableau. Patterns of repetition in the ballet itself reinforce the hypermetrical sevens and fourteens of these structures (in quarter-note beats), and at times the metrical fours and threes as well.[48] The effect of this is often striking, with something of the larger outline exposed and brought to the fore visually.

The 4/4 + 3/4 metrical scheme underlying both the opening fragment and the later hiccup motive allows for the direct superimposition of these components at Rehearsal No. 93 (see Example 5.19c): the main fragment of the opening block, (E♭ D♭ C♭ B♭) in the sopranos, is superimposed over the hiccup motive, D♭-B♭-D♭-E♭ in Piano I. Another version of the (0 2 5) basic motive, here in terms of (E♭ D♭ B♭), D♭-B♭-D♭-E♭ is introduced off the quarter-note beat at Rehearsal No. 93 and is subsequently displaced to the beat in the following measure. The 2–5–2–0 ordering of this particular (0 2 5), D♭-B♭-D♭-E♭, is featured in many of the remaining blocks and passages of the fourth tableau, including, most spectacularly, those at the close at Rehearsal Nos. 133–35. Both ordering and contour are derived from the ubiquitous motive x of the first and third tableaux. As can be seen by the brackets in Example 5.20, the hiccup motive is very nearly the abbreviation of motive x, even the literal transposition thereof if segment b is taken fully into account. Note here as well the small-scale cutting and pasting of these motives and submotives, the mosaic-like repetition to

Example 5.20. *Les Noces*, motivic connections

a)   motive x

Ne klich, ne   klich_____   le - be-dush - ka   ne   klich v pole   be-laia   ne   plach   ne

b)   hiccup motive

[48] Some of these features are discussed in Jeanne Jaubert, "Some Ideas about Meter in the Fourth Tableau of Stravinsky's *Les Noces*, or Stravinsky, Nijinska, and Particle Physics," *The Musical Quarterly* 83, no.1 (1999): 205–27. Jaubert infers a "choreographic" meter from the reconstructed dance complement to a number of passages in the fourth tableau, weighing the agreement and disagreement of this conception with the "printed" meter and an "aural" one.

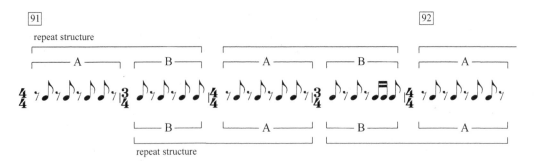

Figure 5.10. *Les Noces*, fourth tableau, overlapping A + B and B + A repeat structures

which they are subject, a central concern above and earlier as well in connection with the motivic succession that opens the second tableau (see Chapter 4). As we shall see a bit more specifically in Chapters 6 and 7, melodic techniques of this kind often replace the figuration identified with tonal practice and the developmental style in particular. Featured is a juxtaposition of sorts, a literal repetition, but with the succession of motives or motivic parts often reordered or rearranged from one statement of a given block to another. As the motives are repeated (sometimes more than once) or deleted altogether, the blocks themselves are lengthened or short-ened as a result. By such means, a juxtaposition of blocks in *Les Noces* is made to coincide with a juxtaposition of these smallest of units. The approach is multilayered.

Consider, too, the ease with which one ordering or succession of motives begets another. As we have indicated, the hiccup motive and its displaced repeat, A+B at rehearsal Nos. 91, 92, 93, and 122, is reversed in terms of B+A at Nos. 114 and 133. (See Examples 5.19 a–f; A stands for the syncopated version of the motive.) However, since the sequence A+B is regularly doubled, a straddling of the bar line separating the initial repeat structure from its double results. As is shown by the brackets in Figure 5.10, B+A straddles the hypermetrical sevens and fourteens of these structures, in obvious anticipation of the full-scale reversal at Rehearsal Nos. 114 and 133. Complications of this kind add to the effect of cutting and pasting, a juxtaposition of single measures, repeat structures, and double repeat structures in the opening section of the fourth tableau.

The rapid octatonic scale passages in Piano III at Rehearsal No. 93 form an accompaniment to the tenors and basses of the chorus. Collection I's 3-cycle is at work here, with transpositions of these descending scales to Db, Bb, and E. And with their jabbing, semitonal verticalizations, the scales may well have been intended to accompany the imagined physically stumbling character of the (inebriated) guests at this point. The motive itself springs from the short Db-Eb-Cb-Bb-Bb inflection that concludes the second measure of the principal motive in the soprano solo.

Finally, Examples 5.19d, e and f acknowledge further appearances of the basic motive, including, enharmonically in terms of (C♯ B (A♯) G♯), the concluding return to the (Db Cb (Bb) Ab) tetrachord at Rehearsal Nos. 133–35.

Octatonic fever

In contrast to *The Rite of Spring*, where the octatonic side of the referential exchange predominates, *Les Noces* is more readily diatonic from the start. As we have noted, octatonic relations intrude occasionally in settings which are ostensibly diatonic. And these relations are confined to a single 3-cycle or transposition. A subset structure of (0 2 (3) 5) tetrachords, triads, and dominant seventh chords intervenes along the lines indicated by the tables in Figures 5.3, 5.4, 5.5, 5.6, and 5.7. In Figure 5.3, for example, the octatonic (0 2 3 5)s are read vertically up or down one of the three transpositional columns; each 3-cycle encompasses a transposition of the given vocabulary. Assuming an element of superimposition, the octatonic sound of this music is defined accordingly.

More specifically, at Rehearsal Nos. 35–40 and 82–87 in the second and third tableaux, respectively, the lengthy passage of lament involving first the parents of the Groom and then the two mothers of the Bride and Groom implicates Collection III. Transpositions of the vocal fragment proceed along Collection III's 3-cycle or (0, 3, 6, 9) partitioning. Similarly, at Rehearsal Nos. 68–70 in the third tableau (see Figure 5.8), transpositions of motive x in terms of (E D B), (C♯ B G♯), (Bb Ab F), and (G F D) proceed along Collection I's 3-cycle.

In the fourth tableau, however, much of this changes dramatically. The octatonic side of the interaction, more extensive in its intrusions, tends to overwhelm all aspects of pitch structure. Indeed, the complexity of the engagement here is quite unlike anything before or after it in Stravinsky's oeuvre. The fourth tableau of *Les Noces* figures among his most octatonic works, in fact, matched in the persistence and intensity of that reference only by *The Rite of Spring*, the first movement of the *Symphony of Psalms*, and sections of the *Symphony in Three Movements* (1945).

The reader will recall the systematic combining of two octatonic transpositions at Rehearsal Nos. 68–70 in the third tableau (see Figure 5.8). Reiterated dominant sevenths accountable to Collection II were superimposed over Collection I's succession of (0 2 5)s in the vocal parts. And in the passage of transition in the first and third tableau, six triads in a descending, stepwise succession alternated mainly between Collections II and III. In Examples 5.13, 5.14, 5.15, and 5.16, Roman numerals identify these collectional affiliations above the quotations themselves. The point here, however, is that, in the ultimately more complex forms of octatonic engagement in the fourth tableau, these rapid juxtapositions and superimpositions of distinct transpositions become the general rule.

And they do so from the start. In the opening block at Rehearsal No. 87 the principal fragment in the chorus is accompanied by another stepwise succession of major triads, here in root position and in Pianos I, III, and IV (see Example 5.18a). Beginning with (B D♯ F♯) and descending step-wise to (E G♯ B), the succession rises and falls repeatedly in a wave-like fashion that can bring to mind the "ribbons of scales" that extend from one page to the next in the actual sketches for this material. Crucially, repeats of the scale-pattern are not synchronized with those of the principal fragment in the chorus. As can be seen by the brackets in Example 5.18a, the scale pattern, spanning five quarter-note beats, conflicts with the principal motive, spanning seven. While (B D♯ F♯) falls on the downbeat at Rehearsal No. 87, (G B D) does so two bars later with the start of the repeat of the principal motive. The two layers acquire a degree of independence by such means, with the layered or stratified effect of this music enhanced. At the same time, the overall structure of the fourth tableau is block-like, mirroring that of the three tableaux that precede it. The opening block at Rehearsal No. 87 is one of a series of blocks, in other words, one that is restated in somewhat modified form at Rehearsal Nos. 89, 93, 115, 119, and 123.

Moreover, as can be seen by the reduction of the first two bars of this opening block in Figure 5.11, the scale defined by the roots of the triads in question refers to Collection I (descending in terms of B-B♭-A♭-G-F-E), while the scales defined by the thirds and fifths refer to Collection II. And the same alternation applies vertically. The triads switch back and forth regularly between Collections I and II. (See the Roman numerals located on top and on the left-hand side of Figure 5.11.) Indeed, the intricacy of the deployment, the extent of the systemization, is extraordinary. Limited to major triads in root position, the succession alternates regularly between Collections I and II on both a linear and harmonic basis, horizontally and vertically. And it does so for the entirety of the opening block, a total of four measures starting with the downbeat at Rehearsal No. 87.

No less systematic at Rehearsal No. 87 is the insistence on a single chordal disposition. This, too, is in line with the "ribbons of scales" that figure

87

4/4 Pianos I, II, IV   **3/4**

	II		I	II	I	II	I	II	I	II	I	II	I	II
I	B	B	Bb	Ab	G	F	E	F	G	Ab	Bb	B	Bb	Ab
II	F♯	F♯	F	Eb	D	C	B	C	D	Eb	F	F♯	F	Eb
II	D♯	D♯	D	C	B	A	G♯	A	B	C	D	D♯	D	C
I	B	B	Bb	Ab	G	F	E	F	G	Ab	Bb	B	Bb	Ab

Figure 5.11. *Les Noces*, fourth tableau, opening block, accompanying triads, alternating octatonic Collections I and II

prominently in Stravinsky's sketches for the accompanying parts of these initial blocks. The vocabulary consists not only of (0 2 (3) 5) tetrachords, triads, and dominant sevenths, but of a number of fixed dispositions as well. And nowhere is this more apparent than at Rehearsal No. 92, the block that immediately follows the introduction of the hiccup motive at Rehearsal No. 91 (see Example 5.19b).

At Rehearsal Nos. 68–70 in the third tableau, the characteristic disposition of the dominant seventh chord involved the spread of a major ninth, with the root of this chord on top, the seventh on the bottom. At Rehearsal No. 92, the same disposition becomes the focus of another octatonic scale pattern, in all four pianos and stretching for some six measures (see Figure 5.12). Again, the chords alternate between Collections I and II, doing so horizontally as well as vertically, both in terms of the actual scale patterns and the dominant sevenths. At the same time, however, the vertical sound is denser here than at Rehearsal No. 87. In an apparent effort to mimic the rushed, stumbling effect of an assortment of inebriated guests (or, quite possibly, as suggested earlier as well, the rattling, off-pitch sound of "primitive" instruments and bands), the added layer of sevenths in Pianos II and IV intrudes (stumbles) off the eighth-note beat, creating bunched cluster-like triadic superimpositions. Stravinsky is careful to preserve the octatonic sound at each eighth-note beat, however, the regular alternation between Collections I and II. In Figure 5.12, vertical lines mark off the eighth-note beats for the first two measures while the Roman numerals on the left-hand side and above the reduction refer to the alternating Collections I and II. The scale patterns continue for six measures through the whole of this block at Rehearsal No. 92.

92

4/4 Pianos I, III   **3/4**

	II	I	II	I	II	I	II	I	II	I	II	I	II	I
I	D	E	F	G	Ab	Bb	B	Bb	Ab		F		D	E
II	A	B	C	D	Eb	F	F♯	F	Eb		C		A	B
II	F♯	G♯	A	B	C	D	D♯	D	C		A		F♯	G♯
II	C	D	Eb	F	Gb	Ab	A	Ab	Gb		Eb		C	D
I		C♯			Bb			Bb	F		Bb		F	Bb

	II	I	II	I		I	II		II	I	II	I	II	I
I	D	C♯	B	Bb		G	F		Ab	Bb	B	C♯	D	C♯
II	A	G♯	F♯	F		D	C		Eb	F	F♯	G♯	A	G♯
II	F♯	E♯	D♯	D		B	A		C	D	D♯	E♯	F♯	E♯
II	C	B	A	Ab		F	Eb		Gb	Ab	A	B	C	B
I		C♯			Bb			Bb	F		Bb		F	Bb

Pianos II, IV

Figure 5.12. *Les Noces*, fourth tableau, accompanying dominant sevenths, alternating octatonic Collections I and II

Still more overtly octatonic is the falling sixteenth-note figure introduced in the tenors, basses, and Piano III in the following block at Rehearsal No. 93 (see Example 5.19c). Another octatonic scale pattern, this one appears as an accompaniment to the main (Eb Db Bb) motive in Pianos I and II, entering on the pitch Bb and then transposed to Db. Initially, it follows the familiar transpositional path in terms of Collection I's (0, 3, 6, 9) symmetrically defined divisions, before ending climactically with a series of descending Collection I scales.

The octatonic frenzy of these blocks and passages, with many of the latter restated extensively throughout the fourth tableau, makes for a congestion of remarkable proportions. (The reader will recall the octatonic complexion of the culminating block at Rehearsal Nos. 133–35. In the instrumental

Example 5.21. Scriabin, Sonata No. 9, Op. 68, opening; alternating octatonic Collections I and II

statement of the (C♯ B G♯) motive at Rehearsal No. 134+6, only F♯ resists the octatonic order in terms of Collection I.) A parallel for the increased complexity of the octatonicism exists in the second part of *The Rite of Spring*. The confinement of a Dorian fourth to within the 0–11 or major seventh interval span in the first part of *The Rite*, octatonically conceived for the most part and articulated by means of varying reiterated, superimposed fragments and chords, becomes something of a self-sustaining chord in the second part, a piece of harmonic vocabulary, as it were. The resultant 0–5, 11 chord, reading down, is sustained throughout much of the "Glorification of the Chosen One" and the "Sacrificial Dance," with transpositions of the octatonic set shifting rapidly and often systematically as well.

No doubt, octatonic passages of a comparable complexity may occasionally be found in the music of Stravinsky's contemporaries in the early part of the twentieth century. Condensed in Example 5.21 are two passages from Alexander Scriabin's Ninth Piano Sonata. As can be seen by the brackets and Roman numerals, an alternation between Collections I and II, inferable from the opening motive, is made the basis of an extended passage at mm.15–19. (Observe that the latter is not wholly without "interference": the 3-cycle C-A-F♯ in the bass at mm.16–17 refers to Collection II or III, while C♯-B♭-G at mm. 18–19 refers to Collection I or III.) Note, however, the vast distinction in the melodic and harmonic vocabulary of these passages. Missing altogether are the simple major and minor triads typical of Stravinsky's approach, the clashing that results from the superimposition of those triads. The difference in octatonic "sound" could not be more pronounced.

Yet, for Stravinsky's music, the octatonicism of the fourth tableau of *Les Noces* represents a pinnacle, with nothing quite like it in the remaining octatonic contexts of his Russian, neoclassical, and early serial works. As we have indicated, only *The Rite of Spring*, the first movement of the *Symphony of Psalms*, and sections of the *Symphony in Three Movements* capture something of the complexity of the invention. And in *Psalms* and the later symphony, the rapid and systematic alternation between transpositions of the octatonic set is not as readily a part of the invention as it is in the fourth tableau of *Les Noces*. From the standpoint of the octatonicism, the construction in these later works is a good deal less intricate.

6 Meter, text, and alignment in *Renard* (1916): Stravinsky's "rejoicing discovery"

The trigger for much of what is characteristic of Stravinsky's music is rhythmic-metric, as we have argued, and involves most fundamentally the metrical alignment and realignment of repeated motives and chords. Compositionally, Stravinsky often began here, in fact, not with a committed set of pitch relations, necessarily, one that was octatonic or octatonic–diatonic, for example, but with a motive or chord displaced in relation to a steady metrical framework. The many works and sections of works which begin accordingly bear this out, as do the many references in his published remarks to starting points and early conceptions.

Even before the birth of concrete ideas, the composer would begin by improvising at the piano, setting himself in motion by "relating intervals rhythmically":

> Long before ideas are born, I begin work by relating intervals rhythmically. This exploration of possibilities is always conducted at the piano.[1]

> When my main theme has been decided I know in general what kind of musical material it will require. I start to look for this material . . . . sometimes starting directly to improvise rhythmic units on a provisional row of notes (which can become a final row).[2]

These quotations refer to his later serial mode of composition, to a time when to compose "rhythmically" was also to compose serially. Yet the approach seems to have differed little in earlier years. To judge from the sketch routines and much additional published comment, matters of rhythm, alignment, tempo, and articulation played a critical role in initiating the compositional process.

Students of Stravinsky's music might begin here as well. In search of a definition of what it is that sets his music apart, they, too, might begin by "relating intervals rhythmically," arranging a theme or motive one way metrically and then another, off and then on the beat of a given level of pulsation. The "same" fragment might be read through placed and displaced in this way, repeatedly and at different locations of a metrical grid, and as a

---

[1] Igor Stravinsky and Robert Craft, *Conversations with Stravinsky* (Garden City, NY: Doubleday, 1959), 11.

[2] *Ibid.*, 12.

way of sensing the disruptive effect displacement can have on an established meter. For it is not as if, in the mind of the listener, meter arose independently of these processes of placement and displacement, as if the materials of Stravinsky's music fell automatically (or mechanically) into place, wholly at the mercy of such a design. Themes, fragments, and motives may be introduced within an established metrical hierarchy, to be sure, acquiring, as a result of that introduction, a strong sense of alignment (or *location*). Yet the processes themselves are reciprocal and work both ways. A sense of meter emerges from the materials and may be subject to modification (or the threat thereof) on a continuing basis.

Our purpose at this point is to inquire after the effects of displacement on Stravinsky's text-setting, notation, articulation, and thematic construction. Any number of passages discussed in connection with *Les Noces* could have served the need for additional illustration. Yet we turn instead to *Renard*, the "burlesque" for which, as we have detailed in Chapter 3, progress on *Les Noces* was interrupted for some seven months in 1915–16. Slighter and less celebrated than *Les Noces*, *Renard* is the bearer of much extraordinary music all the same, including the two passages to be examined below, the *pribaoutka* at Rehearsal Nos. 62–67 and the con brio episode at Nos. 24–26. Both are ideally suited to the topics at hand.

In Chapter 7 we turn again to *Renard*. The opening allegro at Rehearsal Nos. 0–9 offers a wealth and variety of displacements, all conveniently highlighted by a basso ostinato. Ubiquitous in works of all periods of Stravinsky's music, ostinatos are primarily metrical in function. They carry harmonic implications, to be sure, as Stravinsky himself acknowledged, static ones for the most part; they are "anti-developmental" in this respect.[3] Yet the service they render is essentially metrical, with the listener provided with a convenient backdrop, a way of setting alignment in relief.

Origins of displacement

At issue here at the outset of Chapter 6 is Russian popular verse, the flexible stresses that by tradition accompany the singing of that verse. In a celebrated passage in one of Stravinsky's later books of "conversation" with Robert Craft, the composer recalled his "rejoicing discovery" of the "musical possibilities" inherent in this tradition, tracing his familiarity with this and other features of Russian popular verse to his stay in Switzerland during the early years of the First World War. Exiled at the time, he began setting a great variety of Russian folk texts to music, including, in the case of *Renard*

[3] *Ibid.*, 26.

and *The Soldier's Tale* (1918) as well as *Les Noces*, texts which would eventually be pieced together as scenarios.

> My profound emotion on reading the news of war ... found some alleviation in the delight with which I steeped myself in Russian folk poems. What fascinated me in this verse was not so much the stories, which were often crude, or the pictures and metaphors, always so deliciously unexpected, as the cadence they create, which produces an effect on one's sensibilities very closely akin to that of music.[4]

> One important characteristic of Russian popular verse is that the accents of the spoken verse are ignored when the verse is sung. The recognition of the musical possibilities inherent in this fact was one of the most rejoicing discoveries of my life; I was like a man who suddenly finds that his finger can be bent from the second joint as well as from the first.[5]

Such may well have been the means by which Stravinsky was able to free himself from the constraints of fixed accents – in effect, the realist tradition he had inherited from composers such as César Cui and Mussorgsky. In response to the metrical displacement of a repeated musical fragment, he may suddenly have felt himself able to shift the accents of a repeated syllable from one line of a text to the next. Alternatively, the "musical possibilities" inherent in a shifted verbal accent may have prompted similar feelings where meter and metrical alignment were concerned. Either way, what was discovered, evidently, was a novel means of joining the accents and rhythms of Russian folk verse with those of his own thoroughly contemporary musical idiom.

What remains problematic in this episode, however, is the date of Stravinsky's "rejoicing discovery," his "recognition of the musical possibilities" inherent in the variable stresses of sung Russian folk verse.[6] For to place that date in the early years of his stay in Switzerland (possibly as early as 1914), would be to place it after the fact, so to speak, after pieces such as *Petrushka* (1911), *The Rite of Spring* (1913), and the *Three Pieces for String Quartet* (1914). And these are pieces in which, from a strictly musical standpoint, flexible stresses and the element of displacement had already become an established part of the composer's idiom.[7] Such a date would

---

[4] Igor Stravinsky, *An Autobiography* (New York: W.W. Norton, 1962), 53.

[5] Igor Stravinsky and Robert Craft, *Expositions and Developments* (Garden City, NY: Doubleday, 1962), 138.

[6] Richard Taruskin fixes the date of Stravinsky's "discovery" in 1914, at the time of his composition of "Shchuka" or "The Pike," which became the third of the Four Russian Peasant Songs (1917). See Richard Taruskin, *Stravinsky and the Russian Traditions: A Biography of the Works through "Mavra,"* 2 vols. (Berkeley: University of California Press, 1996), vol. II: 1215.

[7] Some of the earliest examples of displacement in Stravinsky's music may be found in the allegro section of the Finale of *The Firebird* (1910). See the discussion of this in Pieter C. van den Toorn, "Will Stravinsky Survive Postmodernism?", *Music Theory Spectrum* 22, no. 1 (2000): 108–13.

seem to overrule the possibility of an early causal relationship, in other words, a role for sung Russian folk verse and its flexible stresses in the early development of the composer's rhythmic practices.

No doubt, such a role could have played itself out at deeper levels of consciousness. Early on, features of Russian popular verse could have been so entirely familiar to the composer as scarcely to have required any deliberate consideration. Stravinsky could have assimilated these features almost without notice, in other words.[8] Just as with the processes of "fabrication" surveyed in the previous chapter, according to which bits and pieces of authentic folk songs were absorbed into the composition of *Les Noces*, the varying stresses that accompany the singing of repeated words and syllables in Russian popular verse could have been assimilated unconsciously at an early date. They could have been "known" to Stravinsky in this way, and could have served as the source of the flexible stresses in his music, the metrical displacements that regularly accompany the repetition of his themes, fragments, and chords.

But if the connection did in fact play itself out in this fashion, there is little evidence of its having done so. For there are no early pieces of Stravinsky's in which the connection is brought to the attention of the listener. And Stravinsky himself was silent on the possibility of such an early influence on his rhythmic practices. He was as reticent in divulging the details of those practices as he was in discussing aspects of his musical language more generally. Not once in his many references to the rhythmic character of his music, to the demands of his music for exactness in tempo and articulation, did he acknowledge the central role assumed by displacement.[9]

What may have struck him quite suddenly at the time was the connection itself, not the flexible stresses of sung folk verse as such (something about

---

[8] This is approximately Richard Taruskin's position in Taruskin, *Stravinsky and the Russian Traditions*, vol. II: 1208. The "rejoicing discovery" was something Stravinsky "had long known, only didn't know he knew it." The shifts in verbal stress "were merely among the superficial decorative trappings of *le style russe*, which advanced musical minds in Russia thought passé." On the whole, however, Taruskin is less concerned with processes of metrical displacement and their origins in Stravinsky's instrumental music than with the composer's "rejoicing discovery" and its implications for text-setting in the Russian period. The connection between metrical displacement in Stravinsky's music and the uses to which the flexible stresses of sung Russian folk texts were put is largely ignored in his otherwise highly insightful account of the latter; see Taruskin, *Stravinsky and the Russian Traditions*, vol. II: 1198–1236. On the other hand, the connection between the displacement of melodic fragments and that of repeated words and syllables is pursued quite explicitly in Chandler Carter, "*The Rake's Progress* and Stravinsky's Return: The Composer's Evolving Approach to Setting Text," *Journal of the American Musicological Society* 63, no. 3 (2010): 553–640. Indeed, Carter underscores a number of strategies common to both sides of this equation. For an earlier account of Stravinsky's text-setting practices, see Pieter C. van den Toorn, *The Music of Igor Stravinsky* (New Haven: Yale University Press, 1983), 244–51.

[9] Recall in this connection the lack of any acknowledgment on Stravinsky's part of the role of the octatonic set in his music, a role whose significance, at least from the standpoint of this present inquiry, would be difficult to exaggerate.

which, as we have suggested, he may have known for some time), but the uses to which those stresses could be put. Before the "discovery" itself the two sides of the equation may have been distinct in his mind. And what may therefore have made the difference was the promise of an accommodation, a way of treating Russian folk texts which could accommodate the shifts in metrical alignment that were already a part of his music. If, in earlier works, fragments had been repeated and displaced relative to a steady metrical framework, words and syllables could be subjected to this same practice.

So, too, a new lease may have been gained by the composer, a new means of exercising his inclination to displace and to run counter to a given musical statement. Stravinsky was free to "dissect at will," treat the words of his texts as "phonetic material."[10] He could direct his attention to the sound and metrical placement of the dissected syllables, the "primary constituent elements," as he later called them.[11] The predilection would remain an integral part of his text-setting in later years as well, regardless as to whether the language was Russian, French, English, or Hebrew.

Pribaoutka

According to another of the composer's recollections, the passage shown in Example 6.1 was "the first part of *Renard* to be composed."[12] Stravinsky identified it as such in another of his "conversations" with Robert Craft. The music accompanies the opening lines of a *pribaoutka*, a form of Russian popular verse resembling a limerick and consisting in the main of riddles and counting games. Designed for children, such forms seem to have had sound as much as sense (or nonsense) as their rationale. The composer's remarks are as follows:

> The word *pribaoutki* notes a form of popular Russian verse, the nearest English parallel to which is the limerick. It means 'a telling,' 'pri' being the Latin 'pre' and 'baout' deriving from the Old Russian infinitive 'to say.' *Pribaoutki* are always short – not more than four lines usually. We all know parlor games in which the same sentence can be made to mean something different when different words are emphasized. In *Renard*, the syllable-sounds within the word itself, as well as the emphasis of the word in the sentence, are so treated. *Renard* is phoneme music, and phonemes are untranslatable.[13]

---

[10] Stravinsky and Craft, *Expositions and Developments*, 136.
[11] Igor Stravinsky, *An Autobiography*, 128.   [12] *Ibid.*
[13] Stravinsky and Craft, *Expositions and Developments*, 137–38.

Example 6.1. *Renard*, *pribaoutka*, five-note segment, displacement

> Translation changes the character of a work and destroys its cultural unity . . .
> [The *pribaoutka* in *Renard*] exploits a speed and an accentuation that are
> natural to Russian. No translation of this passage can translate what I have
> done musically to the language.[14]

Pribaoutki were thus prized for their sounds as well as for their substance,
their play with "syllable-sounds" (often "untranslatable," as Stravinsky
warns) as well as for their tales and "unexpected metaphors."[15] It was the
combination of rhythm and "syllable-sounds" that seems to have proved
irresistible to him, the offering of a kind of "pure mouth music."[16] An

---

[14] See, also, Taruskin, *Stravinsky and the Russian Traditions*, vol. II: 1148–49. "We would call
[*pribaoutki*] nursery rhymes," Taruskin writes, "except that many of them do not rhyme."
They are "jingles or nonsense rhymes." *Pribaoutki* were also closely associated with rough
forms of peasant art, small paintings (*lubok*) often with a narrative content. So entirely
meshed was the poetic, visual, and narrative conception, in fact, that an understanding of
one of these components – the verse itself, for example, the *pribaoutka* – can often be
difficult in isolation.

[15] Igor Stravinsky and Robert Craft, *Themes and Episodes* (New York: Alfred A. Knopf, 1966), 57.

[16] Taruskin, *Stravinsky and The Russian Traditions*, vol. II: 1224.

informal English translation of the *pribaoutka* at Rehearsal No. 62 runs as follows:[17]

> Tyuk, Tyuk, gusel'-tsi, baranovi strunochki . . .
> Tyuk, Tyuk . . . Kak struna to zagula
> Tyuk, Tyuk . . . Da zagula a drugaya prigovarivala:
> Tyuk, Tyuk, gusel'-tsi baranovi strunochki . . .
>
> Tick, Tick, nice little gusly, with little sheep-gut strings
> Tick, Tick, when one string started to twang
> Tick, Tick, another joined in talking, too . . .
> Tick, Tick, nice little gusly, with little sheep-gut strings

Displacements accompanying the first two lines of this stanza are boxed in Example 6.1. If these realignments are read through at a tempo approaching Stravinsky's assigned marking of 152 BPM for the quarter-note beat, they will undoubtedly be found easier to spot on the printed page than to hear. As we shall see, however, the difficulty with their discernment has less to do with tempo than with matters of articulation and small-scale grouping. It involves the grouping and separation of pitches as implied by Stravinsky's slurs, beams, and accent markings. Small-scale as they may be, these articulations play a crucial role in the displacement process.

Falling on the downbeat at m. 2 (see Example 6.1), the boxed five-note segment C-B-C♯-A-A is repeated and displaced at m. 3, where it falls on the fourth eighth-note beat of the 2/4 measure. It is shifted "backwards" by an eighth-note beat in this way, from the first to the fourth eighth-note beat of the 2/4 meter. Another melodic repeat structure is forged by such means, with the initial segment of a thematic statement followed in quick succession by its displacement. (See, in conjunction with Examples 5.29c, d, e, and f, our earlier discussion of the hiccup motive in the fourth tableau of *Les Noces*.) The five-note segment is displaced at mm. 6–7 as well, and along the same lines, namely, "back" by an eighth-note beat.

At the same time, however, the incomplete cycle according to which the displacements of this segment would seem to be arranged is owing in part to Stravinsky's irregular 5/8 bar at mm. 6–7. More specifically, the cycle is owing to the slur and beam markings accompanying the stressed Russian syllable *gu* (*zagula*). (Running alongside the 2/4 meter in Example 6.1, the

---

[17] In the second stanza the term *gusly* refers to an ancient Russian stringed instrument designed for plucking. Much of *Renard* seems to have been fashioned with the gusly in mind, in fact, even if the sound of this instrument, to follow Stravinsky's account of the compositional process, was found to be too small and delicate for the ensemble; it was eventually replaced by the cimbalom. In the first stanza *Zagula* is a nonsense designation for gusly. The use of the Russian diminutive is pervasive throughout this stanza.

changing bar lines enclosed in parentheses refer to the accentuation of the text.) Yet it is not the irregular barring in parentheses that is likely to serve the listener as a form of measurement where metrical placement is concerned, but rather the steady 2/4 meter.[18] And according to it, repeats of the five-note segment at mm. 3–4 and 6–7 fall on the same beat, namely, the fourth eighth-note beat. The placement of the second repeat is identical to that of the first. (Stravinsky abandons the 2/4 meter at m. 6, to be sure, but there is little reason why, in the mind of the conservative listener, it could not be sustained at greater length, given, especially, the synchronized arrival of the alternative irregular and regular barrings on the downbeat at m. 6.)

Strategies similar to the ones played out by the C-B-C♯-A-A segment can also be spotted in the text-setting. At the downbeat of m. 3, the segment's concluding pitch A accompanies the unaccented Russian syllable *ba* (*baranovi*). The segment itself straddles the 2/4 bar line at this point, occasioning Stravinsky's alternative 5/8 measures. At m. 6, however, the same concluding pitch, cut off from the segment, accompanies a stressed syllable (*kak*). Although, in relation to the 2/4 meter, the metrical location at m. 6 is unchanged (the downbeats at mm. 3 and 6 are likely to be felt as such by the listener), the verbal component switches from unaccented to accented; in counterpoint with one another, the former acts as a foil for the latter. In the process, too, Stravinsky's shifting bar lines are interpreted as a form of phrasing or motivic grouping. What changes at mm. 3 and 6 is not the meter, but rather the grouping (or phrasing) of the concluding pitch A.

But these concerns are overshadowed by the larger scheme of repetition. Although it is concealed in various ways, the music accompanying the second line of the text in Example 6.1 is a shortened restatement of the music accompanying the first. And the shortening is achieved along lines that are typical of Stravinsky. The thematic statement is sliced up into smaller units, which are then repeated independently of the initial succession. If the four 2/4 measures of the first line are labeled ABCD, the shortened repeat (with the second measure deleted) would read ACD. On the smallest of scales, the subtraction here of a single bar from the initial thematic statement offers yet another illustration of the sort of cutting and pasting witnessed earlier in Chapter 4 on the part of the motives and juxtaposed blocks of *Les Noces*.

---

[18] Critical above all to the establishment of the 2/4 meter in the opening measures of this passage are the melody's first three attack points (*Tyuk, tyuk, gusel-tsi* . . .), about as strong a suggestion of the quarter-note pulse as could be imagined. In turn, the separation of the first two attacks from the third (the initial D-punctuation separated from C-B-C♯-A, in other words) implies a slower level of pulsation, that of the half-note beat. For a discussion of the criteria likely to be involved in metrical determinations of this kind, see Fred Lerdahl and Ray Jackendoff, *A Generative Theory of Tonal Music* (Cambridge: MIT Press, 1983), 68–88.

Marked off by parentheses, Stravinsky's alternative notation is a rarity. Seldom are alternative barrings introduced in his scores, even if the rationale underlying their application here is straightforward enough. While the 5/8 and 3/8 measures accommodate the naturally stressed syllables of the Russian text (as irregular meters often do in Russian-period works with texts), the steady 2/4 meter exposes the displacements. In addition, the 5/8 and 3/8 measures alternate regularly at points, a pattern above and beyond that underlying the stressed syllables of the text and the 2/4 meter. (Regular alternations of this kind – non-isochronous meters, in effect, attempts on the composer's part to impose a "higher" order on a localized metrical irregularity – may be found elsewhere in Stravinsky's music. See, for example, the alternating 2/8 and 3/8 measures that open his 1947 revision of the *Symphonies of Wind Instruments*, a passage to which we shall be turning in Chapter 8.)[19] In Example 6.1, the successions of 5/8 and 3/8 measures arrive "on target" with the 2/4 meter every other 2/4 measure; five plus three eighth-note beats equal four quarter-note beats or two 2/4 measures. The intersection that results from this "targeting" is crucial where the steady 2/4 meter is concerned, its sensed confirmation by the listener.

The hierarchical implications of the 2/4 meter are sketched both above and below the two opening staves in Example 6.1. The metrical analysis here is doubtless something of an overkill, reflective of a strong reading in this regard, a solid commitment on the part of the listener. And such would indeed seem to be the indication, not just with the notated 2/4 meter here in Example 6.1, but at the outset of Stravinsky's settings of displacement more generally. Themes, motives, and chords are introduced within established metrical frameworks,

---

[19] We should note in caution, however, that attempts on the listener's part to fashion a non-isochronous meter out of this brief and rapid 5/8+3/8 alternation in Stravinsky's *Pribaoutka* are likely to meet with difficulty. Such a meter would presumably consist of a hypermetrical, two-measure beat (whole-note beat), divided by two unevenly spaced beats of five and three eighth-note beats, and then followed by a level of the eighth-note beat. But this conception must contend not only with the conflicting 2/4 meter (a symmetrical rather than asymmetrical division of the whole-note beat), but with a number of interruptions as well; the notated 2/4 measure at m. 1 and again at m. 5 is likely to strike the listener as unmistakable. In the *Symphonies*, the 2/8+3/8 alternation of the opening block reflects a form of metrical parallelism. Yet, it, too, must compete with a conflicting 2/4 meter, according to which the motives of the first two measures are displaced. For a general discussion of non-isochronous meters, see Justin London, *Hearing in Time: Psychological Aspects of Musical Meter* (Oxford University Press, 2004), 100–15. Following London's terminology, the 5/8+3/8 pattern in the *Pribaoutka* is an "8-cycle" (5+3=8), while the 2/8+3/8 pattern is a "5-cycle" (2+3=5). London focuses on the cyclical nature of the metrical process, with meter itself represented not by superimposed layers of dots (with the latter signifying beats), but rather by circles, dots, and lines connecting the dots. In addition, London discusses the role of tempo in the practical application of non-isochronous meters.

only to be followed in quick succession by their displaced repeats. The latter may prove disruptive of those frameworks, but the disruption may be partial and incomplete. If displacement is to be discerned at all, meter must be present in some form.

In Example 6.1, the steady 2/4 meter may be sustained through much of the second line. Beyond this point, however, difficulties are likely to arise. As one displacement follows another, a form of disorientation is apt to set in. Likely to wreak much additional havoc is the timpani fragment, which, beginning at m. 6, undergoes a series of upbeat–downbeat displacements of its own. (Repeats of this fragment introduce a form of stratification.) Attempts to get beyond the quarter-note beat, in other words, to regulate that beat at a "higher" level of pulsation (that of the bar line and above), may cease altogether, as the listener suspends his/her metrical bearings temporarily. And although the psychology of this suspension may vary from one listener to the next, a number of general assumptions are likely to prevail. Conservative listeners, receptive to the least bit of evidence of a periodic mold, may struggle to hold on in the face of much contradictory evidence. Radical listeners, less receptive in this regard, may yield more readily.

The two systems of meter sketched in Example 6.1 share a general understanding of the concept, one to which reference has been made in the Introduction. Below the opening staves in Example 6.1, the metrical analysis follows the Lerdahl–Jackendoff model; above the staves, each bracketed one-two count incorporates a combination of two interacting levels of pulsation. Closest to the stave is the quarter-note beat marked off by the bar line, the half-note beat. The interaction of these levels is duplicated at succeeding hypermetric layers, which are modeled here after Victor Zuckerkandl's "multi-layered texture of subordinate and superordinate phases."[20] Zuckerkandl, using arrows instead of brackets, underscores the "dynamics" of the interaction: the experience of being alternatively on and off the beat of a given level of pulsation is cyclic or "wave-like," one of moving "back and forth" or "to and fro."[21] According to Zuckerkandl, the listener feels herself approaching and then leaving a beat, all as part of a general process of beat-oscillation.

---

[20] Zuckerkandl, *Sound and Symbol: Music and the External World*, trans. Willard R. Trask (Princeton University Press, 1956), 179.

[21] *Ibid.*, 169. "Wave superimposes itself upon wave, the closed cycle; the 'to-and-fro' of the one is, from the point of view of the next higher plane, a mere 'to,' which demands the completing and consummating 'fro'"; 178–79.

The role of articulation in processes of metrical displacement: Stravinsky's slurs, beams, and accent markings

Patterned cycles of displacement are common in the works of Stravinsky's Russian period. Departing from a specific location within a steadily recurring bar line, realignments of a given segment are arranged sequentially, moved "backwards" by way of a fixed unit (an eighth-note beat, for example). If the spans marked off by the displaced repeats are regular, the result is an ostinato. Just as often, however, the spans are of varying length.

The incomplete cycle alluded to above in the *pribaoutka* in *Renard* is typical. Vertically aligned in Example 6.2, the five-note segment C-B-C♯-A-A is moved "back" by successive eighth-note beats. As suggested already, however, the process is flawed. Not only do the spans between successive repeats of this segment vary in their length, but it is only in relation to Stravinsky's changing bar lines that these repeats are cyclical. With the alternative 2/4 meter as a frame of reference, the segment's second and third appearances fall on the same beat, namely, the fourth eighth-note beat of a 2/4 measure.

Even in relation to the changing meter, however, perception of the cycle is likely to be obscured. In Example 6.2, the first and third appearances of the segment fall on the quarter-note beat while the second does not. It is these distinctions in metrical location that, to a far greater extent than those arising from the cycle outlined in Example 6.2, are likely to stand out for the listener. What seems to count most is the sensation of being on or off the beat of a given level of pulsation, on or off the tactus perhaps above all, the quarter-note beat here.

Example 6.2. *Renard, pribaoutka,* five-note segment, articulation

a)

gú   sel' - tsi   ba -

b)

vi   strú____   noch - ki

c)

a   za - gú - la

Example 6.3. *Renard, pribaoutka*, five-note segment, fixed articulation (analytical)

a)

b)

c)

Indeed, the patterned cycle of metrical realignment plotted in Example 6.2 is obscured in other ways as well. The reader will note that the articulation of the five-note segment C-B-C♯-A-A changes with each "backward" shift in placement. The slur and beam markings accompanying the initial C-B unit accompany B-C♯ and then C♯-A as well. These changes accompany the natural stresses of the Russian syllables; they are what underlies Stravinsky's irregular meter. Yet they cut down on the repetition, and so, too, on the displacement process. For the rhythmic character of the five-note segment is changed markedly under these circumstances; the repetition is made less literal from one entrance to the next. And with less repeated, less is ultimately displaced.

At the same time, modifications of this kind are exceedingly rare in Stravinsky's scores. The articulation of a given segment or chord and its subsequent displaced repeats is apt to remain intact. Had it remained so here, then the cycle of displacement in Example 6.2 would have appeared as it does in Example 6.3. In this analytical revision of the articulation, the slur and beam markings accompanying the initial C-B unit of the C-B-C♯-A-A segment accompany all subsequent repeats of this unit, irrespective of their metrical placement. The beam joining C and B on the downbeat in Example 6.3a joins C and B in Examples 6.3b and 6.3c as well. In Example 6.3b, it does so by straddling the bar line, a device common enough in Stravinsky's scores, and common above all when employed for the purpose indicated here. A change in the metrical alignment of a reiterated fragment is thus countered by an absence of change in its articulation. The result is a displacement that lies more fully exposed to the ear.

A useful comparison at this point might be to the thematic fragment shown in Examples 6.4a and b, a fragment repeated at considerable length in

Example 6.4. *Renard*, principal fragment (tp.), displacements

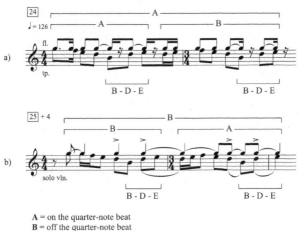

A = on the quarter-note beat
B = off the quarter-note beat

Renard at Rehearsal Nos. 24–26. Like the five-note segment, this one enters first on and then off the quarter-note beat (Examples 6.4a and b, respectively). And the quarter-note beat is the likely tactus here as well, although at a more modest tempo of 126 BPM.

But consider the articulation of the B-D-E segment of this fragment, an (0 2 5) trichord embedded within the larger configuration. Lettered, bracketed, and set apart analytically below the stave in the opening bars of Examples 6.4a and b, B-D-E falls first on and then off the quarter-note beat; it reflects the larger displacement alluded to. Yet, at the same time, its articulation remains unchanged. Notwithstanding the displacement of the B-D-E segment, the tied G in the upper line that coincides with the B of the B-D-E segment in the opening bar of Example 6.4a does so again in the opening bar of Example 6.4b. Striking above all is the instrumental contrast afforded by these examples, the distinction between the flute and brass in Example 6.4a and the solo violin in Example 6.4b. With the repeat in the solo violin at Rehearsal No. 25+4, great care is taken to preserve as much of the original articulation as possible.

Yet there is still greater intricacy in these arrangements. For the fragment itself is composed of a displacement. Just as with the five-note segment of the *pribaoutka*, the second half of this present fragment is the displaced repeat of its first. Bracketed and labeled A and B in Example 6.4a, the fragment's two halves are very nearly one and the same. Each totals seven eighth-note beats and numbers five pitches. And with the displaced repeat of the entire fragment in Example 6.4b, the internal displacement reverses itself. In Example 6.4b, segment A follows segment B.

Example 6.5. *Renard*, principal fragment, internal displacement, reduction

A = on the quarter-note beat
B = off the quarter-note beat

No doubt, the slight variations at the point of connection between the two halves A and B are likely to hinder the listener's apprehension of the construction. Even after repeated hearings, his/her sensed awareness of the underlying repetition may remain dim. The essentials of the invention can be gleaned a bit more closely by reducing them to a stereotypical pattern. Example 6.5a reproduces the notated version for comparative purposes, while Example 6.5b replaces the hinge at midpoint with the original pitch; Example 6.5c then removes the displacement altogether. Crucially, the realignment is a form of compression; segment B, the displaced repeat, enters an eighth-note beat "too soon," shortening segment A to an irregular seven eighth-note beats. And with segment B shortened in the same fashion, a full quarter-note beat is subtracted from the configuration as a whole; following the initial 4/4 measure, the 3/4 measure can be explained in these terms. The circumstances are not unlike those at the opening of the fourth tableau of *Les Noces*, where, at Rehearsal No. 93 (see Piano I in Example 5.19c), the meter underlying the displacement pattern A+B is also 4/4 + 3/4. There, too, the displaced repeat of the motive leads to the subtraction of a quarter-note beat from the larger succession.

Example 6.6. Related fragments, *Renard* and *Les Noces*; motivic segmentation,
(0 2 5), (0 2 3 5)

a) *Renard*, principal fragment, con brio

b) *Les Noces*, first tableau, opening bars

c) *Les Noces*, third tableau

d) *Les Noces*, third tableau

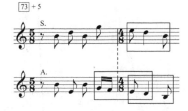

   In fact, this present fragment, shown again in Example 6.6a, may well have
originated with several earlier fragments in *Les Noces*. Example 6.6b reproduces
the opening measures of *Les Noces*, showing, by way of the boxed pitches,
a motivic segmentation different from the one outlined earlier in Examples
4.2a–d. The (E D B) trichord is regrouped in the form of B-D-E, allowing for an
anticipation of a number of subsequent appearances of this ordering in the
third tableau; see Example 6.6c. In turn, the encircled (G F E D) tetrachord in
Examples 6.6a, c, and d points more specifically to the pitch-class priority
assumed by G in the opening sections of *Renard*. Indeed, the three fragments in
Examples 6.6a, c, and d are identical in pitch and segmental content. Although
fragmental in ways discussed in Chapter 5, the contours in Example 6.6c and d
are among the more extended (as well as melodious) in *Les Noces*.

   Yet the tightness of the construction at Rehearsal No. 24 in *Renard* can
still astonish. Example 6.7 reproduces the instrumental accompaniment.

Example 6.7. *Renard*, principal fragment (tp.), octatonic triads

A = on the quarter-note beat
B = off the quarter-note beat

Collection I

And of concern here is the accompanying (G F B) chord in the string section. Repeats of this chord punctuate the individual pitches B and E of the B-D-E segment, doing so irrespective of the changes in metrical alignment. In this way, the chord functions as a form of articulation, one that remains fixed regardless of the displacements to which it is subjected.

Of concern, too, are the corresponding duplicities. The extreme elasticity of the G-F-E-D-B fragment in matters of metrical alignment extends to pitch relations as well. For although the content of segment A (or B) in terms of (G F E D B) is conspicuously diatonic ("white-note"), it is in fact octatonic as well. And it is the octatonic side of this referential equation that accounts for the four accompanying triads in the woodwinds and brass (see Example 6.7). Rooted on G, E, D♭ and B♭, these triads imply a single octatonic transposition, namely, Collection I. And their specific dispositions are arranged no less systematically. G and E of the descending thematic outline G-F-E-D-B are harmonized as triadic roots, F and D as triadic thirds; B, the exception, is harmonized as a triadic fifth. (The system here of alternating roots and thirds would have required B to be harmonized as the third of a (G B D) triad; the C♯, missing from the descending octatonic scale, would have required a (C♯ E♯ G♯) triad.) As set forth in Example 6.7, the changing dispositions of the four triads are determined by (1) the G-F-E-D-B outline they accompany, and (2) the octatonic Collection I to which that outline is accountable. An accompanying ostinato pattern in the cimbalom, wholly octatonic in this regard, further solidifies the commitment.

Motivated octatonically as well are subsequent transpositions of the fragment. They, too, are pursued with unmistakable reference to Collection I. Starting on B♭ and E, the transpositions shown in Example 6.8 are tritone-related. In the given register, the close imitation in the horns produces a rumbling effect, a "dance" meant to accompany the entrance of the Goat and Cat at this point in the scenario. The rumble may be something of a

Example 6.8. *Renard*, principal fragment, octatonic transpositions

A = on the quarter-note beat
B = off the quarter-note beat

Example 6.9. *The Rite of Spring* (1913)

representation, in other words, an attempt on Stravinsky's part to capture something of the imagined clumsiness of the entry.

Finally, the slurs, beams and accent markings in Examples 6.9–6.14 can speak to the tenacity with which, as a general rule in Stravinsky's music, fixed articulations and other small-scale groupings are pursued against the grain of displacement. Included in these examples is a wide variety of materials from, respectively, *The Rite of Spring* (1913), *The Soldier's Tale* (1918), the *Symphony of Psalms* (1930), the Violin Concerto in D (1931), the *Symphony in C* (1940), and *Agon* (1958). In each instance, a thematic

Example 6.9. (contd).

Example 6.10. *The Soldier's Tale* (1918), Music for Scene I, opening

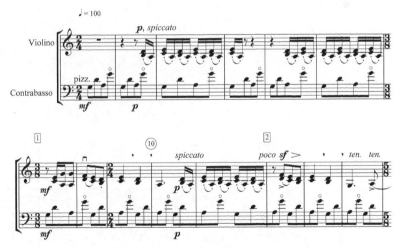

fragment falls on and off either the likely tactus or the interpretative level just above. It falls on and off the half-note beat in Examples 6.9, 6.11, and 6.12, the quarter-note beat in Examples 6.10 and 6.13, and the eighth-note beat in Example 6.14.

Example 6.11. *Symphony of Psalms* (1930), III, opening bars

Example 6.12. Violin Concerto (1931), I, opening bars

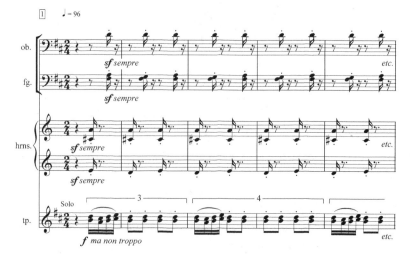

Example 6.13. *Symphony in C* (1940), III, opening bars

Example 6.14. *Agon* (1953–57), Pas-de-Quatre, opening bars

In Example 6.9 from *The Rite of Spring*, a reiterated four-note segment in the horns, A-D-C-D, falls on all four quarter-note beats of a steadily maintained 4/4 measure. It does so successively before settling, in the final bars at Rehearsal No. 70, on a series of equally-spaced repeats on the second quarter-note beat. (Although the notated meter shifts from 4/4 to 6/4 at Rehearsal No. 70, the repetition of the principal fragments continues to underscore the 4/4 design.) Although the arrangement of these placements is not strictly cyclical, it is modestly systematic all the same, capable of conveying the sense of a larger design for the passage as a whole. In contrast, the initial three entrances of the reiterated figure in the violin in Example 6.10 from *The Soldier's Tale* unfold cyclically. As with the five-note segment in *Renard*, they move "backward," starting here with the fourth eighth-note beat of the 2/4 basso ostinato pattern (off the quarter-note beat, in other words, the likely tactus with a marking of 100 BPM). They are then shifted to the ostinato's third and second eighth-note beats, on and off the quarter-note beat, respectively. Entrances of the reiterated (C E G) triad in Example 6.11 from the *Symphony of Psalms* unfold in a similar fashion. Starting on the second quarter-note beat of a 4/4 measure, they are moved "backward" to the first and fourth beats.

Changes in the metrical location of these repeated fragments stand in contrast to the absence of change in the articulation. In Example 6.9 from *The Rite of Spring*, the initial A of the reiterated A-D-C-D fragment is accented while its three-note segment D-C-D is slurred. Notwithstanding subsequent displacements (there are ten repeats in all), this articulation is never varied. Similarly, in Example 6.10 from the *The Soldier's Tale*, the dots and slurs accompanying the reiterated violin figure (spiccato) remain fixed, as do the sforzandos and pianissimos accompanying the reiterated (C E G) triad in

Example 6.11 from the *Symphony of Psalms*. And in Example 6.13 from the *Symphony in C*, the G-F-G figure in the lower strings is treated similarly. Irrespective of the shifts in the metrical alignment of the G-F-G figure, a decrescendo invariably follows a sforzando.

Significantly, too, the fragments repeated and displaced in Examples 6.9–6.14 are starting ideas of individual pieces or movements, "main themes," as Stravinsky would have expressed it. Consistent with our remarks earlier in this chapter, they initiate the compositional process. In Example 6.14 from *Agon*, the idea behind the opening of the Pas-de-Quatre rests not with the D-D-D-A motive alone (in the flutes, punctuated by the strings, pizzicato), but, far more significantly, with the pattern of placed and displaced repeats to which this motive is subjected.

Stravinsky contra Schoenberg

Underlying the stationary character of the articulation in Examples 6.9–6.14 is the same rationale as that which underlies the retention of most other features of the motive in these examples. Left intact from one motivic repeat to the next, the articulation serves as a foil for what *does* change, namely, alignment. In this way, Stravinsky's strategies of displacement overrule many of the traditional processes identified with motives and their development.

Such methods of motivic development have been studied at length, of course, above all as they appear in the music of the eighteenth, nineteenth, and twentieth centuries. Schoenberg regarded them as synonymous with the Classical style, as we have observed already.[22] Stretching from Haydn to Schoenberg's own twelve-tone works of the 1920s, 30s, and 40s, "homophonic" or Classical–Romantic music and developing variation were viewed as one and the same. And such, too, were the means by which Schoenberg sought to identify his music as traditional. Regardless of the style or method of composition, tonally extended, atonal, or serial, his music consisted homophonically of thematic shapes, counter-themes, accompaniment figures, motives, and the like. As he later explained apropos of his Five Pieces for piano, Op. 23 (1923), his method of composition just prior to his discovery of the twelve-tone idea had consisted of working "with the tones of the motive."[23]

Viewed from such an angle, metrical displacement and its melodic, harmonic, and instrumental implications can become defining in character, among the

---

[22] See note 25 in Chapter 1.

[23] Schoenberg, *Style and Idea: Selected Writings of Arnold Schoenberg*, ed. Leonard Stein, trans. Leo Black (Berkeley: University of California Press, 1985): "My Evolution" (1949), 89. This is not to discount an earlier radical, "athematic" phase in Schoenberg's atonal period, one that included, perhaps most remarkably, *Erwartung* (1909). See the discussion of this phase in Bryan Simms, *The Atonal Music of Arnold Schoenberg: 1908–1923* (Oxford University Press, 2000), 66–100.

chief ways in which Stravinsky's music is set apart not only from Schoenberg's but also from the tradition Schoenberg sought to define by way of the motive and its manipulation. Where the construction of themes and the repetition of motives or motive-forms are concerned, processes of alignment and realignment are at odds with Schoenberg's methods of developing variation.[24]

And much of the criticism directed at Stravinsky's music throughout the twentieth century can be understood in light of these large-scale distinctions. In Schoenberg's dismissals of Stravinsky's music, the literal repetition of themes and motives was condemned not only for its "folklorism" but as a matter of principle as well.[25] Literal repetition was regarded as cheap and undistinguished, an unsophisticated way of proceeding musically. As we have seen, folk or popular songs were singled out in this regard.[26] Received and ready-made, songs of this kind could not be broken up into motives or motive-forms, scattered about and grounded into the subsidiary fabric of a development. They could not be submitted to a development without inviting artificiality and the sacrifice of their aesthetic appeal, whatever it was that had caused them to be borrowed in the first place. To paraphrase from the syntactical descriptions of the motivic process employed by Schoenberg: folk songs were complete and sufficient unto themselves. They posed no problems which could be felt to be in need of solutions, no questions that required answers, no incomplete statements in need of completion by way of subsequent elaboration. Such borrowed material could be repeated and repeated again, possibly while varying or rearranging the instrumentation. But this was the extent of its potential.

Ideas of this kind would form the basis of T. W. Adorno's critical understanding of the gulf separating Stravinsky's music from Schoenberg's, as it undoubtedly would for many other composers and critics in the first half of the last century. We will be turning to these issues in greater detail in Chapter 10.[27]

---

[24] Arnold Schoenberg, *Fundamentals of Musical Composition*, ed. Gerald Strang and Leonard Stein (London: Faber and Faber, 1967), 2: "Through substantial changes, a variety of motive-forms can be produced."

[25] See Arnold Schoenberg, Foreword to his *Drei Satiren*, Op. 28. And see the translation of this in Scott Messing, *Neoclassicism in Music: From the Genesis of the Concept through the Schoenberg/Stravinsky Polemic* (University of Rochester Press, 1996), 144. "I also attack the folklorists," Schoenberg wrote, "those who want to apply to the natural, primitive concepts of folk music a technique which is suitable only for a complex way of thinking."

[26] See Schoenberg, *Style and Idea*: "Folkloristic Symphonies" (1947), 163–64. "The discrepancy between the requirements of larger forms and the simple construction of folk tunes has never been solved and cannot be solved. A simple idea must not use the language of profundity, or it can never become popular . . . Structurally, there never remains in popular tunes an unsolved problem, the consequences of which will show up only later. There is nothing in them that asks for expansion . . . A motive, in contrast to this, is incomplete and depends on continuations, explanations, clarifications, consequences, etc." See note 9 in Chapter 5.

[27] Schoenberg, *Fundamentals*, 8–10.

7 Allegro! *Renard* reconsidered

Much of the stage in *Renard* is set not by the prefacing March, which lies outside the main course of events, as it were, but rather by the allegro section which follows at Rehearsal Nos. 0–9. The latter is as much an introduction to the music as it is to the text and narrative. All forces of this remarkable "burlesque" are brought to bear, instrumental as well as vocal, *tutti* and in various lesser combinations. And the effect is stunning. Directly from the start and in a moment's time, all that Stravinsky was able to make of this conflation of Russian barnyard scenes is brought to life, a world of "gentle mockery and fun," as he once described it.[1] The text is as follows:

> Kudá, kudá, kudá, kudá, kudá!
> Da podaite mne yego syuda;
> ya nogami stopchyu.
> I toporom scrublyu!
> I nozhnishko zdesya,
> i guzhishko zdesya,
> i zarezhm zdesya,
> i povesim zdesya!

> Whither, whither, whither!
> Just give him to me hither;
> I'll trample him with my feet,
> I'll cut him up with my axe!
> A knife is here,
> and a noose is here,
> and we'll slaughter him here,
> and we'll string him up here!

This is the Cock's cry, full of contempt for the Fox (Renard) who stalks below. On a perch, the Cock struts about eyeing the Fox with empty heroics. Much of the libretto and music of *Renard* had been completed before Stravinsky turned his attention to this exact starting point, in search of a few fresh lines to convey something of the haughtiness with which he had imagined the Cock's initial taunts. He found them in "The Bear and the Cock" ("Medved' i petukh"), No. 65 in Alexander Afanasyev's *Russian Fairy*

---

[1] Igor Stravinsky and Robert Craft, *Expositions and Developments* (New York: Doubleday, 1962), 139.

Tales. The principal source texts of *Renard* had sprung from the same anthology, of course, but they were largely unrelated to No. 65.[2]

A fragment in the tenor (Tenor I) accompanies the onomatopoeic cock-crows of the first line of the text (*kuda kuda*, etc.), while an extension of that fragment in the bass (Bass I) accompanies the second line. (See the fragments listed as A and B in Tables 7.1 and 7.2. The top-to-bottom ordering in these outlines, with the vocal fragments followed by the instrumental ones, is loosely registral in design.) Assignments of this kind are fairly flexible in *Renard*, however. The main characters of the Cock, Fox, Cat, and Goat are not consistently identified with specific vocal soloists. The eight lines of the opening Cock's cry are shared by all four soloists, which include two tenors and two basses.[3] And the implications of this flexibility are similar to those noted already in connection with *Les Noces*. Attention is drawn away from the individual personalities of the characters, away from the personal and onto the shared, inherited, and universal. What counts is the "geometry" of the plot, the "intersecting of lines," as the composer would later note in connection with the staging of his neoclassical project, *Oedipus Rex* (1928).[4]

But if the ties between the stage characters and vocal soloists are fluid, those between the soloists and the various reiterated melodic fragments are not. Subsequent repeats of the opening fragment are confined to the tenor (Tenor I), while repeats of that fragment's extension in the bass (Bass I) are confined to the latter. The basso ostinato is assigned to the lower strings (viola, cello, and double bass), while repeats of the three fragments introduced by the flute, clarinet, and combined soloists are confined to those instruments and soloists. There are a few exceptions, such as the repetition of the tenor fragment by one of the solo basses at m. 32 (falsetto, however, with the tenor's register preserved), and the occasional substitution of the flute for the clarinet and vice versa later at mm. 38–50. On the whole, however, the principal fragments of the opening section are fixed instrumentally and vocally. And they are fixed registrally as well. Consistent with our earlier observations about the literalness of the repetition in Stravinsky's

---

[2] For a lively discussion of the sources of the scenario of *Renard*, see Richard Taruskin, *Stravinsky and the Russian Traditions: A Biography of the Works Through "Mavra,"* 2 vols. (Berkeley: University of California Press, 1996), vol. II: 1246–80. Taruskin includes a description of the sketchbook of *Renard*, along with a chronicle of the general compositional process.

[3] "I planned the staging myself," Stravinsky wrote much later, "and always with the consideration that *Renard* should not be confounded with opera. The players are to be dancing acrobats, and the singers are not to be identified with them; the relationship between the vocal parts and the stage characters is the same as it is in *Les Noces*, and, also as in *Les Noces*, the performers, musical and mimetic, should all be together on stage, with the singers in the center of the instrumental ensemble." See Stravinsky and Craft, *Expositions and Developments*, 138–39.

[4] Igor Stravinsky and Robert Craft, *Dialogues and A Diary* (Garden City, NY: Doubleday, 1963), 7.

Table 7.1. Renard, opening allegro, principal fragments

A) Tenor

Ku - dá, ku - dá, ku - dá, ku - dá,   ku - dá!

B) Bass I

Po - dái - te mne ye - gó   syu - dá

C) Bass II

ya . no - ga - mi stop-chyu

D) flute

E) clarinet

F) cimbalom

G) horns; combined soloists

H) basso ostinato

Table 7.2. *Renard,* opening allegro, formal layout, mm. 1–62

ensemble	solo	tutti	solo	tutti	solo
measure nos.	①	⑦	㉕	㊱	㊿②
vocal fragments	A　B		C　A B A		A　C
instrumental fragments		D E　E F G		D E　E F　F G　G	
basso ostinato	H —————————————————————————————→				

music, about the connection between literalness on the one hand and the potential for disruption on the other, there are no registral changes. And there are no modifications in dynamics, articulation, or small-scale grouping either. Here, too, all is fixed from start to finish.

In turn, the lack of mobility in instrumental assignment, register, and articulation is in keeping with the idea of a stratification, of which the opening allegro in *Renard* is a prime illustration. Identified by letter, the eight principal vocal and instrument fragments of the allegro are arranged loosely according to register in Table 7.1, and according to formal layout in Table 7.2. The correspondence here to Baroque and Classical concerto forms, with solo and tutti passages alternating with one another, and with each of these passages identified by its own fixed content, is obvious, even if it appears not to have been deliberate. At least, no evidence has been found linking *Renard* to any studied preoccupation at the time with received forms of this kind.

Yet the special resonance of Stravinsky's layered structures has to do with the metrical and vertical (or "harmonic") alignment of the fragments. Given the varying cycles or spans defined by the repetition of these fragments, their alignment will shift in relation to each other and the meter. And, once again, the implications are crucial. For, not only may steady meters be inferred rather consistently from layered structures, but they tend to be acknowledged by the notation as well. Stravinsky's bar lines are invariably conservative in textures of this kind, and the opening section of *Renard* is no exception. Putting aside the irregular 5/8 measure at m. 5, the entire section at Rehearsal Nos. 0–9 is covered by a 2/4 signature. And the evidence in support of that signature may be sensed from the start, in the agogic accents

Example 7.1. *Renard,* opening allegro, mm. 1–7, concluding segment,

displacements

a) score (radical)

b) rebarred (conservative)

that arise from the opening tenor fragment's B♭ and C on the downbeats at m. 3 and m. 4 (see Example 7.1a), and in the steady alternation between the unaccented and accented syllables of the Russian word (or cockcrow) *kuda.* The repetition of *kuda* is treated syllabically, with repeats of the unaccented and accented syllables *ku* and *da* falling off and on the quarter-note beat. A firmer agreement between verbal stress and Stravinsky's 2/4 signature would be difficult to imagine.

And so the stage is set early on. A steady 2/4 meter is introduced, a framework in relation to which the various fragments identified in Tables 7.1 and 7.2 are subjected to displacements of varying degrees of intensity. The displacements are sometimes immediate and, as such, likely to be disruptive of the listener's metrical bearings. At other times, however, they lie more deeply in the background of the metrical framework. But whatever the particulars of location and intensity, they fit into a larger scheme, one that lies at the heart of this music. The "gentle mockery and fun" of which Stravinsky wrote when addressing *Renard* is derived in no small part from the play of these metrical shifts.

Extra eighth-note beats

The irregular 5/8 measure at m. 5 fits into the larger scheme as well, although as the source of a series of complications. This may not be apparent from the score itself, there being no signs of the confusion a 5/8 measure and its extra eighth-note beat (a 2/4 measure plus an eighth) might be expected to create.[5] Experientially, however, the opening page of *Renard* is apt to consist of little else but complication. Indeed, with a view toward unraveling the impact of this single 5/8 measure on the listener, whole treatises might well have been enlisted, inquiries into the special music-historical, theoretical, stylistic, aesthetic, and perceptual terms of the experience. In the process, much light might have been shed on the nature of meter and on Stravinsky's art in particular. And even then, questions are likely to have been left unanswered. Why should the notation have turned radical at m. 5? And why should it have done so in a fashion so singular, so entirely isolated and set apart from the remaining sixty-one measures of the opening section?

And the notation *does* turn radical at this point, and in the quasi-technical sense in which this term was introduced in Chapter 1. As can be seen from the boxed-off areas in Example 7.1a, the concluding segment of the tenor fragment, (G-F-Bb)(G-Bb-C), is transposed down a fifth and repeated as the concluding segment of the bass fragment, (C-Bb-Eb)(C-Eb-F). And these concluding segments are aligned identically. Notwithstanding the 5/8 measure and its extra eighth-note beat at m. 5, the concluding six pitches (3 + 3) of the fragment and its transposed repeat enter two eighth-note beats before the succeeding bar line, with their final pitches falling on the downbeats at m. 4 and m. 7, respectively. And so the irregular 5/8 measure has the preservation of an alignment as its rationale. And the assumption is that the listener will respond accordingly. Seeking to align the transposed repeat of the fragment as before, the listener will do so by adding an extra eighth-note beat to the count at m. 5. And this will allow the segment's final pitch F to fall on the quarter-note beat and bar line at m. 7. It will also allow the stressed Russian syllable *da* in *syuda* to fall on the same beat, directly parallel to its occurrence in *kuda* at m. 4. The clarinet fragment (fragment E in Tables 7.1 and 7.2) will enter similarly, as indicated

---

[5] See note 28 in Chapter 1 for a brief description of the role played by the "extra" beat in radical interpretations of displacement.

already in our discussion of the continuation of this tutti passage in Chapter 1 (see Example 1.2a). It will enter on the beat at m. 7.

At the same time, however, the steady 2/4 meter could have been sustained at m. 5. As is shown by the boxed-off areas in Example 7.1b, this conservative alternative would have left the transposed repeat of the tenor fragment displaced. Beginning at m. 5, the transposed repeat would have fallen off the quarter-note beat. More specifically, it would have fallen on the last rather than next-to-last eighth-note beat of the measures in question. And the clarinet fragment would have entered off rather than on the quarter-note beat at m. 7, a shift which greatly alters its character.[6]

No doubt, these radical and conservative alternatives are extremes. In line with our remarks in Chapter 1, the response to this music is likely to be uncertain and hesitant at points. The impulse to allow (radically) for an interruption of the 2/4 meter in order to align the concluding segment in a parallel fashion (to follow Stravinsky's notation in Example 7.1a, in other words), is not likely to be lost on the conservative listener.[7] Apart from the transposition down a fifth, the repetition of the segment at mm. 5–7 is without changes in grouping or articulation. And the literalness of the repeat strengthens the forces of alignment, as we have suggested, those that would align as before, and do so by breaking up the meter and adding an eighth-note beat at m. 5. "Notes of relatively long duration" are an issue as well, the agogic accents that arise from the long-held pitches E♭ at m. 6 and F at m. 7.[8] Independently of the issue of alignment, in other words, the coincidence of these pitches with Stravinsky's notated bar lines in Example 7.1a is likely to strengthen the radical option.

But however weighty the evidence in support of a radical interpretation of the irregular 5/8 measure at m. 5, it, too, is likely to be sensed with a good deal of qualification. Ignored thus far has been the basso ostinato, a two-measure pattern which accompanies the opening tenor, bass, and clarinet fragments. The pattern extends through the whole of the opening allegro, in fact, and with but a single hitch, namely, the irregular 5/8 measure at m. 5. As can be seen in Example 7.1a, the extra eighth-note beat displaces the

---

[6] The conservative alternative to Stravinsky's radical barring at m. 5 could be made perceptually more apparent by easing the tempo from 126 BPM for the quarter-note beat to, say, 115 or even 120 BPM.

[7] The assumption here is that, while focusing on a given interpretation or structure, whether radical or conservative in nature, listeners can hold competing interpretations or structures at bay. Not only are they able to sense the challenge of an opposing interpretation or structure and be interrupted or disrupted by it, they can also switch "in midstream" without having to backtrack to a beginning. See Ray Jackendoff, "Musical Parsing and Musical Affect," *Music Perception* 9, no. 2 (1991): 223. These perceptual matters were discussed briefly in Chapter 1.

[8] Fred Lerdahl and Ray Jackendoff, *A Generative Theory of Tonal Music* (Cambridge: MIT Press, 1983), 80–85.

pattern, shifting it from the second to the first eighth-note beat of the given
bar lines. After m. 5, it falls on rather than off the quarter-note and half-note
beats. And this results in the emergence of yet another obstacle for the
radical listener: he/she will have to accept a form of displacement after all!
Having struggled with the forces of meter up to this point, forces that would
have allowed for a displacement of the concluding segment, radical listeners
will now have to accept the realignment of the ostinato pattern. Somewhat
sadistically, as it can seem, the stakes are raised just as the battle may well
have seemed won for these listeners, just as they may have thought themselves in the clear, so to speak.

The larger point here again, however, is that, even at this juncture, a very
different response may be envisioned on the part of these radical listeners.
Something altogether less stressful can be imagined, in fact, a much easier
adjustment to the ostinato newly placed at m. 7. Instead of the difficulties
envisioned just above, listeners might adjust quickly to the new alignment
while recognizing the earlier one as having been off track – in effect, a form
of displacement. And to judge from the finished score (see Example 7.1a),
which includes the radical notation at m. 5 and the crossings of the bar line
at mm. 1–5, this is how Stravinsky himself seems to have imagined the
reaction of his listeners.

Of course, to assume that the ostinato pattern is displaced at mm. 5–6 (see
Example 7.1a), is to assume that the beams which cross the bar lines prior to
this point do so rhythmically rather than metrically. It is to assume that they
represent a form of grouping, a joining that might more traditionally have
been acknowledged by phrase markings. Outlined in Examples 7.2a, b, and

Example 7.2. *Renard*, opening allegro, ostinato pattern

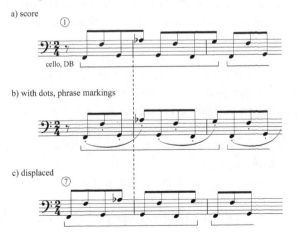

Example 7.3. *Renard*, opening allegro, analytical rebarring, displacement

c, the beams and slur markings are explained in the following terms: they underscore F-F-G-Ab and G-F-F-G as motivic subgroupings of the ostinato. Initially out of phase with the 2/4 meter, these subgroupings enter off the quarter-note and half-note beats, only to be shifted to these beats further along at m. 6. And, as with the clarinet fragment in the conservative reading of this passage, the displacement greatly alters the musical character of the fragment.

Indeed, to assume otherwise on the part of the radical listener would be to assume an alternative metrical structure, and along the lines indicated in Example 7.3. Here, in yet another analytical rebarring of this passage, the tenor fragment and the ostinato pattern enter on rather than off the quarter-note beat. They enter on the first rather than on the second eighth-note beat of the 2/4 measure, a shift "backwards" by a notch. And this ensures, without the necessity of adding an eighth-note beat, an arrival "on target" at m. 7.

For the reasons already cited, however, this latter option may appear far-fetched. The tenor fragment and its concluding segment are far more readily heard and understood as notated, that is, as entering off the quarter-note beat. And it is the tenor fragment toward which the attention of the listener is likely to be directed, and in relation to which the ostinato pattern is likely to be heard as subsidiary. Even as a competing metrical structure, in other words, the rebarring of Example 7.3 is apt to figure only very peripherally.

The plot thickens for the conservative listener as well. Additional obstacles in the path of the radical course are apt to facilitate his/her perspective. In struggling to sustain the 2/4 meter against the forces of parallelism at mm.1–7, listeners can look to the ostinato for support. Holding on to its initial alignment off the quarter-note beat, they can look to the 2/4 meter.

But for how long is this conservative option at mm.1–7 (Example 7.1b) likely to hold out against the radical one (Example 7.1a)? Difficulties are apt to persist with the entrance of the clarinet fragment at m. 7. For there are no subsequent irregularities in the notation, and hence no possibility of evening out the irregular count with, say, the subtraction of an eighth-note beat. So, too, there is no way of arriving "on target" with the notated bar lines; quite simply, the conservative option is abandoned. Accents, spans, alignments, and articulations at mm. 7–17 favor the radical side of the coin, the one represented by Stravinsky's notated bar lines (Example 7.1a). A switch seems inevitable, in fact, with conservative listeners yielding to the notation at some point in this initial tutti passage at mm. 7–17.

The final twist in this metrical tug-of-war comes with the return of the initial solo passage at mm. 25–30 (see Example 7.4). The complications of the opening page are removed altogether, and the passage is barred conservatively rather than radically. Crucially, an eighth-note beat is subtracted from the count at m. 29, leaving the concluding five-note segment in the bass (Bass I) shortened. Conservative and radical readers will thus be able to arrive "on target" with the notated meter at m. 30. For both, the clarinet fragment will enter on the downbeat.

In other ways, however, Stravinsky's conservative barring at mm. 25–30 is consistent with the analytical rebarring of Example 7.1b. With the extra beat of the earlier 5/8 measure missing, the concluding segment in the bass is displaced at m. 29, along with the stressed syllable *go* in the Russian word *yego*; the latter falls off rather than on the beat. Here, music and words are joined by the common purpose that seems to have been at the core of Stravinsky's "rejoicing discovery." Metrically aligned and then realigned, reiterating word-syllables as well as musical fragments partake of the same overall process.

Example 7.4. *Renard*, opening allegro, tenor and bass fragments

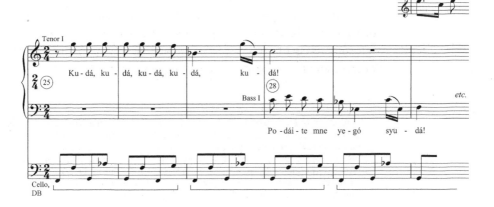

Substructure

A more complete picture of the opening allegro in *Renard* would need to address displacement at intermediate and background levels as well as at the surface. It would need to confront the full range of metrical alignment and realignment. And this would mean, at least initially, turning again briefly to Stravinsky's basso ostinato.

The two measures spanned by the ostinato are a source of hypermeter. At the metrical location of +2 (see Figure 1.5), whole-note beats or measures are added to or subtracted from the count. At the same location, reiterating fragments fall on and off the two-measure beat. In the allegro, for example, the subtraction of a measure early on is not evened out until much later in the second *tutti* passage at mm. 54–55. As we shall see below, the chief yardstick in coming to terms with the long-term "dissonance" initiated by this displacement is the two-measure module.[9]

Yet it is on a much smaller scale that the ostinato's most intriguing features are revealed. Isolated in Examples 7.5a–e are the two halves of the pattern, a five-note segment followed, in overlapping fashion, by its retrograde. The ostinato's opposing halves form a palindrome, in other words, pitch-specific and hence contour-true. Labeled P and R for prime and retrograde in Example 7.5b, respectively, they are marked off by arrows as well.

Affixed to the ostinato in this way, the back-and-forth motion between the two overlapping pitches A♭ and G is repeated thirty-one times throughout the allegro. As the highest of the ostinato's three pitches, A♭ is sounded only once in the single cycle, so that, for the listener, the sensation of repeatedly moving to and from this pitch is what is likely to stand out. To the repetition of the ostinato pattern itself is thus added this internally defined oscillation. So, too, immobility can be sensed as reaching into the smallest detail. Below the surface, the individual segments contained within the ostinato are a product of the repetition, displacement, and reordering that governs the lengthier fragments and blocks at higher and more conspicuous levels of structure. The internal workings of the pattern are a microcosm of what happens above and beyond it.

---

[9] The idea here of a long-term *dissonance* has as much to do with the definition of sonata form or the Classical style in Charles Rosen, *Sonata Forms* (New York: Norton, 1980), 24–25, as it does with Harold Krebs, *Fantasy Pieces: Metrical Dissonance in the Music of Robert Schumann* (Oxford University Press, 1999), 22–39, where conflicting levels of metrical pulsation are termed "dissonant." According to Rosen, the modulation to the dominant in the exposition of the sonata form invests the latter with a long-term structural "dissonance," one requiring, in equally dramatic terms, a resolution to the tonic in the recapitulation.

Example 7.5. *Renard*, opening allegro, basso ostinato

a) score

A four-note segment and its subsequent displacement may also be inferred from the ostinato (see Example 7.5c). The two segments may be spotted more readily in the viola part (arco) and in fragment C (see Examples 7.5a and e, respectively), where the octave displacements of the cello and bass parts are omitted and the pattern is confined to a single register. With A♭ as the point of separation, a shift in the alignment of this segment may be discerned. Still more microscopically, two partially overlapping three-note segments may be inferred as well, G-F-F and its retrograde F-F-G. Bracketed in Example 7.5d, these embedded segments are repeated and displaced from one measure to the next. They fall alternatively on and off the quarter-note beat.

We should mention, too, as another segmentation of the ostinato pattern, the two contrapuntal lines that result from the displaced octaves in the cello and bass parts, F-Ab-F-G in the upper register and F-G-G-F in the lower one. Beginning at m. 6, the syncopation in the first of these lines colors the ostinato, even as the two streams are blurred somewhat by the single registers of the accompanying viola part and fragment C. From m. 52 to the end of the allegro, fragment C doubles the ostinato in the lower of the two registers, a doubling that is not entirely literal, however. As can be seen by the boxed-off area in Example 7.5e, the final G of the ostinato is replaced by a repeated F. And with the G omitted, the displaced repeats of the three-note segments are omitted as well. A form of liquidation may be inferred from this, with some of the fragments and more individual features of fragments eliminated as the section as a whole draws to a close.

Astonishing in their intricacy, these details may be compared to those examined earlier in connection with the basso ostinato at Rehearsal Nos. 68–72 in the third tableau of *Les Noces* (see Example 5.17). There, too, it could seem as if, in a few special instances, Stravinsky had sought to outdo himself in the bass with a repetitive pattern that was something other than just another ostinato. At issue is not only the subtlety of the varying alignments of the given patterns, but also the layer of substructure that is added to the complexity of the whole.

Structure in the large

All eight fragments listed in Tables 7.1 and 7.2 are subjected to displacements of one kind or another, some in more ways than one, and at different locations of the metrical grid. The realignments range from the minute to the intermediate and the large-scale. Most are in the intermediate range of +1; displacements at the location of 0, with fragments falling on and off the quarter-note beat or tactus, are comparatively rare. In fact, the level 0 displacements resulting from the irregular 5/8 measure on the opening page of *Renard* are apt to come as something of a jolt to the listener. It is as if, at the very outset of the allegro, the composer had wanted to jump-start the machinery of the stratification and its separately revolving parts. The remainder of the allegro can seem to coast as a result, with the impact of the +1 and +2 displacements less disruptive of the listener's bearings.

As the principal fragment of the two tutti sections at mm. 7–17 and 36–52, the clarinet fragment has been examined already (see Examples 1.2a and b). Five quarter-note beats in length, it falls automatically on and off the bar line when repeated successively. Similar in construction are the fragments of the flute and combined soloists, shown here in Examples 7.6a, b, and c. Both are displaced relative to the ostinato pattern and its two-measure module. In the

Example 7.6. *Renard*, opening allegro, fl., comb. soloists, ostinato fragments, displacements

first *tutti* passage (Example 7.6a), the flute fragment enters in the second measure of the two-measure module, while, in the second *tutti* passage (Example 7.6b) it enters in the first. The scheme is reversed by the fragment of the combined soloists, which enters in the first measure of the module in Example 7.6a and in the second measure in Example 7.6b.

The +1 displacements in the repetition of these same fragments follow in quick succession. Entering on the second quarter-note beat of a 2/4 measure in Examples 7.6a and b, the flute fragment enters on the first beat in Example 7.6c. Similarly, the fragment of the combined soloists enters on the first quarter-note beat in Example 7.6a, but on the second beat in Example 7.6b.

The graph in Table 7.3 allows for a more comprehensive view of the second *tutti* passage at mm. 36–52, Rehearsal Nos. 5–8. Shown here are the successive repeats of the fragments in the flute, clarinet, cimbalom, and combined soloists, along with the changing alignments of these repeats as they relate to one another and the 2/4 meter; arrows mark off the ends of the repeats. And of particular concern is the segmentation of the clarinet fragment, its eventual shortening and confinement to a single measure. Repeated several times in this way, the confinement reinforces the 2/4 bar line or half-note beat, and just as the +1 displacements of the fragments in the flute and combined soloists get under way. In this connection,

Table 7.3. *Renard,* opening allegro, tutti passage, mm. 36–52

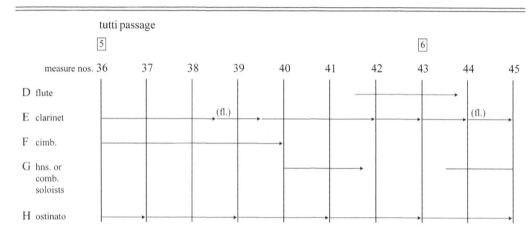

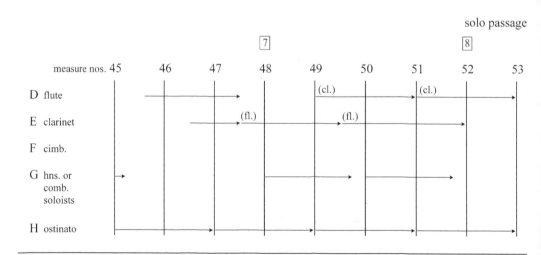

the stratification is a good deal denser in the second *tutti* passage at Rehearsal Nos. 6–8 than in the first at Nos. 1–3. In climactic fashion, there is an accumulation of fragments and doublings as this passage draws to a close.

No doubt, at still higher levels of the metrical grid, levels that would include the bar line and above (hypermeter), meter fades. As we have noted in Chapters 1 and 4, beats at these levels are spaced too far apart for the impression of an up-down, on-off alternation to impose itself; internalized meter gives way to a kind of grouping and, as one music theorist has put it, a more conscious strategy of "counting."[10] Listeners add or subtract measures to and from established norms, with a larger sense of temporal order fashioned accordingly.

In Examples 7.7a, b, and c, the tenor fragment (Tenor I) is introduced off the quarter-note beat; more specifically, on the second eighth-note beat of a 2/4 measure. Toward the close of the opening section, however, at m. 52 (Example 7.7c), the same fragment, although remaining off the quarter-note beat, is shifted to the sixth eighth-note beat of the two-measure span. It is moved from the first to the second measure of the ostinato pattern, that pattern from which much of the listener's sense of hypermeter is likely to be derived. And the result is a displacement involving the two levels indicated; at the highest of these levels, the level spanning two measures, the tenor fragment falls first on and then off the beat.

The origin of this high-level displacement may be traced back to m. 28 (Example 7.7b). There, the fragment in the bass (Bass I) enters three measures after the entrance of the tenor fragment; earlier at m. 5 (Example 7.7a), it had entered four measures after the tenor entrance. (See the brackets in Examples 7.7a, b, and c.) In other words, the bass fragment enters one measure "too soon" at m. 28, cutting off the tenor fragment and effectively shortening it from a four- to a three-measure span. (In terms of the grouping, of course, repeats of the tenor fragment straddle the bar line of a fourth measure; they come to a close accordingly.) And the implications of this irregularity are considerable. All reiterating fragments follow suit. Falling on even- rather than odd-numbered measures, they, too, are displaced from the first to the second measure of the ostinato pattern.

---

[10] See Candace Brower, "Memory and the Perception of Rhythm," *Music Theory Spectrum* 15, no. 1 (1993): 28. "At higher levels of the metric hierarchy," Brower observes, "the listener uses counting to group smaller metric units into larger ones."

Example 7.7. *Renard*, opening allegro, tenor fragment

Not until the close of the allegro at m. 55 (Example 7.7c) is the original alignment between these fragments and the ostinato pattern restored. Answering the tenor fragment, the bass again enters "too soon" (Bass II this time, fragment C), and with the consequence that the tenor fragment is again shortened to a three-measure span. Here, however, the shortening compensates for the earlier subtraction. Beats subtracted earlier are "made good," as the original alignment between the ostinato and the remaining fragments is restored. A long-term metrical "dissonance" is thus resolved in the concluding bars of the allegro. At this highest of levels, conservative and radical listeners arrive "on target."

Large-scale displacements can bring more traditional contexts to mind. Featured in the background of a metrical framework, displacements of this kind involve switches from odd- to even-numbered measures and vice versa. An entire structure may shift in relation to a prevailing two- or four- measure norm.[11]

Of course, unlike the opening allegro in *Renard*, there are as a rule no basso ostinatos in these traditional settings. Instead, the two-measure beat is often reinforced by parallel rhythmic-melodic structures. In Stravinsky's music, ostinatos carry harmonic implications, static and non-progressive ones for the most part. In the main, however, they function as metrical frames of reference, foils highlighting the shifts in placement among reiterating fragments and chords. Indeed, with tonality (or, more generally, a sense of pitch-class centricity) weakened or absent altogether in pieces such as *Renard*, pitch-structural support for meter is weakened as well; the reliance on metrical placement and parallelism for such support (on ostinatos, in the most obvious cases), is that much greater. The irony, however, is that this greater reliance on placement in the establishment of a meter is met by the forms of displacement and disruption surveyed in the chapters of this volume. It is as if processes of displacement had actually materialized as a way of exploiting this increased reliance.

A second outline of the opening section of *Renard* at mm. 1–62 appears in Table 7.4. The bracketed spans in this display trace the entrances of the various fragments in the tenor (Tenor I), bass (Bass I and Bass II), and combined soloists; solo and *tutti* passages alternate with one another. And it is from these spans that a larger sense of form is likely to emerge; the return of the *tutti* passage at m. 36 is especially crucial in this regard. (With the beginnings rather than the endings of the various fragments recorded, grouping, which may overlap occasionally, is only partially represented.) Noteworthy in this regard is the persistence of the even-numbered spanning of two and four measures. Encircled in Table 7.4, the exceptions are the two three-measure spans discussed above, spans which, at m. 25 and m. 52, first displace and then restore the original alignment of the ostinato and the remaining, reiterating fragments.

---

[11] See, in Chapter 1, our brief discussion of the opening of Mozart's G minor Symphony, K. 550.

Table 7.4. *Renard*, opening allegro, mm. 1–62

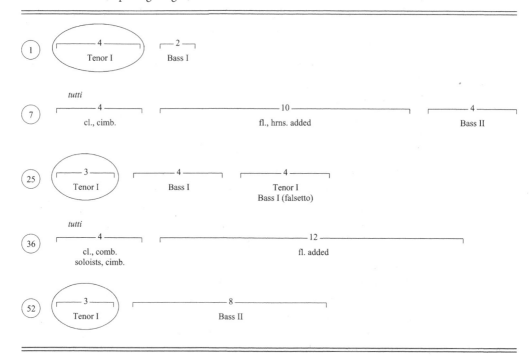

Pitch relations

In contrast to the fluidity of rhythm and meter at the outset of *Renard*, pitch organization is essentially static. This is apt to be true of layered structures generally, of course. Content, including articulation and dynamic shading, is fixed, while, in their alignment, the various fragments shift in relation to each other and the meter. Vertical or harmonic coincidence shifts as well, but as a result of these local changes in alignment. "Harmonic" change will tend to be heard and understood accordingly, that is, incidentally as an effect of metrical placement and displacement. And the variables are not only limited but are set early on as well. The shifts occur without a larger sense of harmonic progress or direction, without the implication of a long-term goal in this respect. In the end, structures of this kind tend to break off inconclusively with a sudden reduction in density or in the number of layers. The opening allegro closes with the ostinato and its doubling by the bass fragment C standing very nearly alone. This can bring processes of liquidation to mind (as described by Schoenberg),[12] according to which, at the close of a section or movement, the most dynamic or characteristic features of a given theme or motive are gradually eliminated from the repetition. Left standing is that which is most common and lacking in implication – in the present case, the ostinato. The role it assumes here is not unlike that of a repetitive pattern in wallpaper.

At the same time, pitch relations in the opening allegro section are overwhelmingly diatonic. They are also modal and even Dorian at times, although articulated not in terms of the (0 2 3 5) tetrachord, as was the case rather conspicuously in *The Rite of Spring* and *Les Noces*, but rather in terms of the (0 2 7 9) tetrachord and its superset, the (0 2 3 5 7 9) hexachord.[13] The latter plays a role in *Les Noces* as well, as we have seen in Chapter 5, but to a far lesser extent than in *Renard*.

All eight fragments listed in Table 7.1 are diatonic. Something of their combined, harmonic sense can be gleaned from the list itself, which, as we have indicated, reflects a registral distribution. The tenor, cimbalom, and clarinet fragments all begin on G, with the first two of these fragments returning to G as well. As a point of departure and return, G is thus apt to acquire a sense of pitch-class priority. Most of the fragments descend, with their initial pitches reiterated or embellished by neighbor-like motions (the A as a neighbor note to the G in the clarinet and cimbalom fragments, for example). Hence the preference in Examples 7.8 and 7.9, as indeed earlier in the illustrations of Chapters 1, 5, and 6 as well, for a descending approach in the representation and numbering of the relevant pitch-class sets and scales.

Example 7.8. *Renard*, opening allegro, overlapping (0 2 7 9) tetrachords

---

[12] See Arnold Schoenberg, *Fundamentals of Musical Composition*, ed. Gerald Strang and Leonard Stein (London: Faber and Faber, 1967).

[13] The normal, ascending form of (0 2 7 9) is (0 2 5 7), set-class 4–23. Numbered, 4–23 plays a key role as a cohesive motivic grouping in Stravinsky's music, as the source not only of numerous ostinato patterns in Russian-period works such as *Petrushka* and *The Soldier's Tale*, but also of melodic segments in neoclassical works from *Pulcinella* (1919) to *Agon* (1953–57). See the discussion of these additional (0 2 5 7) contexts in Pieter C. van den Toorn, *The Music of Igor Stravinsky* (New Haven: Yale University Press, 1983), 176–97; and in Pieter C. van den Toorn, *Music, Politics, and The Academy* (Berkeley: University of California Press, 1995), 160–69.

Example 7.9. *Renard*, opening allegro, overlapping (0 2 3 5 7 9) hexachords

Starting with the opening bars of the allegro, the four-pitch tenor fragment, (G-F-B♭) (G-B♭-C), is transposed down a fifth by the concluding
segment of the bass fragment, (C-B♭-E♭) (C-E♭-F). As shown in Example
7.8, these fragments are forms of the pitch-class set (0 2 7 9); the fifth-related
transposition causes them to overlap by whole steps or 2s. In turn, the
overlapping 2s of these transpositions are the 2s of the fragments themselves, with the fit here between abstract model and presented surface
exceptionally tight. The (0 2 7 9) tetrachord may be arranged alternatively
as a four-note segment of the 7-cycle. In this way, the opening tenor fragment in terms of G-C-F-B♭ may be heard and understood as a form of
anticipation, a point of departure for the fifth-related transpositions that
follow.

At the same time, A♭, the highest pitch of the ostinato pattern (doubled
by the second bass fragment C), can suggest another downward transposition of the (0 2 7 9) tetrachord. And if the pitch content of the resultant
(0 2 7 9)s is filled in, a chain of three overlapping (0 2 3 5 7 9) hexachords
results (see Example 7.9). So, too, the content of the remaining fragments in
Table 7.1 implies a further extension of the (0 2 3 5 7 9) unit, this time
upward by two notches.

Crucial here is the idea of a spread of overlapping (0 2 7 9) tetrachords
and (0 2 3 5 7 9) hexachords along the 7-cycle or circle of fifths. The (G F)(C
B♭) and (G F E D C B♭) units implied by the opening tenor fragment are
central in this regard (see the brackets in Example 7.8 and 7.9), with the
actual sound that largely of a *superimposition* (rather than progression) of
(0 2 7 9)s and (0 2 3 5 7 9)s.

The partial *Tonnetz* of Figure 7.1 allows for a more compact (although
necessarily more abstract) view of the three descending (0 2 7 9)s bracketed
in Example 7.8. Reading from left to right, the (0 2 7 9)s move back and forth
between the 7- and 2- cycles, as plotted along the vertical and horizontal
axes, respectively; graphically, they alternate between the squares and the
parallelograms. (Solid lines mark off the squares, solid and dotted lines,
the parallelograms.) The zigzag motion allows for a parsimonious graph; the
common tones between the fifth-related (0 2 7 9)s are represented at the

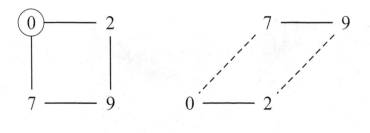

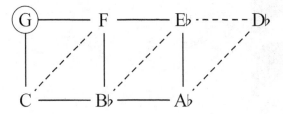

Figure 7.1. *Tonnetz*, (0 2 7 9) tetrachords; *Renard*, opening allegro, tenor fragment, transpositions

vertices of the successive squares and parallelograms, showing them as points of intersection. (There are three common tones between fifth-related (0 2 7 9)s, not just the two that are sustained literally at mm.1–7 between the tenor fragment and its transposition down a fifth in the bass.) Figure 7.1 includes a fourth (0 2 7 9), Bb-Ab-Eb-Db, and largely in recognition of the passage at Rehearsal No. 27. There, a (Bb (Ab) G F Eb Db) hexachordal fragment in the bass is superimposed over a reiterated Bb-Db figure in the cimbalom.

The (0 2 7 9) tetrachord is segmented by its (0 2 9/0 7 9) trichordal subsets in Figure 7.2, with the squares and parallelograms being divided into triangles. The segmentation is implied by the tenor fragment itself, which begins with G-F-Bb and ends with G-Bb-C. More abstractly, the two trichords may be reduced to (Bb G F) and (C Bb G), respectively, and then to the motivic forms (0 3 5) and (0 2 5) to which our attention was drawn extensively in Chapters 4, 5, and 6. Subsets more readily of the (0 2 3 5) Dorian tetrachord in *The Rite of Spring* and *Les Noces*, (0 3 5) and (0 2 5) are subsets of (0 2 7 9) in the opening sections in *Renard* (with (0 2 5 7) as the prime form of (0 2 7 9), reading down, as always). Whatever the superset identification, however, the role of (0 2 5) in particular as a common denominator or basic cell of the Russian period more generally would seem to be confirmed from yet another angle. The role (0 2 5) plays in this capacity is harmonic as well as melodic, coming by way of innumerable

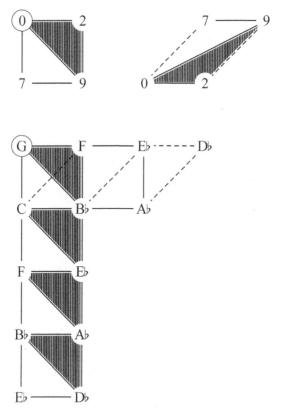

Figure 7.2. *Tonnetz*, (0 2 7 9) tetrachords, (0 2 9 / 0 7 9) trichordal subsets; *Renard*, opening allegro, tenor fragment, transpositions

vertical sonorities, including the dominant seventh chord, as well as linear fragments.

Descending along the vertical axis in Figure 7.2, (0 2 9) and (0 7 9) are inversionally related; the single (0 2 9)s are represented by shaded triangles, the (0 7 9)s by blank ones. Crucially, both (0 2 9) and (0 7 9) are octatonic; while G-F-B♭ refers to Collection I, G-B♭-C refers to Collection III. (The (0 2 7 9) tetrachord is not accountable to a single octatonic transposition.) And it is the first of these trichords, G-F-B♭, along with its affiliation with Collection I, that serves as the bridge to the octatonic in *Renard*. The transition comes by way, first, of a tritone transposition of the tenor fragment, and, second, of the con brio section at Rehearsal Nos. 24–26.

Indeed, the intervention of octatonic relations in *Renard* follows the opening allegro almost immediately, at m. 63 with a flourish in the cimbalom. At m. 91, Rehearsal No. 13, the tenor fragment, reproduced again in Example 7.10a, is transposed not at the fifth, but at the tritone (see Example

Example 7.10. *Renard*, clarinet fragment, tritone transposition and displacement

7.10b). And with G-F-B♭ retained as the connecting link (see the boxed-off area in Example 7.10a), Collection I intervenes. C♯-B-E joins G- F-B♭ in an anticipation of Collection I. (Notice the metrical displacement in these examples, with the tenor fragment falling first off and then on the quarter-note beat.)

With intervals retained, the retrograde form of G-F-B♭ is subsequently introduced as part of the new flourish in the cimbalom at Rehearsal No. 24 (see Example 6.7, as discussed earlier in Chapter 6). And with B♭-F-G transposed to the remaining three (0, 3, 6, 9) partitioning elements of Collection I, G, E, and D♭, the flourish is repeated as an accompanying ostinato to the new octatonic–diatonic theme in the trumpet. The theme itself, G-F-E-D-B at the outset, has been discussed in connection with its built-in repeat structure (see Example 6.4).

Reproduced in Figure 7.3 is the *Tonnetz* of Figures 7.1 and 7.2, only expanded in order to cover this present turn to the octatonic in *Renard*. Located at the bottom of the table is the parsimonious graph of the tenor fragment and its transpositions, the four fifth-related (0 2 7 9)s. Beyond this point of departure, transpositions proceed not along the horizontal or vertical axes, but, starting with the retrograde of G-F-B♭, along the southeast-to-northwest diagonal. As the initial segment of the cimbalom's ostinato pattern, B♭-F-G is transposed along one of the minor-third chains.

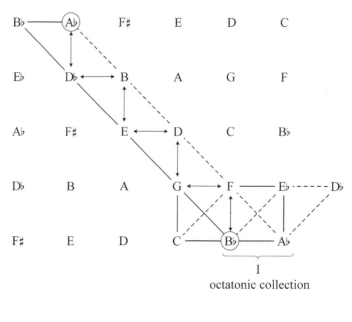

I
octatonic collection

Figure 7.3. *Tonnetz*, (0 2 7 9) tetrachords, (0 7 9) trichordal subsets; *Renard*, octatonic–diatonic interaction

In sum, the intrusion of octatonic relations in *Renard* comes by way of the opening tenor fragment, (G-F-Bb)(G-Bb-C), whose first three pitches, octatonic in terms of Collection I, are joined by C♯-B-E in a transposition at the tritone (Example 7.10b). By way of the ostinato in the cimbalom at Rehearsal No. 24, they are joined eventually by E-D-G and Bb-Ab-Db as well. As with the many contexts examined in Chapter 5, the joining of the octatonic with the diatonic is motivic in conception. Here, the octatonic potential of the tenor fragment, otherwise diatonic in terms of (0 2 7 9), is exploited by means of its trichordal subset (0 2 9). Transposed along the minor-third cycle and with its contour in place, (0 2 9) serves as the connecting link.

Coda: the Royal March in *The Soldier's Tale* (1918)

Most often in Stravinsky's settings of displacement, metrical irregularities are met with subsequent, balancing irregularities. As far as the printed page is concerned, irregular counts are evened out at some point, with added or subtracted beats "made good." Conservative listeners, parting from the radically shifting meter of the printed page, can arrive "on target" with that meter. In the opening block of *Les Noces*, for example, a concealed 3/8 meter arrives "on target" with the rapidly changing bar lines of Stravinsky's notation. The two sides intersect at the end of this block, as the reiterated motive D-E, displaced repeatedly in relation to the sustained 3/8 meter of the conservative reading, is restored to its initial alignment. And in the opening allegro of *Renard*, the early subtraction of a 2/4 measure is eventually evened out by another subtraction in the second *tutti* passage.

But such is not the case on the opening pages of *Renard*. The fiendishness of the extra eighth-note beat at m. 5 arises from the inability of the conservative option to meet up with the radical one of the printed page. Listeners in pursuit of a conservative reading will be forced to abandon it at some point. Instances of this may be found elsewhere in Stravinsky's music, although without the complications of the opening bars of *Renard*.

A case in point is the Royal March of *The Soldier's Tale* at Rehearsal Nos. 9–11. Two thematic fragments are implicated here, a lead-on fragment to the main theme (Example 7.11a), and the main theme itself (Example 7.11b). With the same durations, metrical alignments, and number of notes, the two themes are variations on a set of constancies. They are also "corny Spanish figurations," as Wilfrid Mellers has noted,[14] exemplifying the cosmopolitan turn of *The Soldier's Tale*, a quality shared by other works

Example 7.11. *The Soldier's Tale*, Royal March, main themes
a) lead-on theme

b) main theme

c) earlier:

14 Wilfrid Mellers, *Romanticism and the 20th Century* (New Jersey: Essential Books, 1957), 202.

of the later Russian period, and perhaps most conspicuously by the *Three Easy Pieces* (1914–15) and the *Five Easy Pieces* (1917). In particular, in the Royal March, the style is modeled after the *pasodoble*, a Spanish dance with a strong 2/4 marching character.[15]

Significantly, however, the compositional process remains unchanged. The two themes simulate Spanish popular tunes in the same way that, in *Les Noces* and *Renard*, melody consists in large part of a "fabrication" of Russian popular tunes.[16] Typically in the latter case, the materials are folk-sounding rather than folk-derived. In the Royal March of *The Soldier's Tale*, the two fragments cited in Examples 7.11a, b, and c are clichés of Spanish popular idioms, ordinary and even trivial as such. And so the excitement they generate will stem from the particular use to which this familiarity is put, in Stravinsky's case more specifically from the processes of metrical displacement to which it is subjected.

Indeed, the triplet figure shared by the two themes is a cliché metrically as well as tonally. As a convention, it falls on the downbeat of a steady meter. And, assuming the listener's awareness of this location, his/her impulse will doubtless be to align the figure accordingly, and to do so in the face of any displacements (or attempted displacements) to which, on the basis of a sustained 3/4 meter, it might be subjected.

A more telling demonstration of assimilation, of the means by which borrowed materials were remade in the composer's image, would be difficult to imagine. In Stravinsky's neoclassical works, compromises are struck with all manner of stylistic clichés, forms of gesture from the art music of the Baroque and Classical periods. And what is often appropriated is not the individual or the expressive (the "humanistic," as it has often been dubbed), but the common and the mundane. The explanation for this is straightforward: given the familiarity of the conventional, conditions of metrical placement can be expected to be embedded that much more reliably and firmly in the mind of the listener. And in seeking thus to displace and to run counter to those conditions, Stravinsky may be envisioned as having expected that much more of a jolt, a sense of disorientation on the part of his listeners. The contrariness underlying these methods is evident, as is the sense of counteraction.

As can be seen by the brackets in Example 7.12a, the irregular 3/8 and 2/4 measures of the Royal March add up to an extra eighth-note beat in relation

---

[15] See Stravinsky and Craft, *Expositions and Developments*, 104–05. For further discussion of the Royal March and its origins, see Andrew Westerhaus, "Stravinsky and the Ludic Metaphor," Ph.D. dissertation, forthcoming at the University of Chicago.

[16] Igor Stravinsky and Robert Craft, *Memories and Commentaries* (Berkeley: University of California Press, 1981), 98.

Example 7.12. *The Soldier's Tale*, Royal March

a) score (radical)

b) rebarred (conservative)

a) con'd

b) con'd

main theme:

to the 3/4 meter – in effect, an irregular 7/8 measure. At the same time, however, subsequent repeats of the lead-on theme in the bassoon are aligned in a parallel fashion. In the extended build-up to the main theme in the trumpet at Rehearsal No. 10, all six of these repeats fall off the quarter-note beat, the likely tactus. Putting aside the irregular 3/8 and 2/4 measures at Rehearsal No. 8, they fall on the third eighth-note beat of a 3/4 measure. And, here again, the expectation is that the listener will respond accordingly. He/she will align the lead-on fragment as before, doing so by subtracting an eighth-note beat from the count at some point in the opening measures.

On the other hand, if the 3/4 meter is read through the irregular 3/8 and 2/4 measures of the printed page, the lead-on theme will be read as displaced. This alternative is shown in Example 7.12b; following the irregular 3/8 and 2/4 measures of the printed score, the lead-on theme falls on rather than off the quarter-note beat. And should this conservative barring take hold (as indicated in Example 7.12b), then the main theme itself would be displaced.

No doubt there is little evidence of any follow-through in this regard. Evidence would appear to favor the opposing radical cause, in fact, making a switch likely at some point. Just as with the opening page of *Renard*, the conservative alternative is abandoned.

Once implanted in the musical imagination, however, evidence in favor of either one or the other of these two underlying structures is likely to remain in place. Indeed, efforts to dislodge one or the other would not necessarily be in the listener's interest. Even if the conservative approach to a hearing and understanding of this passage is abandoned at some point, the pleasure gained by pulling the main theme in the trumpet through the displacement of Example 7.12b is likely to materialize as an incentive.

More to the point, the purpose of the irregular 3/8 and 2/4 measures (the extra eighth-note beat) at the beginning of this passage cannot rest solely with the notation and the radical approach it implies. This is not a question of the impoverishment any such partial reading is apt to bring. Rather, it has to do with the two-sided nature of the process. As we have indicated in the preceding chapter, the two sides of displacement and metrical parallelism work at cross-purposes. Even as the listener orients him/herself one way or the other, any such orientation is bound to meet with resistance. For the two opposing sides presuppose one another. While a sense of displacement hinges on meter, meter arises in part from placement, from parallel align-ment; realignment is bound to challenge and in some instances overturn the metrical bearings of the listener, undermining precisely that which allows for an apprehension of change. And so the point (and presumably the attraction) of the invention lies not with one or the other of the two sides, radical or conservative, but rather with the one in relation to the other, with the opposition that is engendered. We have made such a point earlier in Chapter 1, yet it seemed worth rehearsing again in connection with the Royal March, and if only because of the greater obscurity that would here seem to surround precisely the two-sidedness of Stravinsky's methods.

8 Melodic repeat structures in the music of Stravinsky, Debussy, and Rimsky-Korsakov: another look at the *Symphonies of Wind Instruments* (1920)

Just as with the four individual tableaux of *Les Noces*, so, too, with the *Symphonies of Wind Instruments* (1920). In each of these conceptions, a block of material is introduced at the outset and then repeated throughout with very few modifications. In the *Symphonies* (Example 8.1a), the opening block consists of a melodic repeat structure similar to the ones encountered in earlier chapters. Marked off by the dotted line drawn vertically through Examples 8.1a–c, a thematic statement is divided into two approximate halves, the second of which begins with a modified repeat of the first. Even more characteristically here, the second half begins with a metrical displacement of the first, a matter to which we will be turning in due course.

The process of modification proceeds along lines which are no less characteristic of Stravinsky's music. The smaller motivic segments of the first half of this repeat structure are not elaborated in the second half (submitted to a form of embellishment, for example), but are repeated literally, reshuffled, or omitted altogether. In place of a melodic or harmonic elaboration along traditional lines there is an addition or subtraction of eighth-note beats. And the result is a block structure on a miniature scale mirroring that of the piece as a whole. As can be seen by the brackets directly above the quotation in Example 8.1a, the succession of motivic segments, $(a_2+a_2+b_3)+(a_2+b_2+c)$, includes repeats and deletions. In the second half of the structure, the repeat of the initial segment a_2 is omitted, while segment b_3 is shortened to b_2. Segment c, a closing figure, follows as an extension of b_2. It signals a return to the pitch D, which is sustained at varying lengths from one restatement of the block to the next. (The subscripts in these segment designations refer to the encompassed number of eighth-note beats; a_2 consists of the single pitch D extended to a quarter-note beat, b_3 of the same D grouped together with the descending third.)

Observe, however, that the motivic segmentation bracketed in Example 8.1a is complicated by the accompanying parts in the trumpet and trombone. Although the latter are fixed registrally and instrumentally from one block restatement to the next, they vary slightly in the timing of their entrances. In the first half of the repeat structure in Example 8.1a, the

Example 8.1. *Symphonies of Wind Instruments*; opening block A and subsequent restatements

lower pitch F in the trombone is sustained through the repeat of segment a_2, thus allowing the initial a_2 to be distinguished from its immediate repeat. On the other hand, in the restatement reproduced in Example 8.1c, the corresponding pitch D in the trombone is sounded again off the quarter-note. Slight modifications of this kind are not systematic.

Moreover, the bracketed segmentation in Example 8.1a does not correspond with the changing 2/8 and 3/8 bar lines of Stravinsky's 1947 revision of the score.[1] Especially sensitive in this regard are the motivic implications of the composer's 3/8 measures on both sides of the repeat structure. Indeed, a sense of conflict is likely to arise in the following terms: is the first D in the second half of the repeat structure a repeat of the first or the second D of the first half? While the entrances of the accompanying parts in the trumpet and trombone imply the first of these alternatives, the parallelism underlying the 3/8 measures points to the second. The segmentation is ambiguous at these points, and along the lines indicated by the arrows in Example 8.1a: starting with the initial pitch D of the second half of the repeat structure, the bottom arrow points to the initial D of the first half as the source of the repetition, while the top arrow points to the second D.

The opening block A and its repeat structure are stated six times throughout the first half of the *Symphonies*; Examples 8.1a–d reproduce four of these statements. Significantly, the statements in Examples 8.1c and d are transpositions of the original succession of segments. Down a minor third, the transposition allows for continued confinement to the given octatonic collection, namely, Collection I. (With the exception of a few measures of anticipation of the closing chorale melody at Rehearsal Nos. 2 and 5, the material at Rehearsal Nos. 0–6 is wholly octatonic, referable to Collection I.)[2]

At the same time, the restatements shown in Examples 8.1b, c, and d are modified in ways having to do with operations other than transposition. The nature of these modifications can be gleaned by comparing the motivic successions bracketed in Examples 8.1a–d. As a rule, individual segments are either deleted from or added to the initial succession, leaving the latter

---

[1] Although an engraving was made of Stravinsky's original 1920 version of the *Symphonies of Wind Instruments*, it was never published at the time. Instead, a piano reduction by Arthur Lourié was printed by Édition Russe de Musique in 1926. Stravinsky's extensive revisions of the original barring and instrumentation were completed in 1947 for the Boosey & Hawkes publication of the following year. For further comment, see André Baltensperger and Felix Meyer, eds., *Igor Strawinsky, Symphonies d'instruments à vent: Faksimileausgabe des Particells und der Partitur der Erstfassung* (Winterthur: Amadeus, 1991), 28–38. See, also, Stephen Walsh, "Stravinsky's Symphonies: Accident or Design?" in Craig Ayrey and Mark Everist, eds., *Analytical Strategies and Musical Interpretation: Essays in Nineteenth- and Twentieth-Century Music* (Cambridge University Press, 1996), 35–71.

[2] The octatonic implications of the opening section of the *Symphonies* are discussed in Pieter C. van den Toorn, *The Music of Igor Stravinsky* (New Haven: Yale University Press, 1983), 337–44. It should be noted in this connection that a single restatement of the opening block – namely, that at Rehearsal No. 9 – does indeed transgress the octatonic Collection I.

shortened, lengthened, or reordered as a result. In the restatement at Example 8.1b, the initial repeat of segment a_2 is omitted from the first half of the repeat structure (with the ambiguity in segmentation resolved in favor of Stravinsky's 3/8 measures), while, in Example 8.1d, the repeat of a_2 is followed immediately by segments b2 and c, with much of the structure deleted. (The repetition here is such that the restatement in Example 8.1d could be viewed alternatively as a lengthened version of the structure's second half.) In this way, as we have suggested, the internal repeat structure of the opening block foreshadows that of the larger whole. Individual segments are repeated, deleted, or reshuffled, just as blocks are so treated. There is a juxtaposition of segments within blocks just as there is a juxtaposition of blocks within sections. And the cutting and pasting so often alluded to in connection with Stravinsky's block structures can thus be inferred on the smallest as well as on the largest of scales.

The issue of abruptly juxtaposed blocks of material is again brought to the fore. Such a juxtaposition hinges on three related factors: (1) the disparate or relatively self-enclosed character of the individual blocks, (2) the stability of their content from one restatement to the next, and (3) their ability to be reordered with possible deletions and additions. All three factors are

Table 8.1. Symphonies, *Nos. 0–6*

Rehearsal Nos.	0–6	6–
background; sections	A A	B B
middleground; blocks	A B A$_1$ B$_1$	
foreground; motives or segments	A = $(a_2 + a_2 + b_3)$ + $(a_2 + a_2 + c)$	

Example 8.2. *Symphonies of Wind Instruments*, opening section AA

conspicuously evident in the *Symphonies*, above all in the opening section at Rehearsal Nos. 0–6. An abbreviation of this section appears in Example 8.2, while the outline included in Table 8.1 divides the section into three tiers or "structural levels." The first of these tiers consists of the larger sections themselves, beginning with the opening section AA and followed by section BB; to a large extent, the opening section is defined by its tempo, motives, and octatonic content (Collection I). Moving down from the global to the more local, the second tier consists of the block-successions contained within these sections ((A B A₁ B₁) within section AA, for example), while the third tier consists of the succession of motivic segments contained within the blocks. (Only the sequences contained within Block A and its restatement A₁ are included in Table 8.1; those of the remaining blocks, not discussed here, are not specified.)[3]

The impression gained of these blocks and their juxtapositions is thus likely to be one of relative indifference. Within the larger section AA at Rehearsal Nos. 0–6, the actual successions defined by the individual blocks and their restatements are largely unmediated. Cut off abruptly and set apart, block A and its restatement A₁ do not interact with block B, but are relatively discontinuous in this respect.

And it is just this element of discontinuity, as implied in turn by the technique of juxtaposition, that has drawn much critical attention over the past half-century. In the early commentary of Pierre Boulez, for example, the static, non-developmental implications of this technique were dismissed outright as contrary to the nature of composition itself. For Boulez in the 1940s and early 50s, to *juxtapose* in the manner of Stravinsky was not to *compose* at all.[4] (Boulez adopted a similar attitude toward the music of his teacher, Olivier Messiaen. The discontinuity brought about by the superimposition and juxtaposition of self-contained blocks was condemned here as well.)[5] Superimposition was dismissed somewhat similarly, that is, as a static "coagulation," that, for the superimposed fragments of Stravinsky's layered structures, created a "false counterpoint."[6]

More recently, however, a different attitude has prevailed. Analogies to techniques of collage and montage have surfaced in a positive light.[7] Not only the sketches of *Les Noces* but also those of *The Rite of Spring* and the

[3] Mention should be made here of Edward Cone's pioneering study of Stravinsky's juxtaposed blocks in works such as the *Symphonies* and the *Symphony of Psalms* (1930); see Edward T. Cone, "Stravinsky: The Progress of a Method," in Benjamin Boretz and Edward T. Cone, eds., *Perspectives on Schoenberg and Stravinsky* (New York: W. W. Norton, 1972), 155–64. There are three phases to Cone's "method," namely, "stratification," "interlock," and "synthesis"; while his term "stratification" corresponds to our notion of juxtaposition, stratification itself (or layering) signifies in this present volume a very different kind of organization. Cone's idea of a "synthesis" works well with the *Symphonies*, where, beginning already at Rehearsal No. 1+5 in block B (see Example 8.2), the chorale that ends this piece is preceded by a host of anticipations. Yet many of his descriptive terms work less well where other blocks and sections of the *Symphonies* are concerned. Thus, subsequent restatements of the opening block (see Examples 8.1b–d) are unlikely to strike the listener as representing, in Cone's words (156), the "completion" or "fulfillment" of processes begun by the initial statement. Much of the repetition and juxtaposition of blocks in the *Symphonies* can seem less dynamic than he implies, more spatial and static in character.
[4] See Pierre Boulez, "Proposals," in Pierre Boulez, *Stocktakings from an Apprenticeship*, trans. Stephen Walsh (Oxford University Press, 1991), 49.
[5] *Ibid.*   [6] *Ibid.*, 57.
[7] See, for example, Daniel Albright, *Stravinsky: The Music Box and the Nightingale* (New York: Gordon and Breach, 1989), 25–26; Baltensperger and Meyer, eds., *Igor Strawinsky, Symphonies*

Symphonies have been used to document these analogies at the earliest stages of the compositional process.[8] The blocks of *The Rite of Spring* and the *Symphonies* have been likened to the sawn-off images of Cubist paintings, the scattered "scraps" of conversation in *Les Noces*'s libretto to the "strips of newsprint that Picasso glued to some of his canvases."[9] More radically still, the *Symphonies* has been proclaimed the direct precursor of Karlheinz Stockhausen's "moment form." The four blocks of the opening section (A B A_1 B_1 in Table 8.1) have been isolated as "submoments" within the larger "moment" of the section as a whole.[10]

And it is the *Symphonies* which has been heralded in these respects, celebrated as the "auditory equivalent" of Cubism earlier in the century and the precursor of modernist developments later on. Its juxtaposed blocks have seemed exemplary of the process as a whole, and this irrespective of the dance movements of *The Rite of Spring* or the individual tableaux of *Les Noces*, pieces in which the collage-like cutting and pasting is in reality no less abruptly imposed, the blocks and sections themselves no less stiffly set apart at times by fixed definitions of content, instrumentation, and tempo.

Lacking in this celebration of the *Symphonies*, however, has been some further review of the repeat structure of the opening block. Ignored has been the way in which that structure forecasts the larger formation. Displacements lying concealed by the notation have been overlooked, as has meter, for that matter, and meter not only in the abstract, but meter as a living, breathing part of our perception as well. For it is meter of this latter kind that, concealed by a notated irregularity that mirrors the discontinuity of collage and block-like structure, underlies much of what is in fact fluid and continuous in this music.[11]

---

d'instruments à vent, 25–28; Glen Watkins, *Pyramids at the Louvre: Music, Culture, and Collage from Stravinsky to the Postmodernists* (Cambridge: Belknap Press, 1994); and Jonathan Cross, *The Stravinsky Legacy* (Cambridge University Press, 1998), 17–29.

[8] See the references to the "montage principle" in Baltensperger and Meyer, eds., *Igor Strawinsky, Symphonies d'instruments à vent*: 25–28. And see the sketches of the Introduction and "Sacrificial Dance" in Igor Stravinsky, *The Rite of Spring: Sketches 1911–1913* (London: Boosey and Hawkes, 1969), 63, 88. In some of the later stages of the sketching of these particular dance movements, restatements of the various blocks and their orderings are not actually written out by the composer but are identified by upper-case letters. The notation is thus very much in keeping with the designations applied in conjunction with Tables 8.1a and b in this chapter.

[9] Albright, *Stravinsky*, 25–26. In Cross, *The Stravinsky Legacy*, 19–20, the block structures of the *Symphonies* are compared to the abstract shapes and their juxtaposed patterns of repetition in Picasso's *Nude* (1910).

[10] Jonathan D. Kramer, *The Time of Music* (New York: Schirmer Books, 1988), 224–26. For a contrary approach treating the continuous elements of pitch relations in the *Symphonies*, see Christopher Hasty, "On the Problem of Succession and Continuity in 20th-Century Music," *Music Theory Spectrum* 8 (1986): 58–74.

[11] See, for example, the detailed and highly skilled analysis in Alexander Rehding, "Towards A 'Logic of Discontinuity' in Stravinsky's *Symphonies of Wind Instruments*: Hasty, Kramer and Straus Reconsidered," *Music Analysis* 17, no. 1 (1998): 39–53. Refreshingly, Rehding stresses the

The conservative alternative

Shown in Examples 8.3a and b are two alternative barrings of the opening block of the *Symphonies*. The first of these options stems from Stravinsky's autograph of 1920, the second from his revision of 1947. The derivation of the latter from the former is traced by the dotted lines: quite simply, the revised bar lines slice up the earlier 5/8 measures into alternating measures of 2/8 and 3/8. And the logic of the slicing should be apparent as well. The smaller segments more fully expose the underlying repeat structure of the block, in particular, the repeat of segment b. (Stravinsky would later maintain that the "smaller divisions" of his rebarrings were designed to facilitate performance.[12] But practical considerations of this kind could hardly have been divorced from musically logical ones, from attempts on the composer's part to come to terms analytically and theoretically with structure heard and understood.)

More to the point here, however, is the conservative rebarring outlined in Example 8.4b: a steady 2/4 meter is inferred from the bell-like motive D-D-D-B, in relation to which, in the second half of the repeat structure, its shortened repeat D-D-B is read as a displacement. The two segments D-D-D-B and its subset D-D-B are consolidations of the successions of motives

Example 8.3. *Symphonies of Wind Instruments*, opening block A

a) 1920

b) 1947

continuous as well as the discontinuous aspects of the juxtaposition of segments ("cells") and blocks. Yet, here, too, meter and metrical displacement are virtually ignored. And notwithstanding the detail, Rehding isolates the various melodic segments from their accompaniment. As we have seen, the small changes in the entrances of the accompanying parts contribute significantly to the ambiguity and complexity of motivic relations.

[12] Igor Stravinsky and Robert Craft, *Expositions and Developments* (Garden City, NY: Doubleday, 1962), 147. In connection with his 1926 rebarring of the "Evocation of the Ancestors" and the "Sacrificial Dance" in *The Rite of Spring*, the composer explained that his performance experience had led him "to prefer smaller divisions." See the discussion of his revised barrings in Pieter C. van den Toorn, *Stravinsky and "The Rite of Spring": The Beginnings of a Musical Language* (Berkeley: University of California Press, 1987), 44–56.

Example 8.4. *Symphonies of Wind Instruments*, opening block A, reduction

a) notated (radical)

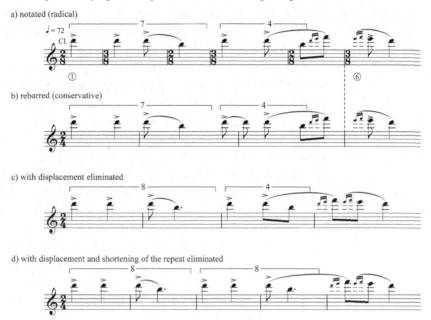

b) rebarred (conservative)

c) with displacement eliminated

d) with displacement and shortening of the repeat eliminated

bracketed in Example 8.1a. They enter on and off the quarter-note beat, on the first and fourth eighth-note beats of the bar line or half-note beat, respectively.

Example 8.4a reproduces the radical barring of 1947 to facilitate comparison; the brackets in Examples 8.4a–d mark off the two halves of the repeat structures. Support for the quarter-note beat comes from the three-fold punctuation of the pitch D, evenly spaced, while support for the half-note beat comes from the descending minor third motive; the latter separates the third punctuation of D from the first two.[13] As a level of interpretation, however, the half-note beat is apt to be felt less securely than the tactus. This is owing in part to the agogic accent that attaches itself to the pitch B, an accent that may well have determined the composer's original barring of 1920 (see Example 8.3a) and the revised one of 1947 as well (Example 8.3b).

The full implications of this conservative alternative are startling. The rhythmic "feel" of the opening block is completely transformed. Underscored above all is the two-part division of the repeat structure:

---

[13] See Fred Lerdahl and Ray Jackendoff, *A Generative Theory of Tonal Music* (Cambridge: MIT Press, 1983), 76–78. Apart from the "well-formedness rules" for meter and its establishment, the "preference rules" stipulating "strong beat early" and "event" are of particular relevance here.

while the punctuated Ds of the first half enter on the quarter-note beat, those of the second enter off the beat. A new sense of continuity is thus apt to arise from the two halves, whether taken individually or, as we shall see below, in moving from the first to the second.

To recapitulate briefly: in opposition to Stravinsky's 1947 revised barring of the opening of the *Symphonies*, a barring that preserves a single alignment for the principal motive D-D-D-B and its shortened repeat D-D-B (Example 8.4a), steady levels of metrical pulsation may be inferred, the level of the quarter-note beat at the very least, that of the bar line or half-note beat more ambitiously (see Example 8.4b). And in relation to these steady levels, the shortened repeat D-D-B may be felt as displaced. At the same time, the displacement, although at a location of 0, is unlikely to be all that disruptive of the quarter-note beat. Not only may the latter be inferred rather strongly from the punctuation of D in the opening bars, but the motive itself is relatively short (and, of course, shortened in its repeat). The displacement may be absorbed with little resistance, in other words, with the shortened repeat D-D-B heard and understood as a syncopated version of D-D-D-B. Notwithstanding the potential for disruption, the reaction to this particular passage is apt to be strongly conservative in character.

The recomposed versions in Examples 8.4c and d provide additional foils for the conservative rebarring in Example 8.4b. In Example 8.4c the displacement of the shortened repeat D-D-B is eliminated by extending the original span from seven to eight eighth-note beats; in Example 8.4d, both the displacement and the shortening of the repeat are eliminated, leaving the repetition literal from a metrical standpoint. Looking back at Stravinsky's invention from this perspective, the displaced repeat D-D-B in Examples 8.4a and b can be seen and heard as arriving an eighth-note beat "too soon." As a result, the initial motive D-D-D-B is left with an irregular span of seven eighth-note beats, an irregularity that underlies the radical notation of Example 8.4a.

Note, too, that the steady 2/4 meter arrives "on target" with Stravinsky's radical notation at the end of the block at m. 6 (see Examples 8.4a and b). The irregular count is evened out at this point, with the downbeat of m. 6 likely to be felt rather heavily as a result. Within the motivic succession (D-D-D-B)-(D-D-B-F-E-D), the pitch E is an upper neighbor-note to the punctuating D, while the pitch-class content, consisting of a gapped (0 2 (3) 5) tetrachord in terms of (E D (C♯) B) inflected by F, may be compared to that of the opening two blocks of *Les Noces*. At the beginning of both the *Symphonies* and *Les Noces*, the octatonic set is implicated in terms of Collection I. In the *Symphonies*, however, the minor-third gap D-B is eventually plugged by the (E D C♯ B) motive introduced by the oboes at

Rehearsal No. 3; see, in Example 8.2, the tail end of the block A₁. Moreover, D assumes priority as a punctuating point of departure and return; F enters as a neighbor note to the E, the latter in turn as a metrically accented neighbor to the D. In contrast, in the opening blocks of *Les Noces*, E assumes priority as a point of departure and return. The two octatonic contents intersect, in other words, but are structured differently.

So, too, inferred and internalized with a degree of authority at the outset of the *Symphonies*, the quarter-note beat may continue into the second block B as a connecting thread. As shown by the brackets in Example 8.2, the massive chords of this block may be heard as entering off rather than on the beat, effecting a form of syncopation. The beat may ultimately be interrupted, of course, retrieved quite possibly with the steady quarter-note motion of the chorale phrases that are interpolated just prior to Rehearsal No. 2. But note, all the same, the arrival of the 2/4 meter "on target" with Stravinsky's irregular bar lines at Rehearsal No. 2. The restatement A₁ of the initial block arrives "on target," with the deletion of the initial segment a₂ accounted for.

Antecedents in the music of Debussy and Rimsky-Korsakov

Ample precedent may be found for the repetition that underlies Stravinsky's melodic repeat structures. Repeat structures appear in nearly all of Debussy's works, for example, early as well as late, and so abundantly as to suggest the flexing of something near-automatic. The opening two measures of the *Prélude à l'après-midi d'un faune* are as good an illustration as any (Example 8.5a), but see, too, in Example 8.5b, the repetition a few measures later in this same score.

Example 8.5. Debussy, *Prélude à l'après-midi d'un faune*, opening bars
a)

b)

In a study of these and similar structures in Debussy's music, the linguist Nicolas Ruwet identified the process as one of "duplication."[14] Ruwet's lengthy analysis followed an earlier study by André Schaeffner.[15] And, from the standpoint of the repetition alone, the cultivation of these structures in Debussy's music is little different from what it is in Stravinsky's: a motive or short phrase, usually no more than a measure or two in length, is followed in quick succession by its "double." The latter is not a reprise or a consequent in the tradition of the thematic period in Classical and Romantic literature. Instead, the harmony of the "duplication" is unaltered; there are no changes in harmonic function or direction.

The effect of a "duplication" is often one of exposure. If only for a few seconds, the motive or configuration is highlighted, set somewhat apart from its context. The listener savors the moment, as it were, some fuller measure of the invention, as the music itself slows to a standstill. Drive and forward motion cease, as does the sense of an ongoing development. It is as if Debussy, fearful of the inattentive listener, had wanted to assure himself of the reception of his invention. A motive or theme is repeated as a way of implanting it all the more securely in the listener's imagination.

Apart from these details, however, the rationale of this process – how and why duplication works – is difficult to unravel. Stressing its elementary character, Ruwet sought to reconcile "the appearance of such a primitive procedure" in music that seemed subtle and complex in other respects.[16] Comparing Debussy's "duplications" to the repeated syllables in baby talk, he referred the reader to several lengthy studies by Roman Jakobson. In the latter, terms such as "mama" and "papa" are indeed viewed as typical of nursery talk; according to Jakobson, they signal the transition in early childhood "from babbling to verbal behavior."[17] Such are the means by which young infants signal their intention to make linguistic sense. The relevant syllables are repeated in order that they might be understood not as babble, but as "senseful, semantic entities."[18]

---

[14] Nicolas Ruwet, *Langage, Musique, Poésie* (Paris: Éditions du Seuil, 1972), 70–99. See, too, the discussion of "duplication" in John Clevenger, *The Origins of Debussy's Style* (Ph.D. diss., University of Rochester, 2002). Clevenger concludes that "reiteration [his own term for Ruwet's "duplication"] is perhaps Debussy's single most recognizable stylistic staple."

[15] André Schaeffner, "Debussy et ses rapports avec la musique russe," in Pierre Suvchinsky, ed., *Musique russe* (Paris: Presses universitaires de France, 1953), 13.

[16] Ruwet, *Langage*, 73. Similarly, Jean Barraqué, in a study of *La Mer*, referred to duplication as "the sole weakness that one can find in Debussy's scores." See Jean Barraqué, "*La Mer* de Debussy, ou la naissance des formes ouvertes," *Analyse musicale* 12 (June 1988), 28.

[17] Roman Jakobson, "Why 'Mama' and 'Papa'?" in *Roman Jakobson: Selected Writings* (The Hague: Mouton, 1962), 542.

[18] *Ibid.*

There is a fanciful side to this analogy, obviously. Yet the elementary nature of the repetition seems integral all the same. Or is this in fact not the case? Is the functional character of duplication different in music from what it is in language and other modes of communication? (In music, duplication may carry metrical as well as rhythmic purposes, with a duplicated idea assisting in the establishment of a metrical framework.)

In fact, contrary to many of Ruwet's conclusions about thematic structure in general, duplication has close parallels in tonal music, the closest of these being the repetition that often opens the thematic sentence or *Satz*. In the sentence, a two- or four-measure unit may be repeated exactly or nearly so; the two samples shown in Examples 8.6a and b are from Mozart's piano sonatas.[19] And these are but the tip of a large iceberg. As the theorist Eugene Narmour has shown on a more comprehensive basis, a+a+b melodic patterns, with the repetition a+a followed by a contrasting unit b, are not only "aesthetically long-lived," but are also hugely prevalent "in all styles."[20] The two additional phrases cited in Examples 8.7a and b are the antecedent phrases of two period structures, transcribed here from Narmour's study; Example 8.7b includes, as a form of repetition, a tonal transposition of a more developmental character.

The point here is that, from a cognitive standpoint, the literal nature of the repetition in many of these repeat structures, tonal or non-tonal, may be foundational rather than "primitive" or infantile. According to Narmour, with the repetition followed by a contrasting phrase, the underlying implication–realization (or denial) scheme is among the most prevalent in all of music. With the establishment of an implication for the continuation of phrase a (a+a), phrase b denies the implication.[21] So, too, the repetition, even when literal from an objective standpoint, may emit a sense of anticipation and

---

[19] Numerous examples of the melodic sentence in music of the Classical era may be found illustrated and discussed briefly in Arnold Schoenberg, *Fundamentals of Musical Composition*, ed. Gerald Strang and Leonard Stein (London: Faber and Faber, 1967), 20–24. For a more detailed study of the melodic sentence within the tradition of a theory of formal functions, see William E. Caplin, *Classical Form: A Theory of Formal Functions for the Instrumental Music of Haydn, Mozart, and Beethoven* (Oxford University Press, 1998), 38–48. The repeat structure is conceived as a four-measure "presentation phase" at the beginning of an eight-measure sentence; a two-measure "basic idea" is repeated as part of a (2+2)+4 design. Significantly, too, in Debussy's music as well, the duplication of a one- or two-measure melodic unit may be conceived as part of the "presentation phase" of a larger sentence. See the discussion of this in Evo Somer, "Musical Syntax in the Sonatas of Debussy: Phrase Structure and Formal Function," *Music Theory Spectrum* 27, no. 1 (2005): 68–83. In Debussy's sonatas above all, Somer argues, "the formal function of [a] duplication should not be heard in isolation but in the context of a sentential presentation – together with a subsequent, possible continuation function" (70–72).

[20] Eugene Narmour, "The Top-Down and Bottom-Up Systems of Musical Implication: Building on Meyer's Theory of Emotional Syntax," *Music Perception* 9, no. 1 (1991): 8–10.

[21] *Ibid.*, 8. Thus, the b unit in a+a+b melodic patterns is not solely a matter of contrast, but of "the denial of an expected continuation (a+a+ . . .)."

Example 8.6. Mozart, piano sonatas

a)   K. 310, I, opening bars

b)   K. 330, I, opening bars

Example 8.7. Melodic repeat structures

a)   Beethoven, Violin Concerto in D, Op. 61, III, principal theme

b) Beethoven, Piano Sonata in E, Op. 109, II, principal theme

continuity. An a+a structure, where a is a segment, configuration, or block of material, may point beyond itself to an overriding train of thought. Not only is the repetition of segment a likely to be qualitatively different from the initial occurrence, but the two units can also add up to something other than a mere sum or total.[22]

In addition to the repeat structures cited in Debussy's *Prélude à l'après-midi d'un faune*, see, in Examples 8.8a and b, the two thematic statements from *Fêtes*, the second of Debussy's *Nocturnes* (1901). Or see, in Example 8.9a, the opening measures of *Nuages*, the first of these *Nocturnes*. Observe, however, that the duplication is modified slightly in the latter. And so it is again in Stravinsky's celebrated imitation of these opening measures of *Nuages*, the repeat structure that opens the first act of his opera *The Nightingale* (1908–14); see Example 8.9b.

But the crucial distinction here hinges on displacement. In the repeat structures cited above in Debussy's music, the second halves are not the metrically displaced repeats of the first. The duplications do not undergo metrical shifts, and the spans they define do not end up uneven or irregular as a result.

At the same time, however, if metrical displacement is rarely if ever a feature of Debussy's repeat structures, it is certainly no more so in the music of Stravinsky's immediate Russian predecessors. And this includes the music of his teacher and early mentor, Rimsky-Korsakov. Repeat structures

---

[22] For an insightful account of the psychology and aesthetics of this type of repetition, see John Rahn, *Music Inside Out* (Amsterdam: Gordon and Breach, 2001), 8–9. The repetition a+a ("a, then-a," as Rahn phrases it) points "beyond the thing repeated to the thing being formed." The focus is "always forward, un-selfish, opening away from the current entity in the direction of something larger and unconfined."

Example 8.8. Debussy, *Nocturnes*, II (*Fêtes*), repeat structures

a)

b)

may be inferred from Rimsky-Korsakov's music, to be sure, and often as frequently as from Debussy's. (Their appearance in Russian music of the nineteenth century may well have figured as part of Debussy's attraction to this repertory. On the other hand, repeat structures appear too early in his own music for their appearance in Russian music to have served as a source.)[23] And Stravinsky's point of departure could just as easily have been here as with Debussy's music, of course, with structures such as the ones cited in Example 8.10a and b from Rimsky-Korsakov's *Sadko*, the symphonic poem (1867) and the later opera (1897).

---

[23] In Schaeffner, "Debussy et ses rapports avec la musique russe," 135, the author claims Rimsky-Korsakov's opera, *The Maid of Pskov*, to have been the source of Debussy's duplications.

Example 8.9. Additional repeat structures

a)   Debussy, *Nocturnes*, I (*Nuages*), opening bars

b)   Stravinsky, *The Nightingale* (Introduction), opening bars

The point, however, is that rarely do the melodic repeat structures in Rimsky-Korsakov's operas and symphonic poems admit to a form of displacement. Instances of notated metrical irregularity abound, but rarely in the form of a displaced repeat of a motive, theme, or configuration.

Cited in Example 8.11b is one of the very few instances of such a displacement. In Act III of Rimsky-Korsakov's opera *Snegurochka* (*Snow Maiden*, 1881), a folk-derived melody, initially in phase and spanning an even eight quarter-note beats (see Example 8.11a), is quite suddenly cut to an irregular count of seven beats.[24] The repeat that follows enters "too soon"; the melody shifts from the first to the second quarter-note beat of a 2/4 measure, from the first to the last eighth-note beat of a hypermetric

---

[24] Brief mention is made of the metrical implications of this displacement in Valentina Cholopova, "Russische Quellen der Rhythmik Strawinskys," *Die Musikforschung* 27 (1974), 444. Cholopova offers a radically shifting meter as an alternative to Rimsky-Korsakov's 2/4 design.

Example 8.10. Rimsky-Korsakov, repeat structures

a) *Sadko*, symphonic poem (1867)

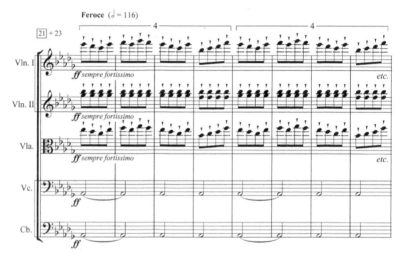

b) *Sadko*, the opera, sixth tableau (1897)

Example 8.11. Rimsky-Korsakov, *Snegurochka*, Act III
a)

b)

beat spanning four measures. And the initial displacement is followed by irregular spans of five, three, and five quarter-note beats. If only for a split second, the metrical bearings of the listener – even those of the highly conservative listener – are likely to be challenged and even disrupted.

Of course, the melody falls on and off the half-note beat or bar line rather than the quarter-note beat (the likely tactus here with a marking of 120 BPM). And this will mean that the disruption will be felt at the level of the bar line rather than at that of the tactus. (The metrical location is +1 rather than 0.) At a slower pace, the listener will be able to react with greater ease. A traditional process of liquidation may be inferred here as well. The displacement is part of a winding-down process, in which segments of the theme are broken up and scattered.

Before and after the displacement itself, the folk-derived melody is repeated thirty-two times, sometimes shortened and other times transposed. Even with modifications in the accompaniment, the sheer quantity of the repetition is likely to overwhelm the listener. And the melody is invariably in phase, too, as well as confined to two-plus-two and four-plus-four metrical spans, confinements which are likely to contribute to a strong sense of metrical squareness. Such a sense may be found emitted elsewhere in Rimsky-Korsakov's music, and in ways that have been acknowledged by critics such as Gerald Abraham and, more recently, Claudio Spies. For Spies, in particular, the effect of squareness in Rimsky-Korsakov's music is so debilitating as to discourage contact altogether.[25] The rhythmic-metric component is judged too uninteresting for the music to have served even the young Stravinsky as an important source of ideas and techniques.

But these contentions are contradicted by the many types of precedents that may indeed be found in Rimsky-Korsakov's music, from melodic repeat structures to octatonic configurations with subset structures similar to the triadic and (0 2 3 5) tetrachordal ones typical of Stravinsky's music. And there are countless specific borrowings as well, many of which have been cited in Richard Taruskin's monumental study of this subject.[26]

Sensitive to the beauty of many of Rimsky-Korsakov's operatic ingredients, the "brilliant colors" and "harmonic subtleties" of a score such as *Sadko*, Gerald Abraham directed his complaints at the "artificiality" of the musical ideas.[27] He thought the repetition of these ideas unmotivated, spun out mechanically by way of "devices." And it was the music of the magical scenes and characters of Rimsky-Korsakov's operas and symphonic poems, music often characterized by the octatonic scale and its symmetrical divisions, that seemed especially vulnerable in these respects:

> The purely intellectual spinning of music in this way, the laying of one little self-contained block of sound against another, the mechanical sense of progress obtained by systematic modulation through cycles of keys, rising or falling regularly in major or minor thirds, the failure of the music to generate a vital impulse from its own nature – all this is frequently characteristic of Rimsky-Korsakov's music even when he is not deliberately aiming at unreality.[28]

The reference here to "self-contained block[s] of sound" is suggestive enough, as an obvious allusion to the repeat structures in Rimsky-Korsakov's music,

---

[25] Claudio Spies, "Conundrums, Conjectures, Construals; or, 5 vs. 3: The influence of Russian Composers on Stravinsky," in Ethan Haimo and Paul Johnson, eds., *Stravinsky Retrospectives* (Lincoln: University of Nebraska Press, 1987), 76–140.

[26] See, in particular, the borrowings in *The Firebird* traced in Richard Taruskin, *Stravinsky and the Russian Traditions: A Biography of the Works through "Mavra,"* 2 vols. (Berkeley: University of California Press, 1996), vol. I: 597–637.

[27] Gerald Abraham, *Studies in Russian Music* (London: William Reeves, 1935), 240.

[28] *Ibid.*, 242.

those similar to the ones cited in Example 8.10a and b. And in Example 8.11a, the folk-derived melody from *Snegurochka* is sliced into two, with the first half repeated independently of the second. This, too, can be counted as a precedent, a foreshadowing of the cutting and pasting of segments and blocks that would play such a large role in the music of Rimsky-Korsakov's pupil.

Yet Abraham's remarks are critical in tone. Consisting of these "self-contained block[s]," Rimsky-Korsakov's music lacked the necessary continuity, a "vital impulse" that could be sensed as organic and as arising "from its own nature." The sense of progress was "mechanical." And what is thus criticized in Rimsky-Korsakov's music is precisely that which would later be acclaimed in Stravinsky's as "modernist" and even as "postmodernist." The static, discontinuous, non-developmental, and "non-linear" features of the "self-contained block[s]" would later be viewed from the perspective first of Cubism and then of a new aesthetic of time, space ("nowness"), and self-awareness. Musical sources as diverse as integral serialism, indeterminism, and "moment form" would join in a new assault on teleology in music, the goal-orientation of the tonal repertory and its "directed motions," developments, and climaxes. (Still later, in the 1990s, *directedness* in tonal design would be targeted by academic feminism as "thrusting" and "masculinist" in character.[29] Here, however, Stravinsky's music as a whole was to prove too closely and conspicuously allied with aesthetic formalism and the Western canonic tradition for it to be embraced wholeheartedly by either the feminists or the postmodernists of the 1990s.)

No doubt, Rimsky-Korsakov's "self contained block[s]" differ from Stravinsky's. The rhythmic vitality that may be lacking in the former may be found in the latter, a vitality that may be traced directly to metrical displacement and to the irregular spans brought about by displacement. By implication, the same vitality may be traced to meter (that which underlies displacement), and hence to the old as well as the new in Stravinsky's music, to the conservative as well as radical forces, and ultimately to the cross-purposes at which these forces are made to work.

Continuity and discontinuity

In brief summary, Stravinsky's juxtaposed blocks can suggest a technique of cutting and pasting, one which can be related to Cubist methods in painting early in the twentieth century. But it can suggest as much only with a good deal of qualification. The discontinuity that would seem to be implied by

---

[29] See, for example, Susan McClary, *Feminine Endings: Music, Gender, and Sexuality* (Minneapolis: University of Minnesota Press, 1991), 112–31.

these block-like structures, with listeners interrupting their train of thought in order to *associate* individual blocks with subsequent restatements, does not entirely supplant the continuous mode. (See the arrows in Figures 8.1a and b; in pursuing first the succession of blocks within the initial section of the *Symphonies* and then the succession of segments within block A, the discontinuous and continuous modes are represented as extremes in each case.) The discontinuous mode is perhaps more accurately described as *associational*, it being understood that, in the mind of the listener, the interruption or discontinuity that may be caused by the abrupt juxtaposition of distinct segments or blocks may be accompanied by connections or

a)   Succession of blocks within section AA

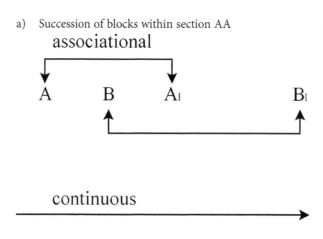

b)   Succession of motives within block A

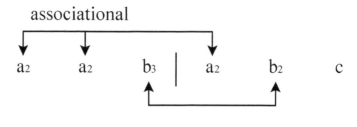

Figure 8.1. *Symphonies*, associational and continuous modes

associations linking such segments or blocks across considerable expanses.[30] At the same time, associations of this kind tend *not* to imply continuity. In the AA section of the *Symphonies*, block A_1 is a modified restatement of block A, not the continuation of an earlier train of thought. Relatively self-contained, its effect on the listener is apt to be spacial.

As a way of distinguishing Stravinsky's music from that of his tonal predecessors (or contemporaries), the question is thus one of degree: just as the continuous mode figures in Stravinsky's music, so, too, the associational one is present in tonal music.[31] More to the point, the associational and continuous modes are closely linked to the distinction raised throughout this volume between radical and conservative interpretations of displacement. An emphasis on discontinuity and the collage-like structure of a piece such as the *Symphonies* will tend to imply a radical interpretation, one in which meter, if present at all, is constantly being interrupted. A barring reflective of this discontinuity will shift in accord with the irregular spans defined by the repetition of a motive or block; it will represent a form of metrical parallelism. In contrast, an emphasis on continuity will tend to imply a conservative interpretation, one in which the meter is sustained to some degree. Here, the irregular spans will be experienced as a form of displacement.

In Jonathan Kramer's detailed analysis of the *Symphonies*, for example, the "nonlinear," non-developmental, and discontinuous features of the various recurring segments and blocks ("submoments," as he labels the blocks) are underscored. Certain "parameters," including instrumentation, are recognized as continuous, while several motives ("cells"), appearing in more than one block or section, are said to usher in a form of change. (Kramer's "cells," "submoments," and "moments" are roughly equivalent to our motives, blocks, and sections, respectively.) Yet it is the stasis and self-enclosure of the blocks and sections that stand out for Kramer, the discontinuities in "tempo, harmony, and cellular material" from one section to another.[32] The *Symphonies* is hailed as a "breakthrough" in the march toward "moment form" in the past century.[33] Not surprisingly, too, Kramer's approach is radical. Underscored is the absence of a "normal beat" in Stravinsky's music, "a reliable sequence of evenly spaced strong beats on any hierarchic level but the shallowest."[34] For Kramer, the extreme

---

[30] In Lerdahl and Jackendoff, *A Generative Theory*, 17, structures formed from the linking of non-contiguous units are termed "associational." In contrast to "grouping" structures, "associational" structures are non-hierarchical.

[31] See the discussion of the scherzo movement of Beethoven's Piano Sonata, Op. 2, No. 2, in Lerdahl and Jackendoff, *A Generative Theory*, 16–17.

[32] Kramer, *The Time of Music*, 224–25.   [33] *Ibid.*, 289.   [34] *Ibid.*, 287.

Figure 8.2. *Symphonies*, opening block; see Kramer, *The Time of Music*, Example 9.3.

irregularity excludes the possibility of such a "reliable sequence" of interpreting or "grouping" levels of pulsation.

In the opening block of the *Symphonies*, for example, no quarter-note
beat is inferred from the three-fold punctuation of the pitch D. In Kramer's
account of this passage, there are no quarter-note beats marking off eighth-
note beats, just as there are no half-note beats marking off quarter-note and
eighth-note beats.[35] As can be seen in Figure 8.2, reproduced from Kramer's
Example 9.3, block A is sliced into three motivic cells, with the second of
these cells acknowledged as the modified repeat of the first. But there is no
displacement of his cell $a_7 1$ by its shortened repeat $a_4 1$. No metrical implications are inferred by Kramer, ones which, concealed by the notated
irregularity, would allow for such a displacement.

Nor are functioning parts inferred by Kramer, parts operating dynamically in relation to a greater whole. Kramer's cell a_2, which corresponds to
our motive c (see Example 8.1a), is not a closing figure, something capable
of bringing the initial block or "submoment" to a close. What he infers is a
string or "sequence" of melodic cells, a loose form of succession, in effect,
not a continuing structure with a beginning and an end. As a consequence,
the sorts of melodic structures surveyed above in the music of Debussy,
Rimsky-Korsakov, and others do not apply. Connections of this kind
between the *Symphonies* and the works of Stravinsky's immediate and
more distant predecessors do not exist. Kramer's conception is wholly
that of a collage-like juxtaposition of segments and blocks, one that is
linked to notions of "moment form" later in the century. It is in no way
qualified by a more traditional sense of meter, alignment, displacement, and
syncopation.

However, for listeners struck by the "square metrical dance schemes"
that, alternatively, may be found lying to the background of pieces such as
the *Symphonies*, the continuous is likely to be stressed as much as the

---

[35] *Ibid.*, 224–28.

discontinuous.[36] For these listeners, a wealth of syncopation is likely to be felt, along with the "metrical dance schemes" of the Western tradition on which that felt syncopation hinges. "Thrown into relief" by those "schemes,"[37] the forward-moving, developmental tendency associated with the upbeat is likely to be experienced as well. According to Hans Keller, a critic who devoted much attention to the psychological dimensions of Stravinsky's music, the explosive character of Stravinsky's rhythmic invention may be traced to precisely this kind of a conservative backdrop. In a giant form of displacement, upbeat figures identified with development and forward movement were shifted to the downbeat.[38] A static kind of downbeating resulted from this. To follow Keller, both the static quality of the invention and the tension that could nonetheless be felt to be embedded within could be explained in this way.

In the same conservative vein, we should note that a displacement, if not too disruptive, can actually have the effect of strengthening the continuous mode. In the conservative rebarring of the opening block of the *Symphonies*, Example 8.4b, the shortened repeat D-D-B is a displacement, as we have indicated, a syncopated version of the initial segment D-D-D-B. With the initial span cut to an irregular seven eighth-note beats, the repeat arrives "too soon." A form of compression results from this, one in which D-D-D-B and D-D-B are made to overlap by an eighth-note beat. Our contention here is that, by way of this displacement, the two halves of the repeat structure are connected that much more closely. The first half flows more continuously into the second. (Compare, in this regard, the conservative rebarring of Example 8.4b with Example 8.4d, where the initial span is extended from seven to eight eighth-note beats and the displacement is eliminated altogether. Our point is that, interpreted conservatively, the displacement notated in Example 8.4b will render the repeat structure as a whole more continuous for the listener.)

Much of the above applies to the three additional thematic statements cited in Examples 8.12a–c. Conservative and radical barrings are shown for each of these repeat structures. At the level of the tactus, the initial span is reduced to an irregular seven beats in each case, with the displaced repeat arriving "too soon" by a quarter-note beat in Example 8.12a and by an eighth-note beat in Examples 8.12b and c. (In Example 8.12c, the displacement arrives "too late" according to the 3/4 meter, but "too early" according

[36] Hans Keller, "Rhythm: Gershwin and Stravinsky," in Hans Keller, *Essays on Music*, ed. Christopher Wintle (Cambridge University Press, 1994), 207.
[37] *Ibid.*   [38] *Ibid.*, 207–09.

Example 8.12. Thematic statements, repeat structures

a)   *The Rite of Spring*, autograph

b)   *Les Noces*, fourth tableau

c)   *Renard*, principal fragment (tp.)

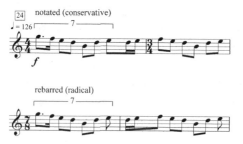

to the earlier 4/4.) The metrical location of the displacement in all three repeat structures is 0.

   Finally, the impact of Stravinsky's music on that of his contemporaries and followers – the matter of its legacy, roughly speaking – must be weighed from the standpoint of the whole as well as the disengaged parts. Jonathan Cross has laid particular stress on the composer's block and layered structures, the influence these structures appear to have had on the music of composers such as Varèse, Messiaen, Carter, Birtwistle, and Andriessen.[39] But this should not obscure the complexity of the issue. While precedents for the repetition in Stravinsky's melodic repeat structures may be found in the music of Debussy and Rimsky-Korsakov, few may be found for the displacement that typically underlies Stravinsky's approach. And while, similarly, in matters of pitch organization generally, precedents for the octatonicism in Stravinsky's Russian-period works (with its vocabulary of (0 2 3 5) tetrachords, triads, and dominant sevenths) may be found in the music of Rimsky-Korsakov and others, they are found scarcely at all for the techniques of superimposition that, in Stravinsky's case, radically alter the harmonic implications of the octatonic employment.

Thus, on the matter of superimposition generally, tritone-related triads may be found superimposed in an extended sketch of Rimsky-Korsakov's composed shortly before his death in June, 1908. (The sketch was intended for an opera, *Zemlya i nebo* or *Heaven and Earth*, which was never completed.) And the same superimposed triads may again be found in the *Prélude symphonique*, an instrumental work composed by another of Rimsky-Korsakov's pupils, Maximilian Steinberg. Richard Taruskin has drawn attention to these passages on several occasions,[40] as a way of emphasizing not only Rimsky-Korsakov's many achievements and contributions, but also, on the basis of his harmony text book and sketch books, the existence of a common practice at the time in St. Petersburg between Rimsky-Korsakov and his circle of students, including Stravinsky.

But if the superimposed triads in these passages by Rimsky-Korsakov and Steinberg did indeed serve as a precedent for Stravinsky, then they could have done so only in a somewhat incidental light. For, when combined already early on in *Petrushka* and *The Rite of Spring* with methods of displacement, juxtaposition, and above all stratification, this technique of superimposition takes on a radically different character. Not just octatonic triads, but all manner of repeated, stratified entities are placed in superimposition; diatonic fragments are superimposed over octatonic configurations and vice versa. The technique becomes fully integrated within a whole that is newly formed as a result. And this is what counts, obviously: less the technique itself than the uses to which it is put as part of a larger dynamic.

---

[39] See Cross, *The Stravinsky Legacy*, 33–80, 104–31.
[40] See Taruskin, *Stravinsky and the Russian Traditions*, vol. I: 407; Taruskin, "Catching Up with Rimsky-Korsakov," *Music Theory Spectrum* 33, no. 2: 169–85.

9 Issues of performance practice and aesthetic belief

The story of the *Symphonies of Wind Instruments* is a checkered one. The solemn chorale with which the piece ends was first conceived as a separate tribute to Claude Debussy, and was published as such in a special issue of *Revue musicale*.[1] The idea had been to start with the chorale and fan out accordingly. This was quickly abandoned, however, in favor of the framework as it exists today, with the chorale featured at the close. Anticipations of the chorale's phrases were worked into the body of the work, occasioning much strenuous effort, from what may be gathered from the surviving sketch materials.[2] Appearing in various guises in block B of the opening section (see Example 8.2, Rehearsal Nos. 1+5 and 5) and then later at Rehearsal Nos. 11–13, 21, and 28, these anticipations underlie much of the cutting and pasting of the *Symphonies*, from the standpoint of both its abruptly juxtaposed blocks and the more continuous structure. While the anticipations interrupt the musical flow, they substantiate the larger design as well. And when the chorale finally does arrive, it does so as an apotheosis. Individual phrases, anticipated at length, are brought together in the form of a sustained culmination. By such means, the larger sense of direction that may have been lost earlier on is gained retrospectively.

For all the exquisite workmanship, however, the *Symphonies* fared little better at its premiere than *The Rite of Spring* had done some seven years earlier. Held in London, June 10, 1921, with Sergei Kussevitsky conducting members of the London Symphony Orchestra, the performance went badly from a technical standpoint. The rehearsal time had been insufficient, and problems developed with the actual staging of the program. Instead of grouping the orchestra's wind ensemble appropriately following a performance of excerpts from Rimsky-Korsakov's *Le Coq d'or*, Kussevitsky allowed the ensemble's members to remain in their orchestral seatings. Laughter accompanied general bewilderment. Reporting in *The Manchester Guardian*, Ernest

---

[1] *Revue musicale* 1/2 (December, 1920): 22–23.

[2] For a brief survey of these materials, see André Baltensperger and Felix Meyer, eds., *Igor Strawinsky, Symphonies d'instruments à vent: Faksimileausgabe des Particells und der Partitur der Erstfassung* (Winterthur: Amadeus, 1991), 28–32. For a detailed study of the sketches, early performances, and later publication of the *Symphonies*, see Stephen Walsh, "Stravinsky's Symphonies: accident or design?" in Craig Ayrey and Mark Everist, eds., *Analytical Strategies and Musical Interpretation: Essays in Nineteenth- and Twentieth-Century Music* (Cambridge University Press, 1996), 35–71.

Newman pronounced the work "the most hideous and most meaningless collection of noises I have ever heard."[3] Few performances followed the premiere, in fact, as Stravinsky resigned himself to the novelty of the invention and to the difficulties posed by its reception.[4] An engraving was made in 1932–33 by Éditions Russes, but the 1920 version of the *Symphonies* was published only later in a pirated edition (1983). For the first thirty or so years of its existence it survived only by way of a piano arrangement by Arthur Lourié (1926), Stravinsky's close assistant at the time. Not until after the revision of 1947 did it become available in an approved form.

But even this grim tale of early incomprehension and abandonment is not without its illumination. The circumstances of the premiere sparked a mini-debate in the popular press about the role of "expression" and "nuance" (or the lack thereof) in Stravinsky's music. In an interview following the concert, Stravinsky pointed to the "counterpoint of sonorities" in the *Symphonies*, the juxtaposition of "mass-sonorities," suggesting that much of this might have fared better had the conductor refrained from expressive "nuance."[5] Kussevitsky replied soon afterwards that, contrary to Stravinsky's claims, the lack of rehearsal time had prevented anything but the most "automatic" of performances. He condemned Stravinsky's band ensemble as musically inferior (it lacked strings), and the material itself as marking a "stage of decline" in the composer's output.[6]

Episodes similar to this followed in the 1920s and 30s. Yet the experience of the *Symphonies* illustrates well enough the difficulties Stravinsky seems always to have faced with conductors, performers, audiences, and critics accustomed to standards of interpretation very different from his own. Chief among these difficulties was the maintenance of an even tempo and the avoidance of any fluctuation of the beat. "Tempo is the principal item," Stravinsky replied when asked about performance problems late in life; "My music can survive just about anything but wrong or uncertain tempo."[7] And the rationale here lies close to the surface: If a juxtaposition of blocks was to make itself felt, a juxtaposition of segments within blocks as well as of blocks within larger sections, then the tempo had to be maintained strictly from one

---

[3] *The Manchester Guardian*, June 16, 1921. Quoted in Baltensperger and Meyer, *Igor Strawinsky, Symphonies d'instruments à vent*, 41. "I had no idea Stravinsky disliked Debussy as much as this," Newman wrote sarcastically.

[4] Later in his *Autobiography* (1936), Stravinsky claimed that the *Symphonies* was not written "to please an audience or to arouse its passions." See Igor Stravinsky, *An Autobiography* (New York: W.W. Norton, 1962), 95.

[5] See Baltensperger and Meyer, *Igor Strawinsky, Symphonies d'instruments à vent*, 42.

[6] *The Sunday Times*, July 24, 1921. Quoted in Baltensperger and Meyer, *Igor Strawinsky, Symphonies d'instruments à vent*, 42–43.

[7] Igor Stravinsky and Robert Craft, *Conversations with Stravinsky* (Garden City, NY: Doubleday, 1959), 135.

repeat to the next. The cutting and pasting of the various segments and blocks had to be rendered in a clean and efficient manner. And if, by the same token, the metrical displacement of a given segment was to have its effect, then here, too, the tempo had to be maintained at an even pace. The point of the displacement would be lost if subjected to any "expressive fluctuation of the beat," as T. W. Adorno phrased it in his lengthy critique of Stravinsky's music.[8] The standard rubato could not be tolerated in this regard, adjustments capable of weakening the listener's sense of meter and alignment.

More specifically, small-scale changes in the tempo or dynamic shading of a theme or motive ("expressive fluctuation") were no different from the changes applied to any other feature of the motive. Cutting down on the actual repetition, they cut down on the displacement, too. And apart from the need for an even tempo in the articulation of a motive's alignments, the need for a certain literalness in the repetition was no less critical.

Expressive timing

Yet it was in the area of expressive affect that the implications of Stravinsky's art of displacement were felt most keenly. Given the need for a strictly maintained beat, little allowance could be made for the conventions of expressive timing, the means by which, traditionally, performers had made their mediating presence felt.[9] Consisting of small-scale cadential retardations and the like, these conventions may always have been a part of music-making, of course, even at the dawn of performance itself. Setting the issue on fire here, however, was the question of their motivation. To deviate from the regular was to be affected. It was to provide an indication of engagement on the performer's part, and of the human capacity for arousal. Even with the deviations stylized as conventions, the ties to passion, arousal, and the personal appear never to have been entirely lost. For the scale of the modification could be altered, the degree or intensity increased or weakened.

According to Carl Seashore, the terms were among the most intimate known to music:

> In music and speech, pure tone, true pitch, exact intonation, perfect harmony, rigid rhythm, even touch, and precise time play a relatively small role. They are mainly points of orientation for art and nature. The unlimited resources for vocal and instrumental art lie in artistic deviation from the pure . . . and the

[8] Theodor W. Adorno, *Philosophy of Modern Music*, trans. Anne G. Mitchell and Wesley V. Bloomster (New York: Seabury Press, 1973), 154.

[9] For a history of the uses of expressive timing or *tempo rubato* (literally, "stolen time") in the performance traditions of Western music, see Richard Hudson, *Stolen Time: The History of Tempo Rubato* (Oxford University Press, 1994).

precise. This deviation from the exact is, on the whole, the medium for the creation of the beautiful – for the conveying of emotion.[10]

As a result, the nerve touched by these Stravinsky-inspired prohibitions was a sensitive one. The conflicts to which they led in matters of interpretation could not have had a more serious effect on the critical reception of his music throughout the twentieth century.

And the issue was by no means one of musical affect alone. Slight modifications of timing and punctuation, whether notated or coming by way of the performer alone, had served as a means of structure. Intensifying (often by exaggeration) the delays and accelerations already a part of the music (the delay of the note of suspension in tonal music, for example), these rallentandos, ritardandos, ritenutos, morendos, and accelerandos had been expressions of structural clarification as well as engagement. They had served to clarify the boundaries of phrases and other large groupings.[11] And it was generally understood that a performer intervened with a purpose of this kind as key. Modifications were not isolated effects (mere caprice or display on the performer's part), but a means toward a larger end. And artistic performances were weighed in this light, that is, by the extent to which they were "true" to the music, placed at the service of a convincing sense of structure.

[10] H. G. Seashore, "An Objective Analysis of Artistic Singing," in C. E. Seashore, ed., *Objective Analysis of Musical Performance*. University of Iowa Studies in the Psychology of Music IV (Iowa City: University of Iowa Press, 1937), 155. Cited in Alf Gabrielsson, "Interplay between Analysis and Synthesis in Studies of Music Performance and Music Experience," *Music Perception* 3, no. 1 (1985): 64. One aspect of this causal chain could be phrased in the following terms: For a performer to deviate from the exact or regular was to be aroused emotionally, and to be aroused emotionally was to falter and to commit error. To be aroused and to err in this way – to fall short of perfection – was to be human rather than machine-like.

[11] The connection between expressive modification and musical structure is pursued at length in Eric F. Clarke, "Expression and Communication in Musical Performance," in Johan Sunberg, Lennart Nord, and Rolf Carlson, eds., *Music, Language, Speech and Brain* (New York: Macmillan, 1991), 184–93. According to Clarke, modifications in performance clarify structural features having to do above all with meter and phrase length; these modifications arise "as a consequence of the performer's spontaneous parsing of musical material" (186). Among the many studies of expressive timing and nuance that involve quantification and an experimental testing of intensity (loudness), slurring (legato), and tenuto, see John A. Sloboda, "The Communication of Musical Meter in Piano Performance," *Quarterly Journal of Experimental Psychology*, 1983, 35A: 377–96; and Bruno Repp, "Pattern Typicality and Dimensional Interactions in Pianists' Imitation of Expressive Timing and Dynamics," *Music Perception* 18, no. 2 (2000): 173–211. For a critique of this approach linking performance nuance to the expression of structure, see Nicholas Cook, "Analyzing Performance and Performing Analysis," in Nicholas Cook and Mark Everist, eds., *Rethinking Music* (Oxford University Press, 1999), 239–61. Cook objects to the "prescriptive" (rather than "descriptive") role assumed by music theory and analysis in this approach, the dualism it presupposes, and the "ultimate authority" invested in music analysis (246). He rejects the idea of performance as a "transparent medium," something expressing or projecting "only what is already 'in' the music, with the performance ideal being a selfless *Werktreue*" (244). Cook would prefer the reverse, with a musical work regarded as "a means of representing or conceptualizing performance" (244).

The ideal could not have been more widely or firmly held. In the interests of a phrase and its articulation, the downbeat marking the end of a cadence might be delayed and then lengthened somewhat. This might occur minutely and almost imperceptibly as part of a hierarchy of such delays and lengthenings, with the weightiest coinciding with the larger phrases or sections.[12] If the foreground of a work could consist of the *prolongation* of harmonic-contrapuntal events lying to the background (endless forms of "artistic delaying," as Schenker described the "detours, expansions, interpolations, and retardations of all kinds" that intervened in the progress of a linear progression),[13] then a performer's intervention could consist of an intensification of that process of delay. Applied in this fashion, expressive timing and nuance could acquire a sense of motivation. They could be felt as being responsive to the internal workings of the music.[14]

The psychology of the alliance was thus no less integral. If "emotion and meaning in music" could be traced to the arrest or "inhibition" of "implications" such as those triggered by the start of a linear progression (as Leonard Meyer argued some time ago),[15] then a performer's small-scale ritardando could be measured in these terms as well. Stretching out a cadence by delaying the arrival of the resolution, the listener's feelings of suspense (of "sweet anticipation," to

[12] See Eric Clarke, "Expression in Performance: Generativity, Perception, and Semiosis," in John Rink, ed., *The Practice of Performance: Studies in Musical Interpretation* (New York: Cambridge University Press, 1995), 27. "Phrase boundaries are marked by a decrease in tempo in proportion to the phrase boundary's structural importance," Clarke concludes. "A large-scale sectional break will typically be approached with a greater degree of slowing than a small-scale group boundary." Or see Neil Todd, "A Model of Expressive Timing in Tonal Music," *Music Perception* 3, no. 1 (1985): 35. "Not only does end-slowing seem to act as a boundary marker," Todd writes, "but, in certain domains, variations in relative lengthening, if perceived, contribute to the recovery of syntactic structure by the listener: the greater the lengthening the more important the syntactic break." Todd notes that end-slowing may be found in speech as well as in music. With a great many languages, evidently, "there is a tendency to lengthen the final elements" of sentences and clauses. In fact, "slowing down at the end is a natural tendency characterizing all motor sequences," and may even be observed "in birdsong and insect chirps."

[13] Heinrich Schenker, *Free Composition*, trans. Ernst Oster (New York: Longman, 1979), 5.

[14] For an alternative theory about the use of expressive affect in performance, see David Huron, *Sweet Anticipation: Music and the Psychology of Expectation* (Cambridge: MIT Press, 2006), 314–18. According to Huron, expressive timing and especially delaying tactics have less to do with structure and its communication than with the predictable nature of events such as cadences and resolutions of suspensions. "High predictability," he writes, "provides for an opportunity to heighten the tension response and thereby to increase the pleasure evoked by [the resolution]. In performed music, highly marked ritards may occur just prior to the resolution of a tendency tone – but this resolution may not necessarily coincide with an important structure division" (216). Thus, the original motivation for slowing down was "to heighten an emotional effect, not to delineate the structure." As we have argued here, however, the drastic reduction in the use of expressive timing in performances of much of Stravinsky's music, as called for by the composer himself, can be traced directly to structural phenomena, and not only to metrical displacement but also to the larger designs of stratification and block-like construction.

[15] See Leonard Meyer, *Emotion and Meaning in Music* (University of Chicago Press, 1956), 22–35.

borrow from David Huron's wording), could be intensified.[16] With the resolution itself, the slowing-down process could prompt a heightening of the sense of release from tension; the beginning of the next phrase could then be accompanied by a slight accelerando. Not just structure plain and simple but something of the psychology embedded within could be acknowledged and clarified as well. The overall impression gained could be that of a dramatic enactment, of performers acting out the events and processes internal to the music (cadences, resolutions, and the like). Performers themselves could be ensured a more active role in the process, with a sense of the human or personal enhanced.

Two dimensions to this question of expressive timing are thus revealed, the one having to do with a performer's expressive response to a musical structure, the other with what the psychologist Bruno Repp has termed "expressive characterization."[17] Reading at sight, performers begin by parsing the music, drawing a mental image of its structure and reacting expressively to that image. Unconscious and spontaneous rather than learned, memorized, and then applied in subsequent readings, the process comes "naturally" to the performer, and to a far greater extent than the deadpan or expressionless alternative. In fact, singing or playing totally without expression is exceedingly difficult, and performers asked to sing or play in this fashion in psychological experiments have invariably been observed to give way at some point to the familiar departures.[18] Even Stravinsky, committed as he was to the virtues of playing in strict tempo, felt obliged to acknowledge (and accept) the irrepressible nature of expression, the residue that would have to remain even under the strictest of conditions.[19] The style he advocated may

---

[16] Huron, *Sweet Anticipation*, especially 314–18. The emotion or psychological stress of anticipation is followed "sweetly" by the release of the resolution. The higher the predictability, the greater the stress of expectation (especially when the resolution is delayed repeatedly), and the "sweeter" the feelings of release at the point of arrival. Huron calls this the theory of "contrastive valence."

[17] Repp, "Pattern Typicality," 174.

[18] See Carl Seashore, *The Psychology of Music* (New York: McGraw-Hill, 1938), 244–53, 247–49; Ingmar Bengtsson and Alf Gabrielsson, "Analysis and Synthesis of Musical Rhythm," in *Studies of Musical Performance*, ed. Johan Sundberg (Stockholm: Royal Swedish Academy of Music, 1983); Gabrielsson, "Interplay between Analysis and Synthesis"; and E. F. Clarke, "Expression and Communication."

[19] See Igor Stravinsky, *Poetics of Music in the Form of Six Lessons*, trans. Arthur Knodel and Ingolf Dahl (New York: Vintage Books, 1956), 127. As evidence of the residue of expression that seems to have been a part of Stravinsky's piano playing and conducting, see the recollections of his son and pianist, Soulima, in Ben Johnston, "Stravinsky: A Composer's Memorial: An Interview with Soulima Stravinsky," *Perspectives of New Music* 9, no. 2 (1971): 16–17. On a nearly daily basis during the 1930s, Soulima played through the orchestral parts of various works in progress; he attended "hundreds of rehearsals" and performed, with his father, in "dozens of concerts." Although the composer was "merciless" about the maintenance of a steady beat, he did not play in the "dry, detached and aloof" manner in which he seems to have "wanted other people to play." He played "much more than the printed signs," and had "a very sensitive and delicate touch." For further comment on Stravinsky's technique at the piano, see Malia Roberson, "Stravinsky as Executant," Ph.D. dissertation, University of California, Santa Barbara, forthcoming.

have reduced (sometimes drastically) the modifications of tempo, dynamics, and articulation, but it did not eliminate them altogether.

In turn, "characterization" refers to an artist's personal contribution, what may transcend the interpretation of a single work. Within an accepted range, there are "individual differences" from one performer to the next, as Repp has noted, a great many characterizations that may be "consistent with a given structural conception."[20] Performers are likely to depart from such a range rather than the abstraction of a deadpan performance. And they are apt to do so by imitating other performers, by being prompted by metaphorical description, and by following the dictates of their individual talents and personalities. The "information" they convey by such means is thus to some extent unique at each instance. It cannot be categorized or held in long-term memory, according to Bob Snyder's *Music and Memory*, and is therefore "ineffable." It accounts in some measure for the ability of a given interpretation to remain fresh even after repeated hearings.[21] Reflecting a performer's individual skills and sensibilities, it is also what we have been alluding to here as *engagement*.

Crucially, however, when applied to Stravinsky's music, the standard modifications of performance practice weakened structure. They obscured the juxtapositions, stratifications, and alignments of Stravinsky's repeated themes, motives, and chords. And they were set aside quite deliberately by the composer and his adherents for these very reasons. At odds with the core of his music, they were dismissed as a form of liberty, one taken at the expense of structure. They were identified as a form of display, a sacrifice made for the sake of a performer's "feelings."

For the composer himself, the personal in music could not have taken on a worse set of connotations. What for the performer had been a matter of structure as well as engagement became one of engagement alone – indeed, one of self-indulgence. (Conductors were always the most heavily censored in Stravinsky's many published remarks on the subject of interpretation; his own experiences had evidently convinced him that, among performing indulgences, those of the conductors were the most severe in their consequences.)[22]

---

[20] Repp, "Pattern Typicality," 174.

[21] Bob Snyder, *Music and Memory: An Introduction* (Cambridge: MIT Press, 2000), 87–89.

[22] Conductors were often pictured as charlatans or "matinee idols" in Stravinsky's comments on performance matters. Unable to adapt themselves to a work, "great" conductors "adapted the work to themselves," Stravinsky complained, "to their style, their mannerisms," and with the consequence that the authority they wielded in the world of performance was "purely egotistical, false, and arbitrary." See Igor Stravinsky and Robert Craft, *Themes and Episodes* (New York: Knopf, 1966), 145–56. Stravinsky tended to maintain that, in a performance of his own music, conductors had merely to sustain the beat evenly, watch for cues, and acknowledge the metrical irregularity and the stress and phrase markings in as clean, crisp, and percussive a fashion as possible; anything else would blunt or smother critical intent. Even the difficulties of a score such as *The Rite of Spring*, so immense and varied in its instrumental layout, were largely imaginary to Stravinsky. "*The Rite of Spring* is

What was required of the meter in a performance of Stravinsky's repeated and displaced themes, motives, and chords was mechanical precision. Fidelity was required, coolness with a sense of restraint. Notes were not to be slurred or tied into. In matters of articulation, a crisp, clean, *secco* approach was essential if the bite of the invention was to be given its due.[23]

Tempo was a factor as well. The larger tempo changes marking the individual tableaux and sections of *Les Noces* and the *Symphonies* often involved the simplest proportions in order that they, too, might imply the tightest of controls. The simplicity of these ratios guaranteed such an effect. And this was especially true of the 1919 version of *Les Noces* for harmonium, two cimbaloms, pianola and percussion. Here, the mechanical piano could provide both the meter and the changes in tempo with an interpretation that was razor-sharp in its accuracy. Stravinsky's many transcriptions for the player piano date from this period, as do the many contracts he negotiated with manufacturers of perforated piano rolls. (A chronology of these negotiations with the Pleyel and Aeolian Companies could fill a hefty volume).[24] However lucrative these contracts from a financial standpoint, their motivation was primarily aesthetic. As he later explained in his *Autobiography* (1936), he had been "anxious to find a means of imposing some restriction on the notorious liberty" that had been widespread in performance at the time.[25] His preoccupation with the pianola was less with the idiom itself (the instrument's capacity for exceedingly rapid passage work, for example), than with its ability to transmit with pinpoint precision. Given the demand of his music for such precision, why should he continue to persevere with performers and the traditions of a performance practice? What need was there for an "interpretation"?

Stravinsky's lifelong battle with rubato and nuance begins here, in fact, not with the aesthetics, necessarily, the formalist ideas with which he had come into contact earlier in the century in Paris, but rather with these practical matters of performance. Lamenting the "deforming" effects of

---

arduous but not difficult," he concluded, "and the *chef d'orchestre* is hardly more than a mechanical agent, a time-bearer who fires a pistol at the beginning of each section but lets the music run by itself." See Stravinsky and Craft, *Expositions and Developments* (Garden City, NY: Doubleday, 1962), 165–66.

[23] See Daniel Albright, *Stravinsky: The Music Box and the Nightingale* (New York: Gordon and Breach, 1989), 4. A question about the ultimate meaning of Stravinsky's music is given the following response: "What is Stravinsky's music 'about'? I am tempted to say *slavery*, so much did he insist on the strictness and rigidity of his processes of composition, on the exactitude of metronomic markings, on *secco* textures and inflexible rhythms."

[24] In 1921 Stravinsky signed a six-year contract with the Pleyel Company in Paris, agreeing to transcribe his complete works. The transcriptions (twelve in all) were "forgotten exercises to no purpose," Stravinsky later mused. Yet they represented "hundreds of hours of work and were of great importance to me at the time. My interest in player-pianos dated from 1914 when I saw a demonstration of the pianola by the Aeolian Company in London." See Stravinsky and Craft, *Expositions and Developments*, 80–81.

[25] Stravinsky, *Autobiography*, 101.

"nuance,"[26] he drew a sharp distinction between "execution" and "interpretation," citing the latter as "the root of all the errors, all the sins, all the misunderstandings that interpose themselves between the musical work and the listener."[27] Still later, in his *Conversations with Stravinsky* (1959), he softened his stance somewhat, acknowledging the existence of a "Romantic tradition" that stood in opposition to a "Classic tradition." While the former depended "strongly on mood and interpretation,"[28] the latter, which included the performing requirements of his own works, was closely tied to the dance.[29] Our point here is that it is only in conjunction with concrete musical concerns of this kind that something of the relentless nature of his pursuit of a strict performance practice can be appreciated. And only when that pursuit is traced to the musical forces that compelled it can his formalist beliefs be placed in a proper perspective. These, too, need to be related to the strict style and to the concrete musical processes underlying that style.

The reader will recall the opening block of the *Symphonies of Wind Instruments*, as examined in Example 8.4b. A 2/4 meter was inferred conservatively above and beyond Stravinsky's radical notation, allowing the second half of the repeat structure to be read as a displacement of the first. Apart from the shortening of the repeat, the motive D-D-D-B underwent no elaborations or changes in articulation. For the reasons cited – ones having to do with the opposing forces of displacement and metrical parallelism, and with the ability of these forces to make themselves felt – the repetition of the bell-like motive was kept as exact as possible. And the rationale underlying the need for an evenly maintained beat is no different. Here, too, as a way of highlighting the displacement, the repetition is stamped as a replica, a carbon copy. Nuance and expressive timing must be kept in check, with the reading left as "straight" as possible.

Indeed, it is not only the literal repetition of the D-D-D-B motive and the maintenance of a strict beat in the opening of the *Symphonies* (Example 8.4a) that assist in exposing the underlying displacement. The shifting bar lines of Stravinsky's radical notation can do so as well. For although the displacement and the quarter-note beat on which it hinges are apt to be felt at some point by the performer, his/her more immediate preoccupation is likely to be with the shifting 2/8 and 3/8 bar lines. (The marking for the eighth-note beat is 144 BPM.) The need to count quite consciously (the twos

<hr />

[26] "Some Ideas about my Octuor," in EricWalter White, *Stravinsky: The Composer and His Works* (Berkeley: University of California Press, 1966), 529. Reprinted from *The Arts*, January, 1924.

[27] Stravinsky, *Poetics of Music*, 127.

[28] Stravinsky and Craft, *Conversations with Stravinsky*, 133–35.

[29] See, too, Igor Stravinsky and Robert Craft, *Dialogues and a Diary* (New York: Doubleday, 1963), 108, where the need for "metronomic strictness," absence of rubato, and "mechanical regularity" is again underscored.

and threes are not entrained) will tend to compel a relatively strict approach on the performer's part, inhibiting his/her impulse to modify the beat expressively. In a curious way, in other words, a shifting bar line invites a strict beat, which is what is needed if, on the other side of this dynamic, the displacement is to be revealed. As pointed out earlier in Chapter 1, the interaction between the radical and the conservative can sometimes be paradoxical.

And so the origin of these Stravinskian requirements in performance can be traced to specifically musical phenomena. No different in this respect from the expressive modifications that can regularly be found accompanying performances of, say, the Beethoven piano sonatas, the requirements for a steady beat in the performance of much of Stravinsky's music are structural in origin. They anticipate more general modernist trends in the twentieth century, to be sure, the preferences at mid-century for "straight," unnuanced readings of all manner of repertory. Yet they are not therefore a fad, a reflection merely of the times or of a conductor's personality. Nor are they traceable to what has been alleged to have been an autocratic, "anti-humanistic" disposition on Stravinsky's part. Rather, they serve musical ends. They are an integral part of the package as a whole, whether that package be viewed from afar or from the specific details of the bell-like motive that opens the *Symphonies*.

By the same token, the reductions in the use of expressive timing need not spell a machine-like disposition on the part of the performer. A crisp, *secco* approach in the articulation of pieces such as *Les Noces* and the *Symphonies* can be sustained evenly and fairly consistently without the listener, conductor, or performer having to imagine him/herself at the mercy of an "ethic of scrupulous submission," as Richard Taruskin has phrased it.[30] And this is because, in keeping to an even beat, performers are better able to expose the displacements underlying the invention and much of its expressive force. The strict beat can carry an expressive purpose, in other words, one that can be maintained sympathetically rather than mechanically or submissively.

No doubt, Stravinsky's music offers less opportunity for expressive variation than the music of many of his predecessors and contemporaries. To a degree far greater than with the music of the nineteenth and early twentieth centuries, the performers of his music are "executants" or "transmitters" rather than "interpreters" (the role of the solo violin in the Royal March of *The Soldier's Tale* can come vividly to mind in this connection). And this may explain in part the relative infrequency of performances of the Piano Concerto (1924), the *Capriccio* (1928), and the Violin Concerto (1931). At the same time, however,

---

[30] Richard Taruskin, "Stravinsky and Us," in Jonathan Cross, ed., *The Cambridge Companion to Stravinsky* (Cambridge University Press, 2003), 283.

an expressive response to the relevant structural characteristics of his music need be no less affective than a response to the characteristics of, say, Chopin's Nocturnes. A fairly straight reading of *The Soldier's Tale* can be as expressive as a strongly nuanced one of Chopin's Nocturne in E-flat. What counts in any given instance is less the amount of rubato or nuance than its appropriateness. Essential is that an interpretation be felt as arising out of the circumstances of the music, as shaping and making sense of those conditions.

Typically, however, critics of the strict style have ignored its rationale. Fashion, temperament, and personality have been cited, with the style itself stripped of its legitimacy. A case in point is Robert Fink's otherwise insightful account of Stravinsky and "the Forging of a Modernist Performing Style," a study of performances and recordings of *The Rite of Spring*, including, starting in 1929, those of the composer himself.[31] Fink appears to prefer a more flexible approach to *The Rite of Spring* to Stravinsky's "grimly geometric" one, noting that it was the former that prevailed early on in the past century. In fact, there are many more indications for rubato in the scores of *Petrushka* and *The Rite of Spring* than in the score of any neoclassical work, with the possible exception of *The Rake's Progress* (1951). Some of these indications are programmatic in design, while others are tied to cadenza-like passages; see, in the latter case, the second movement of the *Capriccio*.[32]

The problem, however, is that Fink's critique of Stravinsky's "modernist style" proceeds virtually without reference to the rhythmic and metrical processes that are affected most immediately and dramatically by performance practice. Little use is made of the many analytic-theoretical and psychological studies of rhythm and meter in general or in Stravinsky's music in particular; psychological accounts of the nature of expressive affect in music are ignored.

---

[31] Robert Fink, "'*Rigoroso* (♪=126)': *The Rite of Spring* and the Forging of a Modernist Performing Style," *Journal of the American Musicological Society* 52, no. 2 (1999): 299–350. See, also in this connection, Hudson, *Stolen Time*, 381–400, Peter Hill, *Stravinsky: The Rite of Spring* (Cambridge University Press, 2000), 123–38, and Nicholas Cook, "Stravinsky conducts Stravinsky," Jonathan Cross, ed., *The Cambridge Companion to Stravinsky* (Cambridge University Press, 2003), 184–90. Although Hudson, Fink, and Cook comment in interesting ways on the practical application of the strict style to Stravinsky's music, they have little to say about the style's rationale. We should point out, too, that Stravinsky's own recordings of his music (with Stravinsky himself as conductor) do not always meet the standards of "metronomic strictness" set forth in his writings and pronouncements (see note 27 above). Addressing his 1929, 1940 and 1960 recordings of *The Rite of Spring*, both Hill and Cook point to the maze of contradictions that arise not only when the recordings are compared to one another, but also when they are placed beside the composer's stated objectives. The ideal of strictness proved elusive, evidently, as differences arose over time and in response to the individual conditions of performances. Yet the practical reality of these recordings does not negate the requirement of much of *The Rite of Spring* and Stravinsky's music more generally for a relatively strict beat. The matter hinges less on the composer's pronouncements, obviously, than on the actual musical processes that compel the need for a kind of "mechanical regularity" (see note 27).

[32] For a brief survey of these rubato indications in Stravinsky's scores, see Hudson, *Stolen Time*, 384–96.

Curiously, too, Fink's neglect of these matters is coupled with hefty denunci-
ations of aesthetic formalism, the specifically musical, and ideas about "the
music itself"; Stravinsky's own published remarks on matters of aesthetics and
performance, scattered and fragmentary as they may be, are treated with
sneering contempt.[33] (That the composer's lifelong attempt to bring a measure
of discipline to the performance of his music might have harbored a legitimate
musical and aesthetic point is a question left wholly unexplored.) Pertinent here
as well is Taruskin's polemic, "Stravinsky and Us," where Stravinsky's arguments in support of a strict performance style are dismissed no less summa-
rily.[34] Like Fink, Taruskin views the style itself as a reflection of modernist
concerns and, more readily, of the composer's "objectivist aesthetics." The
more specifically musical motivation is overlooked here as well.

Indeed, to an extent no less than with Stravinsky's insistence on a strict
performance approach, the composer's formalist convictions are rooted in
the concrete detail and making of his own music. His forays into matters of
aesthetics were provoked accordingly, that is, by the reactions of conductors, performers, and critics during the 1910s, 20s, and 30s. In the face of
much hostile criticism about the lack of expression in his music, he wished
to proclaim the meaning and significance of his music all the same. And he
did so notwithstanding the "cold and heartless" means by which, necessarily
in his music, meaning and significance were conveyed. A persuasive rationale was sought in spite of the fact that, as a formalist, Stravinsky entertained
no illusions about the possibility of an adequate verbal defense or apology.

Music was very much "a world unto itself" for Stravinsky, a world of "relative
autonomy," as he might have expressed it had he been able to avail himself of
Carl Dahlhaus's writings of the 1970s on the subject.[35] His notorious dictum
about the powerlessness of music "to express anything at all" was later amended
to read, "music expresses itself."[36] ("Even the stupider critics could have seen

---

[33] Fink's objections to expressions such as "the music itself" – implying, as they do, a form of
aesthetic autonomy or separateness – echo those in an earlier publication of Taruskin's; see
Richard Taruskin, *Defining Russia Musically; Historical and Hermeneutical Essays* (Princeton
University Press, 1997), 360–88.

[34] Taruskin, "Stravinsky and Us," 282–83.

[35] Although originally a Marxist concept, "relative autonomy" appears frequently in Carl
Dahlhaus's writings, initially in "The Musical Work of Art as a Subject of Sociology" (1974);
see Carl Dahlhaus, *Schoenberg and the New Music*, trans. Derrick Puffett and Alfred Clayton
(Cambridge University Press, 1987), 238–41. See, too, the discussion of the "autonomy principle"
in Carl Dahlhaus, *Foundations of Music History*, trans. J. B. Robinson (Cambridge University
Press, 1983), 27; Carl Dahlhaus, *The Idea of Absolute Music*, trans. Roger Lustig (Chicago
University Press, 1989); and Carl Dahlhaus, "Fragments of a Musical Hermeneutics," trans.
Karen Painter, *Current Musicology* 50: 5–20. Another key text in this regard is Lydia Goehr, *The
Imaginary Museum of Musical Works* (Oxford University Press, 1992), 148–75, where the
"autonomy principle" is similarly approached from an historical as well as philosophical
standpoint.

[36] Stravinsky, *An Autobiography*, 53–54.

that [the earlier dictum] did not deny musical expressivity," he averred, "but only the validity of a type of verbal statement about musical expressivity.")[37] Meaning and significance were not denied, in other words, only attempts to come to terms verbally with the underlying connection of music. Sensed and felt, that connection was given immediately in experience; Stravinsky's scattered reflections on the matter of music's deeper meaning point to an aesthetics of the specifically musical. Music's expressive qualities were qualities at all "only in musically expressive form"; only as they are expressed in music.[38] (Critics have tended to equate Stravinsky's formalism with a disbelief in connectedness altogether, not – as it appears more persuasively in his reflections – with a disbelief in the ability of observers to cope verbally with the nature of that connectedness.)[39]

Distrustful of attempts at translation, of the life such attempts could assume on their own, Stravinsky feared music's trivialization, its "debasement," abuse, and exploitation.[40] Music itself was a creation, not just – or even primarily – a mirroring of something else:

---

[37] Stravinsky and Craft, *Expositions and Developments*, 101.

[38] The phrase "specifically musical" is derived from Eduard Hanslick, *The Beautiful in Music*, trans. Gustav Cohen (New York: Liberal Arts Press, 1957), 47; see note 17 in the Introduction. For an explanation of the "specifically musical" that appears to match Stravinsky's scattered reflections on the subject, see Carl Dahlhaus, "Fragments of a Musical Hermeneutics," 8–9. In seeking to qualify a number of contentions in Hanslick's *The Beautiful in Music*, Dahlhaus remarks as follows: "If one assumes ... that the expressive features inherent in music constitute the actual object of the aesthetic of feeling, then the feelings that music possesses ... prove to be not impulses existing outside and without music, but rather qualities that are feelings at all only as they are expressed by music. That they cannot be translated into language ... means simply that they can be what they are only in musical expressive form ... Musical expression is untranslatable. as a result of its determinacy, which is specifically musical. Inasmuch as a musically expressed feeling becomes the feeling that only musical expression makes manifest, a transformation into language is precluded."

[39] See Stravinsky and Craft, *Expositions and Developments*, 116: "The composer works through a perceptual, not a conceptual, process. He perceives, he selects, he combines, and is not in the least aware at what point meanings of a different sort and significance grow into his work. All he knows or cares about is his apprehension of the contour of the form, for the form is everything." As a critic of Stravinsky's formalist aesthetics, Richard Taruskin concedes the point about "meanings of a different sort and significance" (Stravinsky's acknowledgment of the existence of such "meanings"), but balks at what he takes to be the composer's particularly severe brand of formalism; see Taruskin, "Stravinsky and Us," 264–66. However, Stravinsky's description of the compositional process – of "perceiving," "selecting," and "combining," with an "apprehension" of a sense of "the form" counting for "everything" (and with "meanings of a different sort" materializing unconsciously along the way) – could just as easily be applied to listening and the perceptual process generally. The listener, too, "perceives," "selects," and "combines" in relation to an evolving larger whole, a sense of structure or "form"; this is what following a musical discourse, narrative, or train of thought is generally meant to entail. As has often been remarked in this connection, the sensed beauty of a single musical moment resides at least partially with the evolving sense of the context of which it is a part. So, too, by "apprehension" of the "contour of the form," Stravinsky may not have meant anything extraneous or imposed from the outside, but rather, as in visual perception, a perceiver's unfocused yet dynamic awareness of the frame or background against which a figure takes shape. In fact, it is highly unlikely in the above quotation that Stravinsky would have been referring to "form" in the received, detached, or academic sense imagined by Taruskin.

[40] Stravinsky and Craft, *Expositions and Developments*, 115.

> Composition is something entirely new *beyond* what can be called the composer's feelings ... Does not [Ernst Cassirer] say somewhere that art is not an imitation, but a discovery, of reality? *My* objection to music criticism is that it usually directs itself to what it supposes to be the nature of the imitation – when it should be teaching us to learn and to love the new reality. A new piece of music is a new reality.[41]

The claim of a "new reality" on behalf of art or the musical work would seem to imply the idea of a transcendence. Music is something that can be listened to and appreciated for its own sake ("just for the hell of it," as Terry Eagleton has expressed it),[42] not for the uses to which it could be put or the causes it could be made to serve. It is magically "free of the vulgar taint of utility."[43] (The dynamics here could be compared to those of Romantic Love.)[44] Our transcending experiences can be sensuous and spiritual at the same time, concrete and abstract, intensely personal as well as communal (shared). The recurring motives and chords in Stravinsky's *Les Noces*, while blending into a new unity or whole, retain something of their particularity. However elusive and opaque to the critical eye, such would indeed seem to be the nature of music and its appeal. Music attracts for reasons that cannot be reduced to "rules or doctrines."[45]

We should note, finally, that the "cold and heartless" features attending the performance of Stravinsky's music are not solely a matter of the beat and its strict observance. In concrete terms, features of this kind can be found everywhere, from the composer's instrumental choices (the omission of strings in *Les Noces* and the *Symphonies*, for example), to the use of the piano as an instrument of punctuation and percussion. In applications of various types of layered structures, for example, brass and woodwind instruments, with their hardness of attack and variety of timbre, could better articulate the contrasts between the conflicting, superimposed strata. In *The Rite of Spring*, traditional balances were upset altogether by these imperatives: brass and woodwind sections occupied the leading roles, while the string section occupied the accompanying ones.

---

[41] *Ibid.*

[42] Terry Eagleton, "Coruscating on Thin Ice," *London Review of Books* 30, no. 2 (January 24, 2008): 19.

[43] *Ibid.*, 19.

[44] See, for example, Wagner's depiction of what is commonly understood as Romantic Love in his *A Communication to my Friends* (1851): "Lohengrin sought a woman who would believe in him; who would not ask who he was or whence he came, but would love him as he was because he was what he appeared to her to be." Romantic love is essential love, in other words, love irrespective of lineage, tradition, or social circumstance. Wagner's depiction is cited in Leonard B. Meyer, "A Pride of Prejudices; Or, Delight in Diversity," *Music Theory Spectrum* 13, no. 2 (1991): 248. Pertinent to the present discussion is the relation Meyer draws between romantic love, organicism, and formalist notions of self-contained, autonomous structure, the appreciation of a given work for itself alone.

[45] Eagleton, "Coruscating on Thin Ice": 19.

These preferences were acknowledged by Stravinsky even at the time of the conception of *The Rite* (1911–13): strings were "too symbolic and representative of the human voice," he averred, while wind instruments, with their "drier tone," were "more precise and less endowed with facile expression."[46] In the final 1923 version of *Les Noces* he conceded quite bluntly that he had not wanted "anything so human as strings."[47] What he had sought was a complement to the "intransigent quality" of the material, a sharp, "percussive" approach in the instrumentation. In turn, the material and its instrumentation were designed as a complement to the unbending and archaic severity of the wedding rituals themselves.

[46] "Ce que j'ai voulu exprimer dans *Le Sacre du Printemps*," *Montjoie!*, May 29, 1913. Reprinted in François Lesure, ed., *Le Sacre du Printemps: Dossier de presse* (Geneva: Editions Minkoff, 1980), 13.

[47] *Musical America*, January 10, 1925. Reprinted in Vera Stravinsky and Robert Craft, *Stravinsky in Pictures and Documents* (New York: Simon and Schuster, 1978), 622.

10 Stravinsky and his critics

Beginning early in the twentieth century and extending through Stravinsky's neoclassical and serial eras, the great controversy of his music – the matter of its expressive content – emerged in the following light: given the "cold and heartless" nature of its exterior, what could be made of the interior? Were the insides as "cold and heartless" as the outside seemed to imply? And what about the composer himself? Was his music the reflection of something "cold and heartless" here as well?

Looking to the outside rather than within, critics have sought to answer these questions with a familiar logic. Strictly held beats, a lack of variation, and a curtailment in the use of nuance have been traced to the composer's constructivist or objectivist stance (one lacking in whimsy and passion), and then to the Apollonian virtues of order, construction, and logic (as extolled by the composer himself in his *Poetics of Music*).[1] Stravinsky's aesthetic beliefs have been brought to the fore, the imagined formalist removal of music and its contemplation from the concerns of everyday life, the alleged "price" that is paid for this removal, the lapses in moral judgment that, according to one critic, have come as a result of this insulation.[2] (In T. W. Adorno's critique, Stravinsky's music lacks a *suffering subject*. It speaks for the collective, not for the individual.)

As the reader will have surmised, our intention in these chapters has been to turn this around. A more specifically musical rationale has been sought for the features and belief systems in question, and by tracing them to the underlying processes first discussed in the Introduction. Stravinsky's formalism and performance directives have been viewed here as a *logical outgrowth* of those processes, above all of processes of displacement, juxtaposition, and stratification.

In the area of articulation, for example, the composer's exclamation points, pizzicatos, and frequent staccato doublings of legato lines are structural in design. Forms of punctuation, they sharpen alignment and realignment, crucial where the repetition of fragments and chords is concerned. In passages of stratification, they assist in differentiating between the separate layers and

---

[1] Igor Stravinsky, *Poetics of Music in the Form of Six Lessons*, trans. Arthur Knodel and Ingolf Dahl (New York: Vintage Books, 1956), 66–68.

[2] See Richard Taruskin, "Stravinsky and Us," in Jonathan Cross, ed., *The Cambridge Companion To Stravinsky* (Cambridge University Press, 2003), 276–81.

between the conflicting spans as defined by the repetition of the superimposed entities. Even the absence of strings in *Les Noces* and the *Symphonies* can be understood in these terms. The fluctuation of tone (finger-touch vibrato) is avoided less because of its identification with "the human voice" (as Stravinsky himself speculated at one point),[3] than because of its *lack of precision*. And to the extent that listeners and performers are able to grasp (sense and feel) the connecting thread of logic underlying these features, there should be little difficulty in keeping to a stiff beat.

In fact, our suggestion has been that, compositionally, Stravinsky himself is likely to have followed a similar path. For him, too, the conflicting and potentially disruptive forces of displacement are likely to have served as a starting point. He, too, with displacement as his point of departure, is apt to have felt the need to repeat literally, to fix the articulation of his displaced repeats, to cross the bar line with beams, and to shift the bar line at times so as to expose the opposing forces of parallelism. Any number of instrumentations, punctuations, and strict applications of the beat are likely to have suggested themselves along the way. And if, as a result of this extended rationale, his music lacked expression (as his critics claimed, especially early on), then *all* music lacked expression (in the sense of its being able to express common emotions, moods, or "phenomena of nature"), all music was "powerless" in this respect.[4] Music's attraction lay elsewhere, in fact, not with an ability to portray or reproduce (definitely or indefinitely), but with an ability to stand apart as "a new reality," as Stravinsky insisted,[5] "an alternative vision of the world."[6] "Suprapersonal and superreal,"[7] capable of easing the divisions of our consciousness, our engagement could say something about who we were.

And it follows, too, that to inquire after the nature of music's appeal is necessarily to inquire after its internal processes. In Stravinsky's music, what sort of meaning or significance attaches itself to the displacement process? Why should the disruptive effect of displacement, varying in its intensity from one context to the next, be a source of delight? Similarly, with the

---

[3] See *Musical America*, January 10, 1925. Reprinted in Vera Stravinsky and Robert Craft, *Stravinsky in Pictures and Documents* (New York: Simon and Schuster, 1978), 622.

[4] Igor Stravinsky, *An Autobiography* (New York: W. W. Norton, 1962), 23.

[5] Igor Stravinsky and Robert Craft, *Expositions and Developments* (Garden City, NY: Doubleday, 1962), 115.

[6] Lydia Goehr, "Political Music and the Politics of Music," *The Journal of Aesthetics and Art Criticism* 52, no. 1 (Winter 1994): 99–112. It seems unlikely that Stravinsky would have agreed with most of Goehr's ideas about the political in music. Yet some of her more general conclusions about the "resistance" of separate, autonomous music to the status quo (music's ability to cast itself as "other") might well have gained a sympathetic response. See, too, the discussion of the "separateness" or "apartness" of music (music as a form of "dissent") in John Rahn, *Music Inside Out* (Amsterdam: Gordon and Breach, 2001), 41–48.

[7] Stravinsky and Craft, *Expositions and Developments*, 115.

reiterating fragments and chords of a layered texture, what is the satisfaction in shifting their alignment while leaving other features intact? Why should this excite? (The analogy here might be to the separately moving parts of a piece of machinery, where changes in the alignment of these parts are felt to result from the mechanism itself, the system that is set up beforehand, not from our ability to intervene locally. The mechanism may be ours, in other words, but the working parts, once set in motion, are beyond our control. Invoking the image of a musical subject in this connection, the emphasis might again seem to be placed on the limitations of the individual and his ability to act upon the world. As a reaction to middle-period Beethoven and the heated expectations of the nineteenth century, Stravinsky's music can again seem to stand as a kind of reality check.)

Touching on the psychology and aesthetics of the musical experience, questions of this kind are for the most part beyond the scope (and sometimes beyond the underlying aesthetic convictions) of this inquiry. Yet we shall be endeavoring to pursue them all the same, and as a way of commenting occasionally on the complaints that have arisen in conjunction with the given accounts.

T. W. Adorno

Targeted in Adorno's celebrated indictment of Stravinsky's music are many of the phenomena cited at length in these pages.[8] They include the composer's displacements and the disruptive effect of displacement on the listener. The absence of expressive timing is bemoaned.[9] And instead of the developmental style of the Classical tradition (as defined by Schoenberg, Adorno's point of departure musically and music-analytically), the repetition in Stravinsky's music was often literal. No development could be inferred, no elaboration of motives or motive-forms. So paradoxical in a music that could seem outwardly vital from a rhythmic standpoint, the overall effect was one of standstill, an invention "incapable of any kind of forward motion."[10] "The repetition constantly presents the same thing as though it were something different," Adorno complained. "Farcical and clownish, it has the effect of putting on airs, of straining without anything really happening."[11]

---

[8] See Theodor W. Adorno, *Philosophy of Modern Music*, trans. Anne G. Mitchell and Wesley V. Bloomster (New York: Seabury Press, 1973), and Theodor W. Adorno, "Stravinsky: A Dialectical Portrait" (1962), in *Quasi una Fantasia: Essays on Modern Music*, trans. Rodney Livingstone (London: Verso, 1998), 145–75. In general, the emphasis in this chapter will be on Adorno's treatment of Stravinsky's early works, not the neoclassical or the serial.

[9] See Adorno, *Philosophy of Modern Music*, 154.   [10] Ibid., 178.

[11] Adorno, "Stravinsky: A Dialectical Portrait," 152.

Such characterizations form the liveliest part of Adorno's critique. Descriptions of one kind or another, they address the immediate, psychological effect of Stravinsky's music. At the same time, however, his descriptions are often incomplete and fragmentary, with the task of piecing them together left to the reader. Adorno's approach is unsystematic to the point of being unintelligible ("anti-systematic," as some have suggested more sympathetically),[12] with the analytical descriptions themselves hemmed in by sweeping philosophical and sociological conjecture often no less fragmentary in character. The stream of consciousness can be explained by the dialectical processes at work, but only up to a point, and the suggestion of many of Adorno's adherents, to the effect that the critic-philosopher fetishized this particular aspect of the process (its lack of finality), can seem real enough.[13] Adorno acknowledged the "constellation"-like effect of his thought and prose,[14] but the results can often seem like waywardness all the same. A kind of "poetic obscurity" can seem to substitute for the more determined effort to address head-on the complexity of the issues raised.

Still, the bits and pieces of Adorno's description are worth pursuing. And they are so more for the musical illumination than for the larger philosophical and sociological ideas (Hegelian and Marxist, for the most part) to which they are attached (and from which, as Adorno and his adherents have insisted, they not only derive their meaning but are "inseparable").[15] They are worth pursuing for the music-historical sense that can be made of the juxtaposition of Stravinsky's processes of metrical displacement with the Classical or homophonic style of developing variation.[16]

---

[12] See the discussion of this in Max Paddison, *Adorno's Aesthetics of Music* (Cambridge University Press, 1993), 19–20, and Julian Johnson, "Analysis in Adorno's Aesthetics of Music," *Music Analysis* 14, nos. 2–3 (1995): 296–97.

[13] See Johnson, "Analysis in Adorno's Aesthetics of Music," 298.

[14] See Paddison, *Adorno's Aesthetics of Music*, 19. "The academic treatise . . . was rejected in favor of the idea of a 'constellation' of fragments," Paddison writes, each of these fragments "equidistant from an unstated center, the object of inquiry." Adorno's resistance to the idea of a "whole" in musical works and in systems of explanation generally (the equation of such a "whole" with "truth"), is at work in these predispositions for the fragment and the fragmentary, and this seems to have been the case even with the very earliest of his publications in the 1920s.

[15] Concerning the "inseparability" of the various components of Adorno's argument, see Johnson, "Analysis in Adorno's Aesthetics of Music," 296–97. The "interdisciplinary character" of Adorno's writings is addressed at length in Paddison, *Adorno's Aesthetics of Music*; see, especially, 16–17. Common assumptions about the "self-sufficiency" of analysis in relation to aesthetics and sociological interpretations are questioned by Adorno in T. W. Adorno, *Aesthetic Theory*, trans. C. Lenhardt (London: Routledge, 1989), 477–78. Left unclear in Adorno's remarks, however, is the precise nature of the "inseparability" that he alleges, the dependence of "technical" or "immanent analysis" (Adorno's term) on social awareness and thought. Does analysis automatically presume socio-political awareness? Or does it merely invite philosophical or socio-political speculation? Left alone, analysis is "narrow-minded," Adorno asserts, "positivistic" in its implications. Specific questions of this kind are addressed in Julian Johnson, "The Nature of Abstraction: Analysis and the Webern Myth," *Music Analysis* 17, no. 3 (1998): 267–71.

[16] See note 25 in Chapter 1.

Indeed, the description of Stravinsky's music can be pursued irrespective of the critical verdict. The "no" of Adorno's account need not be accepted in order for the descriptive commentary, harnessed as a means of support, to be appreciated. As Virgil Thomson remarked some time ago in this regard, where matters of musical understanding and criticism are concerned, the actual opinions of critics need not concern us unduly.[17] What matters is the musical understanding that is brought to bear, the features that are noticed, described, and commented upon in one way or another. The Schoenbergian model of the Classical style can serve as a useful foil for Stravinsky in ways wholly consistent with those pursued in the above chapters. And it can do so regardless of the larger and less tangible philosophical and socio-political meanings to which, in Adorno's account, it is attached. On the more speculative side of Adorno's argument, many of the negative images can be detached and replaced by positive, or at least neutral ones.

Briefly, then, we shall be seeking to retrace the steps of Adorno's critique, supplementing the description with the detail and exemplification that is often missing. A number of rebuttals will then be put forward, before turning to more recent attempts to link features of Stravinsky's music to Stravinsky the person. This will lead us to a number of aesthetic issues with some concluding remarks on *Les Noces* and *The Rite of Spring*.

Critical indictments

Adorno is struck above all by the "concentration of accents and time relationships" in Stravinsky's music.[18] The "most elementary principle" of this "concentration" is displacement: motives are constructed in such a way that, "if they immediately reappear, the accents of their own accord fall upon notes other than they had upon their first appearance."[19] Because of the irregularity of these shifting accents, "they can appear to be the result of a game of chance." They can seem to be "under a spell."[20] The game played is an "arbitrary" one, according to Adorno, for its rules lie beyond the listener's control. Stravinsky's displaced accents resist assimilation. They cannot be anticipated by the listener, and so appear as "shock effects."[21] And while "shock" is accorded a legitimate place in the reception of much contemporary music (in that of Schoenberg's atonal and twelve-tone music above all, where it is identified with a recognition of the horrors of the modern world), its effect in Stravinsky's is debilitating. Deprived of an ability to anticipate, listeners

---

[17] Virgil Thomson, *A Virgil Thomson Reader* (Boston: Houghton Mifflin, 1981), 187.
[18] Adorno, *Philosophy of Modern Music*, 178.   [19] *Ibid.*, 151.   [20] *Ibid.*, 155–56.   [21] *Ibid.*, 155.

cannot "make their own" the irregularly shifting accents of displacement. "Shock" overwhelms them, and they lose their "self-control":

> In Stravinsky, there is neither the anticipation of anxiety nor the resisting ego; it is rather simply assumed that shock cannot be appropriated by the individual for himself. The musical subject makes no attempt to assert itself, and contents itself with the *reflexive* absorption of the blows. The subject behaves literally like a critically injured victim of an accident which he cannot absorb and which, therefore, he repeats in the hopeless tension of dreams.[22]

Reference here and elsewhere to "the musical subject" implies dramatization. In Adorno's account, it is the "musical subject" rather than the listener who falls victim to Stravinsky's arbitrarily displaced accents. (The listener is seldom acknowledged, in fact, although listener and "subject" are clearly interchangeable at points, with each the victim of the same set of circumstances.) The music lacks an overriding pattern according to which the irregularly shifting accents can be organized. In turn, the listener's inability to organize these accents becomes the subject's inability. Just as the listener loses his/her metrical bearings, so, too, the subject cannot "heroically reshape" the displaced accents in his/her image; the accents are experienced as "convulsive blows and shocks."[23]

Central to Adorno's argument is the idea of a balance between the musical dimensions of melody, harmony, rhythm, and form. In Stravinsky's music, such a balance is overturned by the emphasis on rhythm and, more specifically, displacement and its effect of shock. That "great" music could consist of an equilibrium of this kind – one good for all seasons, as it were – is an idea traceable to Schoenberg (Adorno's likely source, in any case).[24] Schoenberg, too, wrote of the need for music to develop consistently and "equally" in all directions.[25] Not only were these directions inseparable, but an emphasis on one could come only at the expense of the others. Adorno comments as follows:

> Stravinsky's admirers have grown accustomed to declaring him a rhythmist and testifying that he has restored the rhythmic dimension of music – which had been overgrown by melodic-harmonic thinking – again to honor ... Rhythmic structure is, to be sure, blatantly prominent, but this is achieved at the expense of all the other aspects of rhythmic organization ... Rhythm is underscored, but it is split off from content. This results not in more, but rather in less rhythm than in compositions in which there is no fetish made of rhythm.[26]

---

[22] *Ibid.*   [23] *Ibid.*

[24] See the discussion of this in Carl Dahlhaus, *Foundations of Music History*, trans. J. B. Robinson (Cambridge University Press, 1983), 30–31.

[25] See Arnold Schoenberg, *Style and Idea: Selected Writings of Arnold Schoenberg*, ed. Leonard Stein, trans. Leo Black (Berkeley: University of California Press, 1985),

[26] Adorno, *Philosophy of Modern Music*, 154.

Melody is the first casualty of these imbalances. Instead of a formation of shapes and contours, the melodies subjected to displacement in Stravinsky's music are "truncated, primitivistic patterns."[27] Their features are not subjected to a developing variation along the lines implied by the Schoenbergian model, but are repeated literally and relentlessly. They are not varied, and it is only by means of a process of elaboration, Adorno argues, that the repetition of motives can add up to an overreaching train of thought, something other than a mere sum or total. With Stravinsky's "primitivistic patterns" and their displaced repetition, however, there are only "fluctuations of something always constant and totally static."[28] The much-ballyhooed rhythmic invention "consists of varied recurrence of the same; of the same melodic forms; of the same harmonic patterns, indeed, of the very same rhythmic patterns."[29]

Evidence of a musical nightmare of this kind may be found on virtually any page of Stravinsky's music, but see, once again in Example 6.9, the repetition of the A-D-C-D fragment in the horns in the "Ritual of the Rival Tribes" and "Procession of the Sage" in *The Rite of Spring*. Repeats of this "primitivistic pattern" (ten in all) are without elaboration, transposition or changes in articulation, dynamics, or instrumental assignment. The first two notes of the fragment are always accented, while the last three, D-C-D, are always slurred. What changes is the fragment's alignment in relation to the accompanying parts and the steady 4/4 meter. Entering on the fourth, first, third, and second quarter-note beats, respectively, the fragment falls on and off the half-note beat, the likely tactus here with a metronome marking of 83 BPM. (The half-note beat, along with the sensation of falling on and off it, is likely to define the conditions of displacement in this passage. At a level of pulsation just below the tactus, the quarter-note beat becomes a subtactus unit, the level of the pulse.)

A starker contrast to the world of developing variation would be difficult to imagine. The art of displacement and its many and varied implications preclude the sympathetic give-and-take of that world, the way in which motivic particles, detached from themes, are exchanged between instrumental parts. In Example 6.9, the A-D-C-D fragment is not tossed about from one instrument to the next, made the subject of a "dialogue" in this respect (as it might be in, say, a string quartet of Haydn's). It is not treated "humanistically" by such means (as the character of such treatment has often been imagined, at the very least, since the dawn of instrumental chamber music).[30] And it is not treated expressively

---

[27] *Ibid.*, 150.   [28] *Ibid.*, 155.   [29] *Ibid.*

[30] The association of the "humanistic" with chamber music, dialogue, and the developmental style generally is discussed in Carl Dahlhaus, *Nineteenth-Century Music*, trans. J. Bradford Robinson (Berkeley: University of California Press, 1989), 252–61. "The idea of chamber music," Dahlhaus

either. As has been suggested, if the displacement of the fragment is to have its effect, then the beat must be held evenly throughout.

Consider, too, the extreme irregularity of the spans between repeats of the A-D-C-D fragment in the horns (again, see Example 6.9). Numbering thirteen (twice), seventeen, six, and finally eight quarter-note beats, these spans are reflective of the displacements alluded to, of course, but only in part; a simpler – albeit still irregular – scheme could have accommodated the changes in alignment. The charge on Adorno's part of an arbitrary "game of chance" in *The Rite of Spring* can readily be traced to displacement coupled in this fashion with a high degree of irregularity in the spanning between repeats of the reiterating chords and fragments. (In a recent study of *The Rite of Spring*, the theorist Matthew McDonald has traced number-ings such as those bracketed above the horn fragment in Example 6.9 to intervallic series contained within various chords and configurations, the latter reduced to counts in semitones.[31] That Stravinsky, in *The Rite of Spring*, might have converted intervals into durational patterns is an idea that, as McDonald argues at length, would seem to confirm Adorno's claims about the arbitrariness of the rhythmic patterns in Stravinsky's Russian-period works more generally. We will be returning to these themes in a later section of this chapter.)

But the larger point here concerns the "protest" that, according to Adorno, music has always represented, "the protest, however ineffectual, against myth," against "the inexorable bonds of fate." No cry in the dark could be heard in Stravinsky's music, no "inner self" in its struggle with "outrageous fortune," expressing the inexpressible. All this seemed missing as well, replaced by barking proclamations: "Thus it is, and not otherwise," the composer seemed to be saying from one unvaried repeat to the next. And the proclamations seemed to be those of an authority, of someone in charge, not those of the lone individual. "Stravinsky's music identifies not with the victims," Adorno repeated in one of his more provocative pronouncements, "but with the agents of destruction."[32]

More generally, it identifies "with the collective" along the following lines: Adorno makes reference to a primitive, pre-individual age and a modern, industrial one.[33] The subject behaves ritualistically in the first of these worlds,

---

concludes, "arose as a musical reflection of a humanistic-aristocratic culture primarily centered on conversation. The aesthetic of this genre may be derived from the constantly recurring comparison with educated discourse that each part continuously shows regard for the other. In this way, the whole emerges from an interplay of voices sustained by an understanding of each participant of the overall context, and not as a jumbled amalgam of its parts . . ." (260).

[31] Matthew McDonald, "*Jeux de Nombres*: Automated Rhythm in *The Rite of Spring*," *Journal of the American Musicological Society* 63, no. 3 (2010): 499–551.

[32] Adorno, "Stravinsky: A Dialectical Portrait," 151–52.   [33] *Ibid.*, 157–58.

"regressively" and in an "infantile" manner in the second.[34] In both worlds, however, the subject's behavior is "anti-humanistic." It reflects the powers that be, Adorno insists, various "agents of destruction," not the "suffering subject" and its quest.[35] Locked in repetitive gesture, Stravinsky's subject is unable to move beyond the trance-like stupor of ritual.

In contrast, the developmental style symbolized for Adorno the ability of the musical subject to mature with time, to meet the day's challenges and to develop accordingly.[36] While the world of ritual and ritual-like repetition was enslaved, that of developing variation was relatively free.[37] Such was the nature of the musical opposition Adorno sought to lay bare, the split he attributed to Stravinsky's music and its tear from tradition and traditional sensibility.

Rebuttals

But is there no interaction at all between the style of developing variation and that of metrical displacement? Is the music of Schoenberg and Stravinsky wholly antithetical (as Adorno implies)? And are Adorno's "convulsive blows and shocks" altogether unforgiving? Is there no merit in displacement and the disruption it can cause?

Even in the passage quoted from *The Rite of Spring* in Example 6.9, where displacements in the repetition of the horn fragment A-D-C-D are likely to be disruptive of the meter, the experience can be mixed. Introduced off the half-note beat at No. 67, the horn fragment falls on the beat just before No. 68. Assuming that the shock of this initial shift can be absorbed without too much

---

[34] Adorno, *Philosophy of Modern Music*, 145–47, 157–60.   [35] *Ibid.*, 160–67.

[36] The record is scattered here as well, but see, among several excerpts on the developmental process, Adorno, *Aesthetic Theory*, 315–19. The role of "developing variation" in Adorno's socio-political understanding of the Classical style is discussed in Rose Rosengard Subotnik, *Developing Variations: Style and Ideology in Western Music* (Minneapolis: University of Minnesota Press, 1991), 20–24. In Subotnik's view, the term defines that process "whereby a musical element subjects itself to logical dynamic change while simultaneously retaining its original identity" (20). Especially in Beethoven's middle-period sonata allegros, "subjective freedom" is reconciled with "objective form." Integrated "totalities" are formed, with the individual able to "overtake" or to make his/her own "fixed, external order," the "world of object." The continuation and intensification of the developmental style in Schoenberg's understanding and application of the twelve-tone method is discussed in Theodor W. Adorno, "Vers une musique informelle" (1961), in Adorno, *Quasi una Fantasia*, 283–84. Adorno's argument is summarized in Jonathan Cross, *The Stravinsky Legacy* (Cambridge University Press, 1998), 229–32.

[37] The more immediate aesthetic and sociological implications of these two worlds are addressed at greater length in Robert Adlington, "Musical Temporality: Perspectives from Adorno and de Man," *repercussions* 6, no. 1 (1997): 12–13. While "maturation implies the ability to cope with, and develop in response to, changing circumstances," regression denotes "a reversion to infantile modes of behavior." The latter "is characterized by repetitive urges based on the interminable cycle of need and gratification." While development "signals a proper recognition of the temporal condition," repetition "represents an infantile denial of time" (12).

hesitation (assimilated either as a form of displacement or, by interrupting the meter with an extra quarter-note beat, as a parallel alignment), a second displacement on the beat a few bars later is likely to be more destructive. The uncertainty caused by the initial shift is apt to be renewed and strengthened. Questioned first is likely to be the possibility of such a second displacement, second, the 4/4 meter underlying it. While the quarter-note beat may continue uninterrupted, its interpretation by the half-note beat is apt to be the subject of a breakdown, with the distinction between onbeats and offbeats lost. In the listener's scramble to re-establish his/her bearings, even the metrical placement of the accompanying tuba fragment, otherwise parallel and in phase up to this point, is likely to be questioned.[38]

Yet the disturbance may remain temporary. Although irregularly spaced at first (see the brackets in Example 6.9), repeats of the horn fragment reach the stable duration of eight quarter-note beats at Rehearsal No. 70; seven repeats follow off the beat and on the second quarter-note beat. (Although the notated meter shifts to 6/4 at this point to accommodate a number of conflicting spans in the accompanying parts, the 4/4 framework is likely to persist in the mind of the listener.) And the accompanying tuba fragment is stabilized even earlier, with repeats reaching the duration of sixteen quarter-note beats. Something of a resolution is thus forged as the two dance movements in question draw to a close. Alignment and harmonic coincidence are stabilized, with the disruption of the earlier bars (Adorno's "shocks") capable of being heard and understood as part of a larger plan of action, one with a beginning and an end. Far from being isolated and isolating, the disturbance may be reconciled within a larger, evolving structure.

More specifically, the final placement of the horn fragment A-D-C-D on the second quarter-note beat of the 4/4 bar line may be heard and understood as the "correct" reading. In turn, earlier alignments on the fourth, first, and third beats, respectively, may be read as the displacements. Crucial here is the

---

[38] The steady 4/4 meter on which displacements of the A-D-C-D fragment hinge is likely to impose itself independently and prior to the entrances of the horn fragment and its sustained Ds. The repetition of the G-F-E-D fragment in the first violins is crucial in this regard. As a point of departure and return, the pitch G in this fragment falls on the downbeat, while the fragment's division into two segments, or "cells" (labeled a and b in Example 4.9), with each of these segments spanning the 4/4 bar line, lends further support for the 4/4 framework. Further along, repeats of the accompanying segments in the tuba, although irregularly spaced at rehearsal Nos. 64–67, serve as an additional means of support – indeed, following the removal of the reiterated fragment in the violins at Rehearsal No. 66, as a constant backdrop in this respect. The spans of these entrances are multiples of two and four; repeats of the segments G♯-F♯ (G)-(G)♯ and G♯-A♯-C♯-A♯-(G♯) are aligned in a metrically parallel fashion. In sum, while repeats of the various segments in the first violins and tubas are spaced irregularly, they are metrically parallel in relation to the 4/4 bar line. The two fragments are not ostinatos, strictly speaking, but the displacement that results from the irregular spanning of their repeats is hypermetrical rather than metrical.

fragment's concluding pitch D and the agogic accent of this pitch. The final placement on the second quarter-note beat allows D to fall on the downbeat of the 4/4 barline, and in this way to acquire the metrical acknowledgment and support withheld from earlier repeats at Rehearsal Nos. 64–70. This, too, may contribute to the sense of resolution at Rehearsal No. 70. It is as if, after much trial and error, the horn fragment had finally stumbled into place, finding the metrical location from which a maximum degree of stability could be derived.

Indeed, displacements in Stravinsky's music are not typically as disruptive in their potential as the ones cited in Example 6.9. In Examples 8.4b and 8.12a–c, each of the four repeat structures from, respectively, the *Symphonies*, *The Rite of Spring*, *Les Noces*, and *Renard* consists of a displacement. Whether notated or concealed by a radical notation, a short motive falls on and off the likely tactus. And despite the shallowness of the location and the disruptive potential, a conservative reading is apt to meet with little resistance. The displaced repeats are likely to be read as a form of syncopation.

Indeed, why not interpret the displacements in these examples as *variations* (even as *developing* ones), metrical alignment itself as a feature of the motive along with other such features identified in Schoenberg's *Fundamentals of Musical Composition*?[39] Conservative responses would seem to invite such an interpretation, the idea of a motivic profile that is followed by its variants (displacements, in this case). For the psychology of the conservative response would seem to correspond to that of the motive and its apprehension. Reading through the displacement of a motive as it relates to an earlier placement, listeners are likely to be struck by the change or relationship itself, not by the two or three alignments considered separately or as they might appear in an idealized adjacency. Something of the transformation itself is sensed automatically (effortlessly), and it is this that is likely to excite and to direct their attention conservatively. The experience would seem to differ little from what we know of the perception of more traditional motivic relations.[40]

---

[39] Arnold Schoenberg, *Fundamentals of Musical Composition*, ed. Gerald Strang and Leonard Stein (London: Faber and Faber, 1967), 9–10.

[40] The phenomenology of motivic detection is discussed in Carl Dahlhaus, *Esthetics of Music*, trans. William W. Austin (Cambridge University Press, 1982), 76–77. "The connection between the motivic variant, occupying the present, and the model it recalls is not 'open to inspection'," Dahlhaus writes. "The two motives are not side by side in the same sense as two phrases may be called 'adjacent' ... The fact of similarity between model and variant is clearer than the motive announced to begin with. The general existence of some connection is more striking than what specifically is being connected with what." Also relevant here is the lengthy discussion of the "sensation of difference" and its initial "shock" in William James, *Principles of Psychology*, 2 vols. (New York: Dover, 1950), vol. I: 494–502. In cases of involuntary comparison and discrimination, we become aware of a difference between "terms" (model and variant, for example) before being able "to assign any definite character to that which differs" (496). The "sensation" of

No doubt, there are qualifications. In his lengthy study of metrical non-parallelism and the varied repetition of motives in traditional, tonal contexts, David Temperley has compared the difficulties of the former with the fast, automatic way in which ordinary motivic relationships are assimilated.[41] When reinforced metrically by parallelism, motivic relationships "tend to be detected automatically," he concludes, while, when not so reinforced, they tend to be detected "only with difficulty," if at all.[42]

J. A. Fodor's theories of perception are invoked as a way of explaining this discrepancy. The slow and difficult detection of non-parallel relationships is judged "non-modular," while the effortless detection of parallel relationships is judged "modular" in character.[43]

In terms of the perceptual processes at work, then, metrical placement and displacement may differ from the melodic, harmonic, and rhythmic features of a motive and the subsequent variation of these features. And our perspective has thus far tended to acknowledge as much. Stravinsky's art of displacement has been located in something of an opposition to the Classical style and its methods of developing variation. Stressed in our account has been the reflexive nature of the process of metrical entrainment; meter is assimilated by the listener as a form of motor behavior. Crucially, too, many melodic, harmonic, and articulative features of Stravinsky's music have been viewed as having been shaped and determined by rhythmic–metric forces. The change in emphasis can be highly disruptive of the meter, as we have seen, as well as static in its implications. All this stands in marked contrast to the more immediately continuous, forward-moving aspects of the developmental style.

In other ways, however, and especially where conservative interpretations of metrical displacement are concerned, the analogy to the more traditional forms of variation is difficult to dispel. In the listener's attempt to read through a displacement as it relates to an earlier placement (doing so by sustaining the meter against the forces of parallelism), it can indeed seem as if he/she were attempting to absorb the shift in alignment as a form of variation or modification. Attempts of this kind are difficult to explain in any other way. The displacement is read *motivically*, in other words, with alignment itself read as a feature of the motive. And instead of the sense of stasis that a lack of variation and a disturbance of the meter are apt to prompt, the effect can be dynamic.

---

that difference is "incorporated and taken up into the second term, which feels 'different-from-the-first' even while it lasts." The "second term" is not experienced singly or purely; if it were to be experienced purely, then it would remain "uncompared" (498). For further comment on James's argument see Aron Gurwitsch, *The Field of Consciousness* (Pittsburgh: Duquesne University Press, 1964), 127–32.

[41] David Temperley, "Motivic Perception and Modularity," *Music Perception* 13, no. 2 (1995): 41–64.
[42] *Ibid.*, 153–54.   [43] *Ibid.*, 157.

With Adorno's negative account of metrical disruption generally, however, the concern is less with the variety of displacements in Stravinsky's
music than with the nature of the experience itself. If meter is a "mode of
attending," as one theorist has claimed,[44] a way of focusing the listener's
attention, what are we to make of its disruption? If there is satisfaction to be
gained from letting go, from giving up and breaking away for a time
(allowing, radically, for the regularity of a higher level of pulsation to take
effect), what of the initial confusion of displacement, the disorientation into
which, with varying degrees of intensity, the listener may be plunged?

Theorists engaged in issues of perception have long stressed the emotional
arousal that expectation can bring when inhibited or interrupted. And it has
been some time now since Leonard Meyer first began discussing the affective
experiences that "the deviation of a particular musical event from the archetype
or schema of which it is an instance" can cause.[45] Surely the disruption of an
established meter figures as an instance of musical behavior of this kind.

At the same time, however, the larger psychological and aesthetic question has to do not with arousal as such, not with the state of alertness to
which the listener may be propelled, but with the nature of the emotions
that are stirred in one way or another. Are Stravinsky's displacements and
the disruption they can cause as traumatic and as psychologically damaging
as Adorno insists? Or can they be "exciting" and a "delight," as Meyer
contends in his description of implication and delay more generally?[46] And
if displacement can be a "delight," why should this be? Why should listeners
of Stravinsky's music be attracted to processes that disrupt their metrical
bearings?

Not just meter but meter internalized is the subject of the disruption.
That to which meter attaches itself physically is affected and, in this way,
brought to the surface of consciousness. (As we have suggested, even if the
source of the disturbance is not known at first, it may be sensed and felt all
the same.) And this may be among the *joys of displacement*, of course, the
fact that we are brought into closer contact with what we are deep, down,
and under. It may also be what alertness is, the heightened sense of engagement that is brought about by disruption or the threat thereof.

Meyer's theory of arousal was derived in large part from John Dewey's
"conflict theory" of human emotion.[47] Meyer argued that emotion in music
arose from the same general set of circumstances, namely, the blocking of

---

[44] See Robert Gjerdingen, "Meter as a Mode of Attending: A Network Simulation of Attentional
Rhythmicity in Music," *Integral* 3 (1989): 67–92.
[45] Leonard Meyer, *Explaining Music* (Berkeley: University of California Press, 1973), 213.
[46] *Ibid.*
[47] See Meyer, *Emotion and Meaning in Music* (University of Chicago Press, 1956), 13–16.

expectations, implications, or tendencies. Accompanied by a belief in the eventual resolution of the conflict (or clarification of the ambiguity), the inhibition, blockage, or arrest heightened a sense of anticipation and suspense.[48] "Delay pleasures play," Meyer reasoned.[49] According to the well-known aphorism, "expectation and reverie" could indeed be imagined as being "better than actuality."

In much music of the nineteenth century, delay can doubtless seem to have taken on a life of its own. The ways in which completion or closure is averted, suspense sustained, can seem to have grown ever more elaborate as the century wore on. In poetic terms, the outwardly fragmentary and incomplete nature of much music of this period can be identified with a yearning that is endless, "longing eternally renewed," as Charles Rosen has expressed it in his discussion of the opening song of Schumann's *Dichterliebe*.[50] The emphasis on the purely negative side of pleasure ("negative pleasure," as some have termed it),[51] can seem sadistic or sadomasochistic in its implications. Pleasure can seem to be derived perversely from the inhibition or blockage itself, from the pain of want and desire, the withholding of a sense of arrival, completion, resumption, or release. Adorno himself acknowledged the "sadomasochistic" strains in Stravinsky's music,[52] in the composer's "perverse joy in self-denial" and in the shocks of his metrically displaced accents.[53]

Implications of this kind have doubtless been a part of music in the Western art tradition since, at the very least, the dawn of tonality. And there has been no dearth of acknowledgment. Schenker likened the circuitous routes of the linear progression to real-life experiences of "detours, expansions, interpolations, and retardations";[54] famously, the half-cadence at the close of the antecedent phrase of a period structure was judged an "interruption" of such a progression.[55] In recent studies of the psychology of anxiety, emotions have been identified as "interrupt phenomena" which arise from the "interruption (blocking, inhibiting) of ongoing, organized thought or behavior."[56] More specific versions of this equation involve not one but simultaneously aroused and conflicting implications or tendencies.

---

[48] *Ibid.*, 28–29.   [49] See Meyer, *Explaining Music*, 31.
[50] Charles Rosen, *The Romantic Generation* (Cambridge: Harvard University Press, 1995), 41.
[51] See Jerold Levinson, *Music, Art, and Metaphysics* (Ithaca: Cornell University Press, 1990), 306–35.
[52] Adorno, *Philosophy of Modern Music*, 159.   [53] *Ibid.*, 154.
[54] Heinrich Schenker, *Free Composition*, trans. Ernst Oster (New York, Longman, 1979), 5. "Therein lies the source of all artistic delaying," Schenker wrote, "from which the creative mind can derive pleasure that is ever new."
[55] *Ibid.*, 36.
[56] George Mandler, "The Generation of Emotion," in Robert Plutchik and Henry Kellerman, eds., *Emotion: Theory, Research, and Experience* (New York: Academic Press, 1989), 225. Recent theories of anxiety and emotion are discussed in Renée Cox Lorraine, *Music, Tendencies, and Inhibitions: Reflections on a Theory of Leonard Meyer* (Lanham: The Scarecrow Press, 2001), 4–6.

Here, of course, the fit could not be tighter. Settings of metrical displace-ment in Stravinsky's music involve the opposition of irreconcilable forces, those of metrical displacement and parallelism. To inhibit or interrupt one of these forces (an "ongoing thought or behavior") is to stir the emotions. To displace a repeated theme, motive, or chord metrically is to thwart implica-tions of parallelism, to the point at times of disrupting the meter. It is to invite the "convulsive blows and shocks" to which a good deal of Adorno's specific criticism of Stravinsky's music is directed.

And so the question arises: if inhibition or interruption can be an accepted and even expected part of the listening experience of the tonal (or atonal) repertory to which Adorno adheres, why can it not be so of the experience of Stravinsky's? Even if we grant the distinction in application, the emphasis on pitch structure in the tonal repertory, on rhythm and meter in Stravinsky's, the processes in question substantiate the same general psychology. Moreover, as we have seen in Chapter 1, conflicts between metrical displacement and parallelism are not unique to Stravinsky's music. They may be less relentless in tonal works, to be sure, as well as less immediate. There are fewer displacements, and they tend to be confined to less immediate levels of metrical pulsation. Crucially, too, in earlier hemiola-related contexts, the conflict with an established meter arises in the form of an alternative meter, while in Stravinsky's music it typically materializes *radically* in the form of an outright disruption or interruption. Listeners are unable to switch to an alternative scheme, but must scramble to re-establish something of the disrupted framework. And in line with these same distinctions, the spans between the displaced repeats of a motive are often irregular in Stravinsky's music, while the repetition itself is much more literal.

Notwithstanding the weight of these differences, however, expectation, tendency, and disruption play as large a role in Stravinsky's settings of displacement as they do in earlier contexts. Where issues of perception are concerned, the distinctions are not as cut and dried as Adorno would seem to imply.

Moreover, just as with Adorno's critical verdicts, the larger philosophical and socio-political images can often be set aside and reversed. They, too, are among the detachable components of his analytical description. The same features deplored and dismissed can be interpreted in a positive light. If the lack of expressive timing in the performance of Stravinsky's music can spell coldness and indifference to the plight of the individual (Adorno's musical subject), then it can spell directness and unsentimentality, too, a determina-tion to confront the world "as it is." And if the lack of variation can imply intractability, the refusal of a collective voice to give way to the variations of the individual (a state of unfreedom, as Adorno understands it), then it can also reveal something of the hardness of the outside world, doing so without compromise or falsification. The possibility of such a "negative truth" was entertained briefly by Adorno himself in a later confirmation of the *Philosophy*.[57] He asked whether, in the face of our "impotence" in confronting "the murderous collective," a state of affairs "in which everyone is reduced to the status of potential victim," a direct statement "about the way things are" would not be more persuasive than any "expression of musical subjectivity," any "vain lament":[58]

> Critics might insist that . . . the spirit of the age is deeply inscribed in
> Stravinsky's art with its dominant gesture of "This is how it is." A higher
> criticism would have to consider whether this gesture does not give shape to an
> implicit truth which the spirit of the age denies and which history has rendered
> dubious in itself.[59]

Could Stravinsky's lifelong recoil from the personal in music, from traditional notions of the self and self-expression (his "perverse joy in self-denial," as Adorno phrased it) signal a recoil from vanity and its conceits? Could the static quality of his music announce a more sober view of humankind and its prospects? And could the collective authority Adorno professes to hear so resoundingly in Stravinsky's music, the collective will heard over against that of the individual, be that of an enduring truth or demanding God rather than that of a fascist?[60]

Again, ideas similar to these were entertained briefly by Adorno, but rejected all the same. No sense of an awareness of this predicament could be detected by Adorno on the part of the musical subject.[61] And the static implications of Stravinsky's invention are for Adorno not just a style feature, but the negation of the medium of music itself. Being a temporal art, music must commit itself to "succession," he insists, to becoming something new, to "developing."[62]

---

[57] See Adorno, "Stravinsky: A Dialectical Portrait," 149.   [58] *Ibid.*   [59] *Ibid.*

[60] Similar questions are posed in Chandler Carter, "*The Rake's Progress* and Stravinsky's Return: The Composer's Evolving Approach to Setting Text," *Journal of the American Musicological Society* 63, no. 3 (2010): 633. If something like anti-humanism can be read into Stravinsky and the static, seemingly unyielding qualities of his music, Carter asks, could it take the form not of oppressive political thought, as Adorno and Taruskin have imagined, but rather of artistic and religious values that are sustained absolutely against time, human personality, and "ever-changing Progress"? Carter credits the following in the construction of his argument: T. E. Hulme, "The Notebook," in *The Collected Writings of T. E. Hulme*, ed. Karen Csengeri (Oxford: Clarendon Press, 1994).

[61] See Paddison, *Adorno's Aesthetics of Music*, 268.

[62] Adorno, "Stravinsky: A Dialectical Portrait," 151.

What we may conceive of as musical transcendence, namely, the fact that at any given moment [music] has become something and something other than it was, that it points beyond itself – all that is no mere metaphysical imperative dictated by some external authority. It lies in the nature of music and will not be denied . . .

[Stravinsky] is beset by the crisis of the timeless products of a time-based art which constantly pose the question of how to repeat something without developing it and yet avoid monotony . . . The sections he strings together may not be identical and yet may never be anything qualitatively different . . . [Stravinsky] permanently wrote music about music, because he wrote music against music.[63]

As we continue to insist, however, the distinctive features of Stravinsky's style are not so easily defined. The contrasts afforded by the model of developing variation, however insightful, are often a matter of kind and degree rather than outright distinction or polarity. The literal and relentless nature of the repetition is not without parallel in nineteenth- and twentieth-century music, and there are a great variety of displacements in Stravinsky's music, not all of which are likely to involve disruption. As we have seen, some may actually contribute to a sense of continuity and anticipation.

If Adorno's approach to Stravinsky and his music can serve as a reminder of the hazards general observation is likely to incur when not sufficiently buttressed by concrete analysis, then it can say something of the rewards of immediate impressions as well. Displacement and the conflicts it can cause are more varied and complicated than Adorno cared to admit. And the relationship between the developmental style and that of displacement in Stravinsky's music is not as polarized as he imagined (or as he may have exaggerated, quite possibly for the sake of the argument). Rarely missing from his account, however, is a sense of struggle with what Stravinsky's music is on an immediate level of contact, a determination to come to terms with that level. And it is this that is likely to excite and to move the reader-listener to further reflection.

Today's tendency has been to applaud Adorno's philosophy and sociology as sophisticated and radical, but to reject his analytical description as half-hearted, crude, and dated.[64] This is in part a reflection of postmodernist trends in musicology. As it concerns Stravinsky and the Schoenberg-Stravinsky divide, however, the equation could easily be reversed. A motivic approach to music of the developmental style can hardly be judged inappropriate, and not all of Adorno's analytical attempts along these lines are as

---

[63] *Ibid.*, 151–53.
[64] See Paddison, *Adorno's Aesthetics of Music*, 13–15, or Johnson, "Analysis in Adorno's Aesthetics of Music," 299–300.

piecemeal as those in his *Philosophy* or the later Stravinsky article.[65] Surely the atonal and twelve-tone repertories of Schoenberg and his immediate predecessors can be viewed as intensely motivic in conception. And the juxtaposition of that style with processes of metrical displacement in Stravinsky's music, qualified by the reservations noted here, is surely an appropriate way of proceeding analytically.

In contrast, what can seem old-fashioned and even absurdly naive in Adorno's writings about Stravinsky is a critical judgment that fixes musical value with a single style (with all other styles weighed accordingly), verification with a single method of analysis (drawn from the single style), and musical expressivity with the terms and concepts laid down by that single style. Add to this a view of metrical displacement and its implications that is invariably one-sided (Adorno is steadfastly a *radical* interpreter of Stravinsky's music, never a conservative one), and the makings of a large critical and aesthetic edifice in deep, wobbly trouble are surely unmistakable.

Here again, however, the music to which Adorno refers may end up rescuing both the criticism and the philosophy. As long as Stravinsky's music continues to wield the sort of magic it has in the past, the speculative sides of Adorno's account are likely to be of interest. This is not how the critic-philosopher himself might have envisioned the future, but for anyone less convinced about the nature of music's socio-political content, it may be what we end up with all the same. For it allows for an appreciation of both the music and Adorno's analytical descriptions, setting aside all the while the necessity of having to subscribe to the larger socio-political convictions or to a belief in their musical embodiment (precisely what, as has been argued here, the coming years are likely to find increasingly problematic). Such an outcome can only work to the benefit of both music and its critical reflection.

Stravinsky the person

Only very rarely does Stravinsky the person fall through the cracks of Adorno's lengthy critique of the music. Details of the composer's biography are missing altogether in Adorno's *Philosophy of Modern Music*, and very nearly in his later writings as well. It is as if a thick line had been drawn between what Adorno called "the objective substance of the music and the subjective state of mind of the composer." Holding Stravinsky and his

---

[65] See, for example, Adorno's thematic-motivic analysis of Berg's Piano Sonata in Willi Reich, *Alban Berg: Mit Bergs eigenen Schriften und Beiträgen von Theodor Wiesengrund Adorno und Ernst Krenek* (Vienna: Herbert Reichner, 1937), 21–26. Adorno's analysis of the Sonata is discussed in great detail in Paddison, *Adorno's Aesthetics of Music*, 158–74, and Johnson, "Analysis in Adorno's Aesthetics of Music," 303–11.

attitudes "responsible for certain historical or philosophical implications in his works" would have been "despicable." It would have violated deeply held philosophical principles. As a reflection of larger historical forces, music changed along the lines indicated in response to such forces. "Only if you fail to comprehend the thing," Adorno insisted, "will you seek to make up for your failure by attacking the person."[66]

Nonetheless, such a position has distinguished the critic-philosopher not only from today's postmodernists, but also from the so-called New Musicology of the 1980s and 90s. (Adorno's insistence on a traditional avant-garde and canon of Western art music would have distinguished him as well in this respect.) It separates him from the recent criticism of Richard Taruskin, for example, from Taruskin's attempts to come to terms musically with a number of problematic details of Stravinsky's biography, including the composer's reactionary politics during the 1920s and 30s, his association with the Eurasian émigré movement, and the occurrence in his correspondence of numerous anti-Semitic slurs.[67] From the standpoint of such details, it can almost seem as if Adorno's position on the matter of the composer's biography and person had been accepted as a challenge by Taruskin. Seeking confirmation for Adorno's damning appraisal of Stravinsky's music as unfeeling, tyrannical, and anti-humanistic, Taruskin can seem to have plunged in where, earlier, Adorno had resolved to tread only very lightly.

Central to Taruskin's thesis is the composer's anti-Semitism, which is interpreted as having been deep-seated, pervasive, and "enthusiastic."[68] Scattered throughout the correspondence, Stravinsky's anti-Semitic comments were in no way reflective of something shallow or indicative of the social mores of the time. Nor were they merely opportunistic, attempts to curry favor with German publishers and agents during the 1930s.[69] On the

---

[66] Adorno, "Stravinsky: A Dialectical Portrait," 148.

[67] A typical slur runs as follows: "Is it politically wise vis-à-vis Germany to identify myself with Jews like Klemperer and Walter, who are being exiled? . . . I do not want to risk seeing my name beside such trash as Milhaud." Letter to Gavriyil Paichadze, Russische Musikverlag in Berlin, September 7, 1933; see the commentary in Richard Taruskin, *Defining Russia Musically: Historical and Hermeneutical Essays* (Princeton University Press, 1997), 458. Slurs of this kind were regularly deleted by Robert Craft from his three-volume edition of Stravinsky's selected correspondence.

[68] Taruskin, *Defining Russia Musically*, 448. Taruskin's pursuit of Stravinsky's anti-Semitism mirrors the efforts by present-day historians to come to terms with "ordinary citizens" at the time of the Nazi persecutions, in Germany and elsewhere. The hard line taken in Daniel Goldhagen, *Hitler's Willing Executioners: Ordinary Germans and the Holocaust* (New York: Random House, 1997) may be compared to the mixed experiences chronicled in Victor Klemperer, *I Will Bear Witness: A Diary of the Nazi Years, 1933–1941* (New York: Random House, 1998).

[69] Stravinsky's relations as a composer, pianist, and conductor in Nazi Germany are chronicled in Joan Evans, "Stravinsky's Music in Hitler's Germany," *Journal of the American Musicological Society* 56, no. 3 (2003): 525–72. For the most part, Evans's story unfolds through the composer's correspondence with his German publisher, Schott.

contrary, Taruskin argues, Stravinsky's was a genuinely anti-Semitic mentality. All this figured as part of "the dark side" of modern music, a phenomenon Taruskin has been at pains to pursue with other composers and repertories of the past century as well.

With *The Rite of Spring*, for example, it was as an ugly, anti-humanist tract that this ballet won fame early on, not as a celebration of early humankind or as a tribute to our common prehistoric roots.[70] Both the scenario and choreography lacked human subjectivity; to follow Taruskin, a sense of compassion. Individual characters were made to submit to a collective will, as with the Chosen One and her Sacrificial Dance. Taruskin sees all this as having foreshadowed a host of twentieth-century ills, including fascism and the Nazi regime. Indeed, the same anti-humanist impulses are traced to the composer's formalist aesthetics, Stravinsky's lifelong recoil from the personal in music, his rejection of "psychology," and his insistence on music as a world cut off from everyday forces, including, evidently, those of morality. A more sinister reading of the composer's formalist beliefs would be difficult to imagine.

But the issue from which this argument draws its motivation, that of musical content, must be confronted. The manner in which these antihumanist implications manifest themselves in pieces such as *The Rite of Spring*, *Les Noces*, and the *Symphonies* cannot be sidestepped. "Those who assert the critical relevance of the connection" between society, politics, and music are under an obligation in this regard, Taruskin himself concedes; they share a "burden of proof."[71] Yet it is just here where his argument breaks down. Crucial questions about content, perception, association, and the role of the individual listener are left hanging. Taruskin concludes with the following remark: "Whether [the anti-humanist side] irrevocably taints Stravinsky and his work, as T. W. Adorno insisted, is something we have to decide in keeping with our own liberal traditions."[72]

---

[70] Taruskin, *Defining Russia Musically*, 386.   [71] *Ibid.*, 363, 391.

[72] *Ibid.*, 363. Mention should be made of a number of alternative responses to Taruskin's interpretation of *The Rite of Spring*, his attempt to link the music and scenario to fascist tendencies early in the past century; see, in this connection, Simon Morrison, Review of Richard Taruskin, *Defining Russia Musically*, *Journal of the American Musicological Society* 53, no. 2 (2000): 420–25. To follow Morrison, Taruskin's "metaphoric alignment of *The Rite of Spring*" with fascism and "the German apocalypse" is carefully circumscribed. Stravinsky and his colleagues are pictured by Taruskin not as advancing "a specific political agenda," but rather as "reacting to nebulous, unstructured cultural stimuli." "Shocking" and "frightening," the "revelation" of this alignment "is actually a rhetorical device" on Taruskin's part, according to Morrison, "intended to push the envelope, to enhance discussion about the ballet's music, which, repackaged as a concert work, has been reduced to the status of 'pure' signifier" (421–22). But surely this argument harbors a form of purification of its own, an effort to "sanitize." For Taruskin's "metaphoric alignment of *The Rite of Spring*" with fascist ideology is framed elsewhere in *Defining Russia Musically* with a ferocious attack on Stravinsky's anti-Semitic remarks, on the composer's opportunistic relations with Nazi Germany, early affection for Mussolini and fascist Italy, formalist aesthetics (devoid, as Taruskin interprets them, of a sense of moral responsibility), and insistence on a strict performance style (with, as Taruskin would have it,

But if we, too, were to have to decide on the matter of this music's "taintedness" or "impurity," then, presumably, we would be wanting to do so with a sense of conviction and belief. And such a sense would have to come in response to something tangible in the music. We would not be wanting to activate our censoring "liberal traditions" on a whim, on the flimsiest of associations. Something musically concrete and vital would have to act as a trigger.

But how does music incriminate itself in this way? How does it speak to us in these very specific socio-political terms? Taruskin points to the "long spans of unchanging content" in *The Rite of Spring*, "the long stretches of arrested root motion and pulsing rhythms."[73] And these descriptions mirror Adorno's, of course, the emphasis Adorno placed on the static quality of Stravinsky's music ("unchanging content"), the relentlessness of the repetition, and the lack of a sense of movement or motion. These features are cited by Taruskin as evidence of Stravinsky's anti-humanism, his sense of identity with the darker forces that had emerged earlier in the past century.

Or are they? A few lines on this most crucial of questions, the one having to do with our point of contact with the music, are unlikely to inspire much confidence. Presumably, Taruskin's "pulsing rhythms" (a cliché of nearly a century of talk about this music) embody the anti-humanist evil within, so to speak; the evil that has steadfastly refused to be tamed. Consciously or unconsciously, this is what draws us, an awful truth of some kind.

But what purpose is served by this encumbrance of music? Why should we seek so ferociously to battle its abstraction? Are we not, by so doing, forcing it to become something which it is not? Indeed, it is as if the stimulus of music were somehow insufficient, as if, by making it less abstract and more like a language (and less like music), we could actually work to enhance that stimulus. It is as if, too, there truly were "secrets" of the kind unearthed by Adorno and Taruskin, "secrets" which, revealing something of the nature of Stravinsky's music and its appeal, could act to enhance or diminish it.

Stravinsky may well have cut an unsympathetic figure between the wars. His politics were reactionary (anti-communist, at the very least), pro-order, pro-tradition, and pro-established religion. He was an elitist with a certain fondness for the rich and famous, touting the latter as a way of gaining acceptance and patronage. He admired Mussolini and fascist Italy for a time.[74] Later in the United States, he admired Harry Truman.

---

performance itself reduced to mindless submission). However one may characterize Taruskin's attempt to frame *The Rite of Spring* with a "cultural context" of this kind, it is most assuredly not a "rhetorical device."

[73] *Ibid.*, 383.

[74] The anxieties that may have fueled the composer's obsessive preoccupation with money and financial compensation may also have caused him to curry favor with various right-wing

Taruskin suspects moral indifference. If "great" music and its appreciation could claim immunity from moral judgment, then so, too, on a personal level, could the composer. And this is unacceptable, not only because of the claim of an entitlement, but also because of the chain linking "great" music to flawed, anti-humanist composers.[75] In a world making greater sense, Taruskin seems to be arguing, one in which music's meaning and significance would indeed be tied to the concrete moral and socio-political causes indicated by Taruskin, this would not be the case. And so a number of adjustments are made. Stravinsky's music is judged contaminated, less than "great." It is as if, in the absence of Stravinsky himself, Taruskin had wanted to call the music itself to the stand, and as a way of answering to the composer's socio-political ills.

Another stab at all this is taken with *Les Noces*. The large-scale octatonic–diatonic scheme inferred by Taruskin – with the (0 2 3 5) Dorian tetrachord conceived as a connecting link or melodic "cell" – relates closely to the one introduced here in Chapter 5. Of more immediate concern, however, are the socio-political implications drawn in one way or another.

Taruskin compares the many gapped or "anhemitonic" (pentatonic) melodies in *Les Noces* to those of various ancient Turkic tribes, as transcribed in Nikolai Trubetskoy, *K probleme russkogo samopoznanaiya* (Paris, 1927).[76] (Recall, from our discussion in Chapter 5, the typically (0 2 5) gapped character of the (0 2 3 5) tetrachord not only in *Les Noces* and Stravinsky's Russian-period works generally, but in many other folk and popular repertories as well.) A prolific writer on matters of linguistics and phonetics, Trubetskoy was also a founder of the Eurasian movement, the dream of many Russian émigrés between the wars of an ideal homeland called "Turania." (Turkic tribes were presumed to have been among the earliest inhabitants of Turania.) Evidence of Stravinsky's ties to this Eurasian group is circumstantial, given the absence of references in his correspondence and publications. Several close friends and acquaintances of his were Eurasianists, however, including Pierre Suvchinsky, Arthur Lourié, and Lev Kasavin.[77] For Taruskin, the music of Stravinsky's Russian period, written in Switzerland during World War I, is all essentially "Turanian." *Les Noces*, the culmination of this period, was a "deliberately crafted representation in unmediated musical terms of the Turanian world view conceived by Trubetskoy."[78] And many Eurasianists at the time may have felt likewise, of course, even if Stravinsky's own views remain something of a mystery. We do not know if

regimes in the years between the wars. See the discussion of this in Paul Driver, review of Stephen Walsh, *Stravinsky: The Second Exile*, *London Review of Books* 29, no. 3 (February 8, 2007): 18.
[75] See Taruskin, *Defining Russia Musically*, 386–88; and Taruskin, "Stravinsky and Us," 273–84.
[76] See Taruskin, *Defining Russia Musically*, 405–12.   [77] *Ibid.*, 399–405.   [78] *Ibid.*, 400.

the composer himself thought of his Russian-period music in this way; we cannot be sure of the degree to which his own musical, aesthetic, and socio-political ideals overlapped with those of his Eurasian colleagues. In fact, his early, close ties to a great many literary and artistic currents in Paris, including the constructivist and formalist ones mentioned in earlier chapters, would seem to argue against the deep or comprehensive engagement imagined by Taruskin.

Eurasian politics tended to be anti-West as well as anti-Bolshevik or anti-Soviet; sympathetic publications were critical of the West's "panromano-germanic" origins, its liberal democracies, legalisms, individualism, materialism, and so forth. Eurasianists sought instead a "symphonic society," one of homogeneity, balance, and religious fraternity. But the problem for Taruskin involves the emergence of a dark side here as well. Eurasian visions of Utopia became indistinguishable from fascist and Nazi ideas about race, nation, and society. Taruskin uncovers an anti-Semitic slant as well, bringing Stravinsky's affiliations to the fore. The composer's early jealousies are recounted, among these his apparent envy of Maximilian Steinberg, a Jew and fellow pupil of Rimsky-Korsakov's. Stravinsky's anti-humanism is contrasted with Rimsky-Korsakov's tolerance, humanism, and progressive liberalism. Even after World War II, Taruskin insists, Stravinsky's anti-Semitism continued unabated. He cites the vocal texts of Stravinsky's *Cantata* (1952) and *A Sermon, a Narrative, and a Prayer* (1961) as evidence of this; both incorporate "overtly anti-Semitic content."[79] The *Cantata* text, anonymous and derived from a fifteenth-century "sacred history," rehearses "the old guilt-libel against the Jews as children of darkness," while that of the *Narrative*, taken from the Book of Acts, includes St. Stephen's address to the High Priest of the Temple: "Ye do always resist the Holy Ghost."[80] (It is at least plausible that Stravinsky employed these texts historically and aesthetically and not anti-Semitically, a possibility Taruskin has been willing to consider in a later publication.[81] Condemned in this subsequent essay, however, is Stravinsky's indifference or "lack of concern." More comprehensively, the composer's formalist aesthetic is condemned; that which, to follow Taruskin, permitted music and its engagement to become severely detached from the commonplace concerns of society, morality, and politics.)[82]

---

[79] *Ibid.*, 459.
[80] *Ibid.* The offending lines in the *Cantata* text, "Tomorrow Shall Be My Dancing Day," are as follows: "The Jews on me they made great suit/ And with me made great variance/ Because they lov'd darkness rather than light/ To call my true love to my dance."
[81] See Taruskin, "Stravinsky and Us," 260–84.   [82] *Ibid.*, 279.

Can there be anything worse at this point in time? To be branded an anti-Semite (an "enthusiastic" one) with images of the Holocaust everywhere before us, with issues of race, ethnicity, and prejudice so entirely current? Will Stravinsky's music be able to withstand the threat of an association with these still uglier manifestations of what is alleged to have been an anti-humanist mentality?

Taruskin's own conclusions are somewhat reserved. The attraction of *Les Noces*, he argues, rests with a tension between a Turanian, reactionary vision of society and our obligations as enlightened individuals (our "liberal traditions," in other words). There is an "anxious thrill of a moral risk" at play in *Les Noces*,[83] the risk, evidently, of being sucked back into primitive license, anti-humanism, and collective indifference. Here, however, the familiar "puritanics" of postmodernism are all too evident, the prissiness with which postmodernists have tended to approach matters of aesthetic pleasure and attunement.[84] Listeners are asked to hold back, not to "let go" or to become too rapturously immersed. The loss of such conscious control is anathema not only because of the images of seduction, submission, and exploitation that follow along the prescribed routing system of today's reigning ideologies, but also because of the fear, as with puritanical sects in general, of "nature" and instinct, of being caught off guard, as it were, caught in an ideologically inconsistent act, an incorrectness.

Another interpretation of the vocal texts of the *Cantata* and the *Narrative* suggests itself. According to Lilian Libman, Stravinsky's personal secretary and assistant for twelve years (1959–1971), the composer's anti-Semitism was a "ridiculous fiction," a kind of prejudice that "could hardly have entered [the composer's] scope of thought." In fact, Stravinsky "never bothered to deny" the evidently frequently voiced "theory" that he himself was Jewish.[85] And upon hearing of the offense that had been taken, he and Craft set about changing the word "Jews" to "enemies" in the *Cantata* text. For practical or aesthetic reasons, however, changes of this kind, although realized in a number of concert performances early on, were never made a part of the published score.

A reconciliation of these highly conflicting interpretations may not be possible. Problematic above all is the role of history. Against the backdrop of

---

[83] Taruskin, *Defining Russia Musically*, 391.

[84] These issues have been discussed before. See, for example, Pieter C. van den Toorn, Letter to the Editor, *Music Theory Spectrum* 20/1 (1998): 160–68.

[85] Lilian Libman, *And Music at the Close: Stravinsky's Last Years* (New York: Norton, 1972), 304. Given her official role as a "publicist," the credibility of Libman's testimony on matters relating to Stravinsky's attitudes and conversation has been questioned; see Taruskin, "Stravinsky and Us," 316. Clearly, however, as someone who served the Stravinskys as a secretary and as a companion for over a decade, Libman's position went well beyond that of an employee.

today's heightened awareness of racial prejudice, can we defend Stravinsky without seeming inhuman or, worse, like one of today's legal defense teams, forever splitting hairs in strategies of evasion? Can we condemn Stravinsky for his anti-Semitic remarks while keeping to a historical perspective, one that is mindful of the differences of time and place and of the possible injustice of hindsight, of mixing the composer up with Nazi propagandists and worse?

The hope is that we can. The scattered nature of the evidence in Stravinsky's correspondence would seem to indicate something other than a deep-seated affliction. What is not possible, however, is that today's understanding should be what it appears to have been for the greater part of the twentieth century. Unavoidably, the public today is less tolerant not only of prejudice, whatever the depth or shallowness of its expression, but of ignorance and "blind spots" as well.[86] The three lines of condemnation of the Jews in "Tomorrow Shall Be My Dancing Day" could not be set or imagined today as they seem to have been in 1952 at the time of the *Cantata*; Taruskin's call for an "exposure of the problem" can seem very much to the point.[87] At the same time, in a world not only more sensible but cognizant as well of the historical significance of these lines, the tragedy and folly embodied in one way or another, a performance of the *Cantata* with its original text intact should be possible.

As far as Stravinsky's music as a whole is concerned, however, we remain skeptical of the imagery introduced by Adorno and Taruskin. It is not just the specificity of the images but the manner of their acceptance as a form of content. For the most part, they are introduced not as metaphors or analogies, but as deep-seated truths which, unlocked, speak to the heart of Stravinsky's music and to the nature of its appeal.

Full cycle: *Les Noces* and *The Rite of Spring* revisited

Much early criticism of the music and choreography of *Les Noces* was either Marxist or anti-Marxist in conception. Reactions to the original choreography by Bronislava Nijinska are a case in point. According to this early testimony, Nijinska's designs had stressed the helplessness of the various characters of Stravinsky's scenario, the sweeping away of these individual characters by "mass social forces."[88] Ironically, with the music tied more securely to the scenario and choreography, many of the same images invoked and decried by Adorno as decidedly un-Marxist (images of the "primitive," "regressive," and

---

[86] Taruskin, "Stravinsky and Us," 278.   [87] *Ibid.*, 284.

[88] See Sally Banes, *Dancing Women: Female Bodies on Stage* (London: Routledge, 1998), 118.

ritualistic, as we have indicated) were cited in this early criticism as decidedly Marxist. The emphasis on the communal or collective in Stravinsky's libretto was judged a reflection of Marxist ideas about history and society. (To appreciate fully the chaos of these conflicting associations, something of the composer's lifelong antipathy toward communism and the Soviet Union should be kept in mind. Stravinsky's own conception of an "impersonal," "mechanical," and ritualistic stage action, one with which he later recalled Nijinska's choreography as having been fully consistent,[89] could not have been more sharply at odds with the ideas of these early reviews.)

Thus, for example, André Levinson, writing in the Parisian journal *Comoedia* in 1923, denounced the choreography as "Marxist."[90] He described the individual dances as having been "swallowed" whole by Nijinska's designs, and the art of ballet as having been "leveled" in the process. (Nijinska had favored groups of dancers in her designs, group movement over the development of individual roles. Such an approach had been featured in the original choreography of *The Rite of Spring* as well, as designed by her brother, Vaslav Nijinsky.)

In the past several decades, however, the commentary on *Les Noces* and its scenario and choreography has turned to the "sexual politics" of the early wedding rituals, with Stravinsky's adaptation viewed from a feminist perspective.[91] To follow Sally Banes in this regard, early audiences of *Les Noces* were alert to the "sexual oppression of peasant women in pre-revolutionary Russia." Banes depicts the Bride and her mother as victims of a "patriarchal culture."[92] And in one of Lynn Garafola's biographical sketches, Nijinska herself is depicted as an early feminist, her designs for *Les Noces* as having represented "male power and female pain."[93] Steps assigned to the female dancers at the outset of the first tableau were "stabbing" in their effect, "masculine in their violence," while much of the choreography had sought to enact a "drama of sexual penetration."[94] (Recall Nijinska's use of pointe in the first tableau, the heavy rather than light effect of this employment. According to her own testimony, her intention had been to create an impression of groundedness, of generations of peasants "weighted by centuries of toil.")

In the larger context of *Les Noces*, of course, it is not the Bride alone who is trapped oppressively by "social forces." All are trapped by such forces, including the Groom and his parents. And it is not just the ritualistic

---

[89] Stravinsky and Craft, *Expositions and Developments*, 133. "The choreography was expressed in blocks and masses," Stravinsky recalled; "individual personalities did not, could not, emerge."
[90] André Levinson, "Où sont les 'Ballets russes'," *Comoedia* (June 18, 1923); quoted in Lynn Garafola, *Diaghilev's Ballets Russes* (New York: Oxford University Press, 1989), 126.
[91] Banes, *Dancing Women*, 120.   [92] *Ibid.*, 118.   [93] Garafola, *Diaghilev's Ballets Russes*, 128.
[94] *Ibid.*

movements of Nijinska's choreography that can have the effect of reinforcing this sense of entrapment, but the music as well, by way of the repetition of motives and the rigidities of the beat detailed here and in earlier chapters.

The Bride occupies center stage in *Les Noces*, as she did in the early rituals themselves. The particulars of her distress are underscored, the cruelty of her parting, and the intensity of her fears of sexual violence. (In one of Nijinska's dances, the Bride is shown clutching her fists repeatedly; as Stravinsky himself acknowledged, references at the outset of *Les Noces* to the parting of her braid are sexual as well as spiritual in implication.)[95] Of the 1,043 wedding songs in Kireyevsky's anthology, the vast majority do in fact refer to the bride, and the majority of these sing of "the sorrowful lamentation of the bride about her miserable fate."[96] As we have indicated already in Chapters 3 and 4, the Bride's fate remained ritualistically "sorrowful" even when the particular occasion happened to be a happy and exuberant one.

Yet it seems not to have been as a form of advocacy – a "radical statement" about social conditions in pre-revolutionary Russia, as Banes would have it – that Stravinsky's combination of music, scenario, and ballet succeeded early on.[97] Such a purpose seems not to have been the composer's, in any case, however sympathetic (or unsympathetic) he may have been in real life to the circumstances underlying these causes. Rather, the combination seems to have prevailed as a piece of human drama, a look at how this most basic of human relationships survived in public ritual and more particularly in the vastness of peasant Russia. (The association of all things peasant-like was not merely with the simple or "primitive," but with the deep and abiding as well, with what, concealed, had survived the complications of modern life.) Full of cruelty, pain, banality, hope, and exultation, the picture drawn by the composer is human (if not altogether "humanistic," as Adorno and Taruskin have charged). The emphasis on the communal rites of peasant life was an emphasis on the thoroughly conventional modes of expression associated with those rites. No advice is offered by the composer, no prescription for the future. The play accepts what it enacts, seems transfixed by it, in fact, as if the sources that lay at its foundation had represented a treasure that had been worth preserving for its own sake. Its approach is aesthetic, as we have argued, humane and sympathetic, not sociopolitical or even historical. A distinction of this kind is not without a degree of overlapping, to be sure, yet it is fundamental all the same.

---

[95] See Stravinsky and Craft, *Expositions and Developments*, 131.
[96] Vladimir Propp, "The Russian Folk Lyric," in Roberta Reeder, ed., *Down Along the Mother Volga: An Anthology of Russian Folk Lyrics* (Philadelphia: University of Pennsylvania Press, 1975), 23.
[97] Banes, *Dancing Women*, 120.

Bundled together in a tightly knit package and set aglow, the "typical wedding sayings" of *Les Noces* are not those of a single bride, groom, or mother, but those of any bride, groom, or mother. Passed down through the ages, as we have noted, these "sayings" represent the imagined thoughts of a great multitude of brides, grooms, and mothers. And they bear the scars of this, the wear and tear, so to speak. Yet they are no less moving for the weight of this heritage. Conveyed by such means is something of the struggle brides, grooms, and mothers have had to bear in their confrontation not only with the difficulties of expression but with those of nature and society as well, uncompromising forces for which they are no match. Herein lies the source of the poignancy of these verses.

In the opening blocks of *Les Noces*, the smallest details are marked by a complex system of repetition. In the soprano line, only the pitches D and B of the (E D B) trichord are embellished by grace notes, never E. Similarly, only those Ds which are succeeded immediately by E are singled out and punctuated by the xylophone. At the same time, successive taps on the cymbal are the result of a different system. More to the point, these rules are fixed from the start. Melody, harmony, and articulation are locked in place with little if any change or elaboration along the way.

Nonetheless, within these constraints, variation is not absent altogether. As we have suggested in Chapter 4, repeats of the over-the-bar line succession D-E may be heard and understood conservatively. In relation to a concealed 3/8 meter, they undergo a patterned series of displacements, and may be heard *motivically* in this way, as *variants* of the initial alignment straddling the bar line. So, too, in the larger scheme of things, the system of repetition serves as a backdrop. It highlights the variation that does in fact occur in the form of an irregular spanning and metrical placement.

As in all ritual performance, the private is expressed in public terms. The sobs, gasps, and stutters that can seem to underlie the grace notes of the opening soprano line of *Les Noces* are but a crack in a hardened surface, small openings in what can otherwise seem well-nigh impenetrable to the human heart. Yet they are openings all the same, improvisational in character and capable of easing the hardened surface with the suggestion of an expressive nuance. Swooping down by leaps of a minor third and fourth, they mimic the spontaneous, uncontrollable sobs of a private anguish. More concretely still, the leaps can suggest the cracking of the Bride's voice, the vocal breaks that a character in deep emotional distress may experience. A sense of the personal is conveyed by such means, something of a bride's innermost thoughts and emotions.

In fact, the rigidity of the musico-dramatic expression need not imply a form of submission at all, an identification with the powers that be. Contrary to the views of Adorno and Taruskin in this respect, the severity of the musical constraints need not be sensed as tyrannical or anti-humanistic. The limitations in melodic range, content, articulation, and expressive nuance need not imply compliance on the Bride's part, a passive resignation and surrender to a "murderous collective."

Just as easily, the severity of the message can spell trauma, a body stiffened by distress. The rigidity can signify a voice "choked with emotion," muscles grown tense through strain. The image can be that of a Bride handicapped by mental and physical constraints, unable to sing freely because of them. She can be felt as struggling to maintain her composure, to persevere with a prescribed text and function. Much of the intensity of the opening scene of *Les Noces* can be understood in these terms. Just as the Bride can be pictured as embodying something of the stiffness of the music, so, too, the music can be imagined as incorporating something of her predicament. And the more formidable the constraints, the more intensely is her plight and that of the human condition more generally likely to be felt.

Finally, a few parting remarks here on the critical reception of *The Rite of Spring* have also seemed in order, and by way of the celebrated opening block of the "Augurs of Spring." The notated (and conservative) version of this music, reproduced in Example 10.1a, is followed by the radical rebarring of Example 10.1b. In the latter, the changing bar lines accommodate the irregularity of the spans between repeats of the thick, heavily accented chords. Metrical parallelism reigns supreme in the rebarred version of Example 10.1b, as all accented chords are aligned as downbeats of the bars in question. Implied here is a form of pulsation with little if any suggestion of a meter (a quarter-note beat to interpret the pulsating eighth-note beats). And should the radicalism of this version strike the reader as far-fetched, it is certainly no more so when a portion of it is made to reappear at the end of the "Ritual of Abduction" (see Example 10.2a), or, in conservative notation, at Rehearsal No. 30 in the "Augurs of Spring" (see Example 10.2b) and again at Rehearsal No. 15 (Example 10.2c). The detachment of an accentual pattern in this fashion, the independence it may gain by being separated and applied to different materials, is one of the many "technical" aspects of *The Rite of Spring* and its rhythmic organization that, during the 1940s, 50s, 60s, and 70s, attracted the studied attention of generations of avant-garde composers, including, perhaps most conspicuously, the generation associated with Pierre Boulez.

Shown in Example 10.1c is the octatonic (Collection III) configuration that follows the opening block at Rehearsal No. 14. The intervals of this configuration, measured in semitones, are bracketed above the reduction to the right; as a series of numbers, these intervals match the irregular spans marked off by the changing bar lines in Example 10.1b, with the spans

Example 10.1. *The Rite of Spring*, "Augurs of Spring," opening blocks
a) notated (conservative)

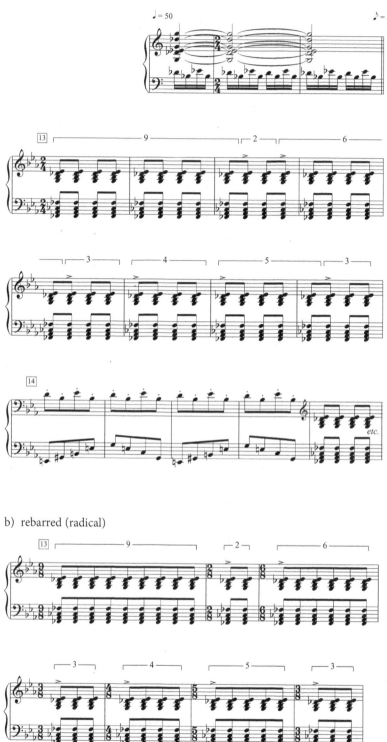

b) rebarred (radical)

Example 10.1. (contd).
c) intervallic series

* first pitch of *The Rite*

reduced to eighth-note beats. In a revealing study of match-ups of this kind in *The Rite of Spring*, Matthew McDonald has identified this and many other rhythmic patterns in *The Rite* as having been derived from intervals in the manner just described.[98] Although we can locate no "smoking gun" or absolute proof of the composer's intentions in this regard (something that eluded McDonald as well), the evidence he presents in support of his findings can be very persuasive indeed.

At the same time, however, as an interpreter of those findings, McDonald is entirely radical. He takes the numbers bracketed in Example 10.1c and elsewhere in his analysis at face value, and so overlooks the role of meter and much of the invention along with it, including that part which, conservative, is capable of converting the quantification into flesh and blood, as it were, drama, excitement, purpose, and subjective feeling. Unavoidably, too, the picture that emerges of *The Rite* is a gloomy one (gloomier even than Adorno's). Even the practice of turning intervals into rhythmic patterns is viewed by McDonald as having been strictly "mechanical," as having prompted on Stravinsky's part an "automatic writing," one that excluded "his own musical imagination, steeped as it was in the Classical tradition, from the compositional process at certain critical stages";[99] composition itself was "dehumanized" in the process.[100] Echoing Adorno and Taruskin in this connection, McDonald stresses the "objective detachment that pervades *The Rite*," its "suppression of any suggestion of human agency." Wholly manufactured, "the simulation of objectivity" implies "the lack of an organizing psychology behind the music."[101]

But such is hardly the only means of interpreting the rhythmic patterns not only of the opening block of the "Augurs of Spring," but at other locations of *The Rite* as well. The conservative (and notated) version of the opening block is reproduced in Example 10.1a. Crucially, the block is preceded by

[98] McDonald, *Jeux de Nombres*: 499–551.   [99] *Ibid.*, 548.   [100] *Ibid.*, 547.   [101] *Ibid.*, 546.

Example 10.2. *The Rite of Spring*; detachment of an accentual pattern

a) "Ritual of Abduction"

b) "Augurs of Spring"

c) "Augurs of Spring"

the (D♭-B♭) – (E♭-B♭) ostinato, a pattern from which, on the basis of the parallelism exhibited, the listener may infer something of the pending 2/4 meter, the half-note beat at the bar line and the quarter-note beat as the tactus. The 2/4 grid may persist through the fourth bar or so, allowing the accented chords to be heard as they are written, that is, as syncopations off the quarter-note beat.

Increased uncertainty and confusion are likely to follow the displacement at Rehearsal No. 13+5, however, where the accents switch from *off* to *on* the quarter-note beat. As the meter gives way to pulsation at this point, the listener may become metrically lost, unable to distinguish upbeats from onbeats. So, too, as with so many of the passages examined over the course of this inquiry, the meter is challenged and eventually overturned by the very forces responsible at the outset for its establishment, namely, those of parallelism. As with the opening blocks of *Les Noces* and the *Symphonies*, too, the conservative and radical barrings arrive "on target" at the end of the block, here at the downbeat of the following block at Rehearsal No. 14. At the point at which these conflicting barrings converge, the parallelism that had preceded Rehearsal No. 13 is restored and further enhanced by the triadic arpeggiation in the bass.

In part, too, the juxtaposition of these opening blocks of the "Augurs of Spring" becomes a matter of meter, its disruption, and of metrical parallelism and non-parallelism.[102] Such are the means by which a sense of purpose and engagement can inform the listener's response to this music, experiences altogether different from the ones singled out by McDonald. Stravinsky's methods need not be viewed from an entirely mechanical or "dehumanized" perspective, and as a confirmation, therefore, as McDonald would have it, of the conditions of detachment and alienation detailed by Adorno and Taruskin. On the contrary, they can be made to represent a narrative physically and emotionally as compelling as any in twentieth-century music. A more conservative take can furnish this dance movement with precisely that which has been found lacking by Adorno, Taruskin, and McDonald, namely, a sense of humanity ("humanness"), expressivity, and an "organizing psychology."

Conclusions

In much music of the common-practice period, the relationship between rhythm (or grouping) and meter adheres to a figure-and-ground dynamic. Against a background of "square metrical dance schemes," melody or song, often out-of-phase with these "metrical dance schemes," is thrown into relief.[103] Meter does "all the dirty work," as Hans Keller phrased it some years ago, while melody "is able to enjoy itself."[104] Above all, melody's "upbeat

---

[102] For a more detailed account of the metrical implications of the opening block, "Augurs of Spring," see Pieter C. van den Toorn, *Stravinsky and "The Rite of Spring": The Beginnings of a Musical Language* (Berkeley: University of California Press, 1987), 67–71.

[103] Hans Keller, "Rhythm: Gershwin and Stravinsky," in Hans Keller, *Essays on Music*, ed. Christopher Wintle (Cambridge University Press, 1994), 207.

[104] *Ibid.*

tendency" is developmental in character, implying anticipation and hence movement or forward motion.[105] And to the extent that, in Stravinsky's settings of displacement, fragments and chords are shifted from the upbeat to the downbeat and vice versa (with, as an essential element in this exchange, the articulation of the given fragments and chords left unchanged), the invention can indeed be heard and understood as embodying a form of counteraction. With upbeat or off-the-beat figures displaced in this way, the developmental potential of melody's "upbeat tendency" is countered, replaced by a downbeating that is static and halting in its implications. The counter-action is not of local significance alone, but involves, as a backdrop, whole repertories, as Keller implies, centuries of music. Much of the explosiveness of Stravinsky's invention can be understood in these terms, quite apart from the disruption that may be associated with the conflicts between displacement and metrical parallelism. For those listeners familiar with the music of the past several centuries, the forward-moving impulse against which the invention directs itself is likely to be one that is deeply engrained.

And the static effect of the invention may be pursued along these same lines, as may, to follow Adorno's commentary, many of the standard complaints about Stravinsky's music. Stravinsky writes "music against music," as Adorno expressed it.[106] In seeking to counter a sense of move-ment and succession, it directs itself not against a style characteristic alone, but against a condition of the medium itself.

Unable to detect either a "square metrical dance scheme" or a develop-mental figure, something capable of serving as a foil for displacement and the downbeating effect, Adorno was at a loss, conservatively speaking. Unable to respond in ways other than acutely radical, he could sense little of the energy or "statically intense tension achieved by [Stravinsky's] oppo-sition to the flow of rhythm."[107] He could discern little purpose in the "anti-expressiveness" of the composer's methods, in the suppression of the upbeat and its forward-moving, developmental potential.[108] The chal-lenge to "the way things are" could not be grasped either, the means by which a traditional sense of progress and forward motion in music (opti-mism?) was being questioned. (In Milan Kundera's *Testaments Betrayed*, it is the anti-expressive character of Stravinsky's idiom that is esteemed above all, the manner in which a traditional sense of progress and expressive affect,

---

[105] *Ibid.*, 207–08. Keller's ideas about the upbeating quality of music in the Classical tradition may have been derived from Hugo Riemann's concept of *Auftätigkeit*. Riemann sought to under-score the end-accented or weak-strong nature of the alternation between metrical beats; see his *System der musikalischen Rhythmik und Metrik* (1903).

[106] Adorno, "Stravinsky: A Dialectical Portrait," 153.

[107] Keller, "Rhythm: Gershwin and Stravinsky," 209.   [108] *Ibid.*

a "human subjectivity" that had grown oppressive and "burdensome," is cast aside.[109] At the root of these Stravinskian forces lay the composer's "refusal to see subjective confession as music's *raison d'être*.")[110]

In many of these same respects, Pierre Boulez's celebrated account of *The Rite of Spring's* independent rhythmic "cells" is as radical as Adorno's criticism. Unlike Adorno, however, Boulez is an admirer of Stravinsky's rhythmic invention. The independence of these "cells" in *The Rite of Spring* (their ability to detach themselves from their original settings and assume a life of their own) was doubtless seen as a prefigurement of the serialization of rhythm (or duration) as a separate dimension in works of integral serialism. Yet Boulez makes little mention of meter and hence ultimately of the role of syncopation and displacement in Stravinsky's music.[111] More recently, too, Jonathan Kramer has underscored the discontinuous features of the *Symphonies of Wind Instruments* and other works of the Russian and neoclassical eras. And he has done so without regard for meter and its role in providing for a sense of continuity.[112] Kramer can locate no "sequence of evenly spaced beats on any hierarchic level but the shallowest."[113] Missing in the opening of the *Symphonies* are levels of pulsation capable of interpreting the eighth-note beat at the level of the tactus and beyond.

For more conservative listeners, however, meter and a sense of the upbeat and its developmental quality are rarely absent from Stravinsky's music. "Stravinsky never forgets to define, by overt or hidden implication, the flow ... against which he moves," Hans Keller observed.[114] And with "square metrical dance schemes" and an "upbeat tendency" brought to the fore, so, too, are syncopation and processes of displacement. Ties to the past are likely to surface in this vein, general as well as more specifically Russian.

Indeed, it should come as no surprise in this connection that historians such as Richard Taruskin have been for the most part conservative readers of Stravinsky's music. Ties to tradition may also account to some degree for the continuing appeal of his oeuvre, why so much of it has survived with fairly large audiences. Even a piece such as *Les Noces*, closely allied as it is with Russian folk texts, music, and ritual, was eventually conceived for large, international audiences, above all, perhaps, Western audiences. The

---

[109] Milan Kundera, *Testaments Betrayed: An Essay in Nine Parts*, trans. Linda Asher (New York: HarperCollins, 1994), 71.

[110] *Ibid.*, 65.

[111] Pierre Boulez, *Stocktakings from an Apprenticeship*, trans. Stephen Walsh (Oxford University Press, 1991), 55–105.

[112] Jonathan Kramer, *The Time of Music* (New York: Schirmer Books, 1988), 221–36.

[113] *Ibid.*, 287.   [114] Keller, "Rhythm: Gershwin and Stravinsky," 208.

expectation must surely have been that, quite apart from Russian popular verse, melody, and ritual (of which little would have been known first-hand or in depth), the great subtlety of the play with meter, alignment, and repetition would not fall on deaf ears. The details of pitch, rhythm, and structure could play themselves out against the backdrop of an inherited tradition.

The early beginnings of *Les Noces* are worth recalling in this regard, the more specifically ethnic conception that was gradually transformed into something more abstract and worldly. The point here rests not with the elimination of the folk element and its replacement by the more abstract, but with the two in combination. And it consists of an assimilation, the creation of something new as well, not merely of a form of quotation, simulation, or parody.

This can bring to mind some of the other forms of opposition pursued in these pages, those of radicalism and conservatism, meter and metrical parallelism, discontinuity and continuity, varied and unvaried repetition, and modernist collage and tradition. Here, too, the key to Stravinsky's art would seem to rest with the interaction of these opposing forces, an inter-mingling as well as a juxtaposition. Much of the vitality of *Les Noces* and other works of the Russian period and beyond can be traced to conflicts of this kind, oppositions, and admixtures. And to the extent that this music attracts in the future as it has in the past, analytical and critical speculation is likely to persist along these lines as well.

Such future study can best be directed along a broad front, with theory and analysis tied to historical, psychological, aesthetic, and critical concerns. This is not to discount specialized study, only to encourage an active engagement between general listeners, theorists, historians, psychologists, performers, and critics. Such an environment would seem to be in the best interests of pieces such as *Les Noces*, *Renard*, *The Soldier's Tale*, the *Symphonies* and their immediate context.

A plea of this kind is hardly new, of course, but it seemed worth making all the same at the end of this rather lengthy inquiry into the nature of Stravinsky's Russian-period works and the larger repertories of which they are a part. We are hopeful that some further interest will have been stimulated in the many theoretical, psychological, and critical issues raised in one way or another. Immediacy and the world of reflection and analysis are complementary, of course, symbiotic as an ideal. Just as calculation draws on heard experience, listeners, unable to stay afloat indefinitely (attuned in rapturous self-forgetfulness, as we have described it), are obli-gated to reflect and regroup in some fashion. They are forced to come to terms with what has been heard, such being the psychology of the matter.

And they reflect, evidently, in an effort to rekindle the immediate sense of rapport that would easily be lost without such assistance. To the extent that more formal analysis can work as an extension of this early reflective impulse, we are hopeful here, too, that this present endeavor will prove helpful. Such a purpose lay at the forefront of its conception, in any case.

Selected Bibliography

Abraham, Gerald. *Studies in Russian Music*. London: William Reeves, 1935.

Adlington, Robert. "Musical Temporality: Perspectives from Adorno and de Man." *repercussions* 6, no. 1 (1997): 5–60.

Adorno, Theodor W. *Aesthetic Theory*. Translated by C. Lenhardt. London: Routledge, 1989.

　Philosophy of Modern Music. Translated by Anne G. Mitchell and Wesley V. Bloomster. New York: Seabury Press, 1973.

　Quasi una Fantasia: Essays on Modern Music. Translated by Rodney Livingstone. London: Verso, 1998.

Afanasyev, Alexander N. *Russian Fairy Tales*. Translated by Norbert Guterman. New York: Pantheon Books, 1945.

Albright, Daniel. *Stravinsky: The Music Box and the Nightingale*. New York: Gordon and Breach, 1989.

Ansermet, Ernest. "*L'Histoire du soldat*." *Chesterian* 10 (October 1920): 291.

Baltensperger, André and Felix Meyer, eds. *Igor Strawinsky, Symphonies d'instruments à vent: Faksimileausgabe des Particells und der Partitur der Erstfassung*. Winterthur: Amadeus, 1991.

Banes, Sally. *Dancing Women: Female Bodies on Stage*. London: Routledge, 1998.

Barraqué, Jean. "*La Mer* de Debussy, ou la naissance des formes ouvertes." *Analyse musicale* 12 (June 1988): 15–62.

Bartók, Béla. *Béla Bartók Essays*. Edited by Benjamin Suchoff. Lincoln: University of Nebraska Press, 1992.

Berger, Arthur. "Problems of Pitch Organization in Stravinsky." In *Perspectives on Schoenberg and Stravinsky*. Edited by Benjamin Boretz and Edward T. Cone. New York: W. W. Norton, 1972, 123–54.

Boss, Jack. "Schoenberg's Op. 22 Radio Talk, and Developing Variation in Atonal Music." *Music Theory Spectrum* 14, no. 2 (1992): 125–49.

Boulez, Pierre. *Stocktakings from an Apprenticeship*. Translated by Stephen Walsh. Oxford University Press, 1991.

Brower, Candace. "Memory and the Perception of Rhythm." *Music Theory Spectrum* 15, no. 1 (1993): 19–35.

Caplin, William E. *Classical Form: A Theory of Formal Functions for the Instrumental Music of Haydn, Mozart, and Beethoven*. Oxford University Press, 1998.

Carr, Maureen A. "Igor Stravinsky and Charles-Ferdinand Ramuz: A Study of Their Artistic Collaboration for *Histoire du soldat* (1918)." In *Stravinsky's "Histoire du soldat": A Facsimile of the Sketches*. Edited by Maureen Carr. Middleton, Wis.: A-R Editions, 2005.

Multiple Masks: Neoclassicism in Stravinsky's Works on Greek Subjects. Lincoln: University of Nebraska Press, 2002.

Carter, Chandler. "*The Rake's Progress* and Stravinsky's Return: The Composer's Evolving Approach to Setting Text." *Journal of the American Musicological Society* 63, no. 3 (2010): 553–640.

Cholopova, Valentina. "*Russische Quellen der Rhythmik Strawinskys.*" *Die Musikforschung* 27 (1974): 435–46.

Chua, Daniel K. L. "Rioting with Stravinsky: A Particular Analysis of *The Rite of Spring.*" *Music Analysis* 26 (March 2007): 59–109.

Clarke, Eric. "Expression and Communication in Musical Performance." In *Music, Language, Speech and Brain.* Edited by Johan Sunberg, Lennart Nord and Rolf Carlson. New York: Macmillan, 1991.

"Expression in Performance: Generativity, Perception, and Semiosis." In *The Practice of Performance: Studies in Musical Interpretation.* Edited by John Rink. New York: Cambridge University Press, 1995, 21–54.

Cohn, Richard. "Maximally Smooth Cycles, Hexatonic Systems, and the Analysis of Late-Romantic Triadic Progressions." *Music Analysis* 15, no. 1 (1996): 9–40.

"Metric and Hypermetric Dissonance in the *Menuetto* of Mozart's Symphony in G Minor, K. 550." *Intégral* 6 (1992): 1–33.

"Neo-Riemannian Operations, Parsimonious Trichords, and their *Tonnetz* Representations." *Journal of Music Theory* 41 (1997): 1–66.

Cone, Edward T. "Stravinsky: The Progress of a Method." In *Perspectives on Schoenberg and Stravinsky.* Edited by Benjamin Boretz and Edward T. Cone. New York: W. W. Norton, 1972, 155–64.

Cook, Nicholas. "Analyzing Performance and Performing Analysis." In *Rethinking Music.* Edited by Nicholas Cook and Mark Everist. Oxford University Press, 1999, 239–61.

"Stravinsky Conducts Stravinsky." In *The Cambridge Companion to Stravinsky.* Edited by Jonathan Cross. Cambridge University Press, 2003, 176–91.

Craft, Robert. *An Improbable Life.* Nashville: Vanderbilt University Press, 2002.

Craft, Robert, ed. *Stravinsky: Selected Correspondence,* vols. 1, 2, and 3. New York: Alfred A. Knopf, 1982, 1984, and 1986.

Craft, Robert, with William Harkins. "Stravinsky's *Svadebka*: An Introduction." *New York Review of Books,* December 14, 1972: 23–29.

Cross, Jonathan. *The Stravinsky Legacy.* Cambridge University Press, 1998.

Dahlhaus, Carl. *Between Romanticism and Modernism.* Translated by Mary Whittall. Berkeley: University of California Press, 1980.

Esthetics of Music. Translated by William W. Austin. Cambridge University Press, 1982.

Foundations of Music History. Translated by J. B. Robinson. Cambridge University Press, 1983.

"Fragments of a Musical Hermeneutics." Translated by Karen Painter. *Current Musicology* 50: 5–20.

The Idea of Absolute Music. Translated by Roger Lustig. Chicago University Press, 1989.

Schoenberg and the New Music. Translated by Derrick Puffett and Alfred Clayton. Cambridge University Press, 1987.

DeBellis, Mark. *Music and Conceptualization*. Cambridge University Press, 1995.

Derzhanovsky, Vladimir V. "Za rubezhom: novïye sochineniya Igorya Stravinskogo." *Muzïka* no. 219 (April 18, 1915): 262–63.

Douthett, Jack and Peter Steinbach. "Parsimonious Graphs: A Study in Parsimony, Contextual Transformations, and Modes of Limited Transposition." *Journal of Music Theory* 42, no. 2 (1998): 241–64.

Driver, Paul. Review of Stephen Walsh, *Stravinsky: The Second Exile*. *London Review of Books* 29, no. 3 (February 8, 2007): 18–20.

Eagleton, Terry. "Coruscating on Thin Ice." *London Review of Books* 30, no. 2 (January 24, 2008): 19–20.

The Ideology of the Aesthetic. Oxford: Blackwell, 1990.

Epstein, David. *Shaping Time: Music, the Brain, and Performance*. New York: Schirmer Books, 1995.

Evans, Edwin. *Music and Dance, for Lovers of the Ballet*. London: Herbert Jenkins, [1946].

Evans, Joan. "'*Diabolus triumphans*': Stravinsky's *Histoire du soldat* in Weimar and Nazi Germany." In *The Varieties of Musicology: Essays for Murray Lefkowitz*. Edited by John J. Daverio and John Ogasapian. Warren, Mich.: Harmonie Park Press, 2000, 175–85.

"Stravinsky's Music in Hitler's Germany." *Journal of the American Musicological Society* 56, no. 3 (2003): 525–72.

Fink, Robert. "'*Rigoroso* (♪=126)': The Rite of Spring and the Forging of a Modernist Performing Style." *Journal of the American Musicological Society* 52, no. 2 (1999): 299–350.

Fraisse, Paul. "Rhythm and Tempo." In *The Psychology of Music*. Edited by Diana Deutsch. New York: Academic Press, 1982, 149–77.

Frisch, Walter. *Brahms and the Principle of Developing Variation*. Berkeley: University of California Press, 1983.

Gabrielsson, Alf. "Interplay between Analysis and Synthesis in Studies of Music Performance and Music Experience." *Music Perception* 3, no. 1 (1985): 59–86.

Garafola, Lynn. *Diaghilev's Ballets Russes*. New York: Oxford University Press, 1989.

Gjerdingen, Robert. "Meter as a Mode of Attending: A Network Simulation of Attentional Rhythmicity in Music." *Intégral* 3 (1989): 67–92.

Goehr, Lydia. *The Imaginary Museum of Musical Works*. Oxford University Press, 1992.

"Political Music and the Politics of Music." *The Journal of Aesthetics and Art Criticism* 52, no. 1 (Winter 1994): 99–112.

Goncharova, N. "The Creation of *Les Noces*." *Ballet and Opera* 8 (September 1949): 23.

"The Metamorphoses of the Ballet *Les Noces*." *Leonardo* 12 (1979): 137–43.

Grave, Floyd. "Metrical Dissonance in Haydn." *Journal of Musicology* 12, no. 3 (1995): 168–202.

Gurwitsch, Aron. *The Field of Consciousness*. Pittsburgh: Duquesne University Press, 1964.

Haimo, Ethan. "Developing Variation and Schoenberg's Twelve-Tone Music." *Music Analysis* 16, no. 3 (1997): 349–65.

Hanslick, Eduard. *The Beautiful in Music*. Translated by Gustav Cohen. New York: Liberal Arts Press, 1957.

Hasty, Christopher F. *Meter as Rhythm*. New York: Oxford University Press, 1997.
    "On the Problem of Succession and Continuity in 20th-Century Music." *Music Theory Spectrum* 8 (1986): 58–74.

Horlacher, Gretchen. *Building Blocks: Repetition and Continuity in the Music of Stravinsky*. New York: Oxford University Press, 2011.
    "Metric Irregularity in *Les Noces*: The Problem of Periodicity." *Journal of Music Theory* 39, no. 2 (1995): 285–310.
    "The Rhythms of Reiteration: Formal Development in Stravinsky's Ostinati." *Music Theory Spectrum* 14, no. 2 (1992): 171–87.

Hudson, Richard. *Stolen Time: The History of Tempo Rubato*. Oxford University Press, 1994.

Huron, David. *Sweet Anticipation: Music and the Psychology of Expectation*. Cambridge: MIT Press, 2006.

Hyer, Brian. "Reimag(in)ing Riemann." *Journal of Music Theory* 39 (1995): 101–38.

Imbrie, Andrew. "Extra Measures and Metrical Ambiguity in Beethoven." In *Beethoven Studies*. Edited by Alan Tyson. New York: Norton, 1973, 45–66.
    "One Measure of Eternity." *Perspectives of New Music* 9, no. 2 (1971): 51–57.

Istomin, F. M. and G. O. Dyutsh. *Pesni Russkogo naroda, sobrani v guberniyakh Arkhangelskoy i Olonetskoy v 1886 godu*. St. Petersburg: Imperial Russian Geographical Society, 1894.

Jackendoff, Ray. "Musical Parsing and Musical Affect." *Music Perception* 9, no. 2 (1991): 119–229.

Jakobson, Roman. "Why 'Mama' and 'Papa'?" In *Roman Jakobson: Selected Writings*. The Hague: Mouton, 1962.

James, William. *Principles of Psychology*. 2 vols. New York: Dover, 1950.

Janáček, Leoš. *Janáček's Uncollected Essays on Music*. Edited and translated by Mlika Zemanova. New York: Rizzoli International, 1989.

Jaubert, Jeanne. "Some Ideas about Meter in the Fourth Tableau of Stravinsky's *Les Noces*, or Stravinsky, Nijinska, and Particle Physics." *Musical Quarterly* 83, no. 1 (1999): 205–27.

Johnson, Julian. "Analysis in Adorno's Aesthetics of Music." *Music Analysis* 14, nos. 2–3 (1995): 295–313.
    "The Nature of Abstraction: Analysis and the Webern Myth." *Music Analysis* 17, no. 3 (1998): 267–80.

Johnston, Ben. "Stravinsky: A Composer's Memorial: An Interview with Soulima Stravinsky." *Perspectives of New Music* 9, no. 2 (1971): 15–27.

Juszkiewicz, Anton. *Litauische Volks-Weisen*. Kracow: Verlag der Polnischen Akademie der Wissenschaften, 1900.

Karlinsky, Simon. "Igor Stravinsky and Russian Preliterate Theater." In *Confronting Stravinsky: Man, Musician, and Modernist*. Edited by Jann Pasler. Berkeley: University of California Press, 1986, 3–15.

Keller, Hans. "Rhythm: Gershwin and Stravinsky." In Hans Keller, *Essays on Music*. Edited by Christopher Wintle. Cambridge University Press, 1994, 201–11.

Kramer, Jonathan. *The Time of Music*. New York: Schirmer Books, 1988.

Krebs, Harold. *Fantasy Pieces: Metrical Dissonance in the Music of Robert Schumann*. Oxford University Press, 1999.

"Some Extensions of the Concepts of Metrical Consonance and Dissonance." *Journal of Music Theory* 31, no. 1 (1987): 99–120.

Krumhansl, C. L. *Cognitive Foundations of Musical Pitch*. New York: Oxford University Press, 1990.

Kundera, Milan. *Testaments Betrayed: An Essay in Nine Parts*. Translated by Linda Asher. New York: HarperCollins, 1994.

Lambert, Constant. *Music Ho! A Study of Music in Decline*, 3rd edn. London: Faber and Faber, 1966. Originally published 1934.

Lawson, Rex. "Stravinsky and the Pianola." In *Confronting Stravinsky: Man, Musician, and Modernist*. Edited by Jann Pasler. Berkeley: University of California Press, 1986, 284–301.

Lerdahl, Fred and Ray Jackendoff. *A Generative Theory of Tonal Music*. Cambridge: MIT Press, 1983.

Lester, Joel. *The Rhythms of Tonal Music*. Carbondale: Southern Illinois University Press, 1986.

Levinson, Jerold. *Music, Art, and Metaphysics*. Ithaca: Cornell University Press, 1990.

Libman, Lilian. *And Music at the Close: Stravinsky's Last Years*. New York: Norton, 1972.

London, Justin. *Hearing in Time: Psychological Aspects of Meter*. Oxford University Press, 2004.

Lorraine, Renée Cox. *Music, Tendencies, and Inhibitions: Reflections on a Theory of Leonard Meyer*. Lanham: The Scarecrow Press, 2001.

Lupishko, Marina. "Stravinsky and Russian Poetic Folklore." *Ex-tempore* 12, no. 2 (2005): 1–24.

Mandler, George. "The Generation of Emotion." In *Emotion: Theory, Research, and Experience*. Edited by Robert Plutchik and Henry Kellerman. New York: Academic Press, 1989.

Mark, Jeffrey. "The Fundamental Qualities of Folk Music." *Music and Letters* 10 (1929): 287–91.

Mazo, Margarita. "Igor Stravinsky's *Les Noces*, the Rite of Passage." In *Les Noces (Svadebka): Scènes chorégraphiques russes avec chant et musique*. Edited by Margarita Mazo. London: Chester Music, c. 2005.

"Stravinsky's *Les Noces* and Russian Folk Wedding Ritual." *Journal of the American Musicological Society* 43, no. 1 (Spring 1990): 99–142.

McDonald, Matthew. "*Jeux de Nombres*: Automated Rhythm in *The Rite of Spring*." *Journal of the American Musicological Society* 63, no. 3 (2010): 499–551.

Mellers, Wilfred. *Romanticism and the 20ᵗʰ Century*. New Jersey: Essential Books, 1957.

Messing, Scott. *Neoclassicism in Music: From the Genesis of the Concept through the Schoenberg/Stravinsky Polemic*. University of Rochester Press, 1996.

Meyer, Leonard B. "A Pride of Prejudices; Or, Delight in Diversity." *Music Theory Spectrum* 13, no. 2 (1991): 241–51.

Emotion and Meaning in Music. University of Chicago Press, 1956.

Explaining Music. Berkeley: University of California Press, 1973.

Music, the Arts, and Ideas. University of Chicago Press, 1967.

Morrison, Simon. Review of Richard Taruskin, *Defining Russia Musically*. *Journal of the American Musicological Society* 53, no. 2 (2000): 420–25.

Morton, Lawrence. "Footnotes to Stravinsky Studies: *Le Sacre du Printemps*." *Tempo* 128 (1979): 9–16.

Narmour, Eugene. "The Top-Down and Bottom-Up Systems of Musical Implication: Building on Meyer's Theory of Emotional Syntax." *Music Perception* 9, no. 1 (1991): 1–26.

Nijinska, Bronislava. "Creation of *Les Noces*." Translated by Jean M. Serafetinides and Irina Nijinska. *Dance Magazine* (December 1974): 59.

Paddison, Max. *Adorno's Aesthetics of Music*. Cambridge University Press, 1993.

Propp, Vladimir. "The Russian Folk Lyric." In *Down Along the Mother Volga: An Anthology of Russian Folk Lyrics*. Edited by Roberta Reeder and Vladimir Propp. Philadelphia: University of Pennsylvania Press, 1975.

Rahn, John. *Music Inside Out*. Amsterdam: Gordon and Breach, 2001.

Reeder, Roberta. "Stravinsky's *Les Noces*." *Dance Research Journal* 18, no. 2 (Winter 1986–87): 30–61.

Rehding, Alexander. "Towards A 'Logic of Discontinuity' in Stravinsky's *Symphonies of Wind Instruments*: Hasty, Kramer and Straus Reconsidered." *Music Analysis* 17, no. 1 (1998): 39–53.

Repp, Bruno. "Pattern Typicality and Dimensional Interactions in Pianists' Imitation of Expressive Timing and Dynamics." *Music Perception* 18, no. 2 (2000): 173–211.

Riess-Jones, Mari. "Only Time Can Tell: On the Topology of Mental Space and Time." *Critical Inquiry* 7, no. 3 (1981): 557–76.

Rogers, Lynne. "Rethinking Form: Stravinsky's Eleventh-Hour Revision of the Third Movement of his Violin Concerto." *Journal of Musicology* 17, no. 2 (Spring 1999): 272–304.

Sonata Forms. New York: Norton, 1980.

Ruwet, Nicolas. *Langage, Musique, Poésie*. Paris: Éditions du Seuil, 1972.

Schaeffner, André. "Debussy et ses rapports avec la musique russe." In *Musique russe*. Edited by Pierre Suvchinsky. Paris: Presses universitaires de France, 1953.

Strawinsky (Paris: Rieder, 1931).

Schenker, Heinrich. *Free Composition.* Translated by Ernst Oster. New York: Longman, 1979.

Schneider, David E. "A Context for Béla Bartók on the Eve of World War II: The Violin Concerto (1938)." *repercussions* 5 (1996): 21–68.

Schoenberg, Arnold. *Fundamentals of Musical Composition.* Edited by Gerald Strang and Leonard Stein. London: Faber and Faber, 1967.

   Style and Idea: Selected Writings of Arnold Schoenberg. Edited by Leonard Stein. Translated by Leo Black. Berkeley: University of California Press, 1985.

Seashore, Carl. *The Psychology of Music.* New York: McGraw-Hill, 1938.

Simms, Bryan. *The Atonal Music of Arnold Schoenberg: 1908-1923.* Oxford University Press, 2000.

Sloboda, John A. "The Communication of Musical Meter in Piano Performance." *Quarterly Journal of Experimental Psychology,* 1983, 35A: 377–396.

Smith, Peter H. "You Reap What You Sow: Some Instances of Rhythmic Ambiguity in Brahms." *Music Theory Spectrum* 28, no. 1 (2006): 57–98.

Snyder, Bob. *Music and Memory: An Introduction.* Cambridge: MIT Press, 2000.

Sokolov, Y. M. *Russian Folklore.* Translated by Catherine Ruth Smith. New York: Macmillan, 1950; rept. Hatboro, Pa.: Folklore Associates, 1966.

Somer, Evo. "Musical Syntax in the Sonatas of Debussy: Phrase Structure and Formal Function." *Music Theory Spectrum* 27, no. 1 (2005): 68–83.

Spies, Claudio. "Conundrums, Conjectures, Construals; or, 5 vs. 3: The influence of Russian Composers on Stravinsky." In *Stravinsky Retrospectives.* Edited by Ethan Haimo and Paul Johnson. Lincoln: University of Nebraska Press, 1987, 76–140.

Stravinsky, Igor. *An Autobiography.* New York: W. W. Norton, 1962.

   Poetics of Music in the Form of Six Lessons. Translated by Arthur Knodel and Ingolf Dahl. New York: Vintage, 1956.

   The Rite of Spring: Sketches 1911-1913. London: Boosey and Hawkes, 1969.

Stravinsky, Igor and Robert Craft. *Conversations with Stravinsky.* Garden City, NY: Doubleday, 1959.

   Dialogues and a Diary. Garden City, NY: Doubleday, 1963.

   Expositions and Developments. Garden City, NY: Doubleday, 1962; rept. Berkeley: University of California Press, 1981.

   Memories and Commentaries. Garden City, NY: Doubleday, 1960; rept. Berkeley: University of California Press, 1981.

   Retrospectives and Conclusions. New York: Alfred A. Knopf, 1969.

   Themes and Episodes. New York: Alfred A. Knopf, 1966.

Stravinsky, Vera and Robert Craft. *Stravinsky in Pictures and Documents.* New York: Simon and Schuster, 1978.

Subotnik, Rose Rosengard. *Developing Variations: Style and Ideology in Western Music.* Minneapolis: University of Minnesota Press, 1991.

Taruskin, Richard. "Catching Up with Rimsky-Korsakov." *Music Theory Spectrum* 33, no. 2: 169–85.

Defining Russia Musically: Historical and Hermeneutical Essays. Princeton University Press, 1997.

"Russian Folk Melodies in *The Rite of Spring.*" *Journal of the American Musicological Society* 33, no. 3 (1980): 501–43.

Stravinsky and the Russian Traditions: A Biography of the Works Through "Mavra." 2 vols. Berkeley: University of California Press, 1996.

"Stravinsky and Us." In *The Cambridge Companion to Stravinsky.* Edited by Jonathan Cross. Cambridge University Press, 2003, 260–84.

Temperley, David. "Motivic Perception and Modularity." *Music Perception* 13, no. 2 (1995): 141–69.

Temperley, David and Christopher Bartlette. "Parallelism as a Factor in Metrical Analysis." *Music Perception* 20, no. 2 (2002): 117–49.

Tereshchenko, A. V. *Bït russkogo naroda [Manners and Customs of the Russian People].* 7 vols. St. Petersburg, 1848.

Todd, Neil. "A Model of Expressive Timing in Tonal Music." *Music Perception* 3, no. 1 (1985): 33–57.

Van den Toorn, Pieter C. *The Music of Igor Stravinsky.* New Haven: Yale University Press, 1983.

Music, Politics, and the Academy. Berkeley: University of California Press, 1995.

"Stravinsky, Adorno, and the Art of Displacement." *The Musical Quarterly* 87, no. 3 (2004): 468–509.

Stravinsky and "The Rite of Spring": The Beginnings of a Musical Language. Berkeley: University of California Press, 1987.

"Stravinsky, *Les Noces* (*Svadebka*), and the Prohibition against Expressive Timing." *Journal of Musicology* 20, no. 2 (2003): 285–304.

"Will Stravinsky Survive Postmodernism?" *Music Theory Spectrum* 22, no. 1 (2000): 104–21.

Walsh, Stephen. *The Music of Stravinsky.* New York: Routledge, Chapman and Hall, 1988.

Stravinsky: A Creative Spring, Russia and France, 1882–1934. New York: Alfred A. Knopf, 1999.

Stravinsky: The Second Exile. New York: Alfred A. Knopf, 2006.

"Stravinsky's Symphonies: Accident or Design?" In *Analytical Strategies and Musical Interpretation: Essays in Nineteenth- and Twentieth-Century Music.* Edited by Craig Ayrey and Mark Everist. Cambridge University Press, 1996, 35–71.

Watkins, Glen. *Pyramids at the Louvre: Music, Culture, and Collage from Stravinsky to the Postmodernists.* Cambridge: Belknap Press, 1994.

White, Eric W. *Stravinsky: The Composer and His Works.* Berkeley: University of California Press, 1966.

Whittall, Arnold. *Serialism.* Oxford University Press, 2008.

"Stravinsky in Context." In *The Cambridge Companion to Stravinsky.* Edited by Jonathan Cross. Cambridge University Press, 2003, 37–56.

Zuckerkandl, Victor. *Sound and Symbol: Music and the External World.* Translated by Willard R. Trask. Princeton University Press, 1956.

Index

Ablesimov, Alexander 56
   The Miller Who was a Wizard, a Cheat, and a Matchmaker 56
Abraham, Gerald 244–45
accent markings, beams and slurs 190–93, 205
Adams, John 2
   El Dorado 2
Adorno, T. W. 1
   music of Stravinsky and Schoenberg 195, 269
   Philosophy of Modern Music 1, 282, 283–84
   Stravinsky's music *see under* Stravinsky and his critics
aesthetic belief *see* performance practice and aesthetic belief
Afanasyev, Alexander 53, 75–76, 196–97
   Russian Folk Tales 196–97
Agon (Stravinsky) 190–91, 194
alignment 19, 194
   changes in metrical alignment 25, 33
   displacement as opposite of fixed alignment 91–92
   dissonances 39
   distinctions between displacement in Classical style and in Stravinsky 32–33
   hemiola 33–34
   Les Noces 108, 112, 221
   metrical alignment and realignment in relief 41
   and metrical interpretations 20–21
   parallel alignment 22–23
   Renard 174, 202, 203, 205, 208, 214
      see also meter, text and alignment in *Renard*
Allegro section of *Renard* reconsidered 11, 196–224
   as "burlesque" 196–97
   con brio section 174, 184–85, 218
   displacement and repetition in the opening allegro 20–21, 28–29, 174, 200–1, 208
      conflicted interpretations 23
      displaced repeats 29–30
      passages heard and understood conservatively in score/ early sketch 22–23
      radical interpretation 22–23
      repeats of the motive 34–35

   extra eighth-note beat 201–5
      notation 201
      response of listener 201–5
   geometry of the plot important rather than individual roles 197
   layered structures 199–200
   metrical analysis following Lerdahl–Jackendoff 17
   octatonic–diatonic interactions 136, 143–44, 189–90, 214–20
   pitch relations 214–20
      Tonnetze 216–17, 219
   stratification 17, 199, 208–11
   structure in the large 208–13
   substructure 206–08
"An Abridged Analysis" (de Schloezer) 13
Andriessen, Louis 2, 3, 251
   De Staat 2
Ansermet, Ernest 79
"Antar" Symphony No. 2 (Rimsky-Korsakov) 147
anti-humanism in Stravinsky's music 12, 89, 261, 286–87, 289, 290, 294–95, 297
Apollo Musagetes (Stravinsky) 115, 121
Arensky, Anton 56–57
articulation 5, 18, 19, 32–33, 267–68, 268–69
   compositional process 173
   exactness in 176
   Les Noces 110, 131–32, 158, 261
   displacement 88
   incompleteness 114, 123–25, 139–40, 148
   percussion supplying extra articulation 79–80
   phrases 256
   Renard 11, 20–21, 199, 205, 214
      displacement 179
   role of articulation in processes of metrical displacement 88, 179, 183–94, 194
   Symphonies of Wind Instruments 261
Autobiography (Stravinsky) 259

Babbitt, Milton 1
Bach, Johann Sebastian 120
   Brandenburg Concerto No. 1 120
Ballets Russes 74
Banes, Sally 292, 293
Barber of Seville (Rossini) 120
Baroque period music 199, 222

Bartók, Béla 67–68, 118, 124–29
    Mikrokosmos 124
    String Quartet No. 3 124, 125, 128
    Violin Concerto 128–29
basic cell
    Les Noces 143–44, 146, 148, 164
        as basic melodic pattern of *Les Noces* 69
        and "hiccup" motive 69, 117
beams *see* accent markings, beams and slurs
"Bear and the Cock" 196–97
Beethoven, Ludwig van 37, 261, 269
bells ringing, suggestion of 69–71, 115–17
    bell-like motive in *Symphonies of Wind
        Instruments* 260, 261
Berceuses du chat (Stravinsky) 55–56, 73–74
Birtwistle, Harrison 251
block and layered structures and textures 3–5
    Les Noces see under meter, motive and
        alignment in *Les Noces*; block and
        layered structures
    *Symphonies of Wind Instruments see
        Symphonies of Wind Instruments*
    see also melodic repeat structures in the
        music of Stravinsky, Debussy and
        Rimsky-Korsakov
borrowing *see* direct borrowing
Boulez, Pierre 1, 70–71, 230, 295, 301
Brandenburg Concerto No. 1 (Bach) 120

Cantata (Stravinsky) 289, 290, 291
Capriccio (Stravinsky) 261, 262
Carnaval (Schumann) 38, 39
Carter, Elliott 251
"Cat, the Cock and the Fox, The" 75–76
Chopin, Frédéric 261–62
    Nocturnes 261–62
choreography 95, 164–65, 291–92, 292–93
church music/Russian Church 71–72, 117, 122
    church bells 69–71, 115–17
    popevki 68, 131
cimbalom 75, 188–89, 215, 217, 218–20
City Life (Reich) 2
Classical period 18, 30–32, 222
    Classical concerto forms 199
    Classical–Romantic literature 194
    Classical–Romantic music 194
    Classical tradition 259–60
    developing variation 119, 195, 270, 278
    distinctions between displacement in
        Classical style and in Stravinsky 32–33
    hemiola rhythm *see under* hemiola
    homophonic style 34, 195, 270
    Schoenbergian model of Classical style 34,
        195, 271
    treatment of fragments 114

Cohn, Richard
    "Hyper-Hexatonic Systems" 46
    neo-Riemannian operations 46, 147
Comoedia (journal) 292
conductors and conducting 6, 261
    Ansermet, Ernest 79
    Boulez, Pierre 1, 70–71, 230, 295, 301
    Kussevitsky, Sergei 252–53
    modernist fashion 5
    Stravinsky's difficulties with 252–53,
        258, 263
Cone, Edward T. 4
    "Stravinsky: the Progress of a Method" 4
Conversations with Stravinsky (Stravinsky/
    Craft) 120, 174–75, 177, 259–60
Copland, Aaron 1
Corle, Edwin 13
    Igor Stravinsky 13
Così fan Tutte (Mozart) 120
Craft, Robert 3, 69
    Conversations with Stravinsky 120, 174–75,
        177, 259–60
    Les Noces 53, 54, 55, 65, 72
    Stravinsky in Pictures and Documents 69
critics of Stravinsky *see* Stravinsky and his
    critics
Cross, Jonathan 250–51
Cubism 231, 245
Cui, César 175

Dahl, Vladimir 124
Dahlhaus, Carl 8, 263
De Staat (Andriessen) 2
Debussy, Claude 162, 252
    Fêtes 239
    Nocturnes 239
    Nuages 239
    Prélude à l'après-midi d'un faune 235, 239
    repeat structures/duplication 235–40, 248,
        251
developing variation 18, 119, 195, 270, 278
Dewey, John 279
Diaghilev, Sergei 54, 55, 56, 74
diatonic system 3–5, 9
    octatonic–diatonic interactions *see under*
        octatonic–diatonic interactions
Dichterliebe (Schumann) 280
Dictionary of the Russian Language
    (Dahl) 124
Die Reihe (music journal) 1
direct borrowing
    folk music in *Les Noces* 120–23, 131
        errors in Stravinsky's accounts of role of
            borrowed folk material 66, 121–22
        "Mitusov song" 122, 131

folk music in *The Rite of Spring* 118–19, 122, 123–24, 129
  opening of *The Rite of Spring* 131–32
  from Rimsky-Korsakov 244
displacement/ metrical displacement 3–6, 8–9, 245, 267–69, 270, 300
  central role 176
  conservative/radical interpretations *see* meter and metrical displacement in Stravinsky
  continuity and discontinuity 247, 249–50
  critical indictments 271–74
  developing variation 273–74, 275–84
  displacements rare in Rimsky-Korsakov's music 241–44
  duplications in Debussy's music not undergoing metrical shifts 239
  effects of *see* meter, text and alignment in *Renard*
  expressive timing 254
  Les Noces see meter, motive and alignment in *Les Noces*; block and layered structures
  and location and intensity *see* meter and metrical displacement in Stravinsky
  meter dimming and displacement fading 16, 29–30
  and metrical parallelism 16
    conflict between 19–20, 22–23, 101–3, 224, 260, 281
  origins of displacement *see under* meter, text and alignment in *Renard*
  overruling traditional processes 194
  Renard see under Allegro section of *Renard* reconsidered; meter, text and alignment in *Renard*
  The Rite of Spring 274, 275–77
  "Royal March" in *The Soldier's Tale* 11
  in Stravinsky's music *see* meter and metrical displacement in Stravinsky
  and superimposition 251
  Symphonies of Wind Instruments 260–61
  syncopation *see* syncopation
  tempo 253–54, 261
dissonance (metrical)
  coloristic in character 151–53
  concept of 38–41
  displacement dissonance 38–39, 40
  grouping dissonances 38, 39, 40
  indirect 33
  and irregularity of Stravinsky's music 40
  Renard 206, 212–13

Eagleton, Terry 265
Éditions Russes 253

Eine kleine Nachtmusik see Serenade, *Eine kleine Nachtmusik*
El Dorado (Adams) 2
entrainment 14–15, 16, 22–23, 29
Eurasianist movement 9–10, 285, 288–89, 290
expression/expressive timing *see under* performance practice and aesthetic belief

fabrication/simulation
  folk songs in *Les Noces* 118–19, 120, 122, 129–31, 135, 176, 222
  folk songs in *Renard* 118, 120, 174–75, 222
  unconscious assimilation of Russian popular verse/borrowed materials 176–77, 222
Fêtes (Debussy) 239
Fink, Robert 262–63
Firebird, The (Stravinsky) 56, 61, 115, 118–19
Five Easy Pieces (Stravinsky) 221–22
Flood, The (Stravinsky) 84–85
Fodor, J. A. 278
folk element in Stravinsky's melodic style *see under* melody and harmony in *Les Noces*
Fundamentals of Musical Composition (Schoenberg) 35, 41, 277

Garafola, Lynn 292
Generative Theory of Tonal Music, A (Lerdahl/ Jackendoff) 13–14
Gestalt psychology 21–22
Gjerdingen, Robert 22
Glass, Philip 2
Glinka, Mikhail Ivanovich 56–57
  Life for the Czar, A 56–57
  Ruslan and Ludmila 56–57
Gogol, Nicholas 60
grouping 17–18, 23, 35–36
  grouping dissonances 38, 39, 40
  hierarchy in works of the Russian period 112–13
  Renard 180, 203–04
  small-scale 179, 190–94, 199

Hanslick, Eduard 7–8
Harkins, William 65
Haydn, Joseph 36–37, 194
  London Symphony, Minuet 37
  string quartets 36–37, 273
Hearing in Time (London) 15
Heaven and Earth (Rimsky-Korsakov) 251
hemiola 33–34, 109
  Classical contexts 33, 36–37
    Haydn's music 36–37, 38
    Minuet from Mozart's Serenade 33–36, 38

hemiola (cont.)
  conflicts involving 110
  grouping dissonances 38
  "hiccup motive" 115, 117, 159–64, 165–66,
    168–69
    origins 68–69, 159–60
    uniting with basic melodic pattern of *Les
      Noces* 69
Histoire du soldat see Soldier's Tale, The
historical background of the Russian period
    9–10, 53–81
  Les Noces
    adaptation from Kireyevsky 53, 54, 60–61,
      63–65, 82, 84
    development of an idea for a choral work
      on a Russian peasant wedding 53
    musical sources in *Les Noces see under Les
      Noces*
    orchestrations 73–75, 77–78, 80–81
    process of completion 53–56
    Russian folk wedding *see* Russian folk
      wedding
    the scenario 60–66, 82
    sources viewed as a natural resource to be
      mined 63–66
  Renard 54, 55, 73–78, 174
    adaptation from Afanasyev 53, 75–76,
      196–97
    authentic nature of music and genre 77
  The Soldier's Tale 54, 55, 73–74, 78–81
    adaptation from Afanasyev 53, 78
    relationship between music and text
      78–79
Huron, David 26–27, 257
hypermeter 16, 29–30, 33
  beats at hypermetrical levels and
    displacements 30–32
  hypermetrical conflict/dissonance 33
  Les Noces 109, 166
  Renard 206, 211
  succeeding hypermetric layers 182
hyper-octatonic network 46–47, 155

Igor Stravinsky (Corle) 13
Istomin-Dyutsh collection 66
Istomin-Liapunov collection 124

Jackendoff, Ray
  A Generative Theory of Tonal Music 13–14
  meter and groupings 17–18
  metrical analysis 13–14, 17, 182
Jakobson, Roman 236
Jeu de Cartes (Stravinsky) 120
Joyce, James 62
juxtaposition 267–68, 270

analogies to techniques of collage and
    montage 230–31
criticism of 230
Les Noces 97, 111–13, 119, 124, 166, 168, 180,
    230–31
The Rite of Spring 230–31
and superimposition 251
Symphonies of Wind Instruments 228–31,
    246–47, 252
  blocks likened to Cubist paintings 231, 245
and tempo 253–54

Kasavin, Lev 288
Kastalsky, Alexander 61
  Scenes of Folk Festivals in Old Russia 61
Keller, Hans 12, 249, 299–300, 301
Kireyevsky, Pyotr 53, 54, 60–61, 63–65, 82,
    84, 292
Kramer, Jonathan 12, 247–49, 301
Krebs, Harold
  dissonances (metrical) 33
    disruption of the meter 39
    grouping and displacement dissonances
      39, 40
    shadow meter 40
  theory of metrical dissonance 38
  levels of metrical hierarchy broken down into
    pulse level and interpretive levels 15–16
Krumhansl, Carol 52
Kundera, Milan 300–1
  Testaments Betrayed 300–1
Kussevitsky, Sergei 252–53

Lambert, Constant 53
Le Coq d'or (Rimsky-Korsakov) 252
Lerdahl, Fred
  asymmetry of diatonic collection and step
    sizes 49
  A Generative Theory of Tonal Music 13–14
  meter and groupings 17–18
  metrical analysis 13–14, 17, 182
  models of diatonic and octatonic "space"
    50–52
    Lerdahl–Jackendoff model/approach
      13–14, 17, 182
Les Noces (Stravinsky) 2, 3, 8, 9–10, 187,
    234–35, 265, 277, 299, 301–02
  "anti-humanism" 286, 290
  articulation *see under* articulation
  block and layered structures *see* meter,
    motive and alignment in *Les Noces*;
    block and layered structures
  choreography 95, 164–65, 291–92, 292–93
  criticism *see under* Stravinsky and his critics
  descriptive factors 7

development of/history *see under* historical
    background of the Russian period
displacement patterns *see* meter, motive and
    alignment in *Les Noces*; block and
    layered structures
Eurasianist movement 9–10, 288–89, 290
features of ritual in text and music *see*
    meter, motive and alignment in
    Les Noces; block and layered
    structures
folk element *see* melody and harmony in
    Les Noces
juxtaposition 97, 111–13, 119, 124, 166, 168,
    180, 230–31
musical sources 66–73
    accidental sources of melody 68–69
    assimilation process/making of
        Stravinsky's Russian-period style 67–68
    bells ringing 69–71
    folk lamentation 73
    melodies built from short melodic units
        resembling *popevki* 68, 72
    Mitusov song 66–67
    Russian Church and liturgical chant 71–72
octatonic scale 43, 46
octatonic–diatonic interactions *see under*
    melody and harmony in *Les Noces*
ostinato *see under* ostinato
performance and staging 77
repeats of the motive 35
revisited 291–99
sexual politics 292–93
solo-instrumental style 56
strings, omission of 265–66, 268
success of 53
    springboard role for much Russian music
        55–56
tactus *see under* tactus
tempo 259
Levinson, André 292
Libman, Lilian 290
Life for the Czar, A (Glinka) 56–57
Liszt, Franz 10, 146–47
London, Justin 15
    Hearing in Time 15
London Symphony, Minuet (Haydn) 37
London Symphony Orchestra 252
Lourié, Arthur 253, 288

Manchester Guardian, The 252–53
Matinsky, Mikhail 56
    St. Petersburg Bazaar 56
Mazo, Margarita 58
McDonald, Matthew 274, 297, 299
Mellers, Wilfred 221–22

melodic repeat structures in the music of
    Stravinsky, Debussy and Rimsky-
    Korsakov 11, 225–51
antecedents in the music of Debussy and
    Rimsky-Korsakov 235–45
    Debussy's music, "duplication" in 235–40,
        248, 250–51
    Rimsky-Korsakov's music, repeats in
        239–45, 248, 250–51
block structures in *Symphonies of Wind
    Instruments* 96, 225–31, 260–61
    conservative alternative 232–35
    continuity and discontinuity 246–50
    juxtaposition *see* juxtaposition
blocks viewed from perspective of Cubism,
    moment form, "nowness" 231, 245,
    247, 248
    continuity and discontinuity 245–51
    discontinuous mode as associational
        246–47
    superimposition 230, 251
layered structure and suggestion of church
    bells ringing 115–17
    sliced into "cells" and repeated 114
melody and harmony in *Les Noces* 10, 114–72
    fragments and motives 114–17
    "hiccup motive" *see under* hemiola
melody and the folk element 10, 117–31, 174–75
    "anhemitonic" character of melodic
        invention 148, 288
    developments from early ballets 118–19
    direct borrowings 120–23, 131
    errors in Stravinsky's accounts of role of
        borrowed folk material 66, 121–22
    fabrication/simulation of folk songs
        118–19, 120, 122, 129–31, 135, 176, 222
    issue of melody sensitive and complicated
        120–21
    juxtaposition 119
    see also juxtaposition
    Schoenberg's arguments against using
        borrowed folk/popular music 119–20, 194
    tapping into "folk" memory 118–19, 122
    tetrachords 123–29
    traits of Russian popular music in other
        folk-song repertories 124–29
octatonic–diatonic interactions 10, 48, 52,
    107, 135–40, 143–44, 144–45
    in the first and third tableaux 147–59
    in the fourth tableau 159–67
    octatonic fever 167–72
    "ribbons of scales" 168
stratification 111–13, 124, 156–57
    layering in the performance of laments 59,
        107–8

melodic repeat structures in the music of
Stravinsky, Debussy and Rimsky-Korsakov
(cont.)
  a *Tonnetz* for *Les Noces*: preliminary remarks
      131–47, 155
    point of *Tonnetze* 143
Messiaen, Olivier 230, 251
meter and metrical displacement in Stravinsky
    8–9, 13–41
  displacement, location, and intensity 28–30
    location defined by interacting levels of
        pulsation 28–29
  earlier examples of displacement 30–37
    distinctions between displacement in
        Classical style and Stravinsky 32–33
    hemiola 33–34
    motivic elaboration 34
  entrainment 14–15, 16, 22–23, 29
  meter and its definitions 13–18
    displacement 28–29
    and grouping 17–18
    levels of the metrical hierarchy 15–16
    measurement internalized/assimilated by
        the listener 13–14, 29–30, 39, 93
    meter synchronized with "internal clock
        mechanisms" 14, 27
    and metrical displacement 16
    see also displacement/metrical
        displacement
    metrical parallelism 16
    nature 13–14
    salience of the middle range of the metrical
        hierarchy 14, 16
  metrical displacement in Stravinsky 18–28
    alignment *see* alignment
    compromises worked out in the notation
        23–25
    conflict between displacement/metrical
        parallelism 19–21
    conflicted interpretations 23
    conservative metrical interpretation
        20–21, 22–23, 24, 25, 27, 110, 247
    predisposition of listeners 27, 28
    radical metrical interpretation 20–21,
        22–23, 24, 27, 31–32, 110, 247
    repetition 18–20
    response-patterns from an initial point of
        contact 26–27
    surprise, reaction response and appraisal
        responses 26–27
    timings of stages varying 27
  metrical dissonance, concept of 38–41
    Stravinsky's metrical displacements
        40–41
  tactus *see* tactus

meter, motive and alignment in *Les Noces;* block
    and layered structures 10, 82–113, 221
  absence of form of resolution in lament 110
    layers in conflict 109, 110
    multi-layered textures of folk rituals as
        source of stratification 107–8
  additional layered structures 107–11
  attraction of the expressive character of ritual
      and ritual performance 84–85
  "anti-psychological" message 84–85
  confrontation between individuals and
      impersonal forces/truths 84
  score in tune with a lament 85
  block structures in the second tableau 96–103
    bride/groom parallel 96–97
    displacements/relocations of motives
        affecting text 101
    juxtaposition 97, 111–13
    see also juxtaposition
    tress/curls parallel 97
  conclusions 111–13
  final version of the scenario an
      encapsulation 84
  layered structures in the second tableau 103–7
  libretto formed as an encapsulation 82–84
  metrical displacement in the first tableau
      89–96, 157–58
    choreography 95, 164–65
  no individual roles 82–83, 197
  precedents in practices surrounding
      performance of the ritual play 83–84
  repetition 85–88
    displacement of metrical alignment 88
  ritual as public exercise mixed with the
      personal 88–89
meter, text and alignment in *Renard* 11, 173–95
  accents of singing and Stravinsky's musical
      idiom 84, 175
  cimbalom 75, 188–89, 215, 217, 218–20
  displacement 164, 174–77, 179–80, 181–82
    role of articulation in processes of metrical
        displacement 183–94
    origins of displacement 174–77
  freed from constraints of fixed accents 175
  pribaoutka music 75–76, 177–82
    alternative notation 181
    displacements 179–80, 181–82, 183–84, 185
    English translation 178–79
    Gospodi pomiluy as a coda 76
    prized for sounds as well as substance
        177–78
    repetition 180
    resembling limericks or folk jingles 75–76,
        177–78
    text-setting 180

"untranslatable" 177–78
"rejoicing discovery" of "musical
        possibilities" 174–76
    role of articulation in processes of metrical
        displacement 183–94
    slurs, beams and accent markings 190–94
    Stravinsky contra Schoenberg 194–95
    text as phonetic material and displacement of
        words and syllables 176–77
    unconscious assimilation of Russian popular
        verse 176–77
metrical accents 18, 91–92
metrical displacement see displacement/
        metrical displacement
metrical location 16, 174
metrical parallelism 16, 40, 295
    and displacement see displacement/metrical
        displacement
    see also melodic repeat structures in the
        music of Stravinsky, Debussy and
        Rimsky-Korsakov
Meyer, Leonard 256, 279–80
Mikrokosmos (Bartók) 124
Miller Who was a Wizard, a Cheat, and a
        Matchmaker, The (Ablesimov) 56
"Mitusov song" 66–67, 117, 122, 131
Mitusov, Stephan 66–67, 117
moment form 231, 245, 247, 248
Morton, Lawrence 122
Mozart, Wolfgang Amadeus 30–31, 37, 237
    Così fan Tutte 120
    Serenade, Eine kleine Nachtmusik see
        Serenade; Eine kleine Nachtmusik
    Symphony No. 40 30–31, 33
Music and Memory (Snyder) 258
Music for Children (Orff) 129
Mussorgsky, M. P. 56–57, 175
Myaskovsky, Nicholai 88

Narmour, Eugene 237–39
neo-classical works 120, 121, 122–23, 140,
        222, 262
neo-Riemannian tables/operations see under
        Cohn, Richard; Riemann, Hugo
New Musicology 285
Newman, Ernest 252–53
Nightingale, The (Stravinsky) 63, 66, 239
Nijinska, Bronislava 95, 164–65, 291–92,
        292–93
Nijinsky, Vaslav 292
Nocturnes (Chopin) 261–62
Nocturnes (Debussy) 239
"Not a Merry Company" ("Ne vesyolaya da
        kompan'itsa") 66–67, 117, 122, 131
Nuages (Debussy) 239

nuance see under performance practice and
        aesthetic belief

octatonic scale and octatonic–diatonic
        interactions 9, 42–52
    distinctions in Stravinsky's scalar ordering
        distinguishing repertories 51
    hyper-octatonic network 46–47, 155
    intervention 3–5
    Les Noces see under melody and harmony in
        Les Noces
    orderings 42–46
    Renard 136, 143–44, 189–90, 214–20
    The Rite of Spring 43, 46, 135, 167, 171–72
    octatonic–diatonic interaction 48, 136,
        143–44, 146
    Russian and neo-classical works 48–52
    scale patterns 7
    scale step and pitch-class priority 48–49
    The Soldier's Tale 136
    Symphony in Three Movements 167, 172
    Symphony of Psalms 167, 172
Octet (Stravinsky) 74, 115
Oedipus Rex (Stravinsky) 84–85, 197
Orff, Carl 129
    Music for Children 129
ostinato
    Les Noces 107, 137
        basso ostinato 105, 153–54, 155,
            156–57, 208
    Renard 17, 22, 188–89, 211–12, 214–15,
            219–20
        basso ostinato 174, 197, 202–04,
            206–08, 213
    The Rite of Spring 40, 132, 133–35
    The Soldier's Tale 193

Paris Opera Ballet 95
pasodoble 221–22
performance practice and aesthetic belief 6–8,
        11–12, 252–66, 268
    aesthetics and Stravinsky's approach to
        music and performance 262–66
    conventions of expressive timing 254–55
    expressive characterization 258
    expressive response to musical structure by
        performers 257–58, 261
    expressive timing 6–8, 11–12, 254–66
    implications of displacement 254
    modernist trends/style 261, 262, 263
    modifications of timing and punctuation
        255–57
        standard modifications of performance
        weakening structure 258–59
    opportunities for expressive variation 261–62

performance practice and aesthetic belief
(cont.)
   piano 259, 265
   rubato and nuance 253, 259–63, 267
      debate about role of "expression" and
         "nuance" 253
      distinction between "execution" and
         "interpretation" 259–60
   strict performance style 5–8, 11–12, 260,
      262–63, 265, 267
   tempo 259, 267
      conventions of expressive timing 254
      maintenance of even tempo 6, 253–54, 265
      and performer's expressive response 257–58
      requirements for a steady beat structural in
         origin 261
      strict beat carrying an expressive
         purpose 261
Petrushka (Stravinsky) 56, 61, 118–19, 136, 251
   flexible stresses and elements of displacement
      175–76
   rubato 262
phenomenal accents 18
Philosophy of Modern Music (Adorno) 1, 282,
   283–84
Piano Concerto (Stravinsky) 261
Piano Sonata No. 9 (Scriabin) 172
Picasso, Pablo 231
Poetics of Music (Stravinsky) 267
"polarity" 139–40, 156
popevki 68, 72, 131
Prélude à l'après-midi d'un faune (Debussy)
   235, 239
Prélude symphonique (Steinberg) 251
pribaoutki
   pribaoutka music see under meter, text and
      alignment in Renard
   pribaoutki in Les Noces 54–56, 73–74
   prized for sounds as well as substance 177–78
   resembling limericks or folk jingles 75–76,
      177–78
   "untranslatable" 177–78
prichitaniye 95
Princeton School 1
Prokofiev, Sergei 88
Pulcinella (Stravinsky) 54
Pushkin, Alexander 60, 63

Rachmaninov, Sergei 121
Rake's Progress, The (Stravinsky) 120, 262
Ramuz, C. F, 78–79
realist tradition 175
Reich, Steve 2
   City Life 2
   You are (Variations) 2

"rejoicing discovery" of "musical possibilities"
   174–77, 205
   date 175–76
   freed from constraints of fixed accents 175
   text as phonetic material and displacement of
      words and syllables 176–77
   unconscious assimilation of Russian popular
      verse 176–77
Renard (Stravinsky) 3, 8, 9–10, 11, 55–56, 277
   allegro and con brio section see Allegro
      section of Renard reconsidered
   articulation see under articulation
   development of/history see under historical
      background of the Russian period
   displacement see Allegro section of Renard
      reconsidered; meter, text and alignment
      in Renard
   Eurasianist movement 9–10
   grouping see under grouping
   imitations of folk songs 118, 120, 222
      folk text set to music becoming scenarios
         174–75
   meter, text and alignment see meter, text and
      alignment in Renard
   octatonic–diatonic interactions 136, 143–44,
      189–90, 214–20
   ostinato see under ostinato
   performance and staging 77, 78
   pribaoutka see under meter, text and
      alignment in Renard
   solo-instrumental style 56
   stratification 17, 199, 208–11
   tactus 183, 184–85, 277
Repp, Bruno 257, 258
Requiem Canticles (Stravinsky) 85
Revue musicale 252
Riemann, Hugo 141
   neo-Riemannian tables/operations 10, 46,
      146–47
   neo-Riemannian theory and analysis 147
   see also Tonnetze
Rimsky-Korsakov, Nikolai 56–57, 124, 162, 252
   "Antar" Symphony No. 2 147
   Le Coq d'or 252
   repeat structures 239–45, 248, 250–51
   Sadko 240, 244
   Snegurochka (Snow Maiden) 241–44, 245
   tolerance and humanism 289
   Zemlya i nebo (Heaven and Earth) 251
Rite of Spring, The 12, 56, 74, 112, 251, 265–66,
   277, 301
   "anti-humanism" 286–87, 294–95
   "Augurs of Spring" 133, 295, 297
   choreography 292
   "Chosen One" 286

criticism *see under* Stravinsky and his critics
"Dance of the Earth" 133
"Danses des Adolescentes" 132
displacement 274, 275–77
flexible stresses and elements of displacement
    175–76
folk music and direct borrowing 118–19, 122,
    123–24, 129
  opening of *The Rite of Spring* 131–32
"Glorification of the Chosen One" 171–72
juxtaposition 230–31
octatonic scale 43, 46, 135, 167, 171–72
octatonic–diatonic interaction 48, 136,
    143–44, 146
ostinato 40, 132, 133–35
premiere 252
"Procession of the Sage" 273
revisited 295–99
"Ritual of Abduction" 295
"Ritual of the Rival Tribes" 40, 273
rubato 262
Russian folk tales incorporated 61
"Sacrificial Dance" 171–72, 286
slurs, beams and accent markings 189–93
tetrachords 124–25, 132, 133, 135, 215, 217
Rolland, Romain 9
Romantic period 18, 30–31
  Classical–Romantic literature 194
  Classical–Romantic music 194
Romantic tradition 259–60
Rosen, Charles 280
Rossini, Gioachino
  Barber of Seville 120
rubato *see under* performance practice and
    aesthetic belief
"Runaway Soldier and the Devil, The" 78–79
Ruslan and Ludmila (Glinka) 56–57
"Russian Folk Melodies in *The Rite of Spring*"
    (Taruskin) 122
Russian Folk Tales (Afanasyev) 196–97
Russian folk wedding 53, 56–60
  bridal shower 56, 59
  bride's wailing and laments 57, 58–60, 131
  portrayals of folk weddings an established
    part of Russian musical culture 56–57
  professional weepers employed to awaken
    specific emotions/thoughts 58, 88–89
  traditions and roles 58
Ruwet, Nicolas 236–37

Sadko (Rimsky-Korsakov) 240, 244
St. Petersburg Bazaar (Matinsky) 56
Scenes of Folk Festivals in Old Russia
    (Kastalsky) 61
Schaeffner, André 236

Schenker, Heinrich 35, 256, 280
Schloezer, Boris de 13
Schoenberg, Arnold 215, 277
  arguments against use of borrowed folk or
    popular music 119–20, 194
  Classical style 34, 195, 271
  conflicts in segmentation between
    Schoenbergian and Schenkerian
    approaches 35
  folk songs, complete and sufficient
    nature of 194
  Fundamentals of Musical Composition 35,
    41, 277
  great music developing consistently and
    "equally" 272
  motives as smallest building blocks 35
  "shock" in music 271
  and Stravinsky 1, 11, 194–95, 269, 275,
    283–84
  Style and Idea 113
  style of developing variation 18, 34, 195
Schumann, Robert 15–16
  Carnaval 38, 39
  Dichterliebe 280
  dissonance (metrical) 38–39
  meter 39
Scriabin, Alexander 172
  Piano Sonata No. 9 172
Seashore, Carl 254–55
Second Viennese School 1
Serenade, *Eine kleine Nachtmusik* (Mozart)
    33–34
  displacement 39
  hemiola cadence 33–36, 38
  Schenkerian graph of Minuet theme 35
Sermon, a Narrative, and a Prayer, A
    (Stravinsky) 289, 290
sexual politics 292–93
simulation *see* fabrication/simulation
slurs *see* accent markings, beams and slurs
Snegurochka (Snow Maiden) (Rimsky-
    Korsakov) 241–44, 245
Snyder, Bob 258
  Music and Memory 258
Soldier's Tale, The (Stravinsky) 3, 8, 9–10,
    55–56, 261–62
  development of/history *see under* historical
    background of the Russian period
  Eurasianist movement 9–10
  imitations of folk songs 118
  folk text set to music becoming scenarios
    174–75
  instrumentation 79–80
  octatonic–diatonic interactions 136
  ostinato 193

Soldier's Tale, The (Stravinsky) (cont.)
  performance and staging 78
  "Royal March" 11, 220–24, 261
    metrical displacement 11
  slurs, beams and accent markings 190–91,
    193, 194
  solo-instrumental style 56
Spies, Claudio 244
Steinberg, Maximilian 251, 289
  Prélude symphonique 251
Stockhausen, Karlheinz 231
stratification 267–68
  the allegro in *Renard* 17, 199, 208–11
  applying to horizontal layering of patterns of
    repetition 4
  implying a form of displacement 5
  layering in the performance of laments 59,
    107–8
  Les Noces see under melody and harmony in
    Les Noces
  meaning in Cone's essay 4
  static/self-enclosed nature of Stravinsky's
    stratifications 42
  and superimposition 251
Stravinsky, Igor
  aesthetics and Stravinsky's approach to
    music and performance 262–66
  Agon 190–91, 194
  Apollo Musagetes 115, 121
  autobiography 259
  Berceuses du chat 55–56, 73–74
  Cantata 289, 290, 291
  Capriccio 261, 262
  Conversations with Stravinsky 120, 174–75,
    177, 259–60
  The Firebird 56, 61, 115, 118–19
  Five Easy Pieces 221–22
  The Flood 84–85
  in France and the United States 3, 259, 287
  friends 9
  Histoire du soldat see Soldier's Tale, The
  improvising by relating intervals
    rhythmically 173
  Jeu de Cartes 120
  Les Noces see Les Noces
  The Nightingale 63, 66, 239
  Octet 74, 115
  Oedipus Rex 84–85, 197
  the person 3, 284–91
    anti-humanism 12, 89, 261, 286–87, 289,
      290, 294–95, 297
    anti-communist 287, 292
    anti-Semitism 285–86, 289–90, 291
    compartmental mind 55
    Eurasian movement 9–10, 285, 288–89, 290

    image 3, 5
    politics 287
  Petrushka see Petrushka
  Piano Concerto 261
  Poetics of Music 267
  politics of Stravinsky's music, changes in 2–3
  Pulcinella 54
  The Rake's Progress 120, 262
  "rejoicing discovery" *see* "rejoicing discovery"
  Renard see Renard
  Requiem Canticles 85
  The Rite of Spring see Rite of Spring, The
  and Schoenberg *see under* Schoenberg
  A Sermon, a Narrative, and a Prayer 289,
    290
  setting Russian folk texts to music 174–76
  The Soldier's Tale see Soldier's Tale, The
  Stravinsky in Pictures and Documents 69
  in Switzerland 3, 9–10, 54–55, 63, 84
  Symphonies of Wind Instruments see
    Symphonies of Wind Instruments
  Symphony in C 190–91, 194
  Symphony in Three Movements 167, 172
  Symphony of Psalms see Symphony of Psalms
  Three Easy Pieces 221–22
  "Three Japanese Lyrics" 77
  Three Pieces for String Quartet 2, 112,
    175–76
    imitations of folk songs 118
  Violin Concerto in D 190–91, 261
Stravinsky and his critics 5, 12, 267–303
  Adorno, T. W. 6, 12, 253–54, 267, 269–71,
    293, 294–95, 297, 299, 300–1
    critical indictments 271–75
    gulf between Stravinsky/Schoenberg
      195, 269
    rebuttals 275, 279, 281–84
    Stravinsky the person 284–85,
      286–87, 291
  anti-humanism 12, 89, 261, 286–87, 289, 290,
    294–95, 297
  "cold and heartless" 263, 265, 267, 281
  conclusions 299–303
  difficulties with conductors, performers,
    audiences and critics 253, 263
  equating Stravinsky's formalism with a
    disbelief in connectedness 264
  expression, music lacking 268
  Les Noces 12, 83, 286, 288, 290
    as "an icy comedy" 88
    Lambert acknowledging the music's
      special status 53
    Marxism/anti-Marxism 291–92
    revisited 291–99
  melody, lack of 121

metrical alignment and realignment
    in relief 41
"objectivist aesthetics" of Stravinsky 12
rebuttals 275–84
    The Rite of Spring 12, 273, 274, 286–87
    role of/reliance on borrowed folk material
        121, 194
    Schoenberg's arguments against
        using borrowed folk/popular music
        119–20, 194
    Taruskin, Richard 293, 294–95, 297, 299, 301
    "Stravinsky and Us" 263
    Stravinsky the person 285–90, 291
Stravinsky in Pictures and Documents
    (Stravinsky/Craft) 69
"Stravinsky: the Progress of a Method"
    (Cone) 4
Stravinsky, Vera 69
strict performance style *see under* performance
    practice and aesthetic belief
String Quartet No. 3 (Bartók) 124,
    125, 128
Style and Idea (Schoenberg) 35
Suvchinsky, Pierre 288
Svadebka see Les Noces
Symphonies of Wind Instruments (Stravinsky)
    8, 11, 54, 265, 277, 299, 301
    alternating bars 181
    "anti-humanism" 286
    articulation 261
    block structures 96, 225–31, 260–61
    the conservative alternative 232–35
    continuity and discontinuity 246–50
        chorale 252
    "counterpoint of sonorities" 253
    displacement 260–61
    imitations of folk songs 118
    juxtaposition *see under* juxtaposition
    problems at the premiere 252–53
        initial survival only as a piano
            arrangement 253
        subsequent debate about role of
            "expression" and "nuance" 253
    setting of conclusion 115
    strings, omission of 265–66, 268
    tempo 259
Symphony in C (Stravinsky) 190–91, 194
Symphony No. 40 (Mozart) 30–31, 33
Symphony in Three Movements (Stravinsky)
    167, 172
Symphony of Psalms (Stravinsky) 2, 84–85
    octatonic 167, 172
    setting of conclusion 115
    slurs, beams and accent markings 190–91,
        193–94

syncopation 160–64, 208, 249
    "hiccup motive" *see under* hemiola
    repeated melody metrically
        displaced 16
    felt by listener 39
    modest 35–36
    syncopation as part of a larger pattern of
        displacement 160–64

tactus 15–16
    conflicting interpretations 24, 110
    Les Noces 92–93, 95, 101, 157–58, 277
        subtactus level 92–93
    meter centered with the regularity of the
        tactus 29
    Renard 183, 184–85, 277
    sense of meter/displacement fading when
        moving away from the tactus 29–30
    subtactus levels 16, 29–30, 92–93
Taruskin, Richard 9, 12, 244, 251,
    261, 263
    "Russian Folk Melodies in *The Rite of
        Spring*" 122
    "Stravinsky and Us" 263
    Stravinsky downplaying his music's
        folkloristic origins 66, 122 *see also under*
        Stravinsky and his critics
Tchaikovsky, Pyotr Ilyich 56–57, 121
Temperley, David 278
tempo *see under* performance practice and
    aesthetic belief
Testaments Betrayed (Kundera) 300–1
tetrachords 10, 42, 51
    Bartók's music 124–29
    and folk songs 123–29
    Les Noces 106, 114, 135–43, 148, 158–59, 164,
        167, 215, 217, 288
    Renard 215, 216–18
    The Rite of Spring 124–25, 132, 133, 135,
        215, 217
text and meter *see* meter, text and alignment in
    Renard
Thomson, Virgil 271
Three Easy Pieces (Stravinsky) 221–22
"Three Japanese Lyrics" (Stravinsky) 77
Three Pieces for String Quartet (Stravinsky) 2,
    112, 175–76
    imitations of folk songs 118
    time-spans 18
Tonnetze 10, 50, 141, 155
    Renard 216–17, 219
    Tonnetz for *Les Noces see under* melody and
        harmony in *Les Noces*
    triadic 146
Trubetskoy, Nikolai 288

Ulysses (Joyce) 62

Varèse, Edgard 251
Violin Concerto (Bartók) 128–29
Violin Concerto in D (Stravinsky)
    190–91, 261

Wagner, Richard 10, 146–47

Webern, Anton 122–23

You are (Variations) (Reich) 2

Zemlya i nebo (*Heaven and Earth*)
    (Rimsky-Korsakov) 251
Znamennïy chant 72, 97, 118
Zuckerkandl, Victor 14, 182